PRAISE FOR
SHY

Named a best book of the year by *Kirkus Reviews*, *Library Journal*, *Town & Country*, *Newsweek*, and *Vox*

"Born into Broadway royalty, Mary Rodgers wrote songs, scripts, children's books—but could a memoir, with an assist from *New York Times* critic Jesse Green, be her masterpiece? Cocktail-hour wit bursts from every page as Rodgers (who died in 2014) recalls an upbringing by difficult geniuses and encounters with pretty much everyone—but especially 'the love of my life,' Stephen Sondheim."

—Boris Kachka, *Los Angeles Times*

"*Shy* is the most hilarious, wise, candid, and tender memoir I have ever read. And with the best footnotes EVER!"

—André Bishop, artistic director of Lincoln Center Theater

"One of the best theatrical memoirs since Moss Hart's *Act One* . . . *Shy* has a conversational style that seems to bring the reader in the room with Rodgers. One feels that she is just chatting away, letting whatever comes out of her mouth go down unedited. [*Not true: It was really edited and expertly so.*] Rodgers comes off as a charming, highly intelligent and cultured Lucy Van Pelt . . . It has to be added that *Shy*'s footnotes—and there are many—are must reading."   —Joe Westerfield, *Newsweek*

"Perfection. Zero notes. Enjoy."   —Constance Grady, *Vox*

"'Outspoken' is a good word for [Rodgers's] memoir, co-authored by *New York Times* theater critic Jesse Green. You just can't imagine anybody saying the things she says about her father in a polite conversation, and she is just breathtaking in her takedowns of absolutely everybody you regard as remotely famous from that era . . . It's hilarious, for four hundred pages."   —Bob Mondello, NPR

"Both a joyful chronicle of a life well lived and a box-seat view on some of the best, brightest, and most idiosyncratic creative minds of the twentieth century." —Leah Greenblatt, *Entertainment Weekly*

"Delectable . . . In part a chronicle of life with father, in part an insider's view of Broadway during a golden age, *Shy* is, most compellingly, an account of a woman finding her power and her voice." —Joanne Kaufman, *Air Mail*

"Having just finished *Shy*, an extremely funny and always fascinating book, I am very sorry I never met Mary Rodgers. But I do feel as if I have, because *Shy* provides the appealing and droll voice of Rodgers, alongside Jesse Green's knowledgeable and witty commentary. For anyone who loves Broadway, or wants to hear about its heyday from a lifelong insider, this duet of a memoir is a welcome compendium of information, anecdote, gossip, and strong opinions—and never anything less than a tremendously good story." —Meg Wolitzer, author of *The Female Persuasion*

"There isn't a dull line in the book." —Celia McGee, *Avenue*

"I read *Shy* in two long, delicious gulps. It is an essential show-biz memoir and a complete portrait, with all the contradictions that make a person real. I'm only sorry that there's no more to read." —Ben Brantley, author of *The New York Times Book of Broadway: On the Aisle for the Unforgettable Plays of the Last Century*

"*Shy* is a funny, ferocious book that highlights the brilliant and delicious voice of a creative force whose greatest project might just have been telling her own story." —*Town & Country*

"Reading *Shy* is like falling into one of the plush sofas in Mary Rodgers's elegant living room, drink in hand, while she regales the room in her unique voice. She is in a talkative—*very* talkative—mood and ready to say, well, anything on her bold and fearless mind. All credit to Jesse Green for organizing Rodgers's thoughts and opinions into a fascinating book. *Shy* gives the reader a full-fledged and revealing portrait of an extraordinary, complex person."

—Ted Chapin, author of *Everything Was Possible: The Birth of the Musical Follies*

"[Rodgers's] tell-all of family dysfunction, a chaotic love life, and a bumpy career read at times like a juicy cross between Moss Hart's *Act One* and Christina Crawford's *Mommie Dearest* . . . Her hilariously barbed bon mots could give Dorothy Parker a run for the money."

—Misha Berson, *American Theatre*

"*Shy* is bound to take its place among the great memoirs . . . One need not be a musical fanatic to appreciate Rodgers's revealing and captivating tale of art, parenthood, and life in mid-century America . . . Combined with Green's annotations—funny enough to catch your attention, informative enough not to be cloying—reading *Shy* feels like listening to the world's most wide-ranging, fascinating conversation."

—Tim Rice, *Washington Free Beacon*

"*Shy* is one of the funniest books I've read this year, and not to be missed if you're a fan of theater. (Not to worry if you don't understand all the references—Jesse Green has included some of the most comprehensive and accessible footnotes I've ever seen in a biography.)"

—David Vogel, *BuzzFeed*

"A future classic of the theater."

—Tom Beer, *Fully Booked*

MARY RODGERS AND JESSE GREEN
SHY

Mary Rodgers (1931–2014) was an accomplished composer, author, and screenwriter. She was the author of the novel *Freaky Friday* and its 1976 screenplay adaptation, and of several other novels. Rodgers also wrote the music for *Once Upon a Mattress*, which was nominated for a Tony Award for Best Musical. She lived in New York City until her death.

Jesse Green is the chief theater critic for *The New York Times*. From 2013 to 2017 he was the theater critic for *New York* magazine. Before that, he covered theater and other cultural topics, as well as writing long-form news features, for many national publications. He is the author of the novel *O Beautiful* and the memoir *The Velveteen Father: An Unexpected Journey to Parenthood*.

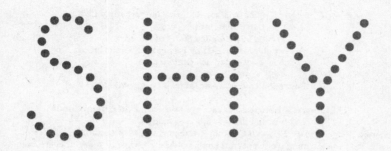

SHY

THE ALARMINGLY OUTSPOKEN
MEMOIRS OF MARY RODGERS

MARY RODGERS AND **JESSE GREEN**

PICADOR

FARRAR, STRAUS AND GIROUX • NEW YORK

Picador
120 Broadway, New York 10271

Illustration credits can be found on pages 465–467.

The Library of Congress has cataloged the Farrar, Straus and Giroux
hardcover edition as follows:
Names: Rodgers, Mary, 1931–2014, author. | Green, Jesse, 1958– author.
Title: Shy : the alarmingly outspoken memoirs of Mary Rodgers / Mary Rodgers and
    Jesse Green.
Description: First edition. | New York : Farrar, Straus and Giroux, 2022.
Identifiers: LCCN 2022018292 | ISBN 9780374298623 (hardcover)
Subjects: LCSH: Rodgers, Mary, 1931–2014. | Composers—United States—Biography. |
    Lyricists—United States—Biography. | Musicals—History and criticism. | LCGFT:
    Autobiographies.
Classification: LCC ML410.R6308 A3 2022 | DDC 782.1/4092 [B]—dc23
LC record available at https://lccn.loc.gov/2022018292

Paperback ISBN: 978-1-250-87290-6

Designed by Gretchen Achilles

Our books may be purchased in bulk for promotional, educational,
or business use. Please contact your local bookseller or the Macmillan Corporate
and Premium Sales Department at 1-800-221-7945, extension 5442, or by email at
MacmillanSpecialMarkets@macmillan.com.

For book club information, please email marketing@picadorusa.com.

picadorusa.com • instagram.com/picador
twitter.com/picadorusa • facebook.com/picadorusa

1   3   5   7   9   10   8   6   4   2

CONTENTS

PART III

PART I

I.

HOSTILITIES

Daddy* is how we have to begin. The only way he knew to have fun with us was by playing ear-training games, challenging us to identify various intervals and, later, chords. He would strike two notes on the piano—say, a G and a B-flat—and my sister and I would race to come up with "minor third." Or he'd try to trick us with ninths, thinking we might confuse them with seconds. It was all quite easy until we got to diminished fifths and augmented fourths, which on a piano look the same. I later learned that this was a routine exercise in elementary music theory classes, universally considered boring. But Linda† and I liked it because Daddy seemed to like us when we answered correctly. And to like himself for having taught us so well. Neither of which likings we saw much evidence of otherwise.

We also played word games at the dinner table; it was one way to get a conversation going. Or we played a form of Twenty Questions we called Who Am I? Good question.

A game called Slapjack was a great excuse for me to slap Linda, which I kept doing, more or less, for seven decades.

....

* If you've read this far, you probably already know that Daddy was Richard Rodgers (1902–1979): composer, womanizer, alcoholic, genius.

† Linda Rodgers (1935–2015): Mary's sister, who outshone Mary as a pianist if not as a composer.

Our mother* drove us crazy with something called Snakes, which involved very rapid arithmetic. When she got to the end of a long series of connected math problems, we were supposed to supply the answer pronto. Neither Linda nor I thought it was fun—especially me, with my complete incompetence when it comes to zeroes—but Mummy, whose friends called her "La Perfecta," sure did: She knew the sums.

Years later, when I had my own kids,† we played better games. A favorite was Camouflage, in which you hid twelve ordinary items in plain sight: things like a battery, a paper clip, a key, a wedding ring. Then the players, in teams of two, were allowed into the room. They could not touch anything; when they located an object, they pretended they hadn't, and quietly checked it off their list. Whichever team completed the list first won. But the fun was really in the cleverness of the hiding. The wedding ring might be sitting right on the lid of that brass canister. A black knee-high stocking on the leg of a piano bench. Once I stuck a banana among the yellow pillows on the sofa: Adam‡ couldn't believe he couldn't find the fucking banana. With enough ingenuity you could make almost anything completely disappear. A Tylenol wedged between the white dust jackets of two coffee-table books. A pair of glasses in the bottom of a crystal vase of flowers. For grown-ups I once devised a version with only dirty things: an enema tip between the black keys of the piano, a tampon in the venetian blind. I had a Tiffany crystal clock with a gold band at the circumference; I put my diaphragm around it. The next morning, Tod,§

....

* Dorothy Belle Feiner Rodgers (1909–1992): decorator, inventor, author, wife. Maybe not in that order.

† With her first husband, Mary had three children: Tod, Nina, and Kim. With her second husband, another three: Matthew, Adam, and Alec.

‡ Adam Arthur Guettel (born 1964) wrote the scores for *Myths and Hymns*, *Floyd Collins*, and *The Light in the Piazza*, with more to come.

§ Richard Rodgers Beaty (born 1952) was originally named Geoffrey Tod Beaty, but his maternal grandparents, never having had any boys of their own, were so outraged at what they perceived as a slight to the patriarch, and applied

who was helping me pick up all this stuff, found it and said, "Mom, where do you want me to put your knee guard?"

We also played the Hearing Game, in which we blindfolded all the kids and made noises they had to identify: nails on an emery board, the waterfalling of a deck of cards. And Rhythm: a kind of Name That Tune but with just the beat, not the melody. And Sardines, in which the person who's "it" hides somewhere, and when you find him—say, perched on a shelf inside a closet—you have to climb in there with him, until gradually you are left with one person still looking, and everyone else incredibly stuffed in a closet full of people.*

And Skin. For that game, you masked someone's entire body beneath sheets and blankets so you couldn't make out their form at all, leaving just one small patch of skin exposed. The players had to guess what part of the body it was. Sometimes it was something perfectly innocent, like a kneecap. Sometimes it wasn't.

That was more of an adult game. We played it, along with many others, at Steve's.†

Steve and I played a game the first time we met. This was at Highland Farm, Oscar Hammerstein's home in Bucks County, in the summer of 1944. Steve was one of the semi-orphans and sad strays with rotten parents whom Ockie‡ and his wife Dorothy§ were always quasi-adopting,

....

such cataclysmic pressure, that the name was changed to appease them. The boy was still called Tod, though; one Richard Rodgers was enough.

* For this you need a large Victorian house.

† Again, if you don't know who Stephen Sondheim (1930–2021) was, you're probably not reading this.

‡ Oscar ("Ockie") Hammerstein II (1895–1960): Richard Rodgers's collaborator from Oklahoma! (1943) through The Sound of Music (1959).

§ Yes, another Dorothy: Dorothy Blanchard Hammerstein (1899–1987). It was her third marriage and Ockie's second. She started out an actress and became—what else?—a decorator.

1957: Stephen Sondheim. "At that moment I thought
I would never be as infatuated with anyone again."

including the fey and fascinating Shawen Lynch and the mysterious,
haughty Margot de Vaulchier, who was either a royal descendant of some
unidentified mini-kingdom like Liechtenstein, or maybe an escapee from
Staten Island—who knew?*

I guess I had come with my parents; maybe Daddy and Ockie were
working on *Carousel*, which opened on Broadway the next spring. Anyway, there we were: a thirteen-year-old girl, fat and ungainly, as my father
kept telling me, and a fourteen-year-old boy genius with a crazy narcis-

....

* The daughter of a French vicomte and a San Francisco socialite, Margot
de Vaulchier (1928–1985) had four children, two husbands, and at least
one spectacular divorce. Shawen Lynch (born 1929) became an unofficial
ward of her mother's friends the Hammersteins after surviving the Blitz
in London. In 1948, she received what Walter Winchell called a "diamond
sparkler" from the journalist Dwight Whitney; they later married and
had several children.

sist divorcée of a mother* who'd put him in military school—which he loved.

With nothing in common except R (me) and H (him), what do you do? You play chess. Three games. He beat me fiendishly, took no time at all. Once we ran through that, we went to the piano, where he played either *Rhapsody in Blue* or *An American in Paris*. I didn't know those Gershwin things, oddly enough. Growing up, I only went to Daddy's musicals; at home, he never played Gershwin records. He didn't play records much in general, but in specific he didn't play Gershwin, the only composer he might have envied—well, maybe not the brain tumor part. Or maybe even that.

I was dazzled by Steve, completely stunned. I knew right away he was brilliant; he just reeked of talent. Which, not illogically, was always the biggest turn-on for me. I married two tall, blue-eyed men,† but the ones I had the most fun with were dark. And, boy, was Steve dark. He wasn't obnoxious, but impatient, a bit snappish. Pleasant, but not boy-girl pleasant. I was just a body there. I don't think he thought I was as bright as he was, and he was right. He knew I wasn't up to his standards. But nobody was. Later, we did become almost equals, except in the brain department. But at that moment I thought I would never be as infatuated with anyone again. Which turned out to be true.

When we were adults, we played much more elaborate games. Steve's

....

* Etta Janet Fox Sondheim, appropriately enough known as Foxy, had recently gotten a Mexican divorce from Steve's father, Herbert. Herbert was a dress manufacturer; Foxy, his star designer.

† Tall, blue-eyed husband no. 1: Julian ("Jerry") Bonar Beaty Jr. (1916– 2011); married 1951, divorced 1958. Tall, blue-eyed husband no. 2: Henry ("Hank") Guettel (1928–2013); married 1961. You will note that almost everyone in the family has a yachty nickname. Richard Rodgers was Dick, of course. Richard, Linda, Constance, and Alexander became Tod, Nina, Kim, and Alec. Adam got Dum Dum from his Aunt Linda; Mary mercifully switched it to Ad. But Mary herself was always just plain Mary, except to her grandchildren, who called her May-May.

scavenger hunts were especially ambitious, and eventually famous—or, in the case of that movie, infamous; the plot was so complicated I eventually gave up.[*] In real life, he'd form a bunch of his showbiz friends into teams and make them follow a series of insanely tricky clues that led all over the city. I remember I was once on a team with, among others, Phyllis Newman.[†] We somehow made our way to a brownstone on East Seventy-third Street that happened to be the home of his lady shrink. Standing on the stoop, if you listened very carefully, you could hear music coming from the gap between the outer and inner doors. Somehow, he'd rigged a record or tape to keep repeating "One for My Baby,"[‡] specifically the opening musical phrase. We all knew the lyric, of course: "It's quarter to three, there's no one in the place except you and me." But what to do with it? Eventually I figured, aha, it's "quarter to three"—two forty-five. So the next address we had to find on the map would be at number 245. I can't remember if we won that time, but I do know that everyone was starving because it took all evening to solve and Steve hadn't warned us to eat ahead. One clue was hidden in the icing of a cake we found somewhere in the process, and poor Phyllis was so hungry she ate the clue.

When kids or huge success arrived in all our lives—usually not both—everyone outgrew the scavenger hunts; they took too long and cost too much. (Steve would send us around town in limos.) But there was always time for Hostilities, and it didn't cost anything, at least not financially. You would sit in a circle, having been assigned a number from one through ten if there were ten of you. On scraps of paper, you'd write an impertinent question for each of the nine other players, fold them up, and "address"

----

[*] *The Last of Sheila* (1973) was written by Sondheim and Anthony Perkins (1932–1992), another member of Mary's theatrical circle. About a murder on a yacht, it involved Dyan Cannon and an illogical acronym.

[†] Phyllis Newman (1933–2019): actress, wife of the lyricist Adolph Green. A completely separate person from Betty Comden, actress and Adolph's writing partner.

[‡] By Harold Arlen and Johnny Mercer.

them on the outside with their number, in pencil. So let's say Adolph was No. 7; you might write, "Who's smarter, your spouse or your collaborator?" then fold it up and address it to No. 7. After everyone got their "mail" they would write answers to the impertinent questions and—this is important—erase the number on the front before throwing it into a pile in the middle. Then they'd all be read aloud. But when they were read aloud you didn't know who wrote the question or whom it was addressed to unless it was you. The supposed point was to match them up.

We ended up calling it Hostilities because it could get very nasty. (That was the *real* point.) One time we played it at Arthur's in Quogue. Are you surprised that Arthur Laurents,* the little shit,† would be associated with a game called Hostilities? Sometimes I'm surprised, and ashamed, that I was associated with *him* as long as I was. But we were still good friends in the mid-1960s, when I was in my mid-thirties and this particular game took place. By then I was married to Hank; out in Quogue on Long Island we were neighbors of Arthur and his partner, Tom Hatcher,‡ four lonely Democrats among the Quoglodytes. Also there was Lee Remick§ and her then-husband Bill Colleran. Lee had recently starred in Steve and Arthur's flop musical *Anyone Can Whistle*; she was lovely in it, even though

....

* Arthur Laurents (1917–2011) wrote the books for two classic musicals (*West Side Story* and *Gypsy*) and a clutch of unclassic ones (including *Anyone Can Whistle* and *Do I Hear a Waltz?*), the screenplays for one brutal movie (*Rope*) and several purple ones (*The Way We Were*, *The Turning Point*), and at least one worthy play (*Home of the Brave*). Plus a series of score-settling memoirs.

† Frequently during our work sessions, Mary proposed new titles for this book. Proposed title no. 1: *What Do You Really Think?*

‡ Mary was not the only person, though perhaps the most vehement one, who found Arthur's longtime companion, Tom Hatcher (1929–2006), even worse than Arthur himself.

§ Much-beloved Lee Remick (1935–1991): a beauty and a real movie star, nominated in 1962 for an Academy Award for *Days of Wine and Roses*.

1972: Arthur Laurents in Quogue. "Are you surprised that the little shit
would be associated with a game called Hostilities?"

she was not known for her voice. Anyway, we were all sitting in our circle
in Arthur's living room, and among Hank's pieces of "mail" (he told me
later) was one asking, "Do you think your wife has any talent?" Well, that
was tricky whichever way you answered it, because even a strong defense
would cast doubt on my talent, which I was sensitive about. But Hank
looked around the room and figured a way out of the trap. His answer
was, "She has talent, but not really for singing." So when it was read
aloud, everyone thought the question had been sent to Bill, not Hank—
Lee's husband, not mine.

Another game of Hostilities took place in my living room with, among others, Arthur, Tom, Lenny,* my *Once Upon a Mattress* lyricist Marshall Barer,† and the Ryans, Johnny and D.D.‡ I wrote this question for Marshall: "How many people in this room have you slept with?" I knew of two: me (between my marriages, even though Marshall was gay) and D.D. But the answer came back, "Three." *That's interesting,* I thought.

One of the rules of Hostilities was that you were not supposed to investigate the answers; you had to let them go, not call someone the next day and ask, "Was that you?" But I called Marshall that very night and asked, "Who was the third person you slept with?" And he said, "Arthur." Which didn't surprise me except that I hadn't known about it earlier, and Arthur always bragged about such things. Two seconds later the phone rings and it's Arthur. "I know it was you who asked that question," he says, "and I know you and D.D. slept with Marshall. But who was the third person?" And I said, "It was *you!*"

He was floored. He didn't remember anything about it. Which was very disappointing to Marshall when, yes, I called him back and blabbed.§

....

* Leonard Bernstein (1918–1990): composer, teacher, conductor—not even he ever figured out in which order. Mary worked for him on CBS's Young People's Concerts from 1958 to 1972.

† Marshall Barer (1923–1998): lyricist, librettist, nutjob, genius.

‡ D.D. (Dorinda Dixon) Ryan, a photo editor at *Harper's Bazaar* with her fingers in everything fashionable. She was an assistant to Halston; she got Kay Thompson to write *Eloise*; she designed the mod duds for *Company* in 1970. While working on the costumes for the 1954 Harold Arlen–Truman Capote musical *House of Flowers* she met Johnny (John Barry Ryan III); he was one of the stage managers. He soon stopped slumming in the theater (and ended his affair with Eartha Kitt) to take up his genetic inheritance as an investment banker. He and D.D. eventually divorced.

§ In case you are wondering, Mary loved the idea of being annotated but, as was the case with the rest of the book, didn't love the actual writing. What you are reading here in the margins, and sometimes outside the margins, too, is therefore a compound of hers, mine, and ours.

2.

LOVE ME TONIGHT

Somewhere, there is a wonderful home movie of Daddy playing with me on a lawn. He looks happy, as adorable as anybody would be with a chubby new baby; I couldn't have been a year old. The first time I saw it I almost burst into tears, though I rarely cry; I taught myself not to because I never wanted to give my mother, who cried constantly, the satisfaction. When I was punished or humiliated for doing something wrong—and I was *always* doing something wrong—I used to look up at the sky and think, *Don't cry, don't cry, don't let her know she got to you.* To this day I let myself cry only at lovely things, like when someone unexpectedly apologizes to someone else. Or at acts of selfless kindness. But watching Daddy in a pair of swimming trunks on the grass, beaming at me with good-natured, silly joy, I thought: *Where did that nice man go?*

I just ached to relive the implied experience—though probably, because he was a showman, and my mother even more so, it was staged.

I certainly have no conscious memory of his being very happy with me, and my conscious memory goes way back. We moved from New York to Beverly Hills in November of 1931: my father to work at MGM on musicals; my mother to mind him; and *her* mother, the very funny but not very bright May, for whom I was named—and whose intellectual curiosity didn't go much beyond the juicy novels she rented at Womrath's bookstore—because she was recently a widow and what else was

1934: Mary and Richard Rodgers. "Where did that nice man go?"

she going to do?* Larry Hart,† whom I loved, also came, and lived with us until my mother couldn't stand it. And ten-month-old me. I don't remember the move, thank you very much, but I do remember, less than two years later, the big earthquake of 1933.‡ Because I was in my mother's arms, not the nurse's, and my mother held me only when Mam'selle, as we called her, had her day off, I know specifically that the earthquake occurred on a Wednesday.§ My mother stood in the doorway

....

* The circumstances of the sudden widowhood of May Adelson Feiner (1878–1954) were so hushed up that it took years (and thirty more pages) for her namesake to get the story.

† Lorenz Hart (1895–1943) was Richard Rodgers's lyricist, as well as a thorn in his side, for twenty-four years.

‡ The Long Beach earthquake, at 5:54 p.m. on March 10, 1933, measured 6.4 on the Richter scale.

§ Fine, but the earthquake occurred on a Friday.

1927: Richard Rodgers and Lorenz Hart. Hart called Rodgers "the Principal."
Rodgers called Hart "the Shrimp."

with me, trying to figure out whether it was safer to be inside or outside, and *that's* what I remember: her indecision. *Is it safer to be inside or outside?*

My father and Larry were in their office at the MGM lot with the story editor of the movie they were writing.* Daddy was playing and

---

* *I Married an Angel*. The version Rodgers and Hart were working on wasn't made, though MGM eventually came back to it in 1942; in between, it was a hit on Broadway in 1938.

Larry was singing when suddenly the room started shaking and the piano started sliding across it. At first Daddy followed the piano, still playing, but as it approached the window, he and the others decided they'd better jump. Because the air conditioner kept the window from opening, Larry threw the piano stool through the glass, and out they went, but it was just the first floor, so nothing happened. They fell into a bunch of shrubbery. An earthquake was just about the only thing that could dislodge Daddy from the keyboard when he was writing, or I suppose that was what he wanted us to know when he told us the story.*

By that time, I was able to talk. Every morning I would say to him, "Where are you going?" and he would answer, not very nicely, as if it were an imbecilic question, "Where do you *think* I'm going?"

"The studio?"

"That's right," he'd say, and pat his jacket pockets on both sides to make sure he had his supply of Lucky Strikes for the day: three green boxes. I'd hear the cellophane crackling as he left.

Two years later, when Linda was born, same thing. "You have a baby sister," he announced.

"What's her name?" I asked.

"Linda."

"What's her *last* name?"

I knew the answer, but this was the kind of pathetic thing I always said to keep him with me longer. It didn't work.

"What do you *think* her last name is?"

Stalling for time, I said, "I thought maybe she'd have a *middle* name."

"No," he answered, and left the room.

Though he was a composer, Daddy was fanatical about words: He demanded, not just from his collaborators but also from his daughters, clarity and concision. He hated having his time wasted with intangible things like emotions, and found excess of any sort distasteful. I've always had a hugely broad smile, apparently too huge for him; when I had my pic-

---

* There are many versions out there; this is the most fun and least likely.

ture taken, he'd say, "Don't smile." And he'd wince every time I'd laugh loudly, which is another thing I do a lot. He would actually recoil. Which is somewhat unfair because, you know, he *made* me. It was like I was a golem, a glob, a repository of all his and my mother's fears about their own excesses. My weight was a constant disappointment, from birth onward. "You are so fat," he once told me, "that your arms swing out on either side like an ape."* And there was my always perfectly slim mother sitting at the lunch table, breezily saying, "Oh well, when I feel I am gaining weight I just don't eat dessert for a while." I wanted to push her face into the soup.

She was even more fanatical about appearances than he, which made her a very difficult parent but a very clever decorator. She once designed a home with all the mechanical systems—pipes and ducts and flues and what-have-yous—color-coded in primary colors. The cellar was like a Mondrian. She started a repair business, patented a line of dress patterns called Basically Yours, invented the Turn and Learn toy, selling it in 1972 to Ideal.† But let's not waste space on her full résumé; you can read about it in her several memoirs. The point is that the contrast between her imaginative ideas (a hollow bracelet filled with refrigerant) and her conventional demeanor (also, in a way, a hollow bracelet filled with refrigerant) made her seem a hypocrite.

Strike the "seem." Among her inventions none was so glamorous as the Johnny Mop, a tongs-like contraption with a detachable, biodegradable pad for cleaning toilets that she sold for a hundred thousand dollars to Johnson & Johnson, which then minimally altered it to cheat her of royalties. This all blew up on the day Tod was born—the same day Nixon delivered his Checkers speech—in September 1952. When I woke from the anesthesia and asked what had happened while I was out, she told

....

* At her heaviest Mary wore a size twenty. But for most of her life she was a size eight.

† Turn and Learn, which involved rotating paper discs in the pages of a book, was meant to be an educational toy, but Ideal used it mostly for tacky Disney promotions.

me about the great mop caper and said she was so hopping mad that she was going to put on her "respectable Republican cloth coat"—though she was of course a Democrat—and sue the bastards, meaning Johnson & Johnson.*

But the point is that the Toilet Queen, as we called her afterward—she was surprisingly good about being teased, even when I gave her a gold key chain charm in the shape of a mop—wouldn't get down on her knees to play with us because she'd then have to send her pants to be pressed. She had imagination about objects and processes and even bookkeeping but none about children. I promised myself that if I ever got out of her home alive, I'd do everything exactly the opposite of the way she did it. And I kept my promise. If you doubt me, ask my kids who taught them all the bad words. I told them they could say *fuck*, *shit*, and *cunt* to me all they liked, but maybe not so much to an Episcopalian priest. The trick children need to learn is how to determine the right context.

I doubt either of my parents really even wanted to have children, not the way children want to be had. Mummy's idea of a daughter was a chambermaid crossed with a lapdog; Daddy's, Clara Schumann as a chorus girl. There was only one, maybe one and a half, of those four things I had any chance of being. And it certainly wasn't the chambermaid, even if Mummy had us cleaning the bathroom and making the beds when we were still in single digits. Which is fine, except that what she meant by making the beds was ripping all the sheets completely off and turning the mattress, then putting the top sheet on the bottom and a new sheet on top. Twice a week! Keep in mind there were no fitted sheets in those days.

What I wanted, desperately, was my parents' affection, but it wasn't there to be gotten. Or I didn't know how to get it. Despite many efforts, I was no chorus girl. And all my childhood curiosity, the normal accidents and mischief of growing up, they took as deliberate provocations. One day when I was three, and not yet fully potty-trained—which was con-

* She did, or rather she dragged them into arbitration, and won. The royalties earned her a nice yearly sum—half of which she assigned to her daughters—until the patent expired in 1962.

sidered nearly defective in those days—I came to my mother's bedroom, where as usual she was just lying in bed, probably pregnant with Linda, and I peed in the doorway right in front of her.* She was so angry that she got up, dressed, packed her overnight bag, and left the house directly for the city. To me, now, that seems like an embarrassing tantrum, but she was very pleased with the story, and would tell it often to show what an effective mother she was. And it *was* effective. But there are other, kinder ways to be effective.

To be fair, she was depressed throughout most of my early childhood. She was certainly depressed in Hollywood. Both she and Daddy detested it. They had moved there for money and got it, but Daddy was frustrated because everything he and Larry wrote, no matter how good, was thrown out. They didn't have any hits during those three years except for the ones from *Love Me Tonight*: "Isn't It Romantic?" and "Lover."† In New York and London they were the toast of the town, not yet fully themselves but getting there. In California they were contract hacks who, far from being celebrated, were silenced. Daddy spent his days playing tennis, his nights playing bridge.

For my mother the problem with California was that she couldn't make the A-list; she was new to Hollywood society and didn't have enough clout. Rather than have the wrong friends, she chose to have none. She was also trying to manage Larry. Once he came home in the middle of the night and flipped an emergency master switch that turned on all the lights, waking my mother, May, Mam'selle, and me. Another time he invited a jazz band over for a midnight concert. More than once, he got the cook drunk. Whatever he did, the next morning we'd stumble upon the forty-seven pots of

....

* The family was back on the East Coast by then, living for the summer in Rye while Dorothy commuted to Manhattan to supervise renovations, or rather re-renovations, at the apartment in the Carlyle Hotel. Why those re-renovations were necessary, we'll get to.

† *Love Me Tonight* (1932) starred Maurice Chevalier and Jeanette MacDonald. It is absolutely charming.

orchids he'd ordered as an apology. We'd also stumble on Larry himself, bashfully smoking big cigars into the curtains, sometimes burning holes in them. Mummy finally made Daddy kick him out.

She had a lot to tolerate, including, no doubt, Daddy's affairs, which she never complained about, probably because she feared he would leave her if she did. Sometimes I think my sister and I were produced as some kind of marital collateral. So even though she didn't want the bother of children, she would have had more if she could. There was another pregnancy, in California, but it lasted only six months; the premature baby, also a girl, died within minutes in August of 1932. Mummy said it was one of the few times I was sweet to her: "It was as though you understood."

Mostly I was a terrible nuisance. I was always doing rotten things, which is where *The Rotten Book* came from.* In third grade, I lit an organdy curtain in my bedroom on fire—not out of bad-seed evil but just to see what would happen. What happened was instantaneous and horrifying: The whole window was aflame within seconds and then the flames leapt to the other window. I ran to the next room where Linda and the nurse were sleeping, the nurse ran into my parents' room, my father ran into my room, yanked both pairs of burning curtains to the floor, and managed to extinguish them.

"How did this happen?" he wanted to know.

Well, I had no idea, I was fast asleep when the smell of smoke woke me up and there it was, this big fire!

"Don't worry. The building super is an expert in how fires get started, and by the time you come home from school tomorrow, we will all know the answer."

In school that day, our class was performing "Hansel and Gretel." I was one of the cookie children who stood front and center, eyes closed, singing. All I could see behind my eyelids were flames.

....

* For reasons that will become clear later, Mary dedicated *The Rotten Book*, published by Harper & Row in 1969, to her fourth child, Matthew, who was anything but.

At home, after lunch, my mother told me my father wanted to see me in his study. The jig was up. As I sat in a chair facing him, he rested his hands on the desk, palms up. "Mary, do you see these hands?"

I nodded.

"These are the hands that play 'Chopsticks' with you. These are the hands that hold yours at lunch." A long, meaningful pause ensued, during which I decided not to say he hardly ever ate lunch with us, and my mitts were too busy trying to hide my calf's liver anyway. "And these are the hands that put out the fire you lit last night."

That was it.

Another time, I corrupted my "English sister," Zoë.[*] That's what I called her, though she wasn't really English or my sister: She was my Scottish French friend. When I was nine and she was ten, she was sent by her parents, whom my parents knew from their trips to London, to live with us during the Blitz. Along with her hateful English nanny, Newton, she arrived in New York in July 1940, giving Mummy and Daddy their very own ward, much as the Hammersteins had Shawen Lynch. They immediately enrolled her at Brearley with me. The following May, my mother showed up unexpectedly at school while Zoë was performing the role of Pitti-Sing in *The Mikado* to tell her that her mother, Myrtle Farquharson d'Erlanger, had been killed in the bombings. Her first question was about what would happen to the Farquharson clan, of which her mother was the titular head. Zoë already had the stiff upper lip.

I hadn't mastered mine yet, which would come to shame me. That Christmas, 1941, my parents gave me a dog—a poodle, of course, because even though we all wanted a collie after reading the novel *Lassie Come-Home*, Mummy held that there were only four possible breeds for families like ours: dalmatians, boxers, collies, and poodles. Poodles? We couldn't have been less interested.[†] Still, she made a wonderful tag for

....

[*] Zoë Caroline Georgia d'Erlanger (1930–2021), later Zoë Hyde-Thomson and Baroness d'Erlanger.

[†] Mary nevertheless had poodles ever since.

1941: Mary, Dorothy, Linda, and Richard Rodgers, with Mary's "English sister,"
Zoë d'Erlanger. "Zoë already had the stiff upper lip."

him to wear around his neck: *My name is Bunthorne* and I belong to Mary
Rodgers.* It was the best thing that happened in my whole childhood. We
called him Bunny and he was adorable, but we quickly decided he was
the only stupid poodle anyone had ever known because no one could
get him to stop chasing cars. When he was killed by one the next year,
and, once again, my mother came to school bearing bad news, I openly
evinced total misery,† but kept thinking about Zoë, who hadn't even
cried about her *mother.* It was probably that kind of thing that later led
my parents to ask if they might adopt her. She politely declined, which
made perfect sense to me.

I'd like to have been adopted by *her* family, though. Or anybody's;

....

* After the Oscar Wilde–like poet in Gilbert and Sullivan's *Patience.* Dorothy's poodle was named after the title character.

† That is, she cried.

I had daydreams about my parents dying in a tractor-trailer crash and my immediately being sent to live with the Hammersteins. Or being kidnapped, like the Lindbergh baby.* I was so envious of that baby, whose fate caused all the celebrity parents in Hollywood in the early thirties to hire security guards to protect their children. At my third birthday party, Helen Hayes's daughter, Irving Thalberg's son, and John Davis Lodge's daughters all had them. But my parents, thinking that my kidnapping was not likely or even perhaps undesirable, wouldn't get me one. I was quite put out.

I call these daydreams, but they were actually at bedtime, which for years was fixed at 7:45, right in the middle of *The Lone Ranger*. I mean, give me a break, would an extra fifteen minutes have killed you? So instead of finding out what happened to Tonto, I had something I called My Think: a few minutes I allowed myself before sleep, in which I imagined better lives I'd like to have or people I'd like to be. Prince Valiant with his wonderful bob. Princess Elizabeth. Even Princess Margaret. And, apparently, "Mary Hammerstein."

It's easy to see why. The Hammersteins seemed like much more fun than the Rodgerses.

Ockie was a big, rumpled guy with a full, friendly mouth, gentle eyes, a soft voice, and badly pockmarked skin that made people think he'd be sympathetic. Dorothy was a great-looking Australian dame with blazing red hair—dazzling Rinso white when she was older—regal posture, a slightly down-turned mouth, a happy laugh, or sometimes a naughty-little-girl giggle to make sure you knew she knew she'd said something reprehensible, which she frequently did. Together, they were a bit exotic† and the epitome of benign neglect, so unobservant that they never noticed, let alone cared, what their kids were up to. Which seemed great

----

* On March 1, 1932, the toddler son of the world-famous aviator Charles Lindbergh and the writer Anne Morrow Lindbergh was taken from his crib by a local carpenter, who later murdered him.

† Ockie, whose full name was Oscar Greeley Clendenning Hammerstein II, was only one-quarter Jewish, and Dorothy no-quarter.

1946: Richard Rodgers, Dorothy Hammerstein, Dorothy Rodgers, and Oscar Hammerstein II on a visit to Oklahoma. "The Hammersteins seemed like much more fun than the Rodgerses."

to me then, though I do think now it fucks you up. Four of the Hammersteins, including their fabulous daughter Susan—who later married Richard Widmark and Henry Fonda, though not at once, with two other husbands strewn in between—went deaf because no one was paying attention. Or at least that's how Mummy, wanting to indicate what an attentive parent she was, told the tale.*

Anyway, after three and a half years with us, Zoë returned to London in February 1943. She didn't get to lead the clan, though; that privilege eventually went to one of her cousins, Alwyne, whose younger brother, Robin Compton, was somebody I really would have gone to bed with ex-

....

* Susan Blanchard (born 1928) is Dorothy Hammerstein's daughter by her second husband, Henry Jacobson; Oscar adopted her upon marrying Dorothy in 1929. If she and three other Hammersteins "went deaf," there must have been a lot of otological negligence—or perhaps a gene?

cept he never asked me. We did write songs together on the Isle of Mull, though. Gorgeous to look at—the Isle of Mull, I mean—but there was nothing to eat there except rabbit and lobster. Every other day I'd go out with Zoë to hunt or trap them. Lobsters were easier. Have you ever tried carrying around a brace of dead rabbits? They get heavier and heavier.

Where was I? Oh, right. So Zoë and I lined the toilet bowl with tissues and, figuring the water would prevent any damage, set them aflame with matches Zoë had stolen while visiting an uncle at the Plaza. But we were dumb enough not to lift the seat, so all the paint on the underside got burned off. My mother was furious and made us pay for the replacement; she also made us light twenty packages of matches one match at a time and drop them into the toilet to cure us of what she called our pyromania. But it wasn't pyromania, it was science. It was high energy and a lack of tact. And maybe something else. My father, along with his fear of tunnels, bridges, the corners of anything, and self-service elevators, had, even more than most people, a terrible fear of fire.

I guess I knew which buttons to press. And because I was so aggrieved, I never felt very guilty. Except once—and it wasn't about anything I did to my parents. We had returned to California after a visit to New York, where I'd gotten an Empire State Building penny bank. I was two. One day, while Mam'selle was kneeling in the closet, straightening my shoes, I thought: *If I turn this bank upside down on her neck it'll flip down her back, and wouldn't that be fun?* But, accidentally, I dropped it on her head, that heavy bank full of pennies, and she cried. Oh my god, the horror of making someone else cry, when I was so loath to do so myself. That's what it took to shame me finally: the unfairness of making someone feel what I never wanted to feel.

I'd had plenty of experience with that, from the other angle. Still, I was surprised when my mother later said, "We love you, but we don't like you." Good to know.

3.

A GENUINE PRINCESS

The whole time I was working on *Once Upon a Mattress** I never noticed how neatly its story tracked mine. How could I? Even if I were the kind of person who studied herself in the present tense, it would not have occurred to me; that's not how I think creativity works. You don't write something because it is personally meaningful, and you don't leave clues all over your manuscript as if it were one of Steve's scavenger hunts. You simply write whatever is before you to write. Maybe Daddy and Ockie could pick stories that consciously reflected their politics and unconsciously revealed their conflicts. But they were the most successful team in the business. At the beginning of a career, whether creative or romantic, you don't say "no" to much. As with children, if what you produce resembles you, it's mostly an accident.

Or so I assumed. *Mattress* wasn't a mission statement: It was a job I fell into, as I've always fallen into everything. By rights, if its story tracked anyone's life, it should have been Marshall's, since the whole thing was his idea; he'd been thinking for years about a Borscht Belt retelling of Hans Christian Andersen's fairy tale "The Princess and the Pea." During the summer of 1958, it was he who wrote the lyrics and co-wrote† the

---

* The 1959 musical with which Mary, with Marshall Barer as her lyricist, made her Broadway debut as a composer.

† With Dean Fuller and Jay Thompson.

book. I was merely the composer, finding notes for his words. Actually, I wasn't even supposed to be the composer; the job only landed in my lap when no one else's lap was available.

But looking at the show from the distance of decrepit old age—and from the other side of several careers, of which musical theater was just the first—certain things, then obscure, seem glaringly obvious. As quickly as we put it together, *Once Upon a Mattress* was built to last.* It has a classic fish-out-of-water theme and an independent heroine in the Jane Austen mold, if Austen got out of the house a bit more—say, to the Catskills. That heroine is called Winnifred of Farflelot, or Winnifred the Woebegone: a big, awkward, loudmouth princess, born to royalty but nevertheless a misfit, likable but unsure of herself.† Despite her exalted provenance, she has to outwit a vain and icy queen to get what she wants and live happily ever after.

Story of my life, if only I'd realized it. At the time, writing *Mattress*, I was in one of my periodic happily ever afters, which, spoiler alert, don't last long. I was twenty-seven, freshly divorced, finally doing what I wanted the way I wanted, even if I was always terrified of failing. But one thing my life had shown me by then was that failing wasn't so bad. In any case, it was inevitable, especially when your father was a god and your mother, well, a vain and icy queen.

So failing to finish college didn't faze me; I would one day end up on the boards of educational institutions.‡ I failed at my first marriage, or

. . . .

* Sixty years on, it remains one of the most popular titles in the musical theater catalog, performed hundreds of times a year by schools and amateurs and revived regularly by professionals.

† "Shy," Winnifred's introductory number paradoxically belted to the rafters, sums it up: "And you may be sure / Way down deep I'm demure / Though some people I know might deny it / At bottom I'm quiet and pure."

‡ Mary served as a trustee of Phillips Exeter Academy from 1977 to 1988

it failed me, but I'd get another chance. (And in the meantime, I could date lots of unmarriageable men.) If I'd failed as a daughter, as I was constantly told, I would eventually earn some grudging respect, both from the god and the queen, in their own difficult ways. Even failing in musical theater, a heartbreak, allowed me to discover in my forties that I had other arrows in my quiver.* And if I failed in some ways as a mother, my kids, I think, have forgiven me. They certainly had a fun ride.

Steve, in his show with the thousand names,† wrote that "you have to learn to bounce." My version of that is learning to swerve. There are few straight lines in life, and how you get from one thing to another—and then to another—is more a testament to resilience than brilliance. It's a testament to ignorance, too: It pays not to know what you can't do and not to add up the damage. Or at least that has been my experience, and even though my circumstances have been unusual, I think the road is pretty much the same for everyone. So if I sound like a poor little rich girl, whining about disapproving parents and being a woman in a man's field and the burdens of tending a creative soul—but I don't believe in a soul—substitute any particulars you like. Jane Austen wasn't an Upper East Side Jew, but I trust she would understand.

....

and on the board of the Juilliard School starting in 1992. From 1994 to 2001 she was Juilliard's chairman.

* The trio of *Freaky Friday* books published between 1972 and 1982 are perennial young adult favorites, frequently remade for film—and musicals.

† The Stephen Sondheim–John Weidman musical about the catastrophic, multitalented Mizner brothers first surfaced in 1999 as *Wise Guys*. It went through many changes and two intermediate titles (*Gold!* and *Bounce*) before emerging in 2008 as *Road Show* at the Public Theater.

4.

TOO GOOD TO BE TRUE

And really, I'm not by nature a whiner. But get me talking about my mother and that comes out. My father was, in many ways, just as inexcusable, yet I excuse him. He gave me music, literally: Very early on, as he reminded me when I almost burned the house down, he put my right hand on top of his to play the upper notes of "Chopsticks" until I could play them without his guidance. Then he taught me to play the first eight bars of "Why Can't I?": a sequence of chromatic thirds I could manage with my two index fingers.* Then we'd put them together: "Chopsticks" and "Why Can't I?" When I asked him how it was possible that the same melody could feel one way the first time but totally different when it was repeated, he explained that I had discovered the secret of harmony.

Best of all, he took me to the orchestra readings of all the Rodgers and Hart shows, which were held a few days before opening to correct wrong notes, set tempi, and, in general, perfect the orchestra's performance. In the thirties, these readings took place not in a rehearsal room, as they do now, but in the pit of the theater. I was plunked down in the first row, where I sat blissfully all day, luxuriating in the live sound of songs I'd already heard, sometimes only fragmentarily, floating up to my

....

* A great, melancholy Rodgers and Hart song, from the musical *Spring Is Here*, which ran for three months in 1929.

bedroom from downstairs while Daddy played at parties or wafting out of our living room as they were being written.

Of course, when he was writing, it was sacrilege to interrupt or disturb him in any way. If we did venture near him at the piano, he instinctively put his hand over its corner, as much to protect it as us. Even so, he would sometimes ask, surprisingly nervously, what we thought. Well, of course we thought whatever he wrote was marvelous—and most of it really was, especially the early stuff. Later, with all those goddamn praying larks and uplifting hymns for contralto ladies, I sometimes hated what he got up to.* Wouldn't it have been more interesting if it had been a shark that learned to pray? Or a narc? And the lovers' songs in *The King and I*—ugh!† All that Brahmsy thickness.‡ I do love some of the stuff he wrote with Oscar, especially *Carousel* and *Oklahoma!*—"Lonely Room" is brilliant dramatic writing.§ But they were doing something different in those "Golden Age" shows.¶ What I first loved were the tickly, funny

....

* A lark somehow learns to pray in the title song from *The Sound of Music.* The hymns are "Climb Ev'ry Mountain," from the same show, and "You'll Never Walk Alone," from *Carousel.* They are very popular among English football teams.

† "I Have Dreamed" and "We Kiss in the Shadow."

‡ Brahms is not the only composer whose influence has been discerned in Rodgers's music. In a radio bit from 1937, Charlie McCarthy, the dummy, accused him of lifting the melody for "My Heart Stood Still" from Mendelssohn. Rodgers's other favorite composers were Puccini, Bach, and Mozart.

§ "Lonely Room": a creepy, scratchy soliloquy for Jud Fry, the twisted villain of *Oklahoma!*

¶ Richard Rodgers was for the most part serially monogamous (in his work). He wrote with Hart from 1919 through Hart's death and then, with only the slightest overlap, with Hammerstein until he died, too. After that came a series of one- or two-show stands, most of them disasters, one of them Mary's fault.

songs he wrote with Larry, and of course the melancholy ones, too. "He Was Too Good to Me"?* "Little Girl Blue"?† It was almost impossible to believe that such songs, so natural and full of feeling, were written at all, let alone by him. He spoiled me for genius, which is why my life ever since has been a joyous talent search. I collect it the way some people collect paintings.

Talent excuses almost anything but Arthur Laurents. So, eventually, does understanding. Becoming a mother, making totally different but maybe just as big mistakes, I began to see my own mother differently. What looked to me as a child like malign hawkishness was really something else. It was *unintentionally* malign hawkishness. Is that an improvement? Yes. You can't stay angry at people when you understand that they couldn't help being who they were. There was a reason my mother was so tentacular, reaching her long arms into every corner of my business and trying to arrange me as if I were a divan in an apartment she was decorating, all the while keeping herself at a great, wintry distance. She was *frozen.* Maybe frigid, too, at least by my father's standards, which were Dionysian. I think it was the owner of the Alvin Theatre‡ who gave him a key to a room of his own upstairs: a place he could take girlfriends anytime he wanted, which was quite often. I would find out about these

....

* Dropped in previews from *Simple Simon* (1930), "He Was Too Good to Me" became a standard anyway. Hart's lyric is exceptionally simple and touching: "It's only natural I'm blue: He was too good to be true."

† "Little Girl Blue" closed the first act of *Jumbo* (1935), the first of her father's shows Mary saw, at a matinee when she was four. Both she and the playwright Edward Albee (separately) remembered this joke from it: Jimmy Durante crosses the stage, leading an elephant on a rope. A cop comes up to him halfway across and says, "Where ya goin' widdat elephant?" And Durante says, "What elephant?"

‡ Four Rodgers and Hart musicals played there, as did *Once Upon a Mattress* for three months of its run. It's now the Neil Simon.

girlfriends years later. Some volunteered the information, like Elaine Steinbeck, eventual wife of John, who when she was Elaine Anderson was an assistant stage manager on *Oklahoma!* Others I just heard about through the theater grapevine: Eva Gabor, who was in the play *The Happy Time*, which Daddy and Ockie produced; Diahann Carroll, who was the star of *No Strings*—that one was supposedly serious. And sometimes there were hints in Walter Winchell,* which my mother told me to ignore, but, really, how could you? Daddy apparently had a big thing with the original Tuptim in *The King and I*: Doretta Morrow, the whitest Burmese slave princess ever. One matinee day when they were having a fine old time in his little sex quarters at the Alvin, he successfully persuaded her to overstay her break, making her late for an understudy rehearsal. He promised to cover for her but didn't and she was fired. Shitty way to treat someone you supposedly cared about. To say nothing of your wife.†

No wonder the facts-of-life lecture Mummy gave me and Linda was so bland; it was like she was reading aloud from a Fodor's guide to some city she never wanted to revisit. "A man and a woman, when they love each other very much, put their arms around each other and"—*blecch!* It put me off sex for years. Linda asked, quite pragmatically, "Do they have to put their arms around each other?"

Later, when I was fourteen, I asked Mummy what "six nine" was, other than "fifteen" in a game of Snakes; I'd apparently misheard "sixty-nine" and thought she'd be the expert.

....

* Walter Winchell (1897–1972) was the leading newspaper and radio gossip of the day, and not above blackmail. Hart mentioned him in a lyric from *Babes in Arms*: "I go to Coney, the beach is divine. / I go to ball games, the bleachers are fine. / I follow Winchell, and read every line. / That's why the lady is a tramp."

† Whether Hammerstein was a man of better character has been debated; he was at least more discreet. He had a longtime affair with a showgirl called Temple Texas, who sounds like a congregation in Dallas but was really named Dora Jane Temple and appeared in *Pipe Dream*.

"I have no idea," she answered.

I also asked how long an orgasm lasted, which I knew perfectly well because I'd had plenty of them under the tub tap.

"Whatever do you mean?" she said.

"I mean how long do they go on?"

"What a question!"

"Twenty-five minutes?"

"Don't be ridiculous!"

She wouldn't tell me. Withholding was all the power she had.

Which was the story of her marriage. She was, or at least was promoted as, a rich East Side girl, a princess, an Edith Wharton character except Jewish—though until she emerged years later as some kind of Lady Bountifulstein she tended to downplay that. She was, au fond, anti-Semitic, even though her mother had helped to create the Federation of Jewish Charities thrift shops. Her anti-Semitism was really a version of class paranoia, and we all had it. I once asked her, about someone we knew, "Is it spelled 'Jacobson' or 'Jacobsen'?"—the former, I knew, being the Jewish way. She said "O." I somehow indicated with my face that that was too bad, and she picked up on it right away, understanding that I was anti-Semitic the same way she was.

Well, maybe not the same way; I would never lie about it. Whereas she, to be more like the Warburgs and the Rothschilds, claimed her people were German Jews, unlike my father's, who were Russian. But when you finally looked into her family's place of origin, it was more like Prussia, which was virtually Poland. And when you finally looked into it, the Feiners weren't so rich, either. It's just that, hoping to jump class, they pretended to be.

Pretense, lies, hypocrisy: Put it in Latin and you've got a family crest.

And Mummy was just as two-faced about race. "It's terrible what they do to colored people," she'd moan, but she wouldn't hire a colored maid. She wouldn't hire even olive-skinned help. We had only French and Irish help, and, for a while, a pair—Elna and Inez, a Finnish cook and a Swedish maid—who were lesbians together. This was totally fine with my mother for some reason, though she disdained gay men even when they were her colleagues and supposed friends.

Daddy was much more coherent about race but much more of a coward; he didn't want to get in trouble. During the entire civil rights movement, I don't remember him ever speaking up for Black people, though he loved sleeping with them.*

I suppose Mummy was no worse than other pampered women of her background. Her father, Benjamin Feiner, was a really wicked man, but she adored him, and he adored her. Her mother, May, had four live-in help, a private masseuse, and a spare nanny for the nanny's day off. Together they saw to it she had only the most beautiful, expensive clothes, often purchased on exhausting daylong safaris through the best Paris shops. For God's sake, she had ermines as a child, even though they were *not* Warburgs or Rothschilds, however much they pretended. Ben was just a lawyer. But I think it went beyond his wanting to spoil her; he took that word to a different level. I've seen letters he wrote her that would give you chills; they suggest to me, if not to my Feiner cousins, who say I'm overinterpreting the literary style of the time, a sort of unseemly relationship, with all that icky romantic language about how much he missed her when she went to college: *My darling dearest Dorothy.*† My father never wrote *me* any *darling dearest* letters.

She went to and hated Wellesley, which is why, two decades later, I went there, too: to prove her wrong. The only trouble is, I hated it as much she had. She left, just like me—but even earlier; I made it through three and a half years, she through only two, after which she traveled to Egypt with her parents. I imagine her forced to ride a smelly camel, which she wouldn't have liked at all. But until she was married, she had very little power to shape herself, except physically; when her father one time—one time!—mentioned her weight, she went all anorexic

....

* As for gay men, can we believe (as has been reported) that he called Larry Hart "that little faggot" while also being very protective of him, sometimes fishing him out of trouble when he got rolled? Mary did.

† A representative sample: "Sweetheart, believe it or not, I have been stunned into silence by an overpowering anxiety at the mere prospect of having my love with me again in a few days."

for years and lived on laxatives. I think that's what screwed her up internally.* Telling, don't you think, that what she really wanted to be, if she'd had her druthers, was a sculptor? She spent a year studying in New York and Paris, in studios her parents paid for on Sixth Avenue and the rue de Châtillon, but she finally realized that she had no talent.

Maybe that's something else I got from her. I don't mean no talent. I mean the ability to be, as she was, clear-eyed about its size and application. My kids don't like when I say that; they want to pump up my perfectly nice achievements into something bigger. But I'm happy with what I achieved by being honest with myself and not letting ego push me further than the circumstances allowed. I was able, unlike a lot of people, especially men, to try new roads when the old ones petered out. As a result, I did very nicely, thank you, in three very different careers, and though I'm proud of that, it is probably just as meaningful to me to have been a mother, especially serving as some sort of conduit between my father's musical talent and Adam's. Adam hates when I refer to myself that way—sandwiched between two geniuses—but tough luck, it's the truth, even if the metaphor sucks. What am I, bologna?

My mother wasn't so much sandwiched as, I don't know, Popsicled. She was very beautiful—though Hank, when he asked her for my hand in marriage, didn't think so—and smelled great, with her lily of the valley perfume and her linens stored in a closet strewn with expensive soap. But she was hard, cold, stuck within herself, even as Ben and May started to bring her out.† They went to Europe every summer on an ocean liner, where she was courted by plenty of eligible men. It was all so promising.

And then she met Daddy—or actually re-met him. Daddy was friendly with Ben Feiner Jr. and crossed paths with his kid sister Dorothy over the years. In 1925, she sat directly behind him in the front row as he conducted the orchestra of *Dearest Enemy*, his first musical comedy hit with Hart. Later that season, when he stopped by the Feiners' to pick up

....

* Dorothy Rodgers suffered chronic pain from abdominal adhesions.

† Jewish girls couldn't "debut" but had other rituals, as Mary would later discover.

Ben Jr. to go to the movies, he ran into Mummy, who, no doubt looking gorgeous in a gown, was on her way out with Andrew Goodman, as in Bergdorf's, to see Jerome Kern's *Sunny*. She was sixteen. Daddy ogled her but decided, in an unusual fit of discretion and temperance, to wait a year before pouncing.

5.

THE BLUE ROOM

He was from the wrong side of the tracks, but the minute you're famous there are no tracks to be from the wrong side of; you pull up the tracks behind you. Moss Hart is a perfect example of that.* He didn't know how to pronounce anything, and if you ever heard him speak you would think, *Shit, who would believe he knew all those words?*

My father was much more presentable, even though he'd dropped out of high school, college, and Juilliard† the minute he grabbed whatever was useful from them. He spoke beautifully, had a great-looking mouth, and dressed in bespoke suits. He was also, by 1926, when he finally made his move on my mother during a transatlantic crossing, a transatlantic celebrity.‡ In demand both on Broadway and in London, he was mak-

....

* Before he became famous as a director, Moss Hart (1904–1961) wrote, with George S. Kaufman, the book for Rodgers and Hart's *I'd Rather Be Right* (1937). Moss Hart and Larry Hart were unrelated, though they were both gay, as anyone but Moss's wife, Kitty Carlisle, could tell.

† Or, really, its forerunner, the Institute of Musical Art.

‡ He and Hart had songs on Broadway ever since "Any Old Place with You," their first copyrighted song, got interpolated into someone else's score for *A Lonely Romeo* in 1919. But they only began to make a name for

ing five thousand dollars a week, and had a reputation, glamorous at the time, as a ladies' man. Anyway, he had ladies. He fucked anything female he could get his hands on.

Except Dorothy Belle Feiner. A year after Ben provided the here's-my-kid-sister introduction, Daddy ran into her aboard the RMS *Majestic*, the largest ship in the world, chugging from Cherbourg to New York. In that setting especially she would have been wowed by him, but you can also see why, despite being just seventeen, she would have maneuvered to keep control of the courtship. She was not going to be one of his discards. For three years she kept him at bay, even dabbling, or pretending to dabble, with the handsome but much older Hollywood star Ronald Colman to make him jealous. Maybe she was afraid of the intensity of her feelings for him, or maybe she was just testing his fidelity, but she also had another problem to manage: her family's snobbery. Daddy's talent and fame opened all kinds of doors, but only for him, not his clan. The Rodgerses—Will and Mamie—weren't the Feiners' sort. (They weren't even really Rodgerses; their name was originally Rogazinsky, with a detour along the way as Abrams.) It was bad enough that they were from Russia; they were also from the West Side.*

Wherever they were from, they were awful. Will had red hair and blue eyes and a terrible temper, maybe not a great quality in a general practi-

....

themselves with the *Garrick Gaieties* in 1925, a revue that included their first hit, "Manhattan." By the time Dick married Dorothy, five years later, eleven more Rodgers and Hart shows (and another *Gaieties*) had been produced on Broadway, with even more hits: "Mountain Greenery," "My Heart Stood Still," "Thou Swell," "The Blue Room." You could do that then. Well, he could.

* The Rodgerses lived in a brownstone at 3 West 120th Street, in the Mount Morris Park neighborhood of Harlem. (Lorenz Hart's family lived around the corner.) At the time, and even fifty years later when Hank and Mary moved to the Majestic on Central Park West, the West Side was considered by East Siders to be only marginally better than living in a stable.

tioner. His bedside manner was prehistoric, at least from the evidence of
how he treated Daddy when Daddy was eight and got osteomyelitis in
his left pointer finger. It was swollen as thick as his wrist. The maid got
a hold of my grandfather and they operated on him in the office downstairs, with no anesthesia, she holding him down as he screamed in pain.
I don't think he ever forgave his father for hurting him so much. In any
case, he carried that scar to his death, and I was obsessed with the missing
nail on the crucial finger.

That wasn't the only scar he carried with him from Harlem. Will absolutely hated Mamie's parents, who lived with them. People literally didn't
speak to each other in that sad house, except when they were screaming.
Mamie herself was adorable, this little round person, quite homely; I just
loved her because she was a completely uncritical ball of Jewish fluff.
But she was so intimidated by life that she was useless to stem the tide
of anger around her. An adult woman, she wouldn't walk to the corner
without her mother at her side. Even when she was old, she remained
scared of everyone, especially Mummy, her imperious daughter-in-law. I
remember a pocketbook she had, with lizard handles; like all children I
wanted to see what was in there. So I would open it without asking, and
Mamie finally said one day, "I wish you wouldn't do that. I don't mind but
your mother does." She died when I was about nine, of a stroke.

I'm surprised she didn't have the fatal stroke much earlier, with that
family. About Daddy's older brother, Morty, I have nothing good to say—
and I will say it later—except that he was a talented obstetrician, if you
include sleeping with lots of your patients and thus landing in Mary Astor's diary as a talent.* He had a filthy temper and was mean as a snake,
constantly torturing the kid at the piano.†

....

* Lawyers threatened to introduce the diary of the actress Mary Astor
(1906–1987) as evidence of adultery during a 1936 custody battle with
her ex-husband. The diary, written in brown ink the press preferred to
call purple, was deemed inadmissible in court, but its details of her many
affairs, including one with "G"—George S. Kaufman—were soon leaked.

† Say this for Mortimer Rodgers (1898–1970): He was directly or indirectly

In a way, you couldn't blame him; when you have a younger brother, as I had a younger sister, who is called the genius in the family, it makes you a little resentful, if you have any brains. Morty was constantly being outshone by Little Smiling Richard, because Little Smiling Richard was the source of the only joy the Rodgers family had. Will and Mamie both loved musical theater, and when Daddy got old enough, they would take him downtown to the latest Victor Herbert, or whoever was writing at that point. Mamie had such a good ear, she would just come home and play the stuff, and as soon as Daddy was able to climb up to the piano, he too would pick out the tunes.

I say Little Smiling Richard, but smiling doesn't mean happy. He just knew to keep his mouth shut long enough for things to pass, and when his mouth was shut in those days it could look like a smile. He wasn't fresh, he wasn't critical, he was not engaged in the family business of hating. Not out loud, anyway. Inside, he must have been at a hard boil, because he was still boiling decades later. He learned early on to cultivate that split, which eventually got so pronounced that what he was like as a person no longer bore any resemblance to what he was like in his music.*

At first, that was a good thing. If he was moody and angry internally, he was joyful and mischievous at the piano.† When he wrote with Larry, he didn't care where his cadences went or what his chords were; he just peed out these insanely charming songs.‡ He wasn't worried; he knew

....

responsible for introducing Richard Rodgers to both Hart and Hammerstein, schoolmates of his at Columbia.

* Perhaps that's why he went to five different psychiatrists before he died, and at one point spent twelve weeks in a stupor at Payne Whitney, the psychiatric hospital.

† You can read all about how he met Larry, how he struggled to get their songs performed, and how he almost gave up on music in 1924 in favor of the children's underwear business in his memoir, a work of fiction punningly entitled *Musical Stages*.

‡ As Noël Coward charmingly put it.

that by doing whatever he wanted he'd get where he needed to go. I mean that musically, but that's how he lived, too—and probably how any very successful very young man, a hit at twenty-three, did and still does. Drinking, though not yet a drunk; smoking, though not yet cancerously; womanizing, though not yet in violation of vows.

You can almost understand how, a few bon vivant years later, he might have fallen for my mother, despite, or because of, her forbidding propriety and reserve. Clearly, she'd make a good home for him, and play the role of Great Man's Wife beautifully. She was curious, an autodidact, and plenty pretty. But she also offered that "interlock" thing you see in some successful couples—I don't mean happy couples. They had complementary neuroses, complementary needs. He needed an anchor, she needed escape. If that wasn't clear to her before, it must have become clear when her father tried to get her to call off the engagement once it came. "If you have a jealous personality," Ben said, knowing that she did, "you mustn't marry this man. Because as you get older the chorus girls will get younger, and it's going to make you miserable."

My mother ignored her father's actually rather accurate advice. She wasn't willful, not with him, but her filial loyalty had been superseded by what she felt, and hoped, about Daddy. They married on March 5, 1930, in her parents' apartment at the Marguery.* She was twenty and he twenty-eight. A family doctor promised to come over the next day to tell them about birth control, but being a Catholic, he didn't show.† She was pregnant within a month.

---

* The Marguery was an elegant residential hotel at 270 Park Avenue. Stephen Wise, the leading Reform rabbi of the day, performed the ceremony, as he had for just about everyone else in the room.

† For reasons that will become clear, Mary is allowed to say that.

6.

LEAVING THE BUILDING

t drove Mummy crazy that Larry Hart, having been invited to the wedding, came along for the honeymoon.* How was the flat Daddy rented in London—in Marylebone, near Regent's Park and Madame Tussauds—supposed to be a newlywed love nest with Larry always underfoot?† Actually, he was overfoot, his rooms directly above theirs; it took just two days for him to flood the joint when he forgot to turn off the bath.

Daddy probably didn't mind as much; for him, the London honeymoon was a perfect case of double-dipping: He had a show in development there.‡ His problem with Larry, which was always his problem with Larry, was that the slippery little guy wouldn't show up when they were supposed to write. His problem with my mother was that her various

....

* Hart joined the newlyweds in Cannes after a decent interval in which they visited Taormina and Rome. After Cannes, he followed them to London.

† Hart was less than five feet tall.

‡ The show was *Ever Green*, with a swell song called "Dancing on the Ceiling," for which a stiffened chandelier was mounted upside down, rising out of the floor. The plot was some nonsense about a mother and daughter who were really the same person.

ailments, made worse by the insta-pregnancy, turned her into a killjoy. He quickly got sick of her always being sick, or pretending to be—I think it was how she got her hooks into him. One time, when she wouldn't come downstairs to greet the guests, he called for her and she slammed the bedroom door. "Is Dorothy unwell?" someone asked. And Daddy said, "When is she not?"

Pretty soon the parties with dukes and swells were replaced by days in bed, and then the doctors told her she'd better go back to New York. There was no question of his going with her while business was brewing. Hadn't he warned her he would brook no interference in his work?

So back home she resentfully came, alone aboard the ship, with me aboard her. Well, not quite home. Just before leaving for London she and Daddy had signed a lease on a nine-room apartment at the Carlyle; Mummy had redecorated it top to bottom, but they rented it out while they were away. This was the Depression, after all. Until *Oklahoma!* they were, despite the money he made, always very hand-to-mouth, a situation my mother managed with great agility, a nose for bargains, and a flair for double-entry bookkeeping. I used to brag about that last one, having no idea what it meant.

So when she returned early, with the subtenants still at the Carlyle, Mummy moved into Daddy's bachelor flat at the Lombardy, at 111 East Fifty-sixth Street. It was a beautiful apartment on the nineteenth floor, with a large balcony and nice views.* But it was not a happy time. She was probably worried that her priapic husband was cheating on her as he raced between London, for *Ever Green*, and Hollywood, where he and Larry had a contract from Warner Bros. to work on *The Hot Heiress*. (That's a movie, by the way, not a person, but doesn't it strike you how

....

* The balcony was shared by his nineteenth-floor neighbor, Edna Ferber (1885–1968), then most recently the author of *Show Boat*, *Stage Door*, and *The Royal Family*. Later she became a kind of proxy parent to Mary, never ratting when the child complained about her real parents or admitted how she'd disobeyed them.

all these titles reflect what was going on?)* Mummy was also in real discomfort: I was a difficult pregnancy, or so she never stopped telling me.
When I finally asked her what was most difficult about it, she answered
that it was being unable to wear all the lovely trousseau lingerie she had
ordered from Paris.

Daddy reluctantly skipped the December debut of *Ever Green* in
London in order to be present for mine, on January 11, 1931, at Lenox
Hill Hospital.† My mother was attended, surprise, by the famous Uncle Morty. Yes, this was profoundly weird. Your nasty brother-in-law up
inside your vagina?‡ But the Rodgerses, shocked and hurt that Dorothy
didn't immediately sign up with Morty when she went shopping for a
New York obstetrician, forced the issue, as it were. So he delivered me. I
was red, wrinkled, ugly, and, at five pounds, twelve ounces, very small.
Not small enough, though; my mother probably would have preferred,
say, five pounds ten. At any rate she said to the nurse, "Take her away and
bring her back when she looks younger." Or so she told me later, and I
think it was probably true. If it wasn't true, is that better?

We lived at the Lombardy for only two months after I was born; I was
lodged in Daddy's studio, with the piano, because bachelor flats don't
have nurseries. As soon as the Carlyle subtenants moved out, we moved
in, around March of 1931. Meanwhile, Ben and May Feiner took over at
the Lombardy; with their daughter now married and Ben Jr. long since

....

* *The Hot Heiress* starred Ben Lyon and Ona Munson as a riveter and a
rich girl who fall in love. It includes the unlikely songs "Nobody Loves
a Riveter" ("she could love a plumber / or someone even dumber") and
"You're the Cats."

† He was back, but not for long; the first out-of-town tryout of the latest
Rodgers and Hart musical, *America's Sweetheart*, started in Pittsburgh a
week later.

‡ Later, Mary pointed out, he would be "up inside" hers; he delivered four
of her children. Why not the last two? Stay tuned.

established in his career of serial failures, they no longer needed that big Marguery apartment. (Stick with me about the real estate; it's important.) So it was a nice game of musical chairs, with a very special surprise *boom* when the last chair was removed.

That happened on October 22. My parents were at the theater, attending the opening night of a play called *Wonder Boy* at the Alvin. At intermission, Daddy was asked to step into the box office for a phone call. When he emerged, my mother, sensing something was up, asked, "Anything wrong, Darling?"

"I'll tell you when we get in the car."

After the show, in the car—Mayor Jimmy Walker's car; they were friends, and he was at the opening as well—Daddy told Mummy that her father was dead.*

She would have remembered at that point the events of the afternoon. And of the last year. Since her marriage, her father had not been himself, as they used to say. He'd been diagnosed with diabetes, and there was some talk about his insulin being off; insulin had become widely available in 1923.

Go ahead, ask me anything medical. I read *The Merck Manual* on the toilet.

But even if his insulin was off, something else was going on. He spoke only in a monotone and spent a lot of time doing jigsaw puzzles in the living room at the Lombardy. He took little comfort from my mother's visits to cheer him up, especially when she brought me along. He would say, every time, "That baby's too fat!"

What is it with my family and fat? You'd think we were a clan of zeppelins.

My mother, hearing this as a criticism of her parenting—and, what's more, as a criticism of the nurse she'd hired—kept insisting that I was

---

* There are several versions of this story in print. In the most dramatic one, Ben Jr. comes to the theater to deliver the news in person. The one Mary tells seems more likely, yet could Richard Rodgers sit on the news for the entire second act? Probably.

merely properly plump for a baby, but each time she visited it would be the same story. She finally got so tired of the comment that, one day, she snapped: "If you say that once more, I'm going to leave the building and never come back."

"That baby's too fat," he said.

As promised, she left the building. And, that night—October 22—so did he.

By the time I was old enough to wonder why my mother didn't seem to have a father, we were in California. I was told he had died, but when I asked how, I got very vague answers. This went on for years, but of course I began to suspect from the very vagueness that something more interesting had happened. It was a Feiner cousin who eventually, if inadvertently, helped me find out what. When my family returned from California to New York in early 1934, I was wildly excited to meet Ben Jr.'s daughter Judy, who was a little more than a year older than I and was furthermore my "poor cousin," though she never rubbed my nose in it, and was rich, rich, richer in the ways that count than anyone I've ever known.*

I immediately adored her but sometimes had an odd way of showing it. When I was six and she was seven, we were taken to the Mother Goose playground in Central Park to have a nice romp in the fresh air. Judy, who by the time we were both fully grown turned out to be a whole foot taller than I, was even then substantially larger, so naturally I punched her. In my own defense I have to point out that at that time I was under the malevolent management of a governess named Miss Kates, née Katz, who the previous summer had beaten me with both the hard and the bristly end of a hairbrush—"and you'll get worse if you tell your mother." The reason? Having been served the same gristly hunk of ice-cold calf's liver for lunch, dinner, and next day's breakfast, with the threat of never getting any other food until I ate it, I had finally resorted to spitting it out in the toilet, and she caught me.

....

* Judith Feiner Crichton (1929–2007) was a pioneer in TV news and the first executive producer of the documentary series then called *The American Experience*.

Let me just say: Don't do this! Why should a child sit for an entire lunch with an oyster in her mouth, holding it there so she can get rid of it later? That was Linda; oysters were her calf's liver. Years later, I sent my kids with our Scandinavian au pair to dine with my parents at the Oak Room, and the au pair told me afterward never to ask her to do that again, because it was too cruel. Mummy was still up to her old tricks, making the kids order and eat things they didn't want. If you just let them come to unusual foods by themselves, they do. The day he got home from camp one year, Alec excitedly said, "You gotta take me to a French restaurant." When we got there, he ordered snails—how marvelous! I try not to think about how he experienced snails at camp, though.

Anyway, poor Jude got punched and promptly burst into tears, which came as a terrible shock. "You punched me in my typhoid shot," she wailed. Boy, was I sorry. Still am.

Where was I?* Please excuse the loopy way I tell stories, one hooking into the next until it's hard to find the way back. Oh yes. When I was twelve or so, Judy and I were at the matinee of something and I asked her, "Do you ever get a funny instinct to do something crazy? Like when the curtain goes up to run up and down the aisle?"

"Sure," she said.

"Or," I added, "to jump out a window?"

"Don't ever talk about that!" she hissed.

I must have looked confused because she quickly shut down the conversation: "Never mind, it's about your grandfather, and don't ever talk about it."

So I went right home and asked my parents, "What is it about Grandfather Ben's death I'm not supposed to talk about?" At which point my mother got up and left the room. My father said he'd had some kind of heart attack. Perhaps he did—as he was falling.

By that point I'd put two and two together, despite my bad math, and knew my father was lying. A little trick soon confirmed it. My grandmother May had a sweet old maddening housekeeper person named

* Proposed title no. 2 for these memoirs: *Where Was I?*

Mrs. McCulgin, whom I casually asked one day, "Why did Grandpa Ben kill himself?"

Without skipping a beat she said, "He was very depressed."

I got the truth, even if it took a decade. I now understood that my mother, connecting her father's jumping off the terrace of the Lombardy to the exchange she'd had with him that afternoon, thought she was partly responsible for his death. And that I in my fatness was, too.

7.

SIX DAYS A WEEK

You'll have noticed the major role played in these lovely reminiscences by what we used to call the help. I was raised, six days a week, then and always, by a nurse or nanny. We also had, in various combinations, a cook, a waitress, a chambermaid, and a laundress. This makes us sound very rich, and I guess compared to most of the world we were, with a lot of my childhood spent in a big duplex in the city and a series of country homes on Long Island and in Connecticut. Mummy always brushed this off by saying that Daddy didn't start to make "real" money until the 1940s, by which point he was in the 99 percent tax bracket, which of course didn't exist. She certainly hoarded her cash as if it did; she liked to play would-she-or-wouldn't-she games, and keep us in a financial fog, as a way of exerting control. As a result, when she died, we were shocked to find that we had to sell their paintings for millions of dollars to cover the huge taxes on the estate. Maybe someone better at math would have known all along.

Anyway, the people we moved among were far richer. In grade school at Brearley,* and before that in kindergarten at Horace Mann,†

....

* The highly exclusive (read: not many Jews; no Blacks) all-girls private school on East Eighty-third Street.

† The somewhat exclusive private school whose girls' division was then

my classmates included Rockefellers and Vanderbilts, Stephen Vincent Benét's daughter Rachel, who got kicked out, and Pammy Woolworth. My friend Leslie Nast, Condé's daughter, had two urns outside the door to her bedroom, filled to the brim with quarters. All I ever got as an allowance was one quarter, and I can't tell you what a temptation it was to reach in and grab a handful. By comparison, my father was just a little Jewish songwriter, and I was part of the 3 percent quota of Jews that Brearley admitted.

Among the others were Irving Berlin's three half-Jewish daughters, Mary Ellin, Linda, and Elizabeth, so maybe they counted only fractionally toward the quota. One day I asked my mother, "Whose daddy is more famous, theirs or mine?" She said, "I hate to tell you this: Theirs is." But when World War II started and we had an air-raid drill in which we all sat against the walls singing songs from *Oklahoma!*, I went home and said triumphantly, "Well, now who's more famous!"*

Anyway, in those days, even middle-class families had help. Probably better help than ours. Some of our nurses and nannies, like Mam'selle, were lovely; Elna and Inez, the lesbian couple, were marvelously discreet and loyal—to my mother. They were the ones who told her, much later, about the liquor bottles Daddy hid in the toilet tank. It was the first any of us supposedly knew about his alcoholism. Turns out he was practically Ray Milland in *The Lost Weekend*: a bottle of vodka a day. Sixteen Scotch-and-sodas after dinner. But aside from a little slurred diction in the evening, it never showed, at least not to us, at least not then. If he'd had any friends, they might have known, but you could count his friends on the fingers of no hands. Jerry Whyte, a big redhead factotum at the Rodgers and Hammerstein office, was probably his most trusted intimate,

---

in Morningside Heights. Dorothy Feiner had gone there straight through high school, graduating just ten years before Mary arrived.

* Probably still Irving Berlin.

but even he wasn't really a friend; he was an abettor and procurer.* A
real character, that Jerry Whyte: A rumrunner during the Depression, he
always smelled of horse shit and leather because he loved the races. He
was comfortable with royalty and gangsters, and especially royalty who
were gangsters. Reader, I slept with him.

But mostly, helpwise, we seemed to attract nutjobs. By the time you
eliminated the option of Black people, and added in the house preference
for starch over warmth, you were narrowing in on a weird population.
Mummy inadvertently favored nannies who were mean because mean
ones were better than kind ones at preventing me from bothering her.

Miss Kates, of the calf's liver crisis, was not just mean but barmy, an
honest-to-God mess of a woman. She told my mother she had two children, one of them dead. Then, while she worked with us, the other one
died. She used to share a bedroom with me, and I would wake up to find
her sobbing, but when I asked her why, she said it was because she'd been
so mean to my mother. Huh? I would lie on the floor to be closer to her
and a comfort. I was seven, but I knew something was wrong; my mother
began to catch on only when someone from Brearley called home and
said, "There's something the matter with Mary. Have you changed help?"
Which was very insightful; kids who can't act out at home act out at
school, and vice versa. My parents must have then spoken to Miss Kates,
because that's when we found out that both her dead children were
fictional.

Soon enough, in fact on the morning of the day of the great hurricane of 1938,† her psychiatrist—even our *nanny* had a shrink!—phoned.
My mother was under the dryer at Elizabeth Arden's when the call came,
so my father, who was playing the piano in the living room, had to get

....

* Jerome Whyte's more polite titles included stage manager, production
supervisor, touring director, and, near the end of his life, supervising director of Rodgers and Hammerstein.

† The so-called Long Island Express hit New York on September 21, 1938.
The city was spared the worst of the damage.

up reluctantly from his work to answer. "Get the kids out of the house," the shrink told him, "and when they return make sure that psychopath is gone."

In those days, fathers didn't know much about children, but Daddy knew enough to explain that Linda, who was three and a half, was in bed with a cold: Maybe she shouldn't go out in the rain? "Wrap her up in a blanket and get her out of there," commanded the shrink, so Linda spent the day at our grandmother May's apartment across the street, where I joined them when I was dismissed early from school to wait out the hurricane.

By the time we got home from my grandmother's, Miss Kates had been disappeared: Her things were gone and her bed was stripped. Daddy was back at his writing, Linda got back in bed, and Mummy, back from Miss Arden's beautifully coiffed, had to give me my bath. Actually, she just sat on the toilet seat and watched me give myself a bath. "How about a little elbow grease?" she inquired.

"We only use soap," I told her.

And then during My Think I leaned out the window with the rain whipping my face, watching saplings bend down to the pavement. It was the best.

You might expect that my own experiences would have led me to renounce nurses and nannies when I became a mother, but no; I had all kinds of household help (and still do, in a way, only now they're once again minding me). I tell myself that my motives were different: I needed nannies if I was going to work, especially in the theater with its crazy hours, whereas my parents would have done almost anything not to have to deal with me themselves. I hope, at least, I picked 'em better than my mother, although I did once have to slap a little British tyrant of a nanny in the face. She was so mean to Tod—who, to be fair, was even more ingenious at being naughty than I was. He unscrewed locks off doors. He threw great big FAO Schwarz blocks out the window, and one time a flowerpot, a piece of which bounced up from the pavement and cut a mademoiselle's stockings as she came back from the park with her charge. I damn near got sued, but sent a dozen stockings to replace the torn one.

And one frigid day when he was six I found him hanging halfway out the maid's-room window, trying to catch a cold so he wouldn't have to perform in the Buckley School Christmas play.

Tod, who now looks just like his father, also kept up the family tradition of unorthodox eliminations. One time, I opened the closet to get his snowsuit and found a turd in a wastebasket. I said, "Oh, Tod, what a good boy!" because at least it was in a container. When Burt Shevelove* heard about this, he gave Tod an enormous flashlight and said, very tactfully, "This is for when you have to go to the bathroom at night." So Tod took out the batteries and peed in it.

If he were my mother's son, I think she would have put him in an institution. But I was determined to be a different kind of parent. You could say I was more permissive, or less finicky, or just selfish in a jollier way. The main thing for me was that I didn't want my kids to feel, as I had spent my childhood feeling, unnoticed. My earliest memory, even before the 1933 earthquake, is not of my parents but of Mam'selle: No doubt at my mother's instruction, she is pasting stars on the headboard of my crib. Red stars if I wet my bed, blue stars if I had to get up in the middle of the night and needed someone to help me to the bathroom, and gold stars if I didn't ask to be taken and didn't wet my bed. With a system like that you quickly learn that you are most admired when least in evidence. You also learn, if you're me, not to comply. Very few of the stars pasted on my crib were gold.

I don't go in for cheap psychology, only the expensive kind, but some things are just too true, too solid-state, to ignore. Everyone becomes a kind of monster of what they failed to get. My father wanted, if he had to have girl children, girls who were showgirls; so I dreamed about dancing in a Broadway show. I was so excited when, at Horace Mann, they skipped me a year in the middle of kindergarten, because first graders not only got these swell blue typewriters, but also a class called Rhythms.

....

* Burt Shevelove (1915–1982): A brilliant play doctor and word man, he wrote, with Larry Gelbart, the book for *A Funny Thing Happened on the Way to the Forum*. When he died, he left Mary his trove of medical books.

We would gallop around the gym in time to recorded music. I tried furiously to show off at galloping, hoping someone would notice me and let me gallop a little closer to Broadway. But no one noticed. I considered it a failed audition and, not having any other ideas of how to get what I wanted, entered one of my periodic childhood funks. I began to steal from breakfast at home those little sugar cubes the waitress put out for coffee, and munch on them at school, like a horse. One day I must have had too many, because I got sick and threw up. The office called home, but my mother wouldn't come for me. I guess they looked down the contact list until they found someone who would. A little later a big limousine pulled up. It was Larry Hart's.

That was fine by me; Larry was fun. Because of his height I thought of him not only as younger than Daddy (though he was, in fact, seven years older) but almost as a child. He certainly had a child's sense of delight and irresponsibility. However much he loved my father the young genius, and I suspect he loved him more than professionally, he was scared of my father the taskmaster.* When summoned to Connecticut to work, he sometimes snuck outside and hid in my tree house. Actually, that story has come down to me every which way. It was my tree house; it was Linda's tree house. (Did we have two tree houses?) Larry bribed her; Larry bribed me. Maybe it never happened at all, though it's nice to think it did, because it helps explain my connection to that kind and tragic little man. We were both on the lam.

Except that what I wanted to escape and what I wanted to get to turned out to have an awful lot in common. My first real composition, written when I was nine, was a collection of little two-piano études I called "Clean Sheets." Miss Kates, not to mention my mother, would have approved.

---

* Hart called Rodgers "the Principal." Rodgers called Hart "the Shrimp."

8.

I DON'T PERFORM

know you're supposed to go in order, but chronology is no fun. It doesn't explain much, either. In real life it sometimes happens that effects come before causes—before causes are uncovered or understood, at least. And sometimes things string together across decades so tightly you'd think they had happened together. I'm only now realizing, eighty-some years after the fact, that it probably wasn't just for money that we hightailed it to California when I was ten months old. It must have been at least as much in response to my grandfather's suicide. Duh. He left the building barely a month before we left New York. Bad luck for me that my mother was so remote in her grief at exactly the time I was waking up as a human. But, if I feel generous enough, I admit she had cause. Her princess bubble had burst. In less than two years, she'd acquired a playboy husband, a pudgy daughter, and a dead father. Her whole life had turned into an earthquake. *Is it safer to be inside or outside?*

At the time, I had no idea that this drama was going on. To me, California just seemed very lonely. The rooms were big and I was small. I was not much in my parents' company, and at one point, when my mother went back to New York for some surgery I assume was gynecological, I was left alone with my father, which probably means I never saw him. The only person I saw who wasn't hired to see me was Frieda Hart,[*] who

* Frieda Hart was Larry Hart's mother, a much-loved and much-forgiving

1934: "Let's face it, most of childhood is the most boring
prison sentence in the world, and you can't get paroled."

came by to give me a taffeta pocketbook, which she called a "poice." I
asked if there was any money in it.

Let's face it, most of childhood is the most boring prison sentence in
the world, and you can't get paroled. Is it a surprise that I became, as the
nursery rhyme says of me, quite contrary? There are home movies of
that Beverly Hills party for my third birthday, with the nannies standing
over their duded-up tots and the bodyguards lurking in the pantry; while
everyone else is singing "Mary Had a Little Lamb" in my honor, I can be
seen (if you are a good lip-reader) singing "The Farmer in the Dell" at the
top of my lungs. I guess it was counterpoint.

Three months later, in April 1934, we finally headed back to New
York. Are you tired of my youthful shenanigans yet? In those days, you
went by rail. Every now and then they would stop the train to water it
or something, and the passengers were allowed to disembark. My father,

German immigrant with a thick accent.

taking me out for a walk at one of those stops, said, "Don't put your foot in the crack or you'll get stuck in the ties." So of course I put my foot in the crack and it did get stuck, and then a train was coming along. Daddy had to undo my foot and put me back on the train and leave my poor little white lace-up shoe to meet its fate. I wasn't doing it to be naughty—but if he hadn't brought it up it wouldn't have occurred to me. It's like saying, "Don't put beans up your nose," which, yes, I also did.

We were headed home but didn't quite get there. The latest subtenants living at the Carlyle while we were in California, a married couple with a new child, had turned the apartment my mother so beautifully decorated into a pigsty, with puppy stains on the rugs, chewed-up chair legs, dozens of shattered glasses, and a broken chandelier. The kitchen, Mummy said, was destroyed. Furious, she refused to move in. From temporary summer headquarters in Rye, where she taught me my lesson about urinary incontinence, she renovated again, commuting daily to the city and complaining all the while to my father about how much work it was to find and deal with all the craftsmen she needed: one who fixed tables, another who repaired china, yet another who cleaned rugs and another to reupholster. "If only there were just one person I could take everything to!" she said. And my father said, "So why don't you start a business like that?" Which she did the next year.*

The summer of the renovations, my mother got pregnant again. She spent, as I've said, a lot of time in bed; devious Uncle Morty gave her Demerol for her pain, which she was still taking the day she died, almost sixty years later.

Now we interrupt this story† so I can say I loved being pregnant, all six times, almost as much as I loved writing music. More than I loved writing music, if I'm honest. People look at me aghast when I admit that, but, among other things, being pregnant gave me an excuse to be fat. I wish I'd been pregnant at fifteen! I also had a great time pushing the little critters around inside me when I'd feel their feet. Or, water being

----

* Dorothy Rodgers ran Repairs, Inc., from 1935 through 1941.

† Proposed title no. 3 for these memoirs: *We Interrupt This Story.*

a great carrier of sound, rapping on the edge of the tub and waking the poor things up. I loved wondering what sex they would be when they came out. But the most exciting thing was discovering that they had a face. It's really a person! And I loved labor—because of my mother, I was determined to. I thought it was the most exciting thing. I never had one that was more than three hours from beginning to end. I think several of them must have been brought on artificially by Uncle Morty, because they were all in the afternoon just before cocktail time. He'd break my water to suit himself. Bad boy!

Anyway, after seventy-two hours of what she always happily called "agonizing labor," Mummy gave birth to my brother, the one named Linda, on March 5, 1935. I say "brother" because my father had spent the previous nine months, as he had spent the nine months of my gestation, calling the contents of Mummy's belly a boy, and I believed him. But the baby's gender was not the only confusion I was laboring under. March 5 was also my parents' anniversary. I was in a little nursery school play that day* and, to explain my mother's absence from the audience, I announced with great solemnity and pride that she had just had a baby and couldn't come because she was getting married.

My mother's happiness was tempered by the knowledge that delivering another girl was an atrocious blot on the Rodgers escutcheon. Grandpa Will was so angry he didn't speak to her for six months. I don't suppose I was angry, but I was something. Anxious? Certainly not jealous, which is what my parents assumed when they took such delight in relating this story for years afterward: While Daddy was talking on the phone in his study, no doubt heralding the arrival of the blot to some relative or other, I swallowed three pennies. By mistake! And they didn't even taste good: coppery and bitter, the way spinach tastes sometimes, or bad red wine, only worse. Frightened, I ran into the study to tell him and asked, "Are you going to call Dr. Schloss?"† By which he deduced that

....

* Mary was almost always in a play when something momentous happened.

† Dr. Schloss was the Rodgers family's pediatrician. At Brearley, if the

1937: Mary with Linda. "It was a bonus that she was not
yet verbal enough to rat on me."

I had eaten the pennies to get attention. I hadn't, but that's what having
a reputation means. It's like getting a carved owl for your birthday and
politely saying how much you like it; soon, everyone thinks that's what
you want and you're overrun with owls.

Linda was put in the same room with me and, at least until she was
five, I was very protective of her.

I actually thought she was a cute little thing, with nice curly brown
hair, and it was a bonus that she was not yet verbal enough to rat on me
when I threw crayons out the window and blamed it on her. A certain
amount of older sister–younger sister mayhem is just human nature.
My own daughters had the same dynamic: Nina was horrible to Kimmy

girls had a sore throat and required a ruling on whether to be sent home,
they were examined by Dr. Spock. Yes, him.

when they were little.* Nina once cut off all of Kimmy's hair, leaving a pathetic fringe, and more than once hid her uniform so she'd be late to school. Now they're fine, I think in part because I refused to pit them against one another. Mummy didn't have such scruples about that with me and Linda. She was forever triangulating us; it was her very clever if not conscious way of maintaining power. She'd tell me that "we" had to work on Linda, and then she'd tell Linda that "they" had to work on me. She'd pump me for horrible information about Linda and, especially, Linda about me. God knows there was plenty to get out of Linda. I refused to play, but she played plenty.

Which, as Ockie wrote, will bring us back to *do*—I hate that line.† I started piano lessons at eight; I thought they were fun. If you completed a piece of Haydn, you got a piece of cake. My teacher, who taught on the fifth floor at the Mannes School of Music, not far from us on the Upper East Side, was Urana Clarke.‡ She was tiny and very homely with severe buckteeth; I don't know how she ate anything. And she had quite a temper. She was a fiend on pupils having short nails; if we showed up with ours over the edge of our fingers she would send us all the way down the five flights of stairs to get her scissors from her locker; we would then have to bring the scissors all the way back up so she could hack at our hands like Sweeney Todd. For years, as prophylaxis, Linda bit her nails.

Linda started playing even younger than I did. At first that was fine. My early compositions, including "Clean Sheets," were written for two pianos; Urana would copy them out because I didn't yet know how, and

---

* It probably didn't help that they were barely two years apart. Linda ("Nina") Beaty was born in 1953; Constance ("Kim") Beaty in 1955.

† From the *Sound of Music* song "Do-Re-Mi," a solfège number with a brilliant structure and a sometimes unfortunately unforgettable melody.

‡ Urana Clarke (1902–1999) taught at Mannes from 1922 to 1949, her pupils including not only the Rodgers girls but the Berlins. She later studied celestial navigation and invented an adjustable piano stool.

Linda and I would play them on the two Steinways in the living room. We weren't in competition; almost the opposite. At Brearley they used to dress us in matching pinafores and ask us to perform at assemblies together. I didn't enjoy that; I don't perform "except at dinner."* But writing those pieces was when I really began to have a use for music. *Use* is a funny word; the use was enjoyment. And something more: pleasing Daddy, which I finally did. Small as those pieces were, they were charming.

Soon the usefulness went sour. I didn't mind that Linda played better than I did, even if she was four years younger. But when one day my mother said, "Darling, you won't believe what Linda has done! She's never had a lesson but she's composed a marvelous piece!" I thought, *Fuck, there goes my childhood.*

I lost, or at least tried to back off of, my interest in piano. I kept asking my father if I could quit and he said, "No." Later I asked if I could have popular music lessons, like a lot of kids were having, and he said, "Those are worthless." It wasn't until I was sixteen when I once again begged, "Please, can I stop?" that he finally answered, "Well, I should hope so!"

It wasn't that I wanted to stop being involved with music: just piano. Daddy was cynical about the difference, being one of those composers, as it turned out I was, too, whose hands did the composing. His method was to whistle the melody as he wrote at the piano, which left all fin-

....

* From the song "Opening Doors," a highlight of Sondheim's score for *Merrily We Roll Along.* It's about three young people in the 1950s scrambling to get ahead in the world of musicals. The line "I don't perform except at dinner" is spoken (in rhythm) by Mary, the bighearted, tart-tongued writer in love with the main character, a composer. Sondheim has said that even though the show draws on his and his friends' experiences as young people in the 1950s scrambling to get ahead in the world of musicals, the character is based more on Dorothy Parker than on Mary Rodgers. Supporting that idea is the fact that the character of Mary is in the original Kaufman and Hart play that gives the musical its title—except her name is Julia. So someone deliberately made her Mary; perhaps the name scans better.

gers free for a richer accompaniment. Later, I copied that method, but I couldn't whistle, so I sang. Or Hank, who read music very well, would sometimes plunk out my melody for me. Adam composes anywhere, on anything or nothing.

But I knew that Urana taught theory as well as piano, and when I said I'd like to study that with her, Daddy seemed to realize that I wasn't completely beyond repair. He set it up. Meanwhile, Linda moved on to a better piano teacher, Fritzi someone. She was still playing, a lot, but claimed that she didn't want to be put on a pedestal or in the spotlight. Performing made her anxious. I think she stole that from me, too.

9.

AWAY WE GO!

Well, we just skipped ten years and a war, much of which the Rodgerses waited out in Connecticut. In those days, rich people got out of town, or at least the wife and kids did, when something bad was happening, be it summer or Hitler. I'm not sure the countryside was always safer, though. When I was quite little, my parents used to rent summer houses on the North Shore of Long Island, in Locust Valley, which was very Gatsby, very *don't-you-know*. Because there was no day camp, I just spent my time wandering around. At some point I wandered into the Italian gardener who came with the house, and he said, "Let me show you something. Let's go here in the woods." Whereupon he whipped out his thing, which I thought was very interesting because I had no brothers and only scarce shots of my father coming out of the shower in the bathroom attached to his library. I thought: *Oh, that's fun. And maybe, if I can't have one, I can be a monkey with a tail and swing from place to place.*

There were several repeat viewings with the gardener. I didn't have to be told by anyone that this was not a good thing to be doing, but I wasn't the least bit afraid. I knew he wouldn't hurt me, and he didn't. It only ended because one day he asked me to kiss it, and, very politely, I said no thank you.

I never told anyone about this until I was twelve, when for some reason I chose to confide in my mother while she was in the bathtub. I guess I figured it could do no harm now, seven years having passed and Mummy covered with soap. Well, it was like a furious whale breaching out of the ocean to call the authorities and get him arrested.

I have to say it thrilled me—Mummy's reaction, that is. Telling tales on myself was like giving her a gift, but she wanted me to spill everything. I couldn't do that; I'd be sent to jail. Sometimes, instead, I'd spill about someone else. When I was fifteen, I had a Brearley friend who kept talking about how much she adored her stepfather. I didn't think much about it until one night when we were on the phone, yakking away as girls do, and I said, "That all sounds fine, but of course it wouldn't be so fine if you'd slept with him!"—and there was a long pause. She answered, "As a matter of fact I did."

I made the mistake of telling my mother: It was like a cat bringing her human a half-dead mouse. Next day, I got a note from the headmistress, Mrs. Mac as we called her,* telling me to come to her office, where my friend appeared from nowhere looking white and horrible and saying, "What have you done! What did you do?" I can't really blame my mother for informing, but my friend never talked to me again; the next year she moved to California. Wait—where was I? I sound like Madame Armfeldt.†

Right. By the time I told Mummy about the gardener, we were living in Fairfield, Connecticut, at the first of three Connecticut houses, which because it was on Black Rock Turnpike we called Black Rock.‡ We'd

....

* After heading Brearley for seventeen years, Millicent Carey McIntosh (1898–2001) became the dean of Barnard College, and later its president. She was an early proponent of the value of women having both careers and families; she herself had five children.

† Madame Armfeldt is the grand old lady in Sondheim's *A Little Night Music*, who in the song "Liaisons" recalls assignations from her past as a courtesan, regularly losing her place in the memories.

‡ The second Connecticut house, where the Rodgerses summered from

moved there after I finished fifth grade at Brearley, and Linda first grade, in June 1941, knowing that the United States would soon enter the war. The war had already begun elsewhere, of course; Zoë, recently bereft of her mother, was with us as living proof. *My* mother was occupied in hating Black Rock because it wasn't chic.* And though I thought it was wonderful, with one of those Victorian sky-blue ceilings over the porch, I spent my first summer there so bored that I tried to fall off the swing to break my arm so I could get a cast and have people sign it. With no friends and no clubs where Jews were allowed, there was nowhere to go except Edna Ferber's pool, and we couldn't even get to that very often because rationing meant there was very little gas.† It was for the birds— literally; my mother was raising Rhode Island Reds.

I was out of the city, one way or another, for a year and a half, but by the end of that time everyone seemed to feel that Connecticut was a worse threat to me than the Axis. Most of this had to do with school. I spent that first winter, sixth grade, at a private school in Fairfield called Unquowa. I liked it well enough; after having screwed myself at Brearley through my pranks and obnoxiousness, any change was good. Also, there were some cute boys at Unquowa, with whom I had my first flirtations, if you don't count the Italian gardener.

Actually, the flirting began in fifth grade, when Zoë and I spotted a couple of preppies in khakis at the boat pond in Central Park. I said, "If

....

1949 through 1965, was called Rockmeadow. By the time Dorothy designed the third, the family had run out of pastoral "rock" names. Hank suggested "Got Rocks"—a joke, based on an ancient stock comedy character called Mrs. Gotrocks, that no one alive today would get.

* Trying to improve things, she spatter-painted the floors in the entrance hall, calling the result her personal Jackson Pollock. Later, an actual Jackson Pollock the Rodgerses owned was sold at Christie's for the bargain price of $275,000 to help pay estate taxes.

† Ferber seemed to follow the Rodgerses around, or they her, first at the Lombardy, then in Connecticut, later at 730 Park Avenue.

we run very fast, they'll pay attention, because they like girls who do things." I made her run with me the length of the boat pond, and by God if they didn't come up and talk to us. So naturally I invited them home for a Coke. Mummy received them but, later, Daddy was apoplectic. "They were perfectly behaved," I told him. "They go to Buckley."* Anyway, I wasn't planning on sex. I was really just fascinated that my plan to get their attention worked; it was like saying "open sesame."

But at Black Rock I felt like a prisoner. I don't remember anything special; my whole life was just no fun. Apparently, that was making my parents' life no fun, too, though I thought the road of blame went one way and they thought it went the other. It was around then that they had me visit a psychiatrist, which made me furious; no kid in those days did that. I would have to take the train in from Connecticut once a week to see David Levy, on the southeast corner of Fifty-seventh and Lex. He started my first appointment by asking, "Do you know why you're here?"

"Yes," I answered. "Because I don't get along with my mother."

"That's right."

"So why isn't *she* here?"

That stopped him for a moment. "That's a very good question."

My mother was concentrating then on how beautiful she was. She claimed that, considering her looks—which she more or less acknowledged, and not in an unattractive way—she wasn't very vain. I think she was right. Her prettiness wasn't a pleasure but a defense; she would blow apart without it, and the power it gave her in life.

Levy must have known that, because eventually he explained that Mummy, though very young, was very set in her ways.† So that if I were to have anything like a pleasant rest of my childhood, I was going to have to be the one to change.

....

* The Buckley School was and remains a predominantly Wasp private school for boys; FDR's sons went there, and so eventually did the only partly Wasp Tod Beaty.

† She was thirty-three when Mary was eleven.

1941: Richard and Dorothy Rodgers.
"My mother was concentrating then on how beautiful she was."

And I thought: *Not a prayer. If she's not going to change, I'm not going to change.*

Levy then handed me one of those articulated sculptor's models and said, "Pretend this is Linda." Really? I knew he wanted me to throw it across the room and admit that I was jealous—or is it envious?—of her. So I said, "Oh, what a darling little sister!"

And he was supposed to be the best child psychiatrist in the country; later, he was engaged by the government to deprogram Nazi children. I hope he had better luck with them than he had with me.

My parents and I were in a three-way stalemate. To break it, someone was going to have to go; guess who? After the school year at Unquowa ended, Mummy announced that she and Daddy were moving back to the city and that Zoë and I—but not Linda, who at seven was supposedly too young—would attend boarding school come fall. The stated reason was that Mummy had had enough of the country, and that Daddy, with *Oklahoma!* almost ready,* needed to be in New York. I didn't care why; it seemed like a dream to me. There was one hitch, however. Mummy, with her very good taste, had found a very tasteful place for us: the Winsor School, in Boston. "Look, Darling, the Eliots of Harvard went there." But even though they would have taken Zoë, who was only part Jewish and had been brought up as an Anglican, they wouldn't take me.

Academic anti-Semitism was old news to me by 1942. In 1937, when I was moving from Horace Mann to Brearley for second grade, Mummy asked Mrs. Mac whether I'd suffer any prejudice there. "If she's popular," Mrs. Mac answered cleverly, "there won't be any problem." Uh-oh.

So Mummy found a boarding school closer to New York that wouldn't mind my being Jewish: Miss Thomas's, in Rowayton, Connecticut.†

Zoë and I arrived at Miss Thomas's with high hopes in September 1942, but they were quickly dashed. For one thing, they walked us to church in Norwalk in our hats, like Madeline; oh, how I hated that.‡ But the whole place was a nightmare, not academically rigorous as promised but merely rigid: If you said *geez*, *gosh*, *golly*, *gee*, or *darn*, you were charged twenty-five cents for Miss Thomas's war stamps book. Miss Thomas herself was a terrible battle-ax who, furthermore, hated me. Hated everyone, probably, sometimes with good cause. We were mostly a bunch of miserable, unmatched kids: orphans of war, orphans of divorce, and, as in my case, orphans of privilege. The only nice thing I remember is that

....

* It wasn't yet *Oklahoma!* but *Away We Go!*—both with exclamation points.

† Officially the Thomas School for Girls, it was later headed by Jean Harris, before she moved to the Madeira School, and thence to Bedford Hills Correctional Facility.

‡ No pictures of the adult Mary wearing a hat are known to exist.

we figured out a way for the girls in my dorm to sneak out like snakes in the middle of the night to hike the three-quarters of a mile up a hill to Zoë's dorm, where we'd all have a festival of cookies we'd cadged. It was a great adventure, crunching our way through the brittle ice by the bright moon, then eating and crunching our way back home.

If I ever really had an eating problem, it began there, after Christmas, when Zoë, prompted I suspect by my parents' talk of adopting her, decided to hightail it home to the war in progress rather than succumb to their affection.* Losing her, depressed as I already was, was appalling. We had become good friends by then; she was my buffer against my parents and Miss Thomas. I was so miserable without her, I started gobbling everything in sight, and though the food wasn't very good, eating a lot of it was worse. At one point, saying I was a terrible influence on the others in my dorm, Miss Thomas moved me to the infirmary, where chronically ill or problem kids were stockpiled; for a roommate I had a sixteen-year-old girl who screamed all night.

If it hadn't been for the music teacher, I might be in that infirmary still. She, at least, liked me; it isn't saying much to say I was her best student. But even if I were a musical moron, she'd have had to like me because of Daddy. Anyway, on a day off in February, I later discovered, she took her academic life in her hands and went to New York to pay a call on my parents. She told them she would lose her job if Miss Thomas learned of her visit, but she had to let them know that I was being horribly mistreated, something I would never tell them, knowing they wouldn't believe me or that they'd think it was my fault.†

"Get her out of there," she said. Sure enough, my father came flying, sweeping down on Rowayton to spirit me off through the snow.

It was the second-best thing that happened in my childhood.

Now I have to say something, because this pushmi-pullyu stuff with my parents is going to go on for a while. They were not all bad. They did

---

* Admittedly, the worst of the Blitz was long over by then. Also, she had a family that may have wished, unlike Mary's, to have her around.

† Proposed title no. 4 for these memoirs: *Bleak House*.

1948: Linda, Mary, Richard, and Dorothy, playing croquet and looking grim.
"They were horrible . . . about little things."

love me, even if (as I'd learned) they didn't like me. I guess I could say the same about my feelings for them. But at times they were glorious. Miss Thomas's wasn't the only situation Daddy rescued me from, physically, financially, or otherwise. This is gross, but when I was pregnant with Nina, I had a terrible cyst on my nose; because of the pregnancy it had to be removed without anesthesia. Daddy was right there, holding my hand—though Jerry, my husband, was not.

I uncover more and more nice things about Daddy as I think through his life. It's also admirable that, being the kind of person who never expressed gratitude, he never demanded it either. But even my mother, who loudly and endlessly did demand gratitude, generally did the right thing in a crisis. That's the point: Straight through my life, everywhere you look, they were horrible, especially my mother, about little things, but important things they were wonderful about.

The trouble is, and this is key, *it doesn't even out.* Even in my admittedly rather eventful life, there weren't as many big things as little.

But this was a big thing, and they handled it well, not just the swooping rescue but the massaging of Brearley to get me readmitted. How glad I was to be back, though it's astonishing how much ground you can lose if you're away for just a year and a half. I needed tutoring for about two years just to catch up. And I needed two years to revamp my reputation. At the beginning of seventh grade, when I mysteriously reappeared, everyone came up to me and said, "Ugh, we didn't want you to come back! We all hated you." Little girls are mean as snakes—and honest. This brought me up very short and I thought: *I'll have to change this.* The teachers and administrators seemed wary, too.* It took me until the ninth grade to win the school over with deliberate super-niceness and have them think well of me. By the time I graduated in 1948 I was very popular. Or, anyway, no longer considered a monster. This was a precious achievement, and something I'd done entirely on my own. I was still rebellious, a loudmouthed liberal; a bunch of us tried to convince the administration to accept Black students or, at least, hire a couple of Black teachers. Mrs. Mac felt it was "a little too early" to convince the board.†
We backed down; if I was going to rebel in any really big way, it wouldn't any longer be through school.

....

* Perhaps they recalled the time in third grade that Mary burst into French class, saying "I have something very important to announce," and then recited: "Ladies and gentlemen, take my advice, pull down your panties and slide on the ice." The school called Dorothy, who said, "You know she comes from a family where people write lyrics all the time."

† Mrs. Mac's successor managed to integrate Brearley, slightly, a few years later.

10.

IS THERE ANY MONEY IN IT?

don't know what grabbed Daddy about *Green Grow the Lilacs*,[*] a folk drama set in the Indian Territory at the turn of the century. But I can easily imagine why, when he proposed it as their next production, Larry declined. Larry's urbanity was all wrong for that kind of story; he may have liked a cowboy in bed, but not in rhyme. By then he was winding down anyway, burning himself up from inside with alcohol. It never made him mean, though, as it later made my father. He suggested that Ockie, who liked Big American Themes, would do a better job with the material, and that he'd be there to cheer them on opening night. He was, too, telling Daddy afterward that *Oklahoma!* was one of the greatest shows he'd ever seen.

I wasn't there. I was back from horrible Miss Thomas's but was still considered, at twelve, too young for an eight-thirty opening night curtain; I was always too young for everything until suddenly I was too old. (I went from "Darling, that's not appropriate for a nice young girl" to "Darling, that's not appropriate for a proper grown woman" in about three minutes.) Instead, I attended the Saturday matinee, three days later. What did I think of it? It was fine.

When I was very little and desperately wanted to please Daddy, I used

* The play by Lynn Riggs, produced by the Theatre Guild, flopped on Broadway in 1931.

to give him poems I'd "written" by secretly copying them from a book. He liked the first one, which I sent to *Child Life* magazine and won a dollar for. My mother told me I must save the dollar to buy something truly wonderful, which even in 1943 was impossible, so I bought a little charm.* The second poem I stole began "The policeman is good and fine." I proudly handed it to Daddy, who read it while he was shaving and said, "*Fine* is a completely meaningless word; you have to describe this policeman better than that." And I was dying to say *I got this out of a goddamn book!* But that would have given me away completely, so I swallowed it.

Oklahoma! wasn't fine, it was thrilling. What I first recognized was that it was radically different from anything Daddy had done before. But as startling as the material may have seemed to audiences at the time, and as definitive as historians now claim the breakthrough to be, I knew he'd for years been preparing himself for a change. He'd taken classical piano lessons for the first time since childhood—you could hear the increased fluency of his playing. He'd lined up Ockie even before Larry bowed out, knowing a crisis was looming. The choice of Ockie wasn't an accident, either: He'd decided that he wanted the drama to dictate the music rather than vice versa, which meant working with a lyricist who swung that way. Larry could only write lyrics to music that already existed; Ockie was bitextual but preferred to write the lyrics first and hand them over for setting.†

I have two images from 1943 in my head. It's unfair to put them together but there they are. One is from the morning after the March 31 opening night: my parents insanely excited as they sit with the seven big rave New York reviews spread out in the dining room. My mother is

....

* A dollar then would be about fourteen dollars today.

† That's one reason why Rodgers's songs with Hammerstein are so much less playful, and more dramatic, than his songs with Hart. Or than Hammerstein's songs with Kern, for that matter. *Show Boat* and the other Kern-Hammerstein shows were written music-first.

clapping her hands in delight, and Daddy looks—what is that?—happy.
I thought it was a very good opportunity to ask them to let us go riding,
which was expensive so they usually said no. They said yes.

His successes with Larry had been hit-and-run, coming and going but
rarely sticking.* Now he had landed something that would last. Or so
everyone kept saying. He was interviewed constantly and became a celebrity, always on the radio or featured at War Bonds benefits.† This fed
but also distended his ego, like a duck liver. The rest of the year, the rest
of his life, was spent succumbing to a case of Great Man–itis.

Possibly to soften the blow of the huge success of *Oklahoma!*—and
the obvious implications of that for their collaboration—Daddy suggested to Larry that they mount a revival of their 1927 hit *A Connecticut
Yankee* later that year. Over the summer they set to work—or, mostly,
Daddy did; Larry was in high escape mode. (This is when he hid out in
whoever's tree house it was.) For opening night, in November, he sent my
mother her customary orchids, which since her honeymoon had been his
way of offering an apology. But for what, this time? Daddy gave instruc-
tions to the management at the Martin Beck to watch out in case the
Shrimp showed up, and to be ready, if he caused trouble, to remove him.
He showed up. From the back of the orchestra he started singing along
with Vivienne Segal as she performed "To Keep My Love Alive," written
for the revival and, as it turned out, his last lyric.‡ When the audience's

....

* Including movies, they wrote thirty-five scores with eight hundred
songs in twenty-four years.

† At these benefits, Rodgers would invite a woman from the audience to
give him her phone number; he would turn it into a melody, write it out,
and auction it off. Perhaps he also kept the number.

‡ It's brilliant, though: a can-you-top-this series of marital murder jokes.
"I caught Sir James with his protectoress: / The rector's wife, I mean the
rectoress. / His heart stood still: angina pectoris / To keep my love alive."
With a wink to one of their first hits: "My Heart Stood Still."

shushing failed to quiet him, he was "escorted" from the theater and disappeared into the rainy night. The next afternoon, Fritz Loewe* found him sitting in the gutter outside an Eighth Avenue bar. And that's the other image I've got stuck in my mind: Larry in the gutter.†

He died four days later, of pneumonia.

The elation of *Oklahoma!* and the despair of Larry Hart: They're related, no doubt. And also not. Daddy wasn't the cause of Larry's alcoholism; he spent years fighting it and cleaning up the messes it left behind. He claims in his memoirs that in those last four days, he did everything he could to save Larry, even contacting Eleanor Roosevelt for a supply of the new wonder drug penicillin.‡ Still, I can't help seeing both of the images I've got stuck in my head as expressions of Daddy's drive, which was the kind you had better jump aboard or get out of the way of. His talent demanded as much. If there was a lot of collateral damage, well, we've got "To Keep My Love Alive" as recompense.

More than one thing can be true at a time. Daddy sobbed at the funeral. He also seems to have been involved, whether directly or indirectly I don't know, in manipulating Larry's finances and will, of which he was an executor. I have trouble following the plot, which has been covered elsewhere in detail; to me, it's all a version of that taffeta "poice" Larry's mother once gave me. Is there any money inside? The gist is this: In the will, Larry's brother, Teddy, and sister-in-law, Dorothy,§ got 70 percent of

---

* With *My Fair Lady* and *Camelot*, Frederick Loewe (1901–1988) would later become a world-famous composer, but at the time he was possibly better known as Hart's poker buddy.

† Obviously, the image is an acquired one. There have been many stories of Hart's death over the years, mostly contradictory.

‡ Other versions say someone else contacted Mrs. Roosevelt. In any case, the penicillin came too late.

§ A well-known comic actor, Theodore Hart (1897–1971) played one of the Dromios in *The Boys from Syracuse*. His wife was Dorothy Lubow Hart (1906–2000). Why is everyone named Dorothy?

the residual estate, but the payout ended with them. Their son, born the summer after Larry's death and named for him,* was in effect pre-disinherited. What would have been his cut went instead to the Feder-ation of Jewish Philanthropic Societies.† The other 30 percent of the residual estate went to Willy Kron, the financial manager Daddy had forced on Larry some years earlier, saying he was protecting Larry from his own spendthrift ways.‡ And though Daddy was not a beneficiary of the estate, he did end up, as executor with Kron, in control of the copy-rights on everything they wrote.

Daddy was a tough businessman, and Larry an impossible collabora-tor. I can imagine that the tough businessman thought, after all the years he'd spent locking the impossible collaborator in rooms to write, and covering for him when he was plastered, and threatening reporters who called him a fairy, that he was justified in arranging things so he could manage their legacy without further interference from beyond the grave. Daddy knew his own worth.§ And the probate court repeatedly found the will to be valid. But I can also imagine how this would seem like a terrible betrayal to the Harts.

I tend to think the truth is somewhere in the middle or at both ends:

....

* Mary later befriended "Little Larry"—Lorenz Hart II (born 1944)—even though he is a conservative lobbyist who worked for Newt Gingrich.

† Hart was nominally Jewish—well, not, in fact, nominally, once the fam-ily changed its name from Hertz. In any case, he was not known to be a supporter of this or any Jewish organization. Dorothy Rodgers was, though; the Federation of Jewish Philanthropic Societies, today called UJA-Federation, was her main charitable outlet. Was the bequest engi-neered by Richard Rodgers as some kind of gift to his wife? As some form of reparation?

‡ Kron was also Dorothy Rodgers's financial adviser.

§ His partnership with Hammerstein was, from the beginning, fifty-fifty, even though Hammerstein usually wrote both the book and the lyrics, and Rodgers just the music. Just!

A justifiable betrayal? A traitorous justice? Maybe that's a charitable interpretation; certainly, it's a convenient one, since Rodgerses have been in charge of the catalog for seventy years.* Understand, none of us ever made an extra penny from Larry's will, just what we would have made anyway from Daddy's share of the songs. Wait, that's wrong. Larry, that dear man, did give Linda and me each two thousand dollars as a gift outright, which my mother made us tithe, and put the rest in savings. So I'm a corrupt witness. My judgment in the matter isn't worth much.

Soon, the copyrights won't be, either. Income from the Rodgers and Hart shows has taken a nosedive; there aren't many major productions of *Pal Joey* and *Babes in Arms* anymore, let alone *Jumbo* and *Chee-Chee*. The individual songs still do well, but the earliest of them, "Any Old Place with You" from 1919, is already in the public domain in the United States, with the rest lined up to start following it off the cliff any day now.†

---

* When the heirs sold the Rodgers and Hammerstein properties in 2009, the Rodgers and Hart properties stayed behind, for a time. The Rodgerses (and the Krons) continued to control the copyrights and receive, along with UJA-Federation, their stipulated shares of the proceeds. Little Larry got nothing.

† "Any Old Place with You" entered the public domain in 2014. As of January 1, 2022, so had (among many others) "Manhattan," "Mountain Greenery," and "The Blue Room."

II.

WHAT'S THE USE OF WOND'RIN?

The year *Oklahoma!* opened and the year Larry died was possibly even more notable as the year I got my period. I'd lost Zoë, lost Bunny, gotten fat, and my face was probably breaking out, but, oh boy, was I thrilled. The faster I grew up the better off I'd be. If I had a child, I thought, then maybe "I wouldn't feel like one."*

But getting to that point was going to be a problem. From the time I returned to Brearley at age twelve, my girlfriends there were atwitter about the events—the horse shows, dances, whatever the hell they were—at which they were eventually going to find beaux. By the time I was fifteen I was basically inflamed from years of anticipation about the fun that awaited me just one more year down the line. I kept pestering my mother about going to the teas: the pre-debutante events at which you were interviewed to see if you were fit to be invited to other pre-debutante events called get-togethers, over Christmas vacation. Finally, she told me, "Darling, that's ridiculous, you can't go to one of those things, you're Jewish. Unless you wanted me to use your father's *name* to get in!" And I thought: *You're goddamn right I do.*

It's not that I wanted to be part of a snob gang that didn't want me,

---

* The line is from "The Beauty Is," a song in *The Light in the Piazza*, the 2003 musical for which Adam Guettel wrote the music and lyrics.

but where was I going to meet boys? There weren't any, of course, at Brearley. I was basically stuck in our apartment the rest of the time. The answer, my mother decided, was Viola Wolff, who taught etiquette and ran a series of what we called Jewish dances in a ballroom on East Sixty-seventh Street. They were awful; the boys were just as snobby as the boys at the proper deb balls must have been. They were all hell-bent for Wall Street or law firms, and I couldn't stand the idea of being married to a stockbroker or lawyer.

But, stuck there, I figured I'd make the best of it. By then I'd realized that the way I could get people to open up and be interesting was to tell them how I felt about things. If you admit to your own shortcomings and guilts and peccadilloes, you're much more likely to get back from others what they feel, and on a deeper level than most people bother to venture. So I remember treating the boys at these terrible dances as if they were just as unhappy as I was. "You're bored," I'd say. "I know you probably want to go dance with someone else, so just leave me behind a potted palm and go to it." Nobody ever left after that. If you go on the assumption that everyone is insecure, boys are bound to be just as insecure as girls are. Anyway, that's what I was counting on; being Richard Rodgers's daughter didn't mean much to these kids, not when you weighed 150 pounds and were jammed into some taffeta nonsense. I made this little rule for myself: You have to go to this dance and get at least two boys wanting to call you up when you leave. Just two; that would indicate that I'd made it through another party. And I was successful. The boys I got to call me weren't all so great, but I thought: *I'm not, either.*

And anyway, I was spoiled for boys. Spoiled in two ways. One was because of the theater. Surprisingly, I had very little access to the theatrical lifestyle at the time; Daddy didn't bring a lot of it home and let us out into it even less. At Brearley, the only theater types I knew besides the Berlin girls were Oona O'Neill and Barbara Bel Geddes. Mildred Dunnock did teach us drama; I made a marvelous Cassandra in *The Trojan Women.* "Lift high in the air a torch to bear." Even now that makes no sense. Maybe I'm getting it wrong? I still remember her elocution exercises, though:

"Come, butter, come. Peter stands at the gate, waiting for a buttered cake." I would say, "Miss Dunnock, that doesn't rhyme."*

But even without much access to that world, I knew about it and craved it. I suppose it began with Larry, so vulnerable and generous. And then occasionally I'd meet an associate of Daddy's, like John Fearnley, the stage manager on *Carousel*, whom everyone loved, including Daddy, even though John was gay. In the spring of 1944, the entire cast of *Oklahoma!* came up to Black Rock for a picnic party my parents threw to celebrate the show's first anniversary. I got to know the actors then, and the big, brawny gay guy then playing Will Parker chased me around the yard with a turkey leg. Yes, I realize all my examples are gay. Well, gay men were nice and fun. Heterosexual men were mean and controlling, and I didn't want to be controlled.

I was also spoiled for boys by the one I met at Ockie's that summer. As I said, Steve floored me. It wasn't his looks, though he was attractive. It was that combination I could never get enough of: great talent and great fun. Intellectual fun, I mean, not touch football on the beach. Word games, puzzles, laugh-your-ass-off remarks. And some sort of pathos, I suppose. I like pathos when it's held in check by craft and wit, not otherwise. I have a third eye for it.

In fact, I have often thought my third eye—for talent, for material—was stronger than my other two. I should have been an agent, and in a way I already was. In 1943, shortly after it came out, I read a book called *Mama's Bank Account* and, thinking it would make a good play, gave it to my mother. She agreed and gave it to Daddy. He agreed and gave it to

---

* The daughter of Eugene O'Neill, Oona O'Neill (1925–1991) was later the last wife of Charlie Chaplin. Barbara Bel Geddes (1922–2005), a daughter of the industrial and scenic designer Norman Bel Geddes, played Maggie the Cat in the original production of *Cat on a Hot Tin Roof*, and later Ellie Ewing on *Dallas*. Mildred Dunnock (1901–1991) was a founding member of the Actors Studio and played Linda Loman in the original production of *Death of a Salesman*.

Ockie. Around this time, Daddy and Ockie were setting themselves up as producers, not only of their own work but of others'. They bought the rights and produced the stage version. I did not get a commission.*

After I came back from Bucks County, I couldn't stop thinking about Steve. Eventually I asked Shawen Lynch—you remember, one of the Hammerstein orphans—to tell him to write me a letter. She did, and I'd go down to the mail room every day hoping to find the result, but it never came. I was thirteen and in love. Then fourteen and in love.

That love was pathetic. I don't mean embarrassing but sad and hopeless, as unlikely to be realized as my younger wish to become Prince Valiant. But I couldn't get rid of it. I kept putting the feeling away and taking it out like a ticket you buy for some later travel.

The ticket came out again, briefly, the next April. With *Carousel*, I was finally allowed to go to one of Daddy's opening nights. Daddy almost didn't, though. A few days before, he had leaned down to pick up a suitcase at the train station in Fairfield and blown some kind of gasket in his back. Sitting or standing was agony, so he lay throughout the show's three hours on a stretcher behind a set of curtains at the side of the orchestra, the kind that lead to the exit hallways, and that ushers close so excitingly as the lights dim. Listening from there, he thought he'd written a flop because the curtains were so heavy they deadened the sound. Only at the end, with the thunderous applause, did he realize he'd written a hit. And not just a hit. It was, of all his shows, his favorite, and probably mine as well.

I was watching from the front of the mezzanine with my proverbial heart in my big mouth, overwhelmed by what he had made. Artistically, it was very nearly perfect, except for the obligatory hymn job, and the comedy scene in which Mr. Snow thinks he has caught Carrie cheating. That was cheating in two senses.†

....

* The stage version, called *I Remember Mama*, ran on Broadway for almost two years, starting in 1944. Richard Rodgers would repurpose it as a musical many years later.

† Yes, Mary would have cut "You'll Never Walk Alone." As for the scene

But the artistry of the show is a separate thing. What moved me so much, even if I didn't fully translate it into personal terms at the time, was understanding *through* his artistry that he understood love. *Fatherly* love. He couldn't have responded to Ockie's telling of the story with such a rush of romantic music otherwise. Because of that, I never think, as most people seem to, that *Carousel* is about Billy and Julie, husband and wife, and what is or isn't forgivable between spouses. Well, I rarely think that, though the subject of an abusive husband is not irrelevant to me. Mostly I think it's about Billy and Louise, negligent father and embittered daughter, reconciled at last. Which touches a universal theme—repairing rejection is a very potent experience for anybody—but also, for me, a very specific one. I find it terribly powerful when Louise says, about Billy, who has returned invisibly from death for one last chance to do good, "He hit me hard. I heard the sound of it, Mother, but it didn't hurt." What a shocking line, especially from Ockie!* And it's true: I have never long resented whatever my father did to me or failed to do for me. It's good conversation to quote him saying, "You are so fat you look like an ape," or whatever it was he said. Complaints make good copy. But I wasn't embittered by him, the way Linda was. It was all about his music; everything loving about him came out in it, and there was no point looking anywhere else. It's also true I didn't have any choice—but it was enough.

Even if I hadn't responded so viscerally to *Carousel*'s themes, and even if my father hadn't written the music, that opening night would have been overwhelming for a totally extraneous reason. Before the curtain, leaning over the mezzanine railing, I saw Steve in the orchestra.

I don't remember a word I said to him, if any, when I found him at

....

with Snow and Carrie, the show does need something there—but not the silly farce it's got.

* There's a lot of misguided criticism of *Carousel* based on this line, as if it were a tract in support of domestic violence. It is about real things that happen to people, and the possibility of redemption. Does *Sweeney Todd* advocate cannibalism?

intermission, but I could tell that he'd been crying. Or maybe that was at the end of the show, where anybody cries automatically; the show practically jabs you with a poker until you do. Either way, there he was, teary-eyed. Bigmouth me didn't have words, and he couldn't have heard me anyway if I did.

12.

DARLING,

JE VOUS AIME BEAUCOUP

At one of Viola Wolff's dances I met a bad girl who was boy crazy. She told me she'd made a date to watch the St. Patrick's Day parade with John Rich, a junior rake no one was allowed to go out with. She offered to get a date for me, too, if I wanted to join her, so I lied to my parents, saying I was going to the parade but omitting the bad girl, John Rich, and the date.

When I got to the girl's apartment, waiting for me there was this boy, Hal Prince.* He was eighteen, but already a sophomore at the University of Pennsylvania; I was fifteen, but came off older than that, or at least wider; I weighed 165 pounds and wore a size twenty. Not only that, but I was wearing a brown wool suit chosen by my mother, who always had my best interests at heart. I looked like a Fudgsicle.

Not that I was any better at dressing myself. Around that time, to

....

* Harold S. Prince (1928–2019) was born Harold Smith Jr.; his father, Harold Smith Sr., was an importer of neckwear. After his parents divorced and his mother, Blanche, remarried, Hal took the surname of her second husband, Milton Prince, a stockbroker. A fragment of Smith remained as his middle initial.

1948: Mary, in a "hideous" taffeta gown, dances with Jimmy Stewart
at a party celebrating the fifth anniversary of the opening of *Oklahoma!*

improve me in that department, Mummy sent me to Jane Engel, the
dress store near us on Madison Avenue and Eightieth Street. "Go get
some nice clothes," she said. Shopping was a huge embarrassment
for me and a terrible time waster for the salesperson, who kept
bringing me things I couldn't wear. Finally, in desperation, I picked a
few dresses, brought them home, and tried them on for Mummy.
"Those are not becoming, darling," she said, and made me take them all
back.

Fudgsicle or not, I had a wonderful time talking with Hal about theater, which he'd gone to throughout his childhood and knew well; his
mother had once been in an amateur production that Daddy wrote.
Daddy may even have been my main selling point: Hal was born clasping
a list of people he wanted to meet. (I was born clasping a list of people I

wanted to get away from.) He was impressed because I would say, "*Blecch*, there's another event for *Oklahoma!* I have to go to; every year there's another damn anniversary."*

Hal could never understand why I wasn't thrilled about all the celebrities. He hadn't had the wonderful opportunities I'd had to pass them hors d'oeuvres and take their coats.

But I bought the whole package. Hal was sophisticated, ambitious, and wanted to be a writer. His taste was fun—he went on and on about *On the Town*, which had just closed and I hadn't seen. I didn't know any people my age like that, except Steve,† and by the end of the parade I knew I wanted to go out with him. Two problems. One: He was going around at the time with a posh Philadelphia deb of the Christian persuasion. Two: My parents.

The first problem took care of itself; overcoming the second involved a series of lies. First, I had to lie about how I met him; I made up a story about dancing with him at the Viola Wolff parties, where he wouldn't have gone in a million years. Then there was the matter of introducing him in the right light. It didn't go well. You would think the fact that he had attended an approved private school—the Franklin School, now part of Dwight—and that his stepfather was a German Jew and a stockbroker, would satisfy them, but Uncle Morty, who was a much worse snob than my mother, implied that, despite this, Hal came from the wrong side of the tracks. Harold Smith was a Schinasi; Bubbles Hornblow was a cousin;

....

* The third anniversary was coming up that month. On the fifth, in 1948, the Theatre Guild threw a bash at the Plaza after the 2,134th performance. A picture of that occasion shows Mary in a "hideous" strapless yellow-and-white-plaid taffeta gown, dancing with Jimmy Stewart, who looks as delighted as an undertaker. Rodgers and Hammerstein blew out the candles on the cake wearing Indian headdresses.

† Mary says she introduced Sondheim and Prince at the opening of *South Pacific* in 1949, but other accounts say it was at a homecoming party for Hal when he got out of the army in 1952.

and they lived on the West Side, which, as you already know, was code for
Polish or at least *not enough money.**

It wasn't true; the family had plenty. But Hal himself didn't. Not that
I cared, except that it forced me into further lies. There were only three
places my parents allowed me to spend time with a boy unchaperoned:
the Plaza, the Pierre, and the Drake. These were also the three most expensive places in New York, where no one I was interested in could afford to take me. Or if they could, we hated it anyway. One time, I don't
know how, I guess Hal scraped up the money for an evening at the Plaza,
where that pretentious Hildegarde sang that fractured-French number of
hers right in my face—you know, the one that, if it were in the key of C,
would go E-F-E-F-G-A-G; C-D-C-D-E-C-G.† Horrible. But usually, with
some poor little rich boy, I'd walk through one door of the Plaza and right
out the other, then head down to the Village, where you could have a
good time and get cheap rum and Cokes. That way I could truthfully say
I went to the Plaza.

My mother eventually found out anyway. A friend told her she'd seen
me at some downtown club. Mummy assured the friend it wasn't possible: "Mary doesn't lie." When she repeated this to me, hoping for confirmation, I said that actually, yes, I'd been to that club. She was furious
because I'd made a liar out of her, but what did she expect me to do? I was
lying in self-defense, to preserve my own life, such as it was. Then as later,
I did what I had to. I broke a lot of rules, but they weren't mine.

Eventually my parents got used to Hal. They still didn't approve
of him; they said he was going about everything in the wrong way and
would never get anywhere.‡ They meant they found him oily and self-

---

* The Schinasis were Turkish Jews who made a fortune in cigars; Bubbles
Hornblow (née Leonora Salmon) was not a stripper in *Gypsy* but a socialite, recently married to the movie producer Arthur Hornblow.

† "Darling, *Je Vous Aime Beaucoup*," written for the chanteuse Hildegarde
(1906–2005) by her manager and lover, Anna Sosenko.

‡ Twenty-one Tony Awards later, he proved them wrong.

promoting. And, even a year into our relationship, they thought I was too young to be dating a college boy. (I was seventeen by then.) In a failed attempt to get me away from him, they loosened the strings on other forms of socializing. I was shoehorned into a few debutante events, many of which would have been whited out that winter by the Blizzard of 1947 were it not for hormones. While most of New York stopped dead in its tracks, we boy-crazy girls of upper Park Avenue—is there any other part of Park Avenue?—origamied our evening clothes into suitcases, sloshed our way in galoshes or, for those who had skis, skied our way to the hotels.

Not that I met anyone interesting there, and so things with Hal kept on. Two years into our relationship, my parents were getting desperate; they sent me on an all-girl Viola Wolff cross-country trip, and later— change of strategy—on a coed one to Europe. The first plan backfired because Hal showed up in California just as soon as we girls did, the sec- ond because all the boys were gay.

By this time Hal and I were practically engaged, but I still couldn't visit him in Philadelphia on my own. When my mother nixed my plan to go to some kind of prom extravaganza they had right before commence- ment at Penn, I went upstairs to my bedroom and put on the biggest act of wailing and sobbing until she finally came back with what she called a compromise: "I'll be your chaperone." She knew that I would rather die than bring her, but I called her bluff, and she came, not very hap- pily. Within minutes of arriving, and claiming the situation looked safe enough to her, she hightailed it to the Hammersteins in Doylestown, an hour away.

Maybe she should have stayed. I can't remember the party except that I had my first screwdriver and pretended to myself for quite a long time that I didn't know there was any booze in there. After several of them, I said to Hal, "I think I don't feel well."

"It's all in your head."

"No, it's in my stomach," I said, at which point he ran me to the bath- room, where I threw up.

"I still don't feel good."

So we got a cab to go back to my hotel, constantly opening the back door so I could throw up some more. I threw up all over Philadelphia.

The next day Hal, in his cap and gown, chewed gum to cover his alcohol reek all the way down the aisle to his diploma. There was no gum powerful enough for mine.

Hal and I have had a lot of ups and downs since then, at least one down per decade, and they were usually my fault. Or my big mouth's. When he was producing his first musical, in 1954, he asked me to invest in it, and instead of saying, "No, I can't afford to," which was true, I said, "No, I can't because I've heard the score and I really don't think it's very good." Which was also true. The songs were catchy and likely to be popular but not good in the way I later knew Steve was. Hal was angry, and it was a stupid decision, too, because anyone who did invest in *The Pajama Game* made a fortune.* Then, in 1966, after he got rudely ejected from the musical version of *The Member of the Wedding* I was writing with Marshall, he was even more furious. And he wasn't wrong.

There are others, but somehow we've always more than recovered, even from the no doubt tactless way I broke up with him the autumn after my Philadelphia Vomit Tour. He had graduated from Penn by then and was working as an unpaid office boy for George Abbott;† I had just arrived at Wellesley. I don't remember how I told him I did not want to be a genuine Princess, but he was much more furious and upset than I would have thought, snarling: "You're just going to go off and marry some goddamn Wasp from Princeton!"

He nailed it completely. That's exactly what I did.

....

* The original Broadway production ran for two and a half years; it was a hit in London; it was a hit movie; it was a hit everywhere. Backers nearly quadrupled their investment.

† George Abbott (1887–1995) had by then been the Big Man of Broadway—director, producer, writer—for decades, with at least another decade to come.

13.

MYOPICS

By eleventh grade at Brearley I'd mostly straightened myself out. I was decently popular and a more-than-decent student. I'm not sure the popularity was good for me; it made me a coward, too eager to please. That trait, which is not really a trait but a maladaptation, is pretty much still with me. I don't like people to be mad at me. I have file cabinets full of nice letters people have written, to counteract the bad ones.

But the good-studenting was entirely positive, giving me for the first time a sense of achievement that meant something even to my parents. At my graduation in 1948 I was awarded two honors: the music prize, which I split with another girl, and the Latin prize all by myself.[*]

Despite that, it wasn't a very happy occasion. My mother, then thirty-nine, had recently gotten pregnant after what I suppose were years of trying to produce additional collateral for the marriage. The pregnancy had us all thrilled. I felt close to her for the first, and last, time, doting on her slightly swollen belly and reading aloud from the What to Expect books, or whatever the prehistoric version of those was. But she wasn't

---

[*] Mary's yearbook quote, beneath a pretty picture, was a slight misquotation from Kaufman and Hart's *You Can't Take It with You*: "Gold stars, then blue stars, then some bombs, then a balloon." The subject, in the play at least, was firecrackers.

MARY RODGERS

"... Gold stars, then blue stars, then some bombs,
then a balloon. . . ."
You Can't Take It With You

Entered II
Absent VI and ½ of VII
Temporary Prefect V, VII-XII
Volley Ball Numerals XI
Song Committee XI, XII
Dance Committee X, XII
Dramatics IX, X
Choral Dramatics VIII
Yorkville Project XII
Year Book Board XII

1948: Mary's Brearley yearbook page notes that she was "absent" for
one and a half years. "By eleventh grade . . . I'd mostly straightened myself out."

destined to carry that child to term. She had a miscarriage and didn't get
to the graduation; Daddy cried and cried because it was obviously his last
chance to have a son.*

I had by then been accepted into Wellesley and Smith, and had chosen
Wellesley for at least two dumb reasons. One was, of course, my mother's
having hated it and dropped out. The other was even more pathetic,
something straight out of my old bedtime ritual of My Think. I had been
hearing for years about the perfumed elevators at the Ritz-Carlton, where
Daddy stayed when he had a show trying out in Boston. Wellesley is only

----

* It was a girl.

about forty minutes away from downtown Boston, and I wanted to experience that splendor for myself. I somehow imagined that if I went to Wellesley, he'd call me up some Friday after classes and invite me to stay at the hotel for the weekend. We'd see the evening performance of the new show, dine at Locke-Ober, and discuss what had worked and what hadn't over lobster.

No such luck. For one thing, Locke-Ober didn't seat women. And when *South Pacific* blew through Boston on the way to Broadway[*] in March of my freshman year, it blew away again without a summons to the Ritz-Carlton.

Whatever my reasons for going, Wellesley was a mistake. The place was filled with Amazonian jocks who just wanted to row across Lake Waban; hoping to please even them, I at some point wrote the crew song. I'd been a minor freak for a while at Brearley, but at Wellesley almost no one knew what to make of me at all. A Jewish faux debutante and the daughter of a famous composer? Some of the girls had never seen a musical; some of them had never seen a Jew. It took me a while to adjust to expectations, which was not then and is not now my forte. My first year, continuing the process of socializing myself I'd begun in high school, I deliberately changed my personality completely, from someone who was fun and funny, but not someone to respect, to someone who could very carefully get elected president of my house. Unfortunately, that's as far as my plan went; I was not, once I got the job, a very good president. Or so they told me. *Back to the drawing board*, I thought; time for more revisions. It was my own out-of-town tryout. By my second year I had myself, if not yet my eating, pretty well under control.

But I'd made a mistake academically, too. Smith, which I'd rejected, had a great music department; Wellesley's was tiny and dismal. There were no courses in composition because they thought women had no reason to learn it; why bother putting it in the curriculum for students

....

[*] It opened at the Majestic—not the ocean liner or apartment building but the Broadway theater—on April 7, 1949.

who would end up, at most, as high school music teachers, if they didn't get married first? The offerings were limited to the more ladylike history and theory. I was good enough, thanks to Brearley and Urana Clark, to skip the 100-level courses and go directly into the sophomore curriculum, but as a result I was behind all the time and intimidated by the older kids. The teacher, an organist and Nadia Boulanger disciple called Howard Hinners, was terrifying; he apparently had a son he'd taught to detest music. He always seemed to be examining me for the true lineage: *Hmm, Richard Rodgers's daughter, let's see what she knows.* Not much, it turned out. We were given hellish assignments, like intuiting the other voices of a four-part invention from the one voice provided. I would sit there as if I were playing it on the piano, miming the keys on my desk, and then translate what I came up with into whichever clef it belonged in. I don't know how I passed any exams.

It takes at least four years, and really more, to become fluent in musical notation; the pencil is harder to play than the piano. Luckily, I had a good ear—too good, sometimes. My introductory Spanish teacher thought I must have lied to get into the class because I spoke as if I'd studied before. I was just mimicking her sounds; I had no idea what I was saying. Which is why I had so much trouble when I started doing musicals later: I could hear what I wanted but didn't know how to find it. As a result, I wrote very slowly, creeping my way forward. I would often start with some kind of little vamp, and once I got an acceptable tune to go with that, maybe not more than a couple of bars, I would know where I wanted it to go harmonically. But the harmony I heard in my head I couldn't find on the piano. It was hidden there somewhere, often in a place that other people, like Daddy and Steve and Adam, could have spotted immediately. For me, it was another game of Camouflage, trying to see the enema tip between the black keys. I would sit there at the piano perfectly happy for ten hours, smoking and drinking coffee and carving my roadway to death, then get up to go to the john; when I came back, there it was. I loved the mystery of that.

I was also very lucky because, by then, Steve was studying with Milton Babbitt, and he'd pass on to me everything Babbitt had passed on to him. Well, everything he thought I'd understand.* I guess I absorbed some of it. When I was writing *Once Upon a Mattress*, Marshall would often give me, after the chorus of a new song we were working on was done, the lyric to the verse. And no matter where I started the thing, in whatever key, I somehow found my way to the first bars of the chorus as if I'd been following an invisible map. What fun!

But that was later. At the time—at Wellesley and for a few years after—it was lucky I had low expectations of myself; that way I could fulfill them. I was so conscious of working in my father's field that I would choose to cultivate corners of it where no one was looking or would notice if I flopped. Children's songs. Christmas songs. I knew I could grind them out, at least. In November of my sophomore year, I wrote a little thing called "Christmas Is Coming," with a lyric by a girl in my class named Janet Parker. We decided to sell it as a Christmas card for other girls to take home to their families. A girl called Doddie Troopin did illustrations, and I ruled nine million staves on shirt cardboards covered with white paper and copied out the song. We sold the cards for three dollars each, in the lobby of the dorm. After dinner, to promote sales, I'd go to the piano in the common room and audition it. Yes, I was a song plugger at Wellesley, probably the only one ever.

That was about as aggressive as I got, but I guess my name, or maybe just Daddy's, was spreading around campus because the following summer I was asked to write songs for the junior fall musical. By then my parents had moved from Black Rock to Rockmeadow, in Southport; mo-

---

* Upon Sondheim's graduation from Williams College in 1950, the school awarded him a Hutchinson prize: a two-year, three-thousand-dollar fellowship for further musical study. He chose to spend it on lessons with Milton Babbitt (1916–2011), which was odd, because Babbitt was an avant-garde composer, all tone rows and electronica. But Babbitt was able to teach Sondheim what he needed to learn—one definition of good pedagogy. Years later, when Mary became the chairman of Juilliard, she found Babbitt still there, "scratching away."

mentously for my virginity, and for my life in general, I was also working that summer at the Westport Country Playhouse. But we'll get to that later. This was in its own way as momentous, at least concerning Daddy and me; has any girl's life ever been so linked—so chained!—so long, to her father's? Anyway, I was having lunch at Rockmeadow with my parents one day that August when I got a call from a classmate I'll call Sally. Because she was the only other girl in the entire class of 1952 who admitted to writing music,* she was also composing some songs for the show, which for reasons I not only forget but can't imagine, was to be called *Myopics in the Tropics*. Monkeys with glasses?†

Sally, who couldn't find her way up a C-major scale, came right out with it. "Listen, a lot of people have been saying to me that they think the only reason you're writing so much of the show is because you've got a famous father," she said. "So what I'm proposing is that I put my name on a lot of your things so they won't think that anymore."

I was so stunned, I said, "Oh, well, okay."

I came back to the table with my face apparently the color of chalk. Daddy said, "What's the matter?"

When I told him, he was enraged. "You get right back on that phone and tell her you're pulling all your stuff."

So I did. I said, "Sally, I'm withdrawing all my stuff since clearly you're capable of doing it on your own."

With rehearsals scheduled to start in a month, the theater group was so badly stuck that they came crawling back, as Daddy knew they would.

....

* Not quite: Natalie Allyn Wakeley, a classmate and fellow music major, also contributed songs to the fall musical, but used the masculine nickname Nat Wakely. She later composed, under her married name, Sleeth, more than 180 hymns and anthems for church and school.

† No monkeys were involved, but according to newspaper reports, *Myopics in the Tropics* featured a "world-reforming Wellesley alum" and a banjo-strumming cowpoke. At one point, the chorus, dressed in sarongs and shorts, brandished giant prop toothbrushes while singing a song called "Brush Teeth."

He was very good that way, and whether or not he thought I had talent he taught me to behave like a professional. At some point in rehearsals that fall, I realized that my numbers weren't getting any attention, because guess who was the director? Sally. I was so disgusted that after the first performance, on a Friday night in late October, I hopped a train and came home to Rockmeadow. Daddy said, "What are you doing here? Don't *ever* leave something you're working on! You have to protect your work investment."

My work investment? It was a silly amateur musical I was too embarrassed to want him to see. And he, surely knowing what a bunch of girls would write at Wellesley, wasn't about to trundle up there anyway. As for my mother, she was now fully embarked on her lifelong course of deathly illnesses to bravely overcome. Some families support their children's work even if it isn't good. Not ours.

Anyway, it was too late to go back—it always is.

14.

MORE THAN ONCE UPON
A MATTRESS

t was at Ann Loeb's second coming that I met my first husband. Ann was the younger sister of my friend Judy Loeb, who lived in the same building in the city as my parents. My mother was slightly in awe of the Loeb girls because they were also, on their mother's side, Lehmans, both families being true German Jews who considered themselves, and were probably considered in this country, equal to the Rothschilds.

Ann's first coming out hadn't worked—they couldn't find a boy for her—so the next year they gave her another one. I guess the second worked better; she married Edgar Bronfman a couple of years later and before you know it popped out five children. Later, she turned up gay.

That second coming occurred, fittingly, just before Christmas of 1949, in the middle of my sophomore year at Wellesley, while my immortal song "Christmas Is Coming" was burning up the charts in the homes of my classmates all up and down the Connecticut seaboard. The party was held in the rooftop ballroom at the St. Regis. I was seated at a table for ten, and this great-looking man was sitting around the other side from me, so we couldn't communicate. Eventually he came over and introduced himself—Julian Bonar Beaty Jr., an impressive mouthful but known as Jerry—and asked me to dance. We very quickly got into a conversation about mutual attraction, and he said, "You'd never marry me because I'm much too old"—he was then thirty-three.

circa 1948: Jerry Beaty, possibly while still "in the Intelligence."

And I said, "Oh no? Just ask me."

"Okay," he replied. "Will you marry me?"

I said yes.

So I came home from the second coming and woke up my sister, to whom I was then speaking, and said, "Guess what? I've met the person I'm going to marry." She was absolutely agog. The next day I told my mother—that I'd met this wonderful guy, not that he'd proposed. She said nothing.

Others might have laughed it off, but I took the proposal very seriously. I didn't like the pickle I was in, a pickle in which every available boy was dull and every exciting boy was forbidden. Okay, it was a crowded pickle—and it also had a door, because Jerry looked like a great way out. He was sexy, in a TV lawman way: tall, slim, a good mouth and teeth, with thick, dark brown hair pompadoured in front. Since my values were a trifle skewed in those days—I was almost as much of a snob as my parents—it didn't hurt that he was also a catch socially. The Beatys* were

....

* Warren Beatty, who added the extra "t" to his name in the late 1950s, was a distant relative.

considered one of the really good families of Rye, with a big house on Dogwood Lane backing up on the Apawamis Club; Jerry's father, Julian Sr., had even been the mayor and, perhaps less excitingly, a secretary to Grover Cleveland. Jerry himself went to Loomis,* where he was kicked out and then allowed back in, which I thought was exactly right. Then he majored in English at Princeton, followed by law school at the University of Virginia. As a junior partner at Reeves, Todd, Ely & Beaty, his father's law firm, he represented copper mining interests in British Columbia and earned what was to me the unbelievable sum of ten thousand dollars a year. Even more exciting, he had been in the Intelligence, as he put it; during the war, which was still immediately recent, he was an army counter-intelligence officer in the European theater.

Years later, when I was already remarried, I went to see the movie *Judgment at Nuremberg*, which included documentary footage of the actual trials. There he was, wearing headphones and taking notes; I was so impressed I rushed to call him afterward, but he was blasé.†

I was not in the Intelligence, apparently. For the next few days I waited for my husband-to-be to contact me, much as I had spent the previous few years waiting for a letter from Steve. After two weeks of no news I thought, *Oh well, I guess that's a big fat nothing*, and trudged back to Welles-ley for the spring semester.

But then, on January 12, 1950, the day after I turned nineteen, I got

....

* A Waspy boarding school in Windsor, Connecticut, now known as Loomis Chaffee.

† If Jerry Beaty was blasé, perhaps it's because his work in "the Intelligence" was more of a desk job; he wrote phrasebooks for GIs to use in Europe and, near the end of the war, helped to organize the withdrawal of troops from Cherbourg. He may well have been at Nuremberg during the trials, but Mary is likely wrong about seeing him in the movie; the courtroom scenes are not documentary footage but fiction, featuring Hollywood actors including Spencer Tracy and Burt Lancaster.

a letter from him, addressed "Dear Nellie," and signed "Love, Emile."*
He wrote that although our fifteen-year age difference was surely a difficulty, he meant what he'd said and would like to see me while in the
area. (Among his four younger siblings, who came in very good-looking
and very ugly varieties, one was a sister at Wellesley.) I ran all around the
dorm showing everyone the letter, and must have called home as well,
because soon enough my mother got back to me with intelligence of her
own. Her friend Mildred Creen, she explained, was Jerry's godmother;
she'd gone all the way through school with Jerry's mother, Constance
Saltonstall Dawbarn Peck Beaty. This godmother, Mildred, who'd known
Jerry since birth, had told my mother: "Don't let her marry him."

I didn't ask why, and it didn't matter. I would have married him if he
had two heads. Which apparently he did; he made mixed emotions into
an art. When he showed up to see me the next week at Wellesley, we
went for a drink fifteen minutes away in Framingham; he seemed more
delighted that the bartender asked him to prove his age than that we were
finally face-to-face. About us he remained evasive: I couldn't pin down
his intentions. Really, I didn't dare. But looking back, I see that keeping
me uncertain was his modus operandi. He would reconfirm my puppy
love, then fade into the mist again. During one of his reappearances that
spring, he invited me to a cocktail party in New York. I remember saying
to Daddy, because Mummy was abroad, that I was coming down from
school to attend a party that Jerry Beaty was giving. Daddy said: "Are you
asking me or are you telling me?" and of course I was telling him. But I
wish I'd been asking. Jerry had gathered and edited all these friends for
the party: I was being auditioned. I guess I failed, because he immediately
disappeared again, this time, it seemed, for good.

After a springful of this, I was depressed and panicked, ready to grab
somebody, anybody, else.

....

* Nellie and Emile are the age-discordant—and everything-else-discordant—
lovers in *South Pacific*, which had opened on Broadway the previous
April.

Do I seem like a horse's ass? I can only say I was desperate to have some kind of life that felt like my own. I didn't yet understand how hitching your horse's ass to someone else's wagon was just another kind of servitude, worse even than being a child. I just wanted to *start*. I was still, at nineteen, a virgin, which everyone in the world would have wanted me to be but me. I have mixed feelings now about premarital sex—the consequences, not the morality—not to mention intermarital sex, both of which will be rehearsed here. When there's nothing to hold you back, you can give too much away. On the other hand, I made a lot of big mistakes, some of them rather late in the game, that I might not have made if I'd had a little more freedom at the beginning. Or maybe I'd have made not fewer, but better mistakes. Either way, it doesn't pay to be schoolmarmish about them now; though I was raised to be a prude—I don't know how old I was before I stopped calling my breasts my "front"—I got over it fast. Let's all get over it, shall we?

Especially women. Women's stories get squelched, or swallowed, so that other women don't get the benefit. My mother didn't get the benefit, God knows; her idea of what it meant to be a woman was dictated almost entirely by her creepy father. The books she wrote about life with Daddy were basically fantasies. I didn't get the benefit, either, but I went looking for it and found it and was determined to pass it along. You—yes, you down there in the notes—once described me as having "a personal style you might call knee-jerk transparency, except that you do not need even a tiny rubber mallet to get the goods."* That's true—even the implication that my honesty sometimes spills over into indiscretion. But it's not a reflex, it's an innate quality. I'm not trying to embarrass my kids or needle

....

* While working on a profile of Adam Guettel for *The New York Times Magazine* in 2003, I visited Hank and Mary's Central Park West apartment, never having met them before. Mary had set out, along with the tea service, "a dossier of Adamic memorabilia: prep-school report cards, early compositions, joke photographs of the kind you'd usually burn, letters of filial love and apology." Hank kindly offered a large manila envelope to transport the trove back to my office.

my dead mother or shock my few remaining Brearley classmates who are still compos mentis, though I admit it gives me a nice bubbly feeling inside to imagine members of the board at Juilliard or the snobs in Quogue bug-eyed over my misadventures. Those are just bonuses. The real reason to tell the truth, or truth within reason,* is that it's healthier for everyone, like airing out a house that's been closed for too many seasons. I speak from knowledge, on both counts.

So: The following summer, the summer of 1950, the summer Sally tried to steal my songs and Jerry kept not reappearing, was the summer I finally got deflowered, at age nineteen and a half, by Chilton Ryan in the darkened wings of the empty theater at the Westport Playhouse—on a mattress!

I'd been begging my parents to let me be an apprentice at Westport ever since they'd moved the previous spring to Rockmeadow, which was practically next door.† They said I was too young, and too impressionable. After a year they gave in, despite the same misgivings, which were absolutely right. I wasn't there more than twenty minutes before I thought: *This is what I love. These are the people I want to spend my life with.* They were theater people, you could smell it, the way dogs smell certain things, only instead of meat it was imagination, iconoclasm, fearlessness, a gift for fun. They were visible, exposed, making the gray groups I'd been forced to hang out with at school seem like pencil sketches of people. Here they were all slashes of color and action. And none of that snobbery. They weren't all from the Upper East Side; they came from all over. They didn't care if I was Jewish and, even better, they didn't care who my father was. When I'd say I was there at the non-behest of my parents, they laughed as if they understood.

But that's not the only reason I loved Westport immediately. On my first day, wonderful surprise, a boy stuck his head out of the stage man-

....

* "Truth within reason" is a paradox like being a little bit pregnant, which is itself a story to be told in good time.

† The Westport Country Playhouse, then considered one of the country's leading summer theaters, is three miles from Rockmeadow.

ager's window and said hi as I ran past on some apprentice errand. It was
Steve.

Though he had not responded to me in any way in the years since I'd
met him, I would hear about him indirectly* and stew. But by the time
I saw him again I'd finally gotten over my fourteen-year-old's crush and
we became terrific friends. On Saturdays, we went to his father's house
in Stamford—Herbert was now remarried to a very attractive, big blond
half-Cuban woman named Alicia Babé—for the all-white lunches they had
there. I mean the food was all-white: cold boiled potatoes covered with
sour cream and herring. And we'd play with Steve's little half-brothers,
whom he loved.† I was sublimely happy about that. In the way that can
happen only around that age—and if you miss the train it's too late—he
and the others that summer remade my life.‡ I'd been disappointed in the
fancy-shmancy debutante department and disappointed by my counter-
intelligence agent, who seemed to have moled himself underground for
the duration. It was such a relief to find that there was a group for me, and
I loved them all. Well, not all. There was one girl, Eunice, whom Steve and I
both hated, but she got polio and landed up in an iron lung, so we felt kind
of evil.

....

* In 1947, Sondheim worked as an assistant—basically a gofer—on *Allegro*, Rodgers and Hammerstein's self-conscious turn toward the avant-
garde after *Oklahoma!* and *Carousel*.

† Alicia Babé and Herbert Sondheim married in Connecticut in 1943,
with the slight hitch that his Mexican divorce from Foxy Sondheim was
not yet recognized in New York State and Alicia's from her previous husband was likewise not quite official. Their son Herbert Jr. was born later
that year; his brother, Walter, in 1946. At that point, their divorces having
come through, they married again.

‡ Many of the twelve interns at Westport in 1950 went on to careers
in show business, including the film director Frank Perry, the theatrical
agent Peggy Hadley, and the Actors' Equity bigwig Conard Fowkes.

1950: Surrounding the stars Dennis King and Gertrude Lawrence (center) are apprentices and other young workers at Westport Country Playhouse, including Frank Perry (in front with cigarette), Peggy Hadley (middle row in checked dress), Mary (next to her, far right), Chilton Ryan (behind Mary), Conard Fowkes (next to Ryan), and Stephen Sondheim (top, of course).

We were also working like crazy, learning at least a little of every job there was to learn in the theater. We drove the professional actors around, took tickets, built sets, hung lights, typed press releases, called cues, cleaned the johns—without a Johnny Mop. I honestly don't remember much about the shows themselves, just the intense satisfaction of doing them and then the intense satisfaction of undoing ourselves. In Westport, everything closed up tight as a drum at one in the morning. We wanted to party but couldn't find a place to drink. So Chilton and I, under the auspices of the trumped-up Westport Culture and Bird-Watching Club, laid in some alcohol during the day and ran our own bar at Frank Perry's house at night, often accompanied by a low-stakes poker game. Like me and Steve, Frank lived nearby. His mother was AA, but so solidly AA—she'd bring drunks home off the railroad track and give them coffee and sober them up—that she didn't mind our running a bar. We served thirty-five-cent shots in cups stained tar black from her Maxwell House ministrations.

My parents would have been appalled, if not by the alcohol then by how little we made from it; we only charged enough to cover our costs and a few drinks each. Luckily Mummy and Daddy were in Europe. Which is why I had such an easy time sleeping with Chilton after the big deflowering on the uncomfortable mattress: Rockmeadow was empty except for me and the maids. Most of the other apprentices were billeted in boardinghouses and, poor me, I had to live in this fancy manse with a pool and a lake and fluffy beds and wisteria; it was humiliating. The *house* felt like a chaperone.

Chilton, the oldest of six in an Irish Catholic family from Wilton, wasn't an apprentice—he was a year older than I—but a low-level staff member of some sort.* I spotted him the first night, after an organizational meeting, when we all went to somebody's house for some getting-to-know-you drinks. He was fabulous-looking and very sexy, over six feet tall, with dark hair, brown eyes, wonderful teeth, and an absolutely chiseled movie body. He was also, amazingly, a virgin. I don't see how; if I was ready to climb aboard, wasn't every other girl there, and not a few boys as well? Anyway, we began paying attention to each other, and after a few weeks of flirting we decided: This is the night. So we planned it all out, waited until everyone else left the theater. It wasn't "I want this done"—though it was high time; it was "I want *him*." It didn't feel at all morally wrong, though it's just damn luck that I never got pregnant; neither he nor I used any birth control and I didn't dare ask my gynecologist about it because my gynecologist was Uncle Morty. But it felt a little *physically* wrong, what with my being a virgin and his being not just tall. But I got over that. Afterward we were a couple and everyone knew it.

I don't remember a proposal, but that winter, as Chilton and I talked

....

* After Westport, William Chilton Ryan (1929–2020) worked in theater and radio and television and advertising; he acted in local Connecticut theaters well into his eighties.

to my parents in the little library of Rockmeadow, I kept looking, lovingly and childlike, at the tiny emerald-cut diamond on my finger. I'm not sure how conscious I was of the line between an escape route and an engagement ring; I just wanted to get out of that house.

Mummy and Daddy were surprisingly placid. They asked mild questions, like what we were going to do for money. Which would have been a reasonable concern—Chilton had none at all—if my parents hadn't been sitting there in that tastefully appointed fifteen-room, seven-thousand-square-foot house with the view of the gardeners and the lake beyond.

Mummy, showing fortitude, didn't burst into tears and leave the room for ever so long. Not until Chilton announced that I was going to convert.

15.

ET QUATENUS MASCULINUM
ET FEMININAM

From the age of about sixteen I wanted to be a Catholic. "I'm thinking of converting," I'd say to Mummy's Irish maids. "How would I go about that?"

I thought the Roman Catholic Church was so glamorous, so fun and crazy, with the Latin and the swinging censers and the whole panoply of religiosity. However moronic that sounds, I wasn't totally snowed. I knew that choosing to be a Catholic would involve certain compromises. When I visited a church for one reason or another I was always underwhelmed by the priests' sermons, and, much later, when they started saying Mass in English, so much of what they were saying turned out to be silly. Still, I was looking for a loving father—not in Jesus, particularly, but in God. And God, as the Catholics presented him, with all his theatrical accoutrements, was the best showbiz father I could find.

I've thought a lot about it over the years and concluded that the whole thing was really about my being depressed. My parents kept saying over and over that I wasn't a nice person. *We love you but we don't like you.* I thought that becoming a Catholic, with the required acts of devotion and penance, would give me a chance to prove them wrong. It was also, obviously, a way to rebel, not so much against Jewishness as against our house brand of Jew-flavored atheism. When I was twelve and asked my father if he believed in God, he said no without even giving it a thought.

I said, "I don't, either. But why don't you?"

"If I have a sick child I don't pray," he answered, reciting what might as well be the New York Jewish creed. "I get the best doctor in town."

There was no poetry in that. Catholicism seemed less rigidly practical. It was also the only religion I thought might be open to me. I didn't dare consider becoming any kind of Protestant, because then I would have been accused of being anti-Semitic. My family had no respect for people, and there were plenty, who pretended they weren't Jewish by joining Fifth Avenue Presbyterian. But the Catholics were almost as unpopular as the Jews, so no one could think you were converting to raise your status. You could only be doing it for something even more disreputable: a genuine need.

Chilton was really just an excuse, and not much of one at that. Despite going to Fairfield University, a Jesuit school, he was, as his sleeping and tending bar with me demonstrated, a lousy Catholic. His parents weren't, though. His mother was a very pretty little woman, gentle and devout despite many sorrows. She refused to institutionalize her daughter Lisa, who had Down syndrome, choosing instead to work with her at home and managing eventually to teach her to read and even play the piano a bit.* Another daughter, Margo, died of leukemia when she was seventeen. Chilton's father, the William for whom he was officially named, was very good-looking in a bony, austere, Irish way, like a tenant farmer in an O'Neill play, but he didn't have a job, let alone a farm. They were land rich, without much land. Their house in Wilton was big, though, big enough that one room was devoted entirely to the Infant of Prague, not to be confused with the Infant of Quogue,†

....

* Even so, Lisa told her parents she was going to die when she was nineteen, and did.

† As Hank and Mary later called their first grandchild on a visit to Long Island.

and the first evening of my first visit there we spent what should have been cocktail hour on our knees praying with rosaries to a little blond doll.

I had no idea what I was doing, and was afraid of getting something wrong, but the thing about the Ryans was that they were so unscary. I wasn't used to that; I was always terrified of my parents and at war with myself over whether to tell them what I thought of their behavior. With the Ryans, I had no terror, and no cause for it. They were kind with each other—and with me. That first night there, I noticed these little ashtrays screwed into all the doorjambs, and I thought *How considerate!* as I went around flicking my ashes into them. The Ryans never said a word to me about it; it wasn't until later that I learned I'd been defacing Catholic property. How was I to know they were holy-water fonts?

Clearly, I needed lessons. During the fall of my junior year, Chilton arranged for me to take instruction from Father Harkins, a classics teacher he liked at Fairfield. Harkins was not, evidently, popular; he'd been banished to a fourth-floor classroom, where most of the students wouldn't bother to climb. That appealed to me—it seemed like an opportunity for Christian charity on my part—but I didn't meet with him there. Instead, once or twice a week, I visited him at the seminary he belonged to in Weston, not far from Wellesley. I could see immediately why Chilton liked him; he was wonderfully bright and honest, and grubby, too, with his cassock, unlike the other priests', always rumpled and stained. He was clearly a renegade in any number of ways. He'd read the books on the banned-book list to find out why they were banned. When I asked him to explain to me what the phrase "the occasions of sin" means, he thought about it for a moment and then answered, "For me, an occasion of sin would be any street in Boston with a bar on it."

That's when I understood why he always looked so grubby. If Boston bars were his occasions of sin, then he was probably getting drunk and therefore spilling his food. His failing only made him dearer; admitted alcoholics are so much jollier than the closeted kind, unless they get too sober. Over the next few months—on an accelerated schedule, I now realize, because it's supposed to take a full year—he taught me the rituals

and the responsibilities of being a Catholic woman, and the catechism and
the Profession of Faith. There was something musical about the study that
reminded me of piano lessons.*

I was attracted to the drama of Catholicism; I couldn't have known
it would soon turn into an absurdist comedy, with me as the fool at the
center. When Father Harkins deemed me ready for conversion in early
1951, I began making plans to be baptized in the little Catholic chapel in
the town of Wellesley. A week before the ceremony, I called the seminary
to provide the details, but when I asked to speak to Father Harkins, the
person who answered the phone said, "Who?"

"Father Harkins," I said. "I don't know his first name."

"I'm sorry, there's no Father Harkins here."

"But he's supposed to convert me a week from Saturday!"

They sent a ringer priest.

I don't remember the ceremony very well; I know I felt that something was off. My family didn't come, of course, though one of Daddy's
buddies, a wonderful Irish guy called Mike Kelleher who was the fire
commissioner in Boston, showed up in his big red truck with dozens of
nieces and nephews. My best Brearley friend, Nancy Ryan, who was then
at Radcliffe, also came, but all I could think was how pissed off I was that
I hadn't gone to Radcliffe with her. I'd stupidly bought into that myth
that Radcliffe was full of unwashed, stringy-haired, intellectual freaks,
and there was Nancy taking classes with world-famous writers and looking great while doing it.

I kept looking around for Father Harkins, sometimes wondering if
I'd made him up. Other times I imagined he was so ashamed of his lack
of control over alcohol that he felt he wasn't good enough to lead a new

....

* In *The Light in the Piazza*, Clara also receives instruction from a priest
prior to her conversion. At one point she sings, in Latin, from the Profession of Faith: *Et quatenus masculinum et femininam sese mutuo complent.*
When I told Mary it means something about man and woman completing each other, she said, "If only!"

person into the church—and thus selflessly told the seminary to act as if he didn't exist. Or maybe they defrocked him and sent him away: *The Laity Vanishes?* In that scenario, I imagined him ending up on the island off the coast of Connecticut where they send priests to dry out. But I'll never know; I never saw or even heard of him again.[*]

Anyway, the deed was done. Or partly done. It wasn't enough that I'd become a Catholic in name; I wanted to be a super-good, grade A, fully signed-and-sealed one. So sometime very soon after I was baptized, I made my first confession. While Chilton waited for me in the main sanctuary of the church, I entered the booth, very excited, as if I were having a professional portrait made. I cheerfully recounted all my peccadilloes to the priest, especially and thoroughly my sexual misdeeds. Wow, that felt great! But when I emerged, Chilton was barely managing to contain his laughter. No one had told me not to use my regular voice, which in an empty church on a Saturday afternoon must have resounded like a carillon. He and a few old ladies and a janitor had heard everything I said.

I was not deterred from my plan to go all the way. Rather, I decided I wanted to be confirmed as soon as possible, which is something you ordinarily do, if you're a born Catholic, when you're about seven. I chose the confirmation name Elizabeth, in honor of Lisa Ryan, Chilton's sister with Down syndrome. I booked, if that's the right word, the church, a big wooden one nearer to Boston—or, really, I asked whoever was in charge there if I could be part of the confirmation group that spring of 1951.

....

[*] Rev. Frederick A. Harkins, S.J. (1909–1999), did leave the Weston seminary in 1951. It seems unlikely that he went to the St. Edmund's Retreat recovery center on Enders Island, off the coast of Mystic, Connecticut, as Mary imagined; in his book *Father Fred and the Twelve Steps: A Primer for Recovery*, published anonymously in 1996, he wrote that he did not attend a recovery program until 1959, while teaching theology at the College of the Holy Cross. He remained active in pastoral work, including twelve-step programs for alcoholism, until his death.

But somewhere along the path I must have tripped an alarm, because in March, after the baptism but before the confirmation, I got a call from Daddy, who was in Boston with the tryout of *The King and I*. He wanted to see me! Well, that was ominous, but at least I was finally being summoned to the Ritz, whose elevators, I sadly discovered upon arrival, contained no discernible hint of perfume.

"If you had told me that you wanted to go to Paris and be a bubble dancer,"* Daddy said, "I would have thought, well, that's peculiar, but go and have a good time. What I cannot understand is that you've never discussed this Catholic nonsense with me at all."

Apparently, he hadn't been listening when Chilton announced my conversion in the library at Rockmeadow. Nor did he notice, every Friday dinner that year when I was home from college, that Mummy served the most succulent of filet mignons or double-ribbed baby lamb chops for the pleasure of watching my sanctimonious refusal.† Nor how I showed up on Ash Wednesday with a gigantic slash of soot across my forehead.

But it's true I hadn't discussed it with him; Mummy had warned me not to. "Your father is so disgusted with you; he never wants to hear about it again." Meanwhile, she immediately rejoined Temple Emanu-El, on Fifth Avenue, where she'd been confirmed in 1923—going rarely, and Daddy not at all.

Classic triangulation and, back at the Ritz, here came more, from Daddy. Saying "I thought this might interest you," he handed me a telegram he had just received from Walter Winchell. "Dear Dick," it began, with words to this effect: "There is a lot of gossip about how Cardinal

---

* The stripper Sally Rand, always on the lookout for a new gimmick, was famous in the 1930s for a semi-naked dance she performed behind a large translucent ball.

† A decade later, Mary would not have had to refuse. In the 1960s, the church modified meatless Fridays and did away with what she called "all the other interesting and meaningless prohibitions," while keeping "the one that was flat-out disastrous: birth control."

Spellman* is going to confirm your daughter in the Catholic Church. I assume you would not like me to print this."†

I didn't know what to make of it; it seemed so ridiculous. And yet, Daddy explained, it might well be true that Spellman hoped to get involved. Conversions were very important feathers in the caps of the Catholic hierarchy. That vicious anti-Semite Bishop Sheen—then merely a monsignor—was still making hay four years after converting Clare Boothe Luce, a prominent Protestant. And I was an even better plum, the daughter of a prominent Jew. As for Winchell, his motives were clear. Daddy wrote him back saying thank you and yes, he'd be grateful not to have the information printed, which was like signing an IOU. I never learned whether or how he paid it off.

At least *The King and I* was good. I was amazed then, as I am now, that Daddy and Ockie, these two mid-century men, each a tyrant in his own way, could write so beautifully about subjugated women. I wonder if Catholicism was for me what Siam was for Anna: a Hail Mary pass at independence.

Anyway, awful Spellman did not confirm me. I don't know how I did it, but I somehow had the opportunity to decline his supposedly kind offer. Instead, I was confirmed by someone I can't even remember, with a lot of boys in white suits and girls in white dresses with big white bows. At twenty, I was a bit conspicuous.

Several years later, Daddy and Spellman were seated next to each other on the dais for some benefit. Spellman said, "How's your daughter?"

"Which one? I have two."

"The one who married the Catholic boy."

"As a matter of fact, she didn't marry the Catholic boy," Daddy said. "She married a Protestant boy and has three children."

"Well," said Spellman, "that's almost as good."

And then he added: "But don't worry, we'll get her back."

....

* Francis Joseph Cardinal Spellman (1889–1967) was archbishop of New York from 1939 until his death.

† The telegram is lost, possibly (Mary says) eaten.

He was wrong. Almost as soon as I was confirmed I started having serious doubts, realizing that I had concocted this whole Catholic Fantasyland as an escape route, not a destination. The Chilton Fantasyland as well. He was ungodly sexy, and a genuinely nice guy, but once I got him wanting to marry me, I'd used him up. A week or two after my parents reluctantly placed an engagement announcement in *The New York Times*,* I returned the pretty little diamond ring. They were thrilled; I was unhappy. But better to be unhappy than bored.

---

* The announcement appeared on June 26, 1951, under the headline MARY RODGERS, DAUGHTER OF THE COMPOSER, ENGAGED TO W. C. RYAN, FAIRFIELD GRADUATE.

16.

HOLIDAY FOR HEARTSTRINGS

At Wellesley in 1951 there was one phone on each floor of the dorm. When you got a call, the girl who was "doing bells" that day would yell or maybe intone over a public address system, "Phone call for so-and-so." How I longed to hear "Phone call for Mary Rodgers," and to find a man on the other end of the line. But as I returned for my final year that fall, I began to think that I had boarded the wrong ship, heading irreversibly into old-maidhood. All the girls of that time, except those who were exceptionally confident and sophisticated, were in the same boat, but mine seemed to be leaking like crazy. If you didn't have an engagement ring by senior fall—and, even better, a wedding planned for the June of graduation—you were dead meat.

Remember, this was before even the earliest squawks of liberation. For Chrissakes, Madeleine Albright, a Wellesley grad in 1959, married minutes after commencement.* By the time Hillary Clinton graduated, another ten years along, feminism was entrenched and all that stuff about going to college only to get your "MRS degree" was archaeological. But girls of my vintage were in the dark, staggering around like zombies. We were not prudes: We knew about and wanted sex. We wanted careers,

....

* Well, three days after commencement. Her husband left her twenty-two years later, naturally for a younger woman, but Albright then became the first female secretary of state.

too—well, some of us did. But the society that had begun to allow us to accept these ideas about ourselves had not yet found a way to make acting on them a coherent part of our identity. It was like trying to play the piano in an earthquake. You make a lot of clams.*

Like this one: A few days after I broke up with Chilton I got a call from a great-looking guy called Rabbit I'd met one summer in Westport.† He was short but swell and sexy, unlike the awful braggart bankers' sons I'd met at Viola Wolff's dances, and despite being from a rich real estate family and going to the Harvard Business School, he was very modest. But when he took me out to some local steak house, I did nothing all the way through dinner but sob about Chilton and my need to get married. What a great way to ruin a date! Rabbit was quite ready to fuck me but not to get engaged over T-bones.

It sounds so stupid now. At the time, though, I felt I would drown if a man didn't rescue me. Desperate people do desperate things, as the return of Jerry Beaty, sometime in September, demonstrated. He was now curiously eager to marry. I came down to New York and we met for lunch, a block north of Bloomingdale's.

"I thought you were otherwise engaged," he said.

"I've broken it off."

"I'm not interested in being a substitute for anyone else."

"No, no, no, I'm finished with that."

"How can I be sure you won't go back?"

"Because the only reason I got involved with Chilton in the first place was that you were so elusive."

I didn't actually say that. I was too afraid of angering him to have risked even mild criticism. But I must have pledged my troth, because I left the restaurant engaged to be married right after graduation in June.

If the moment was less than romantic, I got what I wanted. I'd be out of my parents' house and control before I turned twenty-one. With any luck, I'd have a kid before I was twenty-two, and plenty more thereafter.

....

* Musicians, especially brass players, call a botched note a "clam."

† Rabbit (1927–2017) was not his real name; it was Rabinowitz.

But what was in it for Jerry? He was now thirty-five and, I supposed, in as much of a hurry as I. In the two years since we'd met at Ann Loeb's second coming, he had not yet found anyone else. I vaguely understood that he needed to lock me down while he still could. I was not his best-case scenario, but I didn't mind; he wasn't mine, either. And I believed you could make a go of that if you stayed upbeat and didn't look too hard.

I did my part by completely agreeing to all his plans and directives. One was religious: Jerry was a nonpracticing Protestant, an elder in the Madison Avenue Presbyterian Church.* He said, "You can be anything you want, but I do think it's unfair to bring up children as Catholics without giving them a choice." By then, my vestigial Catholicism didn't matter to me, and I realized that dropping it would be an advantage, if not for his reasons then for my own. For one thing, my grandmother May wouldn't come to a wedding in a Catholic church. So when I told my parents that I was (a) getting married to Jerry and (b) giving up being Catholic, they were so relieved by (b) that they bit their tongues about (a). It was like giving them four Christmases in a row.

I presented my apostasy as a triumph for everyone. And I felt it to be. But it was harder to make Jerry's next demand seem like a good thing. Possibly as late as early November, while I was home for a weekend, he called and told me to meet him on a particular park bench on Fifth Avenue, near my parents' apartment. "I have something very important to talk to you about," he said, ominously. If I worried he was going to wriggle out of our engagement, or extend it indefinitely, I was not completely relieved when the opposite turned out to be the case. He wanted to get married as soon as possible. December, in fact. I couldn't figure out why, any more than I could figure out how to assemble a wedding in just a month or so. But he put enormous pressure on me; being even more easily push-aroundable then than I am now, I went home and very nervously told my parents that "we" had decided to get married over Christmas break. And, oh yes, that I was therefore leaving Wellesley at Thanksgiv-

....

* A highly desirable church, even to children, because it had a swimming pool and a bowling alley.

ing, never to return, though I did write that crew song, for the Class of 1952 I was no longer a part of.

My mother burst into tears, absurdly explaining that she had always looked forward to shopping with me for my trousseau but now there wouldn't be time. Besides, she didn't feel well and was in no shape to plan a proper wedding. Daddy just looked grim. To his credit, he never said a word against it, though his disapproval was obvious. I think he knew, and my mother, too, that I was being pressured, and I'm sure they guessed why.

The date was set for December 7: Pearl Harbor Day. "This is going to be a disaster," we joked.

Had I really talked to anyone about it, maybe I would have insisted on graduating. Even if I wasn't getting what I wanted in college, and didn't enjoy it, it was ridiculous to drop out with just one semester to go. But I didn't confide in anyone because I was both stubborn and embarrassed. My parents, who in the past didn't wait to be asked before delivering their opinions, were overcome by a spell of delicacy, a kind of deference to me as an engaged lady that I'd never felt as a daughter. They neither mentioned the unwisdom of the decision nor repeated the dire warning of Jerry's godmother. Should they have? Not necessarily. By this time, they'd figured out, both of them, that I was too bloody-minded to manage. If they objected, it would merely have shoved me further into my reckless plans.

They came as close as they could. A few weeks before the wedding, my mother said, "Have you slept with him?" Which was weirdly up front and liberated of her. I said yes, and that it was wonderful. But that was a lie. I didn't sleep with him until about two days before we got married, and then it was only moderately entertaining. I was probably fantasizing about someone else the whole time. Him, too.

Would I have said at the time that I loved him?*

I don't know. I certainly admired him and respected him. He was tremendously bright and very well-read and very liberal politically except

....

* Please enjoy a snack or beverage as the pause between question and answer lengthens intolerably.

1951: Mary and, to her right, Jerry at their wedding.
"By then I'd got myself believing I was very happy."

for one occasion when a little anti-Semitic crack leapt out inadvertently. Though I wasn't drawn to him physically, the way I was to Chilton and Rabbit—or drawn to him essentially, the way I was to Steve—he was so handsome with his thick dark brown hair and he solved a lot of my problems.

So I guess so.

Though the wire photograph* makes it look as if the wedding took place in the palace at Versailles before an audience of thousands, it actually took place in my parents' seventeen-room duplex apartment at 730 Park Avenue, with barely a dozen people attending. No invitations, no nothing—just my father; my mother, risen from her sickbed; my sister;

....

* "NEW YORK, Dec. 7—WEDDING TUNE FOR COMPOSER'S DAUGHTER— The former Mary Rodgers, daughter of tunesmith Richard Rodgers of Rodgers and Hammerstein fame, cuts herself a piece of cake with the assistance of her new spouse . . ."

my grandmother May; my cousin Judy; Jerry's parents and four siblings. We had a pianist who had also played twenty-one years earlier at my parents' wedding, and two clergy: a rabbi from Temple Emanu-El and a minister, the Rev. Samuel Carson Wasson, from Jerry's church. Rev. Wasson had a delicate job to do. May was fine with the Father but even without knowing them personally harbored an unshakable grudge against His Son, Jesus Christ, and His cohort, the Holy Ghost. So Rev. Wasson laboriously removed all mention of Them from the service, which resulted in weird gaps: "In the name of the Father and"—pause, pause, pause—"Amen." I still have the pretty little white Presbyterian wedding book, in which Jesus Christ and all his appurtenances are penciled out.

It was late afternoon. I wore my mother's wedding dress, an ivory satin gown with lace trim. Of course, it was let out, even though by then I was skinny again, having starved myself down to 130 pounds. We also cut off some of the train; something about a living room wedding did not seem to call for one.

You wouldn't think it possible, but by then I'd got myself believing I was very happy. You can see in all the pictures the huge smile Daddy hated. Fairy tales usually start out nice, and there was something of the fairy tale in this for me. *Sleeping Beauty*, maybe. When I was upstairs in the bedroom getting fitted into the dress, the dressmaker pricked her finger, leaving a spot of blood on the bodice of the gown. I was horrified, but my mother said, "I know what to do." She always did, regarding a stain. She just got an ice cube and rubbed, and it came out almost immediately—a trick to remember when you are old and decrepit and bleeding all over everything from the Coumadin.*

Jerry had planned a monthlong Caribbean cruise for our honeymoon, with a Christmastime stay in Jamaica as the centerpiece. This too was a rush job, so after the ceremony, after an awkward exchange of champagne toasts, and after my mother went back to her sickbed, we hurried down to the pier to settle into our cabin. Three of my friends, who had only recently met Jerry, joined us there for a little party before sailing.

---

* A blood thinner often prescribed to prevent or treat blood clots.

One was Ford Schumann, officially and rhymingly Ward Ford Schumann, a painter and sometime composer who was a friend of Steve's from Williams. One was Caroline Schumann, his first wife. They would later divorce, and Ford would fall out with Steve over *Merrily We Roll Along.* (Having read the bad reviews, Ford decided not to fly in from Aspen to see it. Oops.) But it was Ford who taught us the Robert Burns toast that would, in an English version, become a motif in that show: "Here's to us! Who's like us? Damn few."* The third guest was Steve himself.

That summer, when I was between grooms, Steve and I had gotten closer. By then he had finished his studies with Milton Babbitt and was looking for a way to translate what he had learned, along with his natural gift, into something he could sell. I was also trying to find a way into the business, so we talked a lot about songwriting, though I knew I was not in his league. Steve suggested we collaborate on something more pop-oriented than theatrical. We knew that Christmas songs did very well, and calypso was fashionable at the time, so we wrote, yes, a calypso Christmas song called "Christmas Island at Christmas Time":

> There's an island in the Pacific
> Where the weather is perverse.
> All year long the heat is terrific,
> But at Christmas time it's worse.

He says I wrote the music; clearly he wrote the lyrics.†

We often worked at my parents' house and would sometimes sit, writing or gossiping, under one of my father's pianos. During one of those conversations, not quite innocently, I mentioned that a certain boy we both knew was probably gay, though I'm not sure that's the word I used.

Steve said, "Maybe I'm that way, too."

....

* Sondheim omitted from his lyric the final phrase: "And they're all dead."

† In *Look, I Made a Hat*, Sondheim writes that the song was "probably aimed at a television program or a record company."

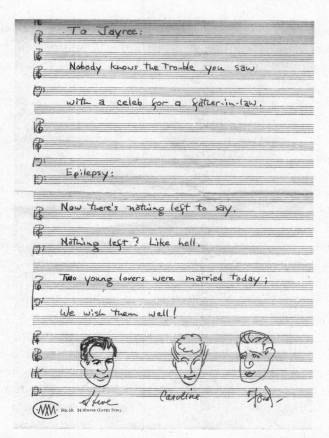

To Jayree:

Nobody knows the trouble you saw

with a celeb for a father-in-law.

Epilepsy:

Now there's nothing left to say,

Nothing left? Like hell,

Two young lovers were married today;

We wish them well!

Steve   Caroline   Ford

1951: Final page of the "Holiday for Heartstrings" manuscript, signed by Sondheim, Caroline Schumann, and Ford Schumann. "No Beaty knows the trouble you've seen."

"Oh, you can go to a psychiatrist and get that changed," I responded blithely.

He nodded—we all thought that way back then. "But maybe I don't want to change," he said.

The intimacy of nineteen, twenty, and twenty-one is not like any you ever experience again. It's very deep and very narrow. You are dumb and brave and maybe they are the same thing. I nodded, too, though I guess my heart was breaking.

Six months later, Jerry and I boarded the ship, where Steve and the

Schumanns threw us the little farewell party. They had written a wonderful "have a nice honeymoon" song, making fun of my parents and their disapproval of the wedding, which the three of them performed for me and Jerry.*

But then something terrifying happened: My father showed up unexpectedly to say goodbye. Suddenly, he was standing in the doorway as the five of us, wedged into the cabin, were laughing uproariously. Had he heard the song? What if he saw the manuscript the lyrics were written on, and decided to have a look? He already hated Steve, and had from the moment I'd begun talking about him. That feeling was overdetermined. Not only was Steve obviously a brilliant boy but he was Ockie's brilliant boy. There was also envy involved, if it's possible to be envious predictively—and I think it is. By then, too, *Allegro*, on which Steve had been a gofer, had crashed. And of course, anything I brought home was *treyf*.

But surely Daddy didn't hear the song or see the lyrics. Right? He just stood awkwardly at the door for a while, looking sad and dour.

Maybe I'm making this up; Steve doesn't remember any of it. Anyway, it *should* be true, and would make a great moment in a novel. Can't you see it? Those three men—Daddy, Jerry, Steve—each more or less hostile to each of the others, each representing a different aspect of the deluded heroine's not-yet-started life, all cramped in the same small space with the "all ashore" about to sound.

....

* "Holiday for Heartstrings" appears to have been a collaboration among Sondheim and the Schumanns. The manuscript, which has the lyrics but no tune, is not in Sondheim's hand, though he has signed it, along with Ford and Caroline, each beneath a charming little cartoon portrait, presumably drawn by Ford. Most of the lyrics, addressed to "Jayree" and "Mayree," are generic epithalamic ribaldry: "Jayree's a laddie / Sharp as a tack, / Maybe a Daddy / When he gets back." But at least one couplet, addressed to "Mayree," is too zingy and insightful not to be Sondheim's: "Ev'ry day Mother turned a bright green; / No Beaty knows the trouble you've seen."

PART II

17.

SOMEONE'S GETTING
WORSE

My parents' wedding gift to us was too big for our apartment. And also for our marriage.

It was a beautiful grand piano, a Steinway. The apartment was Jerry's bachelor pad on the fourth floor of a nice brick and limestone building at Seventy-fourth and Fifth, with one small bedroom and another even smaller. (While still under the covers you could reach out and touch the two opposite walls.) Originally a walk-up, the building had at some point acquired a tiny self-service elevator, which so panicked my father the first time he came for dinner that he never came again. The piano couldn't get up the elevator, either, let alone the bendy stairs.

Before the wedding, I'd begun writing a collection of children's songs. The idea, of course, had been Daddy's—always the businessman. Having seen me through the *Myopics in the Tropics* crisis, he wanted me to do something with both music and lyrics so I could control the whole package. And having praised my Wellesley Christmas song well enough, he asked why I didn't write more songs like that. I knew that "like that" meant small and low-ambition; he wasn't about to say to me, "Why don't you write a symphony?" Or even a musical. But children's songs were just the ticket, so I quickly came up with a few ideas for subjects that might work; I figured there might be twelve if I could only grind them out. He, very pleased with himself, came up with the title.* As a parent he was surprisingly pushy on my behalf, but it was tricky: He had very high standards that he rightfully worried I wouldn't meet, yet also the fear, common among insecure geniuses, of hearing something too good. At this point in my life, the first was far more likely than the second, but either way it created a feeling of ambivalence; his ambition for me was real enough but his appreciation was theoretical. He never asked to hear any of the songs, of which I guess I'd finished six when Jerry reappeared on the scene and I tossed the project aside. Did I mention that when we discussed getting married, I disavowed any passion for a career and especially for writing music? Being a wife and, especially, a mother would be enough for me, I told him honestly, or so I thought.

But after I got back from the honeymoon, Daddy and Steve began pestering me: What's happening with your writing? One weekend at the Hammersteins', even Ockie took me aside and asked about the songs. I said I'd written some and had others in my head but didn't have the energy to put them on paper. And he said, very quietly and persuasively as if he were telling me to climb ev'ry mountain, "Do one a day."

I wasn't aware of it, but I must have sensed that, despite my promise to Jerry, I'd better get back to work. I knew without knowing that things were already awry. After the honeymoon, Daddy kept saying, looking at me very searchingly, "Well, how are you?" And "How was it?" I could tell, because that was a level of intimacy that we'd never gotten into, that he was deeply concerned. Of course I lied to him, as I had lied to my mother, and said it was wonderful. Which in bits and pieces it was. But from Chilton and my own experimentation I knew what good sex was, and it wasn't "bits and pieces." It was full-out fun, like a hayride or something, not constantly interspersed with worries and passive-aggressive comments. "I'm beginning to think I'm frigid," I told Jerry one morning on the cruise; naturally, he was very insulted. "That's a nice thing to tell me on my honeymoon!"

....

* *Some of My Best Friends Are Children.* Richard Rodgers was very big with puns. He later named the advice book Dorothy and Mary wrote together: *A Word to the Wives.*

I didn't really think I was frigid; saying so was just a funny, or devious, way of raising a subject I couldn't otherwise. I had already learned from Jerry's example that our relationship would have to proceed by evasions and half-truths and something even worse, like when your computer freezes up and you get that whirling ball. That's what it was like sometimes, looking in his eyes. He would stare back and I would feel: *He's not there.*

That wasn't always a metaphor. Soon after the frigidity incident, I woke up in our hotel in Kingston, the depressingly un-Christmaslike sun pouring into the room and Jerry nowhere to be found. Because it was Boxing Day, an earsplitting steel band festival was going on outside, and as I waited and waited for him to come back, those drums hollering, I became terrified. Had he abandoned me in a foreign land? Fortunately—or maybe unfortunately—not; he finally resurfaced, late in the day, with the excuse that he had merely gone out to enjoy the music and fun. I knew it was very aberrant behavior for a man on his honeymoon, but I didn't dare say anything about it; in any case, he must have felt the need to atone, because by the time I arrived home I was (I later realized) pregnant.

Looking back, I assume he was out getting sex. Of course. What else?

If he walked into a room today, I think you would know, not from his manner but from the pains he took at concealment, that he was gay. In fact, he walked very stiff-legged, like his knees wouldn't bend. I later spent many years watching gay people move and realized he had been trying not to walk like them but way overshot.

Apparently, my parents also knew the truth, thanks to Mildred Creen of "Don't let her marry him" fame. My former shrink David Levy knew, too, though I wouldn't find that out until a few years later, when, at a dinner party, he very unprofessionally engaged my father in a conversation about why I kept landing up with gay men. I guess everyone knew but me, and even I did, too, but only in the way you know you will die someday. You say, "Yes, that could happen," but it keeps not happening so maybe it won't. It's an idea you puff but don't inhale. To be fair, Jerry did try to tell me once—I think:

"What would you do if I admitted something truly shocking?"

"Like what? That you don't love me?"

"No, not that."

"Well, like what, then?"

We both gave up.

And was it such a bad thing? I *liked* gay men. Don't most women who aren't homophobes? Everyone should marry a gay man at least once. A few years later I introduced my sister to one, a good friend of Jerry's who was great-looking and the editor of a fashion magazine. I didn't have a clue he was gay, or maybe I did, but my parents were furious. I was obviously married to a gay man, and now I was introducing their unwed daughter to another one? She didn't marry him, but maybe, given the alternative, she should have.

After all, gay guys, being warmer, more accessible, more tolerant, and more emotional, listen to you. They understand what you're talking about, and once they know you're on their side, they're eager to confide in you, too.* As for a rewarding life in bed, there are myriad ways to skin that cat, and I'm not going to spell them all out for you.

But of course I'm talking about openly gay men. Guys in the closet, like Jerry, spend so much of their emotional energy disguising themselves, there is little left over for all those wonderful gay traits. I don't blame him in the slightest—now. Anyone under the age of fifty can't possibly imagine what a nightmare it was to be gay in those days. Hairdressers were gay. Dress designers, set designers, florists. Actually, in the fifties even *they* weren't gay; they were faggots, pansies, fairies, or, in extra-polite company, light in the loafers. (In Quogue, I know people who still say that.) But Julian Bonar Beaty Jr., Esq., the lawyer from Rye and Loomis and Princeton, was not supposed to be any of those words and he damn well knew it.

And he was, much of the time, an extremely good guy. A funny and well-informed conversationalist, a raconteur, a devoted wordsmith, an outspoken liberal, and, crucially, someone who not only liked me but needed me. He was also giving me a child—and I was inordinately proud

---

* Two words of counterevidence to this benign stereotype: Arthur Laurents.

1951: Mary and Jerry. "Anyone under the age of fifty can't possibly imagine what a nightmare it was to be gay in those days."

of being the first to be married and have kids from my whole class at Brearley. When my friends at Wellesley were getting ready to graduate, I went back to visit them, flaunting my front.

Of course, I was giving Jerry a child, too, though that turned out to be less protection than I imagined. One night at the Drake Room, where we liked to hear the pianist Cy Walter* play, I craved beef Stroganoff but couldn't eat it when it came. (This must have been during my standard one week of gestational vomits.) Jerry was furious. "I have to pay for that!" he shouted. And I said, "You have to pay for it whether I eat it or not."

Let that be a life lesson. You pay for it whether you eat it or not.

In any case, I was getting pregnant-er by the day and bored-er by the minute. As soon as we moved into a bigger apartment, on East Seventy-eighth, in early 1952, I took receipt of the Steinway and went back to

....

* The Art Tatum of Park Avenue, as he was called, Cy Walter (1915–1968) specialized in heady improvisations on Broadway classics. He was for many years a fixture at the Drake Room, the fancier restaurant at the Drake Hotel in midtown Manhattan.

work. In a few months I had finished notating enough of the songs that Daddy made an appointment for me to audition them for his publisher. This was, of course, arrant nepotism; how many twenty-one-year-old girls whose fathers hadn't written *Oklahoma!* landed meetings at Chappell with Dr. Albert Sirmay* and the dreaded Dreyfi?†

Actually, I met only half the Dreyfi: Max, who ran Chappell's New York office, at Rockefeller Center in what was then called the RKO Building.‡ He was very formal and welcoming when I showed up, great with child and small of résumé, or perhaps he was just being nice because of my father. Either way, he and Dr. Sirmay listened as I played and sang however many of the songs I'd written; I was nervous enough that I auditioned from memory, not trusting myself to read from the page. Afterward, crickets. We smiled at one another. Finally, in his thick German accent, Max politely explained that all musical phrases must consist of an even number of bars. When I asked why, he said, "That is the way it is done." Dr. Sirmay nodded, and I nodded, too, having heard this repeatedly from Daddy.§

....

* In his native Hungary, Albert Szirmai (1880–1967) was a successful operetta composer; in America, under his Anglicized name, he was the music director at Chappell & Co., in which position he edited hundreds of Broadway works for publication, including those of Gershwin, Kern, Porter, and Rodgers.

† The "Dreyfi" were Max (1874–1964) and Louis (1877–1967) Dreyfus. They owned the joint, and in that position exerted huge control over Broadway musicals from the 1930s on.

‡ The building is now just plain 1270 Avenue of the Americas. Radio City Music Hall is at the bottom. Louis Dreyfus ran the London office.

§ It wasn't a rule so much as a cultural habit that traditionalists clung to. Even when lyrics would clearly work better in a seven-bar setting—like some that Sondheim wrote for *Do I Hear a Waltz?*—Richard Rodgers insisted on stretching them to eight, adding padding as needed to fill out the phrase.

1953: Jerry, Mary, Tod: "He was an active, crawly, impatient little guy
who would crash around his playpen for all of five minutes."

To my surprise, they did agree to publish *Some of My Best Friends Are
Children* once I finished all twelve songs and corrected the bar counts. I
know it took me the better part of a year, because I was still working on
it after Tod was born, on September 23. Tod didn't make things easier.
When I got him home from the hospital, I tried to put him next to my
face. No. That wasn't happening. He had the strongest neck in the world.
And almost immediately, he was an active, crawly, impatient little guy
who would crash around his playpen for all of five minutes and then yelp
to get out before I had a chance to get more than two bars on paper. That
was my first child.

Maybe the songs' contents had affected him prenatally; the lyrics were
based on nursery rhymes ("Finders Keepers," "The Woodchuck") and
street games ("Allee in Free," "Kick the Can, Willy!") that suggested the

mischievous, rambunctious child he would turn out to be.* Or maybe it wasn't so much prenatal as autobiographical; if the songs didn't describe Tod a few years later, they certainly described me a few years before. Most of them are about a kid who wants to be allowed to act like a kid but no longer wants to be treated like one.†

The sheet music was published in a pink folio, with some sort of Aubrey Beardsley–in–kindergarten illustration on the cover, in early 1953. It sold for a dollar. Through a deal that Chappell had with Golden Records, a bright yellow, six-inch, 78-r.p.m. "Little Golden" recording of four of the songs, performed by Anne Lloyd & the Sandpipers and destined to be lost behind radiators everywhere, was released around the same time, for twenty-five cents.‡ I'd probably be embarrassed if I heard the songs now,§ but I sure liked receiving a check in my name.

Or a version of my name. Chappell wanted "Rodgers" in the byline, thinking it would help sales. I wanted "Beaty" in the byline, thinking it would appease my husband for "Rodgers." So the pink folio and the yellow 78 and the green check all said Mary Rodgers Beaty, which satisfied no one.

....

* "'Who has been poking in my room?' said nurse, / 'Seven sticks of chewing gum are missing from my purse. / Someone has been naughty and someone's getting worse,'" goes one verse of "Couldn't Have Been Me."

† In the last of the twelve songs, the child asks a rocking horse to take her to a place where her face "isn't patted by people who think I am three." It ends a bit desperately: "Rocking horse, take me wherever you care, but rocking horse take me there."

‡ The orchestra was led by Mitch Miller (1911–2010), about whom more soon.

§ They are charming and well-constructed and perfect for their audience.

18.

SOME OF MY BEST FRIENDS

already knew there was no satisfying my father; now I was learning how hard it would be to satisfy Jerry. Our first summer together it was already clear that he was, at best, ambivalent about my work, my friends, and the theatrical world I was cultivating. Not that his own world thrilled him much. At dinner on the second night of our honeymoon he told me he didn't like what he was doing, specifically being a junior partner in his father's law firm. This came as no surprise to me; what was to like? Copper litigation? His fusty colleagues? His father was a self-made cock-a-doodle-dandy from South Carolina, valedictorian of his class at Princeton, an unattractive, stocky, beetle-browed fanny-pincher. Fortunately, Jerry took after (and, less fortunately, resembled emotionally) his mother, Constance, who looked like a fat Ethel Barrymore: statuesquely handsome but no prize package. Not to mention bossy, and overly protective of her five children—Jerry, her first, in particular. Once, when he was suffering from an "incipient ulcer" that I and my young friends apparently caused, she delivered Jell-O and junket* to our apartment every day for a week.

That night on our honeymoon I told Jerry that if he was unhappy

....

* Junket, a watery, sloshy, milky concoction of sweetened milk and rennet, was usually served to small children as dessert or when ill. At the time of these sickbed deliveries, Jerry Beaty was nearing forty.

doing what he was doing, the time to make a change was now, before we had any children. But when I asked what he had in mind for himself, he was flummoxed. Though the diplomatic corps appealed to him, he was too old to take the civil service exam; the cutoff age, he told me, was thirty. And he wasn't rich enough to be a political appointee. At some point, he woke me up in the middle of the night to announce with great excitement that he'd realized his destiny: He'd be a minister. A minister with a former-Catholic-Jewish-atheist wife greeting parishioners in the vestibule of the church every Sunday? I told him he was nuts. Next, he thought he might like to be a theatrical lawyer. I told him to forget about that too: a non-Jewish theatrical lawyer? Such an anomaly didn't exist. Well, there was one, John Wharton, a partner in the firm of Someone, Someone, and Someone, now known as Someone, Someone, Someone, and Someone Else. He was the goy that proved the rule.

A few months after we returned from our honeymoon, with the question unresolved, Jerry paid fifty bucks to take a three-day battery of aptitude tests given by the Johnson O'Connor Research Foundation. O'Connor, a psychometrician, had developed a fascinating way to describe your basic personality: You were either objective or subjective, depending on whether you were innately focused outward or inward. Lawyers were counterintuitively said to be, for the most part, subjective, interested in the law itself, not the client. Well, of course the tests showed that Jerry had an objective personality, as anyone afraid to be discovered must, making him wrong, wrong, wrong for that kind of work.*

The information was useless for him, but Steve, my friend Nancy, and I were fascinated by the tests. They not only measured your objectivity and subjectivity but read the tea leaves for specific qualities that supposedly matched with specific careers. Like lemmings, we all plunked down our fifty bucks† and rushed to find out what we were.

Steve went first. He was rather cool about the experience; he said they

---

* Jerry Beaty remained a lawyer until he retired, fifty years later.

† The tests, still available, now cost $750.

didn't tell him anything he didn't already know about himself. I don't mean this snidely, but has anybody, ever?

Nancy* went next. Having been the most brilliant member of my graduating class at Brearley—excelling at physics, Greek, Latin, and English, and able to concoct original Chaucerian prose or Shakespearean sonnets or a play in the manner of Euripides faster than I could write a grocery list—she graduated from Radcliffe, a veritable kudos-collector, but then what? Her mother, Mrs. (Janet) William Rhinelander (Ryan) Stewart, a great beauty of the 1930s, was one of the first socialites to appear in advertisements, including one for Pond's cold cream. Nancy was considered beautiful, too, but not as delicate as her mother; she took more after her father, a big, rawboned, blond swimmer from Yale. Put them together and you got the kind of shiny, intrepid, super-smart woman you'd find in a Truman Capote story—and in fact Truman and Nancy were friends.

But also like a Truman Capote character, she didn't know what to do with herself. Neither did Johnson O'Connor. The test told her she had too many aptitudes.

This turned out to be true. After becoming a member of the stage electricians union, she hung around with the young theater crowd in New York, then married the English critic Alan Brien, making her, absurdly, Nancy Ryan Brien. She went to live with him in England and had two terrific children: a girl named Jane and a boy named Adam, the same age as ours. (The two Adams got into plenty of trouble together.) Soon, though, Nancy and Alan divorced—Alan's fault, not hers; every ten years or so he got tired of his wife and married a new one, which was not an easily detectable shortcoming. After that she had an affair with the columnist Leonard Lyons, which was just too silly.† Having avoided an-

....

* You will recall that Nancy Newbold Ryan (1930–1987)—no relation to Chilton, D.D. and Johnny, nor even the upcoming Ginny and Nin—was the only friend to attend Mary's baptism in 1951.

† Lyons was married and had children—one of them eventually the film

other near rhyme, she went to the London College of Furniture, where she learned how to make Renaissance musical instruments, one of which my mother bought as a gift for my Adam's Yale graduation in 1987. She then studied Czech, an impossibly bizarre and difficult language, in order to teach instrument making in Czechoslovakia. Who knows how many other lives she might have led if, before arriving in Prague, she hadn't taken her Adam whitewater rafting in Nepal, where she became terribly ill with pancreatitis and died before she could be medevacked to a proper hospital because it was the king of Nepal's birthday and he had commandeered the only helicopter in the country? Further hindered by the cost and red tape of shipping the body home, her Adam decided to give Nancy a nice, traditional Brahman Hindu funeral, pyre and all, down the Ganges,* which I hope she enjoyed. The rest of us missed it. And continue to miss her.

Now it was my turn. I was three or four months pregnant and in the middle of trying to make the manuscripts of the kiddie songs. The first testing day covered math and spatial relations, about which I was clearly a moron—either that or they purposely gave me a set of mismatched blocks that were never going to fit together. No matter; I didn't want to be an architect. The second day was about language. One of the language tests, called Ideaphoria, included a section in which they counted how many words you could spew out within a minute. No surprise, I was good at that. But then came the third day, the one that mattered most to me because it included musical assessments. These began with a simple

....

critic Jeffrey Lyons—and so Nancy told him it wasn't going to work. He got very angry and stormed out of the apartment and immediately came back because he forgot his coat. And left again. Thank god! Otherwise she might have been Nancy Ryan Brien Lyons.

* Nancy Ryan's remains were released into the Bagmati River, which eventually joins the Ganges. Her children believe she would have died in Nepal regardless of the king's birthday, and that her death was in any event more peaceful in the idyllic mountains there than it would have been had they been able to get her out.

rhythm test, which was no problem, but soon got much harder. By the end, my eardrums were flailing around in a maelstrom of tricky, continuously varying rhythms. On to the melody test! Equally disastrous. It, too, started easily, asking you to repeat melodies like "Row, Row, Row Your Boat." This was followed by more and more difficult examples until it got to Schoenbergian twelve-tone tunes that were impossible to reproduce and, furthermore, were beginning to give me a stomachache. Meanwhile, an ugly thought was crossing my mind: What if their analysis of my results, which could be picked up the next day, said I had no aptitude for music? They might be mistaken, of course, and surely if someone like Steve got such a dire diagnosis, he would ignore it. But I knew I'd believe them if they said so; I'd never write another note. Oh, what a bad stomachache I had now!

Only it wasn't a stomachache. When I got home, I started to bleed. I called Uncle Morty, who said I was showing signs of a miscarriage; I was to go to bed immediately with my legs propped up and stay there for a week. Not only did this get me out of a little dinner party I was supposed to make but also out of returning to Johnson O'Connor for my results. How considerate of my innards to provide me with an excuse to flee that place! Nothing medically ominous developed from the bleeding and, five months later, with the ease of a peasant field worker in *The Good Earth*, I produced a perfectly healthy seven-pound boy. Meanwhile, I never went back to Johnson O'Connor; I never even called. To this day I have no idea if they thought I had any musical aptitude. It was the best fifty bucks I ever blew.

Still, without drastic new insight into our ideal careers, Jerry and I were left to keep plodding along with the ones we already had. If he was antsy, I was worse; by August, very hot and very fat with forty pounds' worth of child and other stuffing, I thought I might crawl out of my body before the baby could. Remember, no one had air-conditioning back then; all we wanted was to get out of town, somewhere near water but far from family.

So did our impoverished friends—which is to say my impoverished friends. Ten of us, all at the stage of our lives when we were pitifully flailing for attention on the margins of showbiz, rented a big house and a spillover annex for very little money on the main street of Quogue. There was Steve, of course, whose great achievement as the clapper boy during the filming of John Huston's *Beat the Devil* still lay before him. There was George Dale, a writer of liner notes for Columbia Records. Ford and Caroline Schumann were there, too, along with several of Steve's other college pals: Chuck Hollerith and his wife, Dinky;* Howard Erskine, who was not yet a snob;† and Nick Dunne.‡

It was a friend of Jerry's who found us the "cottage." In beach territory, the residences, no matter how big or small, are called cottages as long as they're brown and covered in wood shingles, usually with genuine shake roofs. It's a reverse-snobbery thing; on the outside they are supposed to look ramshackle and unloved, even if inside they are pristine—chockablock with comfy bedrooms, well-appointed kitchens, and gracious living rooms. Ours scored well for its outside decrepitude, but unfortunately the inside matched. It was a dump. There were the requisite many bedrooms, yes, each with a disconnected call button to summon a lackey who no longer existed. But they were dank, with sagging mattresses, mouse droppings, dead flies, live flies, all of them lit by bare twenty-five-watt bulbs.

Did we care? Not a bit. We were like kids let out of school; whatever

----

* Charles Hollerith (1927–2011) would go on to produce a number of Broadway plays and serve on the board of the Actors Fund. Dinky, actually Catherine, was his first wife; she soon had a baby and then killed herself while pregnant with a second. She was twenty-seven but, as always, they called it a heart attack. Chuck's second wife died young of cancer. The actress Hope Lange was his third wife; he outlasted her as well.

† Howard Erskine (1926–2011) would eventually become a successful director and producer but was then working as an actor, getting bit parts on television.

‡ You probably know the journalist Dominick Dunne (1925–2009) from his *Vanity Fair* days; when Mary met him, he was a floor manager of *The Howdy Doody Show*.

we were working on, we let it go. For ten days we played millions of games—the kind that would become such a central part of our social life later. It may even be where we invented what we called "the" game, a mad combination of charades and a relay race that lost ground in our repertoire as quickly as our smoking gained.

Smoking was not our only bad habit. As we tried out every restaurant up and down Montauk Highway, we cursed like characters in a David Mamet play. Everything was *fuck this* and *fuck that*, which was something you rarely heard in those days. My favorite new phrase was: "I'm going to take a dump." I was so immature, or so straitened despite my attempts at rebellion, that I thought this was the funniest thing ever. Unless it was this: Nick Dunne showed me one day that a little bathroom downstairs had a window; my idea of humor was to creep around the house when we knew Steve was on the toilet, climb—or rather, in my case, waddle—up a ladder, look in, and shout, "Boo!"

Jerry appeared to be enjoying himself but maybe he was just trying to be a good sport. He was a decade older than the next oldest of the gang, and we must have seemed so childish. For him, "the hills of tomorrow" that Steve would write about in *Merrily We Roll Along***** were already beginning to recede in the rearview mirror. Between that and whatever was going on inside his head about sex, or outside our bedroom for that matter (as I later came to understand), he was not what you'd call a carefree man. Had I known the truth I'd have been sympathetic. We were, after all, stuck in parallel traps, having been drawn to each other thinking: Here's a way out.

For me, hoping to escape the tyranny of my mother, it was mortifying to realize I hadn't escaped her: I had married her. Jerry was exactly as exacting as she, as finicky, controlling, puritanical, and elusive. Over the next few years, we argued constantly about my role as a wife. Unfulfilled according to him; unfulfilling according to me. We bickered about big

----

* An optimistic anthem sung by graduating high school seniors. "Behold, begin: There are worlds to win. / Let us come to trust the dreams we must fulfill." In later versions of the show, the song was cut.

things, small things, all things. Breakfast, for instance. When he finally arrived at the table, he would complain that his eggs were cold.

"Okay, let's set an exact time for breakfast," I said one day. "How's about seven thirty? Then I can time them for that."

"Fine."

The next day: "My eggs are cold."

"Of course they are; it's now seven forty-five."

"My mother had five children and she got up from the table and made eggs fresh for each one of us individually."

"I'm not your mother."

This sort of raking-Mary-over-the-coals ritual was what I got married to get away from. Every morning of my younger life, I'd come into Mummy's bedroom before breakfast. She would reach for the tear-off pad on the night table to her left and this beautiful little Cartier pencil with a ball at the end that hid extra leads and an eraser that of course she didn't need. Then she'd tick off the list with the pencil. *Did you write your thank-you notes? Wash your hairbrushes? Hang up your clothes—your room is a mess. Where's ten percent of your three months' allowance, please? Did you? Why didn't you? When are you going to?*

For Jerry, I was only as good as the cover I provided; I worked very hard to convince him that I was the domesticated creature he wanted. But it's impossible to bang out songs on the sly the way you can scribble sonnets, say. "Composing for the theater," I wrote in an article some years later,[*] "is not a nice quiet kind of thing you can do around the house—

....

[*] COMPOSERETTE TALKS TURKEY (as the newspaper headlined it) appeared in the *New York Herald Tribune* in 1960. Though it disclaims feminism per se, it is nevertheless a kind of feminist manifesto, a borscht belt version of *A Room of One's Own*. The reason there are so few women composers, it argues, is that women are forced to give up too much if they want that kind of life. "Working in the theater is fundamentally a collaborative effort. There are constant meetings, auditions, rehearsals, late hours. If you've written a book, you don't have to go on the road with it, but if you've written a show, your husband may have to phone you at the Taft

it's excruciatingly noisy and maddeningly repetitive—and your husband knows perfectly well what you're up to." I did try, though. I wrote as much as possible while he wasn't home, covering my tracks. Even that article was eked out when no one could say I was skipping my home duties. On Milton and Amy Greene's* boat during a picnic outing in Quogue, I sat in the back where you do deep-sea fishing, scribbling away while getting horribly seasick from watching the horizon bob up and down.

I really was as much of a liar as Jerry. We were both in the closet—separate closets.

....

Hotel, Kayseys, or the Shubert Theatre in New Haven in order to tell you that he can't find the children's snowsuits. By the time you get home after a seven-week tour, you'll find the snowsuits, but you just might not find your husband. Few women want to risk that."

* Milton H. Greene (1922–1985)—not to be confused with the Broadway music director Milton Greene, who conducted *Once Upon a Mattress* at Tamiment—was a photographer famous for his portraits of Marilyn Monroe. Monroe lived with him and his wife, the Cuban model Amy Franco Greene (born 1929), for four years in the mid-1950s.

19.

DUBONNET

Clearly in need of more closet space, we did the traditional thing: We moved to the suburbs. Ours happened to be smack on the border between Port Chester, New York, and Greenwich, Connecticut; the state line crossed through our driveway. The declared intention of the change was to give our little rascal more room to play than an apartment permitted, and me more time to write—even though, oh yes, by the summer of 1953, at twenty-two, I was pregnant again.

Jerry was in favor of the move because, having grown up nearby, he was familiar with the territory. His brother, Dick, and sister-in-law, Judy, lived a few miles away in Purchase.

Judy was Judy Loeb, my Brearley friend and the older sister of double-debutante Ann. Judy was very positive in the way that only rich, wellborn people can be, like Maggie Smith on *Downton Abbey*: They're right about everything. Well, almost everything. Twelve years later, in 1965, after Dick was caught cheating with another woman and took an overdose of pills, Judy found him stone cold dead next to her the next morning, with a note: *Dearest Judy, I'm terribly sorry for having hurt you.* Which is nice, but there she was with five children, a great deal of money, and a regretful corpse.*

Jerry liked living in his native clime and even liked the commute to

---

* Following the rulebook, they called the suicide a heart attack. Richard Beaty was forty-five.

circa 1953: Mary and Jerry Beaty, with Dick and Judy (Loeb) Beaty.
"Dearest Judy, I'm terribly sorry for having hurt you."

the city, with its early departures and late returns and the neat folding of his newspaper in quarters. But we were so far out in the country that I would have had to get up at the crack of dawn to drive him to the station in Greenwich if I hadn't bought him a cute little green Morris Minor* so he could chauffeur himself. Meanwhile, I drove an ugly Pontiac station wagon that my parents gave us and that we called, after a gardener's mispronunciation, the Peeontic.

The move was a mistake, the result of an idle "Gee, wouldn't the country be nice?" comment I'd made to Jerry on a crowded, noisy New York Sunday with Tod in the pram at the zoo. For one thing, writing wasn't any easier in the house; Tod used the extra space for constant, dangerous explorations. He kept sticking little things, like forks and fingers,

---

* A British car that looked like the love child of a Volkswagen and Winston Churchill.

in baseboard sockets.* In desperation, I put him in a baby carriage harness attached to a long rope and tied him to the trunk of a big tree near a window so I could plink away at the piano while at the same time keeping an eye on him playing with his toys. When he started eating those toys, I switched to walking him endlessly up and down the road to enjoy the scenery. Mostly he enjoyed the crows.†

In December, Nina was born—early. She was a tiny little sweet thing, only five pounds and change; I'm sure her premature arrival was due to my lugging her thirty-pound brother in and out of the stroller a million times a day. I loved her, but a second child within fifteen months of the first made writing more than twice as difficult. During the summer and fall, I could just about swing it. Steve would visit and we would work together on a one-hour musical we were trying to make out of "The Lady, or the Tiger?"‡ We had a faint idea that we might be able to sell it to television, though neither of us had sold a thing at that point, other than my children's ditties. Still, we mapped it out like professionals, and wrote maybe nine numbers, of which, to my knowledge, only one, called "Once I Had a Friend," survives. This was intended for a scene in which the girl reveals her feelings to the boy, explaining how the "mental" relationship they shared has turned, in the girl's mind at least, into something else:

I used to think how pure it is,
This friendship we've made.
But now I'm not so sure it is.
Something's changed and I'm afraid.

....

* Tod Beaty's first word was "Hot!"

† His second word was "Caw!"

‡ Frank R. Stockton's 1882 short story, heavily anthologized, often adapted, long out of copyright. It shows up as the second act of Bock and Harnick's 1966 musical, *The Apple Tree*.

I can't remember who wrote what, musically, but the gist of the lyric, being highly autobiographical, is clearly mine. Even as he methodically improved it, cleaning up the bridge and adding internal rhymes, I don't think Steve ever noticed what I was saying. If he did, I hope he forgave me.*

Winter put at least a temporary end to our work and, at the same time, vastly multiplied the annoying, stultifying chores of motherhood in a cold, lonely suburb. I will now force you to sit through a paragraph that you should consider yourself lucky goes on only for a minute instead of several months. We are in the dead of January with snow and ice on the driveway. I've run out of some necessary food item. The man from the garage comes out to put chains on the Peeontic. The garageman leaves. I stuff the two babies into the car—I don't remember where I stuffed them, but there were no seat belts, let alone car seats, in those days, so they were probably bouncing around in the back like lotto balls—and set out for the supermarket twenty minutes away. I get as far as the road, where the chains instantly break because it, unlike my driveway, has been cleared. I trudge back to the house to call the garageman again. By the time I get the eggs home safely, the kids are grown and I am dead.

And so, by spring, I'd had quite enough of country living; Jerry must have had quite enough of it, too, because he willingly acquiesced when I suggested we move our rapidly growing ménage back to the city. Do you know the way a dog circles and circles a small space before nestling down

....

* It wouldn't be the first time this song caused trouble between the friends. After their version of "The Lady, or the Tiger?" fizzled, "Once I Had a Friend" (or "I Wonder Why," as it was also called) went into what Mary called her very little trunk—"more like a jewelry case." Years later, in 1993, it came out again to be used in a revue of her work called *Hey, Love*. Somehow it happened that the song was assigned to be sung by a man, which made it even more wistful but should not have been done without Sondheim's permission. To apologize, Mary sent him a large French porcelain serving piece. In a note accepting the apology he responded, "Thanks for the platter, but where was my mother's head?"

for sleep? My life on the Upper East Side was like that: sniffing around a few square blocks, over and over. This time we ended up at 50 East Seventy-second Street, just west of Park Avenue: thirteenth floor, eight rooms, one cleaning woman—please don't make me say "cleaning lady," which is a feeble attempt to compensate in language for how little they are paid—and a series of now-you-see-them-now-they've-left live-in au pairs. One was a Jamaican who, when Tod came down with a cold, insisted that the only cure was to put rum on his head. I demurred politely; the local drugstore had something that would work just as well, I said, and immediately went around the corner to get some. By the time I returned, the whole apartment smelled like a distillery and Tod was gleefully bouncing up and down in his crib, high as a kite on contact fumes, his hair sticking straight up, gummy and damp.

The new surroundings were better—I could at least see my friends without an hour's drive—but Jerry's behavior just got worse. On the rare occasion when he psyched himself up for sex with me, if I told him I wasn't up for it he threatened me with divorce, which seemed to me to be overkill. And then one night I woke to find him standing over the bed in the dark; I could hear the tinkling of ice in a glass, and I could see the lit end of a cigarette. When I asked what was going on, he said, "Would you like to go to a party?"

"Now? What kind of party?"

"Oh, you know, with people. Having a good time."

To keep my mind off strange portents like these, I gave myself the challenge of writing a song a day, no matter what. At the end of a week I had seven bad ballads. I think I had seven bad ballads at the end of a month as well, because it just wasn't possible to keep up that pace. For me, writing music, or prose as I later discovered, requires long vistas of open time. Or at least a few hours without vomit on my blouse. Not that I thought I was such hot stuff, but the weak spark of entitlement I brought with me into the marriage still kept blinking its little message. I should be doing something more fun and meaningful, it said, than heading east to the supermarket with my wire basket to buy cheaper food than at Gristedes and/or heading west to the Seventy-second Street playground

1954: Jerry holding Tod's hand while Mary pushes Nina in the stroller.
"The weak spark of entitlement I brought with me into the marriage
still kept blinking its little message."

where I spent most of my time trying to prevent Tod from bashing some
other kid over the head with a shovel.

This, while simultaneously fishing three-quarters of a Kent cigarette
out of the back of Nina's throat, rushing her to the doctor, then rushing
both kids home to give them lunch (the doctor was unimpressed), then
naps, then back to the playground, then home for baths, supper, and a
martini for me, then fixing dinner and waiting for Jerry, who, despite the
much-reduced commute, was frequently very late.

And frequently very angry.

Oddly, I associate the first time he hit me with an aperitif. Dubonnet was, and is, a sweet and somewhat lethal fortified wine, especially when combined fifty-fifty with gin. My parents drank it that way every day at lunch, in old-fashioned glasses. As it happened, Ruth Dubonnet* shared an elevator hall with us on East Seventy-second. Her study, across the air shaft, faced a table in our apartment where the children ate; she would put fun things, like stuffed animals, in the window to amuse them. One Christmas we all ended up waiting for the elevator together. She said Merry Christmas, and the kids who could talk said Merry Christmas back. Then she leaned down to give Tod, who was three, a kiss, and he bit her on the nose.

Admittedly, this has very little, even for me, to do with the subject. It's just that it was in the same elevator hall that Jerry first slapped me, hard, across the face. We were heading out to a party at Morty Gottlieb's,†

....

* Someone should write a book about Ruth Obre Dubonnet (1900–1992). Or maybe someone has: She was one of several women said to be the model for the gold-digging flapper Lorelei Lee in Anita Loos's 1925 novel, *Gentlemen Prefer Blondes*. Ruth's marital history bears out the contention: Born the daughter of servants on the John Jacob Astor estate near Rhinebeck, New York, and having been widowed by her first husband, the Greenwich Village painter Walter Dean Goldbeck, she moved to France, where she became the Countess de Vallombrosa and, when that paled, the wife of the aperitif heir André Dubonnet. The immediate postwar years, spent partly in confinement as a suspected German collaborator, were not so glittering, but once cleared of all charges, she returned to the States to restyle herself as a Great New York Broad. By the time she and the Beatys became neighbors, she had separated from Dubonnet and was the girlfriend of the composer Jule Styne—who, bringing things full circle, had written the music for the 1949 Broadway musical version of *Gentlemen Prefer Blondes*. Still, Ruth wouldn't marry him, she told Mary, because (a) Jule was a gambler, and (b) doing so would endanger her generous alimony from the fortified wine family.

† Morton Gottlieb, then a Broadway general manager, later produced many slick hit plays, including *Sleuth* and *Same Time, Next Year*.

arguing as usual, or maybe more than usual. Even so I had no way of expecting it. All the violence I grew up with was verbal, except of course when it came from me.

I froze, but the slap seemed to loosen something within him, to jiggle open a lock. There would soon be other slaps and shoves and, almost worse, threatening gestures that didn't leave bruises. Once, as I was wearing a raspberry cashmere sweater, he clawed at me with his fingernails so hard that he ripped the sweater in half from neck to hem. I didn't dream of retaliating—for one thing, he was so much bigger than I. But I did once throw a glass of, yes, Dubonnet and gin, fifty-fifty, at him. I missed by a mile and ruined a lampshade; I was never very good at gym.

20.

A CRAW FULL

So what did I do about all this? Did I contemplate a divorce? God, no! What a terrifying prospect! I was so scared of being alone with two kids, and in that configuration having to find a guy, that I practically raped Jerry one night in order to get pregnant again. That way I would be locked in: No one but a fool would divorce a man when she had *three* kids. Nor, I thought, would a man divorce me. Dilemma solved. The only downside was that I would have to spend the rest of my life being miserable.

The misery got off to a good start that year of my third pregnancy, when a Connecticut house we rented for the summer turned out to come not only with linens but fleas. One night, still scratching, Jerry and I got into a big fight about Steve, beginning at a party in Lake George where he swung around on me seething, "You're in love with him!" Every man I knew was envious of that friendship, and Steve, too, had a way of finding anyone I took an interest in not smart enough or too boring to be worthy of me, as if I were such a prize. Jerry was smart enough, God knows; and he wasn't boring. But he was too old for the kind of fun Steve wanted us to be having.

When I gave a big party back in the city for Jerry's thirty-ninth birthday in September, Steve wrote and sang a song for him called "You're Only as Old as You Look" that was just hilarious enough to cover the hostility:

Of your in-laws
You've a craw full.
The demands that they make are in-lawful.
Well, you're only as old as you look—
*And you look awful.**

The fall was no better. A few days before rehearsals for Daddy's show *Pipe Dream* were scheduled to begin, he was diagnosed with cancer of the gum. Not surprising when you've smoked since childhood. Of course, everybody smoked then—none more enthusiastically than I. That may be why I have a total of half a lung left.

Daddy was always very squeamish about illness, but oddly enough, having waited his whole life for something terrible to happen, he experienced the diagnosis as a form of relief. He liked being taken care of and was very serene, possibly because doped up, while recovering from the removal of the left half of his jaw† and all those teeth with it. He was still vain, though—or my mother was on his behalf. When I went to visit him in the hospital, she warned me to take my glasses off to make him less self-conscious. Which was terrifying because, being nearsighted already, all I could see was this gauze-wrapped thing on a pillow.‡

He returned to *Pipe Dream* ten days after the operation: surely too soon, as he was still in a wheelchair and drooled constantly into a hand-

....

* In his collected lyrics Sondheim calls the song "an aggressive triple act of conveying affection, making someone acutely uncomfortable, and showing off."

† The jawbone was replaced with titanium.

‡ Dorothy stage-managed all of her husband's medical dramas, which later included bladder cancer and a bout of laryngeal cancer that required a tracheotomy. And there was something she knew but never told him, which is that he was born with only one kidney, one big kidney. She used to say it was a good thing he never tried to give it away—not that he would.

1955: A Christmas greeting from Sondheim. The handwritten melody is from
"The Two of You," a song written in 1952 for Kukla, Fran, and Ollie. The lyric:
"Every day I think anew of you / How I love the two of you."

kerchief. But he had something to prove. The most recent Rodgers and Hammerstein show, *Me and Juliet*, had run only a year, which wasn't so bad except in comparison to the previous two: *The King and I* (three years) and *South Pacific* (almost five). For men at the top of the heap—and I say men advisedly—every step is a likely fall. And *Pipe Dream* was not looking promising even before Daddy had to recuse himself. It was a weird attempt to merge the gritty realism of John Steinbeck with R&H uplift, which, despite constant rejiggering and a few lovely songs, never worked.* Daddy knew it, as Leonard Lyons hinted in a column.† *Pipe Dream* closed seven months later, a flop.

Lyons's item made it sound as if Kimmy were born that same night; actually, it was the next day, on December 1, 1955. But it was, as he wrote, an easy labor—without benefit of a father or even a doctor in attendance. Jerry's absence was expected; he attended none of his children's births. As for Uncle Morty, he simply didn't make it to the floor in time. I was left alone in the operating room with a very frightened nineteen-year-old nurse. No problem. As Daddy later reflected, I didn't need an obstetrician anyway, I needed an outfielder.

I also, clearly, needed a shrink. I was twenty-four going on twenty-five, with three children under four years old, a gay husband, a stalled career, and a tendency to double down impulsively on bad choices. My parents, now fully aware of how unhappy I was—they could see that for

....

* The female lead was so watered down from the source novel, *Sweet Thursday*, that Steinbeck barely recognized her. He famously complained that Hammerstein had "changed his whore into a visiting nurse."

† Just after the Broadway opening on November 30, Lyons wrote: "Richard Rodgers' daughter, Mrs. Mary Beaty, is a determined woman. She told her father that despite her imminent motherhood she would see the premiere of Rodgers and Hammerstein's *Pipe Dream*. . . . Mrs. Beaty did attend Wednesday's premiere of *Pipe Dream*, then went to Lenox Hill Hospital and gave birth to a daughter. She was in labor only one hour. . . . 'One hour?' said Rodgers, who'd just suffered through a two-and-a-half-hour premiere. 'I think I had the tougher time.'"

themselves and besides, I finally admitted it to them—agreed to pay. Top dollar then was forty an hour, and that's what it cost to undergo treatment with the Hungarian genius Sandor Rado* at Columbia Psychiatric Institute. He had been analyzed by an analysand of Freud, which was kind of like being a grandson of God, and his other patients included not just cultural stars like Lenny B. but, it was rumored, Joe DiMaggio. Despite his reputation I was somewhat resistant to him. I never lay down; I didn't want to give anyone that control over me. Instead I would sit in the chair opposite and have coffee brought to me, as if I were at Bergdorf's and he was my personal shopper.

Rado may have been a genius, but he wasn't a very good shrink, or not a very objective one anyway. He openly disapproved of my marriage—on moral grounds, though that was the pot calling the kettle gay. When I once said, "What kind of marriage do you have? I hear you play around all summer in Provincetown," he chuckled malevolently.† He also spent a lot of time trying to pick my brains about Lenny, which I thought was a poor use of my parents' forty bucks. And when, two years later, I'd finally had enough of him and said I thought we were finished, he got very upset. "No we're not, you're way too sick to be finished!"

Still, there was something clarifying about his rigid and old-fashioned ideas, if only as a counterweight to mine. The major theme of our discussions was divorce: Should I or shouldn't I? His advice was that unless I already had a man eager to meet me at LaGuardia and marry me when I returned from my mandatory six-week stint in Las Vegas, he was opposed. Did I have such a man?

"Absolutely not," I told him, huffily. "What kind of woman do you think I am?"

....

* Sandor Rado (1890–1972) was the founding director of what was then known as the Psychoanalytic Clinic for Training and Research.

† Rado's theories helped pathologize homosexuality and lead psychoanalysts to embrace the idea that therapy could provide a successful "treatment."

I was the kind of woman who would quasi-lie to the grandson of God. I certainly didn't have anyone waiting to marry me. What I did have was a series of increasingly indiscreet would-be infidelities. One was with a great guy who was the entertainment editor of *Life* magazine. We used to get bombed (Dubonnet cocktails for me; martinis for him) in a place called Robert on West Fifty-fifth. We even got into bed a couple of times, to no avail; he was gay. Then there was a photographer's agent with a tiny German accent whom horrible Arthur introduced me to.* He was so attractive I practically made him ask me out. But he too was gay. See a pattern? I sound like an ass, but I rather hoped I might convert someone, perhaps because I had not known in time that I needed to convert Jerry. Nor that conversion was impossible, and loathsome.

In my defense, remember that the straight men I had access to as a wretchedly unhappy married woman with three children were almost by definition unhappily married themselves. One of them, let's call him Elwin, was a second cousin on the Rodgers side, a colleague of Daddy's, and not a nice person. But at least he'd sleep with me. I would graduate to a better quality of infidelity as my marriage continued to crumble.

Jerry's infidelities were presumably more frequent and successful, but I was never dead sure until years after the fact. He did disappear at the oddest times. On Easter Sunday when Kimmy was four months old, she had a cold that turned into a cough that quickly turned into something worse. Jerry was at church, of course, leaving me alone with this terribly sick baby and the two other ankle-biters; when he got back, he announced he was heading out to meet someone.

"Where?" I asked. "Who?" I was always thrown back with Jerry to the basic reporter's questions.

He said he wanted to bring this terribly good friend of his, an epileptic, for a visit.

---

* Laurents borrowed the agent's last name—Schub—for a very unpleasant character in *Anyone Can Whistle*. In that, Schub got off easy; many people had not just their names but their secrets stolen.

"Now?" I asked. "I don't want anyone around here who is going to have a fit around my children, especially when one of them is so sick."

"That's not very Christian of you!" he replied—an evil thing to say, if you think about it.

And so he disappeared with the guy until late at night, while Kimmy got worse.

The next morning our wonderful pediatrician, Dr. Anderson, came over, took one look, and said, "We're taking her to the hospital right now—I think we can save her." He and I, with Kimmy in my arms, rushed into his car, which in those days was allowed to park in front of buildings, and sped to Lenox Hill Hospital. I thought, as they immediately wheeled her off to X-ray, *My God I just brought her back from here.* And also that I didn't want to be alone. Crises are telling in that regard: When I picked up the phone in the emergency room, a phone usually used for staff, it was my mother's number I dialed. She said she'd be there at once, but where was Jerry? Had I called him?

"Not yet, but I will."

"Why did you call me first?"

"Because he sometimes keeps me on the phone for twenty minutes," I answered, hedging. She understood.

I did call Jerry, who rushed to the hospital but flew into a rage when he found my mother had gotten there first. Out he stalked again.

Kimmy's pneumonia was quickly brought under control. While she slept in an oxygen tent, Mummy took me to lunch at a restaurant near the hospital. She asked if I'd like a Dubonnet cocktail to calm my nerves and was surprised when I said no. I told her I'd noticed myself drinking too much whenever I was around Jerry, or angry at him. She turned all sorts of colors, but said nothing at the time about Daddy's alcoholism, which she'd recently learned of from Elna the cook and Inez the waitress. When she did tell me, a while later—she actually said, "Darling, you must know, Daddy is a drunk"—it was because she feared I might have inherited the disease. I wondered, too, but found, as drunks like to say, that I could stop whenever I wanted.

Daddy was an extreme case, but you have to remember that drinking, like smoking, was a central element of social life, especially theatrical life, in those days. No one gave any of it a second thought; there was no such thing as a smoke-free environment, let alone a drink-free one. I think I was allowed to smoke in the hospital. A meal wasn't over, or for that matter well begun, without a couple of drinks. Even my mother had two dry Rob Roys after dinner, plus those Dubonnet cocktails at lunch; I shudder to think what she would have been like without them. But it worked the other way on some people, inflaming instead of calming their worst selves. Their true selves, perhaps. It was only with the help of liquor, I think, that Jerry could seek the companionship he wanted; it was an unfortunate side effect that the liquor made him behave badly with me. And indirectly with the kids. Later the same winter as Kimmy's pneumonia, when Tod decided to have it, too, Jerry showed up at the hospital saying he had to leave for two weeks.

"You're going to leave me alone with this sick child?" I asked.

He said he had to: It was time for his gig with the army reserve, though I had my doubts, and anyway you could get out of it for an emergency. I don't know how many drinks he needed to make that kind of choice. Would it have been better if it were none?

I finally went to my mother's lawyer, Ralph Colin, hardly a divorce expert, but he was the only lawyer besides Jerry I knew. He asked: "If we put a detective on him, do you think he could be caught?" I said I didn't know; only later did I learn that he could have been caught every night of the week. But a detective was going to cost about a hundred dollars a day, which to me was a fortune, and my parents were already paying for Rado and whatever schooling existed for the kids at their ages.

And there was something else: Jerry had warned me that if I ever tried to divorce him, he'd take the children. He said, "I'm a lawyer, I know how, and I will."

That paralyzed me. I had wedged myself so tight and deep into this impossible situation that release could only come with a blow from outside. Rado continued to suggest that I simply line up a proper new husband so I could get safely divorced.

"But how?" I asked. "I'm married. You want me to go to parties with a placard around my neck saying that despite appearances I'm available?"

"This is up to you."

My jaw must have dropped. After a minute of silence, he changed tack. "All right then. Why don't you get back to writing music?"

That was the first and only sensible suggestion Rado had ever offered, and I took it.

21.

AND THEN I WROTE

How do you write a song? For me it never came spontaneously, as it did for Daddy. Until he began to dry up—you can hear it starting, ironically enough, around the time of *Pipe Dream*—he was a natural spring with an overflowing tap; you just had to put a bucket under. I had to wander around with a divining rod, trying to guess where the moisture was. And then dig for it with the little spoon of my technique.

Like all of us hoping to get ahead in show business, I tried everywhere. At home, I continued writing innumerable practice songs, music and lyrics both, all of them excruciatingly sappy. Well, maybe not all of them. Sometimes when I finished one, it was such a joyous feeling I had to leap up immediately and play it for someone, but there was no one to play it for at home, so I'd run down Park Avenue to my parents' place and play for Inez the waitress.

But it wasn't like writing with Steve, who by 1954 had no more time for our version of *The Lady, or the Tiger?*; in 1953, he'd landed a job writing scripts for the television series *Topper*—scripts I often typed for him, poorly.* Meanwhile, I spent several months working on a proposed chil-

---

* *Topper*, which debuted on CBS in 1953, concerned a convivial couple who, after dying in an avalanche, come back to haunt a stolid banker.

dren's show called *Tickle, the Trolley Mouse* with Shari Lewis,* but it was an idiotic, horrible thing with lyrics like "I am Tickle the trolley mouse," *blecch*, and no network seemed to want it.

A real story to tell, with characters and complications, might have lifted me out of the rut, but without that kind of framework I was stuck writing a series of ditties, jingles, and kiddie numbers. Write what you know, I guess. I added lyrics to a stock instrumental called "Puffin Billy" that was being used as the *Captain Kangaroo* theme song. I wrote lyrics for several commercials, the most memorable of which, ten years later, was for Prince Spaghetti. ("Wednesday is Prince day, say what a treat! / Wednesday is Prince day, up and down the street.") And then I wrote—I hate that phrase—music and lyrics for something called "What Did You Do Before You Had TV?"; it featured these immortal words in the verse: "Have you learned to neigh like Trigger? / Can you bark like Rin Tin Tin? / If the TV set were bigger / would you probably fall right in?" Speaking of which, I also developed a subspecialty in dog numbers. I wrote "Lassie, My Four-Footed Friend" for the popular TV series and, under duress, turned out five songs in two days for Rin Tin Tin himself.†

TV this, TV that: It wasn't what I'd meant to do, but it had a lot to recommend it. For one thing, it kept me out of Daddy's territory. It paid well, and I'd begun to feel I had better have a source of income that didn't depend on him or Jerry. But also, television just kept knocking, one job leading to another; in its adolescent growth spurt, it had an almost insatiable appetite for disposable material and a quaint faith in New York talent. For a novice like me, that was in some ways a boon and in some ways a trap. I was learning how to write faster and better, but with no obvious way of making good on the improvements.

Escaping that professional trap would prove no easier than escaping my obviously failed marriage. Step one for the former if not the latter

....

* The wee puppeteer and ventriloquist, born Phyllis Hurwitz (1933–1998), would eventually hit it big as the voice of Lamb Chop, a sock.

† Proposed title no. 5 for these memoirs is the name of one of those songs: *Cold Nose, Warm Heart*. No?

involved roping in a collaborator. There was no shortage of people in those days who were interested in trying their luck on a pop song or show, maybe especially with Rodgers spawn; fewer had adequate skill and follow-through. Forget "And then I wrote." "And then I *didn't* write" was the story of my life.

Not for lack of trying. One night in 1954, Steve took me to a party given by Johnny and D.D. Ryan at El Morocco, saying, "You're going to meet someone whose voice is so incredible that you're going to want to scream with laughter the minute he opens his mouth." And I nearly did— it was Truman Capote.* By the end of the party we were planning to write a musical together: some kind of fairy story, which seemed safe and had the advantage of not requiring the purchase of rights. Of course, it never happened; Truman was a hoot but confessedly unreliable. "People accuse me of being a terrible gossip, but if they ask me not to tell anyone I never do," he said at the party. "If they are dumb enough to leave their personal correspondence on their desk, though, that's their problem."

There was a circuit of these parties; we'd all audition new material and tell each other how great we were. I'm sure I was the only woman, certainly the only woman composer, which was fun in a way, but also nerve-racking because it made me stand out. (So did my parental affilia-tion.) Steve had to force me to play my stuff. Compared with his—he was then working on *Saturday Night*, which was due on Broadway in the fall of 1955—mine was a little dreary. But compared with his, so was almost everybody's. One exception was Dean Fuller, who played some very good songs he was writing with a guy named Marshall Barer. Tall and

....

* At the time, Truman Capote (1924–1984) had published two novels: *Other Voices, Other Rooms* and *The Grass Harp*. He was also writing the book and lyrics for the adaptation of his short story "House of Flowers"; with music by Harold Arlen, it would soon make a beautiful flop. Much later, *The Grass Harp* would be turned into a musical as well, sans Capote, but starring Barbara Cook. It too was a flop. The delicacy of his sensibil-ity in those early works could not support a Broadway show. But even the sturdier *Breakfast at Tiffany's* made a disaster of a musical.

wellborn, a trained composer who could also write lyrics, Dean seemed like a professional in a room of wannabes. He and Marshall were already writing real shows for real audiences, if not in New York then at least at Tamiment, the Poconos resort and theatrical colony that was a kind of summer camp for emerging talent.

Marshall I had met by that point: He was the lyric editor at Little Golden Records, which meant he had either to write the words for the songs they recorded or procure them somewhere else. After *Some of My Best Friends Are Children*, the head of Golden, Arthur Shimkin, who was missing one finger, put us together. Marshall explained to me that Golden paid him six thousand dollars a year as an advance against earnings but that, at three hundred dollars per song, which is what they paid for lyrics, "earning out" would require him to write twenty songs, which was more doggerel than he could tolerate. It clearly behooved him to identify a needy substitute, and based on what he'd heard of my work, he figured I would do. I gladly accepted on one condition: I'd write all the lyrics he wanted as long as he'd let me write the music, too. Fine with him.

My first "olive out of the bottle"—that's how Daddy always referred to the first song in a new score—was an Easter ditty I wrote in 1955 for Roy Rogers and Dale Evans.* Marshall, holding his nose, gave me the assignment, telling me that the Rogerses, as opposed to the Rodgerses, were quite religious, so the song had to be reverential. Well, I knew they were conservative, nice-nelly types, so I wasn't about to write "Screw Easter, I'm an Atheist." Maybe I went too far in the other direction. "Easter Is a Loving Day" was treacly enough to make your teeth ache.† Still, Arthur Shimkin, Marshall, and presumably the King of the Cowboys and

....

* By the 1950s, Roy Rogers (1911–1998) and his wife, Dale Evans (1912–2001), were major radio, movie, and television stars, noted for their theme song, "Happy Trails to You," and their explicitly Christian wholesomeness.

† Get out your insulin: "Spring is full of many fine surprises / Spring has green and yellow trees to climb / That's when everybody realizes / It's Easter time, it's Easter time."

the Queen of the West were delighted. I was delighted, too, with my success and with my check for six hundred dollars: three for music, three for treacle.

Not delighted was Daddy. When he learned that I had sold my copyright in exchange for a mess of pottage, he nearly killed me. How often had he explained to me the value of royalties! (Often.) How could I have accepted a deal like that! (Easily.) Would I promise never to do such a stupid thing again?

Here I protested: There were writers lined up around the block to sell their souls for six hundred a song, copyright be damned. But Daddy had a misplaced sense of entitlement about me, combined with a cavalier attitude toward my actual gifts.* He thought I should be able to call the shots, whether or not I deserved to. Or perhaps he was just under the impression that I was he.

If so, he wasn't the only one, as I would soon discover.

After the success of my Easter number, whenever there was any garbagy song Golden needed, or one Marshall didn't want to dirty his hands with, he'd flip it over to me. I'd write it and play it for him on the spinet in his apartment, or on the grand in mine, and he would steer me. If it wasn't right in certain measures, he'd stand over my shoulders and practically beat me with a stick until I came up with something better. And he knew what he was talking about; he had an incredible ear, as you have to, to be a good lyricist.†

I dispatched several songs for Golden Records, just happy to receive the finished platter when each was done, even the one that credited me as Mary Rodger Beatly. Eventually I found out that, as the composer, I was allowed to attend the recording sessions. I remember my first with real chills and a joy that was otherwise lacking in those marital dissolu-

....

* So did Dorothy. "The public," she said, "will value you at the value you place on yourself."

† That he was one of the best was not necessarily obvious from his first hit lyric: "Here I Come to Save the Day," otherwise known as the theme from *Mighty Mouse*. He lived off it, while trying to live it down, for years.

tion years. Marshall had presented me with a challenging assignment: to make a musical out of Dickens's *A Christmas Carol*, featuring Howdy Doody as Bob Cratchit, that was wee enough to fit on a six-inch disc. It was a tight squeeze, but I did it. In the recording studio, as the opening church chime rang out the introduction, I burst into tears and cried for three minutes—the length of the piece.*

As he had done for *Some of My Best Friends Are Children*, Mitch Miller led the orchestra. Best known for his *Sing Along with Mitch* records, thousands of them, he was also a classically trained oboist, a very successful producer and arranger, the head of A&R for Columbia Records, and a world-class lecher. After one or two recording sessions together, he invited me, sometime in 1956, to have lunch. On the assumption that this would be good for my career, I made a date with him, only to be phoned at the last minute by his secretary, who said he was running late; could we meet at the same place but at three instead of twelve thirty? It's not a time I like eating, but I figured why not, so I showed up at the little Italian place on the East Side to find no one there but Mitch and an unctuous headwaiter. I was, as always about such things, oblivious; people have to practically take their clothes off before I know what it is they have in mind. On I nattered about songwriting until Mitch finally suggested, over dessert, which I didn't eat, that we go to bed. Right there? On the banquette? I politely explained that I was separated from my husband but not yet divorced and therefore had to be very cautious.† He nodded and possibly stroked his weird, long goatee, signifying his sophistication. Two years later, on the very day after I returned from securing my divorce in a sleazy town in Alabama, he called to ask if I was unencumbered yet. I don't know how he knew. Uncanny!

Predatory men, or just opportunistic ones, tend to think they're doing girls a favor by mashing on them. Maybe the ones who mashed on me knew about Jerry and believed I would be grateful for sexual attention. And I might have been, too, without the subterfuge. But to exploit

---

* Mary wishes to remind you that she cries only at happy things.

† This wasn't exactly true. The separation came later and the caution was intermittent.

1956: Richard and Dorothy Rodgers. "Why in the world would my father want to write my music? He doesn't even want to *listen* to it."

a woman's ambition just seemed squalid and mean. The next summer, when I really was separated but not yet divorced, I was giving a dinner party in a house I had rented in Westport. For some reason, Jule Styne* was there, I suppose with Ruth Dubonnet. Jule was doing the music for a documentary about kids learning to sail on a schooner, he said, and perhaps we could meet soon to discuss the possibility of my contributing lyrics to it. Well, now it sounds fishy, but back then I just thought, *Jule Styne thinks I'm good enough to write with him*. When I later came down to his apartment in the city, having gotten a babysitter to watch the kids for the day, there was no schooner, no job, no nothing. He just came at me. I turned around and walked out, humiliated.

....

* Jule Styne (1905–1994) was so busy chasing girls that he didn't marry until he was fifty-seven, and when he did it wasn't even Ruth Dubonnet. But he was a terrific composer, not just of shows like *Gypsy* and *Funny Girl* but of pop songs, too; in Mary's special talent-accounting system, which resembles a chiffonier except for the mirror on top, he got stacked above almost everyone in the crowded second drawer.

This kept happening, especially with musicians. Maybe they thought, as Cardinal Spellman had, that the daughter of Richard Rodgers was an especially valuable conquest. Or that in some Oedipal way bedding me might raise them to his level or bring him down to theirs. I do know they tended to confuse us. At some point during the Golden years, Marshall let on that Mitch Miller was telling people far and wide that Daddy wrote all my music. I could only laugh. "Why in the world would my father want to write my music? He doesn't even want to *listen* to it." The rumor—maddening in one way, flattering in another—was finally dispelled when, a few months later, I had to turn in manuscripts for some new songs for Golden on a fast deadline. The day I did, pictures of my parents at a London opening the previous night appeared in the New York papers. So unless he was writing them by spirit medium or transatlantic cable, I was now in the clear.*

There were a million insults like these, but when I was insulted I didn't pack up my marbles and go home. I worked harder to make my music sound less like Daddy and more like me. Every song I wrote, I'd ask people if it sounded like him, and if they said yes, I'd tear it up. I figured that my talent, separate from his name, would eventually speak for itself if I plugged hard enough. I'm not saying I was at his level; he may have begun drying up, but, as *Cinderella*† proved, he still had a lot of

....

* But not forever. Years later, a trashy roman à clef called *The Princess and the Goblin*, by the lyricist Paul Rosner, featured a cameo by a spoiled, neurotic, talentless composer named Shirley Fleischer, who was said to steal her melodies from her genius father. When one of her shows appears to be heading toward success, and someone says, "Shirley Fleischer's done it again!" the main character responds: "Done what again? Taken sleeping pills?"

† On March 31, 1957, CBS's live broadcast of Rodgers and Hammerstein's *Cinderella* was watched by more than 100 million people. The score includes a clutch of perfect musical theater songs, including "In My Own Little Corner," "Impossible," and "Do I Love You Because You're Beautiful?"—as well as some of Rodgers's loveliest waltzes, including "Ten Minutes Ago" and "Waltz for a Ball."

gorgeousness left in him. (And so much for television being my exclusive preserve.) I hadn't gotten anywhere near that and arguably never would. But I was competent and, when I think back on some of those songs, more harmonically adventurous than you might expect of a twenty-five-year-old with three kids and insufficient training. Plus, I was dogged—and not just with Rin Tin Tin. I did just about anything offered to me, and gradually what was offered got better. And bigger. In 1957, I finally got to write for a record that was more than three minutes long and six inches wide. This was the quasi-musical of *Ali Baba and the 40 Thieves* I wrote with Sammy Cahn* for Bing Crosby. Cahn would send me the lyrics from California, and I would set them: maybe eight songs in all. A few are quite good, despite or maybe because of Der Bingle's lazy swooping.† They hang together pretty well to tell a story: a story, of course, of escape. But perhaps the most significant thing about the recording is that, on the back of the sleeve, I'm just "Mary Rodgers." "Beaty" is gone, as he would soon be in real life, too.

---

* Sammy Cahn (1913–1993) was a successful Hollywood lyricist with two Oscar-winning songs to his credit by 1954, and two more to come, neither written with Mary.

† In the *Times*, Herbert Mitgang wrote that Cahn and Rodgers "have combined to make some outstanding songs, especially one called 'My Own Individual Star.' Singing these songs, Crosby is his amiable self, but as a narrator he occasionally sounds as if he has not removed his pipe stem from his mouth!"

22.

MY OWN INDIVIDUAL STAR

You might think that a marriage that never really took off would not have far to fall. But coming apart, or admitting and formalizing the coming apart that had already happened, was so much worse than I expected. By the time Nina was born, Jerry and I were effectively over as a couple; that winter I heard him tell Tod, who was three, "Don't bother to put on your galoshes, never mind what your mother told you. She doesn't love you or me; all she cares about is her writing." To me he said things like, "You told me clearly before we married that you didn't want to have a career," as if I were in violation of one of his copper mining contracts. We were both consumed with guilt about the sour secret we shared—in Jerry's case due to fear; in mine, denial. But he was the one who played dirty, setting my kids against me, and however sympathetic I am now to the fact that he was in agony, I didn't give a fat fuck about it then. I had to get out—but how?

Indiscretion on my part apparently wasn't enough. Jerry knew about my affair with "Elwin," the unpleasant Rodgers cousin, but despite its Freudian incest-by-proxy ickiness (Elwin even worked with Daddy) said nothing at the time. Maybe he figured I deserved an affair, given all of his, or maybe, knowing that Elwin was such a creep, he thought I deserved *that*. More likely, he was just relieved to be relieved of the burden of—how you say?—servicing me properly, and happy to keep the knowledge of the affair in reserve as ammunition. But he didn't know about the much better affair I was soon having with somebody else.

That one began, as most did, with work. The theatrical manager and producer Jean Dalrymple, who then ran City Center, invited me to her office in early 1957 to discuss a possible holiday project for kids. I was hoping for Christmas, but what she actually had in mind was the much duller Thanksgiving. Did I have any ideas? The first thing—the only thing—I could think of was *The Courtship of Miles Standish*, which, like everyone else, I'd read in school.* She liked the notion and sent me off to find a collaborator.

I think it was Hal who put me in touch with Leslie Stevens.† I called him up, we met to talk, and pretty soon I discovered that he was a fabulous bedmate. It wasn't just that he was very good-looking, in that shiny Aryan way: tall, blond, square-jawed, and very male. It was that he *wanted* to be with me. I knew what that felt like from Chilton six years earlier. Even though I could hardly remember why I felt so infatuated with him, it was impossible to forget the feeling of his infatuation with me.

Leslie suggested we get an apartment together, and not for writing. He even showed me a real estate ad about a place that could serve as our own little love nest. Maybe he'd seen too many of those Broadway comedies in which people get away with that. In any case, a film job came up and he had to move to California, thus ending both the Standish affair and ours. Ours for obvious logistical reasons. Standish's because a mail-and-phone collaboration is no way of developing a musical. You could write separately but you had to think together. I had watched that dynamic for years with Daddy and Ockie: They discussed everything first, sometimes for weeks, before Ockie would go off and put a scene or a lyric on paper. Then Daddy would sit with the lyric, perhaps for as long as a half hour, and pour out the music—not to minimize the work involved,

....

* Longfellow's 1858 narrative poem is a quasi-historical ballad set among the Pilgrims of the Plymouth colony. It's about . . . a love triangle.

† Leslie Clark Stevens IV (1924–1998) was a playwright and screenwriter. He ran away from home at fifteen to join Orson Welles's Mercury Theatre, helped to inaugurate the off-Broadway movement with his play *Bullfight* in 1954, and later created the TV show *The Outer Limits*.

as some anecdotes about his speed do.* The work went on all the time, in his head, sometimes for weeks; that's why it came out of his fingers so quickly. He absorbed everything he ever heard and saved it for when he needed it, like one of those plants that lives a thousand years but doesn't flower until it finally gets water.

However long it takes each partner, you have to be, literally, on the same page at the same time. But I was writing the score—music and lyrics—on my own and in the dark, without a book, which kept not coming from California. Of course, I was able to pick out places in the story where songs probably belonged, but that's not the same thing, and I tended to overpick ballad spots because I had a hard time writing funny lyrics. There may have been several lullabies: not a good sign. One of them had a great title, at least: "So Near and Yet So Far." I was excited about that one enough to tell Daddy. "Too bad Cole Porter got to it first," he said.†

It didn't matter, because Leslie's book was not only late but awful, totally inappropriate, and obviously dashed off. I submitted it and my songs to Jean anyway, but when I called to check in a few days later, she let me know that the deal was off. There goes that! My first full score, ten or more songs, vanished! And not highly trunkable songs either, being all Pilgrimy.‡

What made it worse was that I got the bad news in Jule Styne's apartment, on the day he tried to mash me. I had borrowed his phone to check in with Jean; the second I got off, he let me know he wanted to get off, too.

That was a fun train ride back to Connecticut. Once there, I'd find the

....

* Hammerstein said, "Hand him a lyric and get out of the way!"

† Porter's version was for the 1941 film *Never Get Rich.* Not only did he pre-steal the title but he had the audacity to set it to better music.

‡ "Mistress Mullen and Master Alden," "The Mayflower Will Sail," "Clap Your Hands, All Ye People," to name three songs unlikely to find other contexts.

kids hopped up from a day with the babysitter, and I would not be feeling my most motherly. To recap: I'm twenty-six. Tod is four, Nina three,
Kimmy one. I have almost no income of my own, and what I do have is
highly intermittent; my most notable success is a lyric I wrote for Captain
Kangaroo, a fat guy in a bowl haircut who named himself for a marsupial
and looked like a little child molester.* My career is going nowhere, even
though I've apparently sacrificed my marriage to it, and it isn't even clear
I can get a "good" divorce.

Jerry and I were by then in the midst of our extremely unpleasant
separation. This had begun in earnest when, during a fight earlier
in the year, he threw me across the bedroom. Really *slung* me. I had
a carpet burn in the middle of my back from the way I skidded after
landing: not the dainty pink blush of a child's elbow but an angry crimson
welt. That was the last straw. I couldn't reach Mummy's lawyer, Ralph
Colin, so I spoke to an underling of his that night, quietly after Jerry
went to bed. The lawyer said, "Get to a doctor first thing tomorrow and
have him substantiate the injury, otherwise you'll never be able to show
cause."

I did go to the doctor, who wrote up his observations and—am I re-
membering right?—took a picture. I assumed I would sue Jerry for physical cruelty, but Ralph, when I later reached him, advised against it. I was
to let Jerry divorce *me*, as he had threatened to do, for non-cohabitation,
which was a legal euphemism for my having had an affair and was highly
hypocritical under the circumstances. Never mind, Ralph said: I wasn't to
contest or argue the charge but to let the accusation stand. "Someday you
may come into a lot of money," he explained, "and if you divorce Jerry,
he has a better chance of getting it away from you. Whereas if *he* divorces
you, he's up a creek."

I understood but couldn't have cared less. For one thing, I wasn't sure

....

* The odd phrase "little child molester" comes from, and is a key clue to
the solution of, Sondheim and Anthony Perkins's screenplay for *The Last
of Sheila*. Please enjoy pronouncing "molester" as Mary did, with just two
syllables.

I'd ever "come into" a lot of money. Coming into a pittance from my parents was hard enough. But more than that, I didn't want anyone who learned of the divorce—which is to say, everyone—to think from my nolo contendere that I was the guilty party. I became non-cohabitational long after Jerry did, and without mauling him, either.

That point of pride turned out to be moot, though; Jerry perversely refused to act unless I did first. He wanted to stay married, even horribly married.

So we had to serve papers on him, which was tricky; the lawyers scripted it for me like a thriller. They said: When Jerry leaves for work in the morning, you will look out the window. There will be somebody on the street looking up at you. That's the process server, and because he doesn't know what Jerry looks like, you are to point at Jerry from the window as he exits the building and starts walking toward the subway. Once the server starts to follow him, you can leave the window. Then call a locksmith, whom you will have already engaged, to come change the locks, while you also pack a suitcase with Jerry's immediate needs. Leave the suitcase with the doorman.

And that's exactly what happened one late spring day in 1957, except that I almost fell out of our thirteenth-floor window, pointing so vigorously straight down at my husband, the man with the very stiff-legged gait and the hat. Does anyone still wear a hat? All men did, anyway, so it took a lot of semaphore to single him out.

The precautions seemed silly, but the lawyers feared that if Jerry were served too near the building, he might rush back in a rage. Their plan was to serve him thirty minutes away, at his office:* enough time and distance to fortify the apartment and alert the doormen. As it happened, the precautions were unnecessary, because as soon as the server, who'd followed him downtown, handed him the papers, Jerry would of course understand why he'd been served in that manner. Anyway, he didn't rush home; he never came home at all.

....

* Reeves, Todd, Ely & Beaty was located at 165 Broadway, near the corner of Liberty Street.

1948: Burt Shevelove with his self-portrait as a balloon.
"The best friend a divorcée could have."

Aside from the locksmith, I had pre-arranged for Burt Shevelove—
whom Jerry had introduced me to in the first place—to keep me company that day, and to be there when I talked to the children. Burt would
turn out to be the best friend a divorcée could have. Between my marriages, he'd take the girls to Bergdorf's and the boy to Brooks Brothers,
when he had money; when he was broke, which was just as often, he'd
say, "Hello, come see what's in my pockets," and they'd come running
because he'd stuffed them with Hershey bars and chewing gum.

But even with him there, I didn't know how to start the conversation; I kept waiting for the kids, or the two who could talk, to notice that
Jerry was missing and say, "Where's Daddy?" Perhaps it's telling that they
never did. So when they had their baths that evening, Burt and I sat there,
trying to maneuver the conversation around to the subject. Kimmy was
too young to understand any of it, but even Nina and Tod had very little
reaction. At least at first. Later I realized that Tod, who seemed like such
a wild child, was actually taking it very hard.

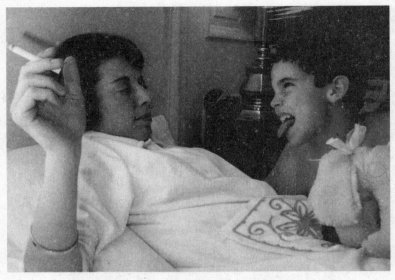

1960: Tod, not enjoying Mary's smoking—or her divorce from Jerry.
"He'd like to be married to you again," Tod said.

Trying to demonstrate that people who were divorcing could still be nice to each other, I asked him one day what he thought Daddy would like for a house gift now that he'd moved into his own apartment, just a couple of blocks away, on East Seventy-first.

"He'd like to be married to you again," Tod said.

"Oh, Toddy, I hope you don't remember this, but we used to argue so much. I'm sure he doesn't really want that."

And he said, "You don't know."

Divorcing a lawyer isn't easy. The legal maneuvering took another nine months. Alimony wasn't the problem because I didn't try to get any. Jerry knew perfectly well that my parents could take care of me; that I had so much trouble asking them to do so, and that they had so much trouble consenting, was my problem, not his. But I was furious about the child support. He refused to go above $375 a month, which barely covered food, let alone babysitting, doctors, clothing, and Betsy Wetsy dolls. He kept saying, "Search me, that's all the money I've got," even though his parents, too, were very rich, with an apartment on East End

Avenue and the big house on Dogwood Lane. "Remember, you're the one who wanted the divorce," he would add, infuriatingly, as if I'd had a choice.

Meanwhile, thrown back on Mummy and Daddy, I was a dependent and a suppliant once more.

They lived around the corner, so it wasn't far to beg—and, I have to admit, they restrained themselves admirably from the raised eyebrows and I-told-you-sos. They became positively sympathetic when I finally told them that Jerry was physically abusive—straight out of *Carousel* except without the redemption. And they paid all the legal bills silently; I never saw even one. As I say, they were good on the big things.

By then, they had other problems, anyway. Whether from the depressive effects of the alcohol or from the emotional fallout of his cancer or from the tranquilizers that his doctors prescribed to stabilize his mood, Daddy had become, by the summer of 1957, a zombie. Seldom talking, hardly moving, never writing, he was wholly emptied out. "We're going to have to put him in Payne Whitney," Mummy told me in early July. He stayed there for fourteen weeks: at first on suicide watch,[*] later placidly. In his largely fictional account of the period in *Musical Stages*, he made it sound like a vacation.

I could have used a vacation myself. Life was calmer, of course, once Jerry moved out; there were no more fights. The situation, as I told even the press, was not ideal, but workable.[†] I was relieved of the fear that he would, as he'd threatened, snatch the kids from me. I was even hopeful that he and I could be friendly someday, and eventually, very slowly, we were. But at the time I felt more overwhelmed than relieved: sore and unattractive, washed up yet barely started, not having a clue what would happen to me.

The kids don't like this part, even now: the part where I scramble

....

[*] Linda Rodgers has said she had to buy him pajamas without strings.

[†] In a *Newsday* feature on May 20, 1959, Mary "admitted that it isn't easy to be a career girl as well as both mother and father to three children" but added that she's "never been happier."

around like a booby looking for a place to nest. Sorry, kids, I was a separated and then a single woman; I slept around. More on that later. Rel-
evantly now, I had an affair with Sheldon Harnick,* even though he was
neither married nor gay nor rich; he was as broke as I was and living in
an apartment where the ceiling dripped on your face. This is relevant,
as I say, because *The Body Beautiful*, his first show with Jerry Bock, was
opening on Broadway the same evening I returned from that sleazy town
in Alabama where Ralph Colin, who was not used to such low-class legal
shenanigans, had escorted me to obtain my swifty-nifty one-day divorce.†
I promised Sheldon I'd be at the opening; I changed into evening dress on
the plane, rushed to the theater directly from the airport, and made it in
time for the second act.

It was fine.

Anything would have been fine, I suppose, now that I was out from
under my bad marriage. But before we say goodbye to Jerry, I want to
give him his due as a good father if not a good husband. It's easier for me
to do so now, having long since forgiven him, as I had to forgive myself.
What a wretched time to be a gay man! And what a wretched time to be
a naïve, overly protected, headstrong young woman. Years later, when
Hank and I were visiting Key West, a man came up to us in the lobby
of the hotel and introduced himself as Bob Butterworth. I'd met Bob
once with Jerry, wondering, stupidly, why such a great and funny and
good-looking guy wasn't married. Years later I realized that Bob and Jerry
had been lovers. Now he sat down with Hank and me for a good long
chat, recalling how Jerry, back in 1951, had asked Bob what he thought
of a thirty-five-year-old homosexual man marrying a nineteen-year-old
heterosexual girl. He'd told Jerry, he now said, that it was fine as long as

....

* Starting a few years later, Sheldon Harnick (born 1924) wrote, with
Jerry Bock, a string of superior musicals including *Fiorello!*, *She Loves Me*,
and *Fiddler on the Roof*. Later he'd collaborate with Mary on several occasions, and with Richard Rodgers on his late-period failure *Rex*.

† The divorce was granted in the central Alabama city of Marion, for-
merly Muckle Ridge, on January 23, 1958.

he told that girl the truth, and was horrified to learn, from me, that Jerry never did.

I now know that he couldn't, in part because I wouldn't let him. We both did better with time, finding more honest ways to live. And though he never untangled himself from the law—he stayed with his father's firm until it was dissolved in 1975, then went on to another, and then into solo practice in Bridgehampton until he retired in 2001—he seemed calmer and more accepting of himself.* More accepting of me, too. When I re-married, he came by every Wednesday to play poker with the kids or read to them from Poe or join us for dinner. Prince Spaghetti Day.

---

* Jerry Beaty eventually settled down with the landscape architect Paschall Campbell (1923–2003), though for many years he said they were just housemates.

23.

LENNY: A RHAPSODY

As bad as things were for me professionally during the dissolution years, I was in good company. Steve couldn't catch a break, either. *Topper* was canceled in 1954, and after the producer of *Saturday Night* died suddenly in 1955, so did the show. A year later, what was supposed to be his next first Broadway musical wasn't.*

But around the same time, Leonard Bernstein asked Steve to write, or rather co-write, the lyrics for what would become *West Side Story*. Lenny had planned to do the job himself; he was a decent lyric writer. But with another show in the works—*Candide*—and his classical activities also at a boil, he knew he wouldn't have time. His usual collaborators, Betty and Adolph, said no, and thank God, because they were so wrong for it. I don't know who else was asked. Finally, Arthur, who was writing the book, loosely based on *Romeo and Juliet*, suggested Steve for the job; he'd heard Steve's score for *Saturday Night* and admired the words if not the music. But Steve wasn't interested in writing just lyrics, let alone co-writing

....

* *The Last Resorts*, a 1952 book by Cleveland Amory about "American society at play," had already defeated Irving Berlin's attempts at musicalization; Sondheim and the playwright Jean Kerr—Mary's friend and the wife of the theater critic Walter Kerr—didn't fare any better. The project was shelved.

them. It took Ockie to convince him to swallow his pride and see the job as a learning experience.

For me, and I should know, it was all a bit incestuous. At one point it even looked like Rodgers and Hammerstein might produce *West Side Story*, but when that fell through, Hal, flush off the recent success of *The Pajama Game* and *Damn Yankees*, took it on. Jerry Robbins* was to direct and do the dances, once he finished re-creating his stage choreography for the movie of *The King and I*. With so many people I knew involved, I naturally became a *West Side Story* camp follower, a *fille du regiment*, albeit with three kids in tow. But it wasn't until early 1957, around the time of Operation Expel Jerry—Beaty, that is—that I understood just how good it would be. That's when Steve started coming over to play what he and Lenny were writing. Not that I liked everything; I had the bad taste not to appreciate arias like "Maria" and "One Hand, One Heart," which seemed awkward and arbitrary. I loved the rest, though, especially the restlessness of "Something's Coming," and the "Jet Song," and the nasty wit of "Gee, Officer Krupke." When I went to Washington that August to see the show in tryouts, I was overwhelmed: musically, theatrically, dancily. As for Steve's lyrics, they were so exceptional that it was hard to know what to say.†

After the Washington preview I attended, a bunch of us went out for drinks: Steve and Lenny and I guess Hal and Arthur, to whom I'd recently been introduced by Steve. Arthur was almost obsequiously nice to me—he liked women in trouble—and bracingly mean about everyone

....

* The choreographer Jerome Robbins (1918–1998), né Rabinowitz, was a groundbreaking figure in both ballet and musical theater. Sondheim considered him the greatest genius he'd ever known; not disputing that, many others considered him the greatest prick.

† Maybe the critics had the same problem; they ignored Sondheim completely.

else, which at that time in my life I appreciated.* Hal, who knew I was semi-single again, seemed to be making gestures toward a renewal of our relationship; for the moment I ignored them. Anyway, it was hard not to pay attention to Lenny, who made sure that was always the case by always being fascinating. At some point the talk turned to his new job as music director of the New York Philharmonic. Along with the directorship, he said, he'd inherited the Young People's Concerts, a tired institution† he hoped to spruce up, in part by televising them. "But what do I know about children?" he moaned.‡

Then he turned to me. "You write for children, you know about children, you want to work on this?"

"Sure," I said.

As soon as I got back to New York I sent him what I considered a foxy letter, inverting the usual format of such things, which would suggest my praising *West Side Story* for three paragraphs before squiggling a meek little query about the job at the end. Instead, I began by saying I was dying to work on the Young People's Concerts, and practically saved the praise for a postscript. This seemed more honest: I really did want the job. It wasn't writing music, but it was something, and even if money weren't a concern, I was the kind of woman who needed to be busy, beyond what three small children could dream up to exhaust me.

The letter must have worked because I got the job, and for fourteen years—for as long as Lenny continued to conduct them and even a little longer—I was officially Assistant to the Producer of the Young People's Concerts. Unofficially, I was Lenny's script editor and someone he just liked having around. He liked having a *lot* of people around; "gregarious"

---

* Later, it would become a nasty double bind.

† They had begun under that name in 1914.

‡ At that point, Bernstein and his wife Felicia had two, the same ages as Tod and Kim: Jamie (born 1952) and Alexander (born 1955). Nina—"their Nina"—came along in 1962.

doesn't begin to describe him. At the time, he and Felicia* and the kids and their Chilean nanny-housekeeper Julia, pronounced Hoolya, lived at the Osborne: an old, rococo building catty-corner to Carnegie Hall. Elsewhere in the building Lenny kept a small, dark studio where the production team, about six of us, crammed in for meetings. In Stygian gloom, we would await the Entrance, which Lenny, clutching a fistful of yellow legal pad pages, would make explosively, despairingly, energetically, or like a fainting Mimi, depending on what he'd been doing the previous day and night, and on how he had most recently been treated by the music critics who were sometimes (he bellowed) insulting, denigrating, obtuse, insensitive, ignorant assholes.

Once he got that off his chest, we all settled down to cutting and honing his inevitably overlong script. The musical elements were dealt with by my more musicologically informed colleagues, including Jack Gottlieb and, soon, little Johnny Corigliano, whose father, the highly respected but ill-tempered concertmaster of the Philharmonic, was mean as a snake to everyone, especially his son.† The rest of us worked on the timing and the tone, which on very rare occasions struck me as too sophisticated or academic for kids. The mot juste was my bailiwick and my glory; while writing an early episode I made a tiny suggestion that brought forth an orgasm of praise from Lenny in the form of a letter‡

....

* Bernstein's wife, Felicia Cohn Montealegre (1922–1978), was a Chilean actress and singer.

† Jack Gottlieb (1930–2011) had success later on with liturgical music, but at the time his ambition was totally overshadowed by his role as Lenny's aide de camp and amanuensis. He even wrote his dissertation on Lenny's compositional methods. John Corigliano (born 1938) survived his father's temper to become a famous and much-honored composer.

‡ "My dear little Miss Rodgers: I am happy to inform you that you have won the contest for the best word to replace 'classical'. Your magnificent choice of EXACT will ring down through the centuries, and no doubt enter Webster's 567th edition, if only as a footnote."

and a fifty-dollar check. I never cashed it; I wasn't *that* broke. CBS paid me five hundred dollars a show, four shows a year, for fourteen years, which I thought was just swell; I was too dumb about money ever to ask for a raise.

The first episode—called "What Does Music Mean?"—was broadcast live from Carnegie Hall on Saturday, January 18, 1958, five days before I got my Alabama divorce. The music rehearsal with the orchestra was on Friday; at three in the morning on Saturday, we and the CBS television crew staggered through the stage door for the technical setup, with cameras all over the front of the hall and fat black cables snaking up the fire stairs to the control booth in the men's room. Not that I ever went inside the men's room—no girls allowed. Which is more than I can say for the men's rooms at Philharmonic Hall, where the broadcast was moved in the fall of 1962. The brand-new building featured many men's rooms— many, many men's rooms—four on each tier, two of them labeled *Ladies*. A new mother at the time, I briefly visited every one of these, searching fruitlessly and more and more frantically for a place that did not feature a wall of urinals, but owing to a contractor's mistake, there was no such place to be found.*

Anyway, I was too busy down on the floor to keep looking for non-coed toilets. There was an invited dress later in the morning, followed by the live performance at noon. With no tape and no teleprompters, the burden was on Lenny to stick to the scripts we had prepared and set out for him in various locations, but he didn't really need them. By the time he'd written the thing, nitpicked it with us, and reread it a million times, he had every word, every note, every piece of blocking and camera position pretty well memorized.

The performances went remarkably smoothly, never running over-time, which was a good thing because a second more than an hour would

---

* Eventually they corrected the problem, but Dorothy Rodgers's remark about the subsidized housing complexes she visited, which inevitably lacked ramps for baby carriages, remained apt. "Typical," she said, "when you don't have any women on the design team."

1961: Mary with Leonard Bernstein, onstage at Carnegie Hall before a
Young People's Concert. "'Gregarious' doesn't begin to describe him."

have gotten us in trouble with CBS. Afterward, we would find Lenny in
the greenroom, exhausted, exhilarated, happy with himself, happy with
us, happy to see Felicia; Jamie; Hoolya; his sister, Shirley; his brother
Burtie and Burtie's wife, Karen; their daughter, Swee'Pea; and a million
other people. It was airless, it was claustrophobic, it was mayhem, and
Lenny, dripping with sweat and smoking, always smoking, positively
basked in it. He loved being loved, did our Lenny—who doesn't? But
Lenny more than most, and he sure gave it back, if not always carefully.
When Adam was three, I brought him to one of the early-morning technical rehearsals, at the end of which Lenny lifted him onto the podium,
put the baton in his hand, turned him to face the orchestra, and ordered
him to conduct. Down came the stick and out of the orchestra came such
a cacophonous, one-note, mega-decibel blast that the poor startled kid
nearly fell backward into the dark.

Lenny's hugeness of spirit, however much collateral damage it caused, made you forgive almost everything else. Well, it's easy for me to say that; I don't know what it was like for Felicia. It was she who hosted the Black Panther event that Tom Wolfe made infamous for its lefty posturing.* What I want to know is how come I wasn't there posturing right along with Steve and Adolph and John and D.D. and the dozens of other attendees I knew; it was right up my alley. I'd probably have raised a Black Power fist, or whatever they were doing, along with the rest.

Felicia was tiny, tinkly, blond, delicate, immaculate, charming, and cold, reminding me a little too much of—well, Ockie said it better: a kind of sweet and petite little tintype of my mother. She spoke with a pleasing remnant of a Chilean accent and unintentionally made every other woman in the room feel like a Clydesdale. How difficult it must have been for someone like that to be married to a gay man who wasn't at all discreet.† At least there was love between them, and their kids all ended up terrific.

They certainly ended up musically informed. Over the course of the program, Lenny continuously if unconsciously upgraded the intellectual content of the scripts to match his own children's increasing sophistication. At the end of fourteen years, I and possibly half the adult audience barely understood what he was talking about. But the kids who watched seemed to. They responded uncritically to his drama and silliness, his high-low grab bag. I'm convinced that of all Lenny's talents, teaching was by far his favorite and probably his best. His conducting garnered him huge attention but not always unanimous admiration. (He wriggled around like a puppy on the podium.) As for his composing, well, I'm no critic. I'd put him in the top drawer of that chiffonier of mine for his early theater music, from *On the Town* through *West Side Story*, and I love

....

* Felicia's 1970 Black Panther fundraiser became, in Tom Wolfe's snarky retelling of it in *New York* magazine, "Radical Chic: That Party at Lenny's."

† It was well known that he'd had affairs with Aaron Copland, Dimitri Mitropoulos, and Tommy Cothran, the lover he finally left Felicia for, two years before her death.

his early concert works, too, especially *The Age of Anxiety*, which Steve introduced me to. But most of his later, serious efforts sound like musical homework: music he forced himself to write for his reputation. When he had a deadline, he'd sadly excuse himself from whatever house party or anagrams game was transpiring, then slouch to his studio to scratch out some bars. He wasn't excited about it the way Daddy, and Steve, and even I were. It was maestro music.

The less fun it was for him, the more adulation he required and the more needy he became. Years later, in 1979, at Schuyler and Betty Chapin's,* he swept through the door beyond-the-pale late, in Serge Koussevitzky's cape, while Betty dutifully reheated the pasta. He proceeded to flirt mercilessly with Richard Wagner's young and pretty great-grandson, Wolf Siegfried, holding forth on every damn thing and getting glassy-eyed drunk. Afterward, Nin Ryan, a gossipy grande dame encumbered with wealth by both birth and marriage,† offered us all a ride home in her limo. The second we got in the car, Lenny asked if we'd seen *Sweeney Todd*, which was then in previews.‡ Before we could say "Yes, and we adored it," he launched into his appraisal: *Disgusting, enough to make you want to throw up in your galoshes! I guess Steve finally got to write a musical*

....

* During his days as a record executive, Schuyler Chapin (1923–2009) worked closely with Bernstein; later he had every arts job in New York, including vice president of Steinway & Sons, the piano firm Betty's grandfather had founded. Their son Ted joined the Rodgers and Hammerstein office in 1981 and ran it, in its various incarnations, from 1983 to 2021.

† Nin—Margaret Kahn Ryan (1901–1995)—was both the daughter of the financier Otto Kahn and the wife of the railway and diamond heir John Barry Ryan. Her son, Johnny, has already come into the story; her daughter, Ginny, soon will.

‡ *Sweeney Todd: The Demon Barber of Fleet Street* opened officially on March 1, 1979. Sondheim, who wrote the music and lyrics, had a little thriller in mind, but Prince, who directed, wanted a large-scale Grand Guignol. It was, amazingly, both.

that suits his temperament perfectly. Or words to that effect. Appalled at his obvious envy, let alone his treachery toward Steve in front of the old gossip, I must have been staring daggers, because when we stopped to drop him at the Dakota, where he was then living, he stuck out his lower lip and said, "You're mad at me, aren't you?" and looked as if he would cry.

"Yes," I seethed.

What he would have envied most in *Sweeney Todd* was the absolutely unlabored flow of its music. It was scary, brilliant, and gorgeous, yes, but also fun, the one thing Lenny couldn't do anymore.

But my God, when he could!

24.

FOR THERE IS MUCH
TO DARE

The universe may be expanding, but the world you actually live in only gets smaller and smaller. So guess who worked at CBS when Lenny hired me? Our friend Elwin. He was, among other things, executive producer of the Young People's Concerts. Now that I was divorced, I'm not sure what he thought would happen between us; he himself was married, to an extremely nice woman who knew a lot earlier than I did what a shit he was. But I soon caught on. At one point during the first year of the show, he threatened that if I didn't get Steve out of my life, he'd (a) stop seeing me and (b) get me fired. He was both jealous and envious, which I've only recently learned are different things: jealous of me, envious of Steve. But everyone was envious of Steve, even Lenny, as we've seen; his talent drove them mad. Anyway, (a) was fine with me, but (b) wasn't, so I hung on to Elwin for a while, ignoring his ultimatum.

Despite his title, and mine, Elwin was not the producer I officially reported to. Instead that was a wonderful funny sweet tall homely and adorable guy named Charlie Dubin. Anyone that wonderful funny sweet tall homely and adorable is dead meat in TV; sure enough, after the first three episodes of the Young People's Concerts, he was subpoenaed by the House Committee on Un-American Activities, where he refused twenty-two times to answer the "Have you ever been?" part of the famous question, and promptly lost his livelihood.*

His replacement for the rest of the season, and forever after, was the presumably never-been-Red Roger Englander. Roger earned extra money on the side as the producer of Thomas Scherman's Little Orchestra Concerts at the Hunter College auditorium, four of them a year, which were attempting to ape the Young People's Concerts but didn't come close. Tommy Scherman was what we call an ick: an effete jerk who talked way down to his captive juvenile audience, boring them and their captive parents and Roger Englander to death. Roger decided that a new scriptwriter might help, and although he scarcely knew me at that point, he invited me to give it a whack, at fifteen hundred bucks for all four scripts. I said yes, naturally, and pitched right in. Then he added that he needed a theme song for the series: Would I write that, too? He even had a title in mind: "It Takes Three to Make Music"—the three being, as he explained, "the man who writes it, the man who plays it, and the man who hears it."† Not a bad hook, so I wrote a lyric and, with no melodic idea coming to mind, wondered whom I could get to write the tune.

Here I must detour a bit, into a Divertimento on Linda.

As I've already told you, my twerpy kid sister stole my childhood. My musical childhood, anyway. When she was six, she was already so much better at the piano than I that it was humiliating. When she was eight or nine, in order to cut down on the opportunities for sibling competition, the Mannes School assigned us different teachers. Linda got Fritzi, while I continued with Urana the nail-clipper. It must have been Fritzi who contacted Juilliard when Linda was twelve to alert them to the existence of a radiant new prodigy; Juilliard promptly contacted my parents to inquire about her availability and was promptly turned down flat. The life of

....

* It took Charles S. Dubin (1919–2011) a few years to get good work again; among the first to hire him was Richard Rodgers, for whom he directed the television remake of *Cinderella* with Lesley Ann Warren in 1965. Later he directed forty-four episodes of *M*A*S*H*.

† Yes, all men, even though he was talking to a woman.

a concert pianist was not at all what they envisioned for their already
nervous and spotlight-averse daughter: It was too demanding and, in the
long run, a thoroughly unrewarding existence. Whether or not they were
right about that, the world will never know, but I do know it was an arrogant mistake that they never asked Linda. They never even told her—I
did, many years later. If you are a twelve-year-old with demonstrable talent, you're plenty old enough to understand the sacrifices you'd have to
make in order to succeed, and you're more than willing to make them.
Or not, which is also fine.

Steve gave the character of Philia in *A Funny Thing Happened on the
Way to the Forum* the great lyric "Lovely is the one thing I can do." At
twelve, piano was the one thing Linda could do, or at least wanted to do.
She was extremely bright but hated school. She was shy, had only one
good friend, didn't care about athletics, and although she was very cute
to look at, with enviably curly hair and a nice trim little body, she didn't
think she was attractive. But give her a hunk of Mozart, Bach, Debussy,
whatever, and she ran the world. By the time she was nineteen, though,
having tried and hated a year of boarding school and a year of Smith,
Linda's priorities had changed. Number one on her list, as it had been on
mine, was getting out from under our parents' thousand thumbs. In 1955,
a few weeks before her twentieth birthday, thus beating me by almost a
year, she married Danny Melnick,* then an aspiring television producer.†
I liked Danny, even though he wore all black, thinking it was stylish.

....

* Linda's wedding was a near carbon copy of her sister's, in the same
apartment with the same ivory satin gown and the same rabbi from
Temple Emanu-El. No reverend, though: Melnick was Jewish. The gown
turned up again in 1983, when Nina wore it at her own wedding in the
same apartment. Still later, Mary offered it to Alec's fiancée, Christy, but
quickly rescinded the offer: "Actually, all the marriages from that gown
were a disaster. You can't have it."

† Daniel Melnick (1932–2009) was soon hugely successful, producing television shows for CBS and then ABC like *Get Smart* and *The Untouchables*;
he even green-lit *The Flintstones*. In the seventies he moved to movies:

Anyway, back to our story, the minute they married, Linda pretty much stopped playing the piano seriously, and instead began writing music, because that's what I had done.

Jump ahead to 1957, when Marshall was putting together an LP for Golden about jazz in America. He and I wrote the text, which surveyed the history of the form from African drumming to bop; not quite logically, it was to be narrated by our favorite marsupial. Maybe I was just feeling sorry for Linda, or maybe we all thought that my musical style didn't scream "jazz," but when it was decided that we needed a theme for the album, Linda somehow got asked to provide it. Marshall and I wrote the words. I don't remember the resulting song at all, but *A Child's Introduction to Jazz*, as the album was called, was enough of a success that Linda felt somehow confirmed as a composer—a composer of children's songs, no less. Terrific: Now there were two Rodgers daughters competing for space in the kiddy ditty rat race.

Never again, I told myself.

Cut to that fall: "You know, dear, poor Linda so wants to make a success of her composing," said Mummy, doing that look-ahead-but-whisper-to-the-side trick during a High Holiday service at Temple Emanu-El that she must have dragged me to. "And she can't get a good lyricist!"

"Good lyricists are hard to find," I answered blandly.

"Well, why don't *you* write them, darling? You're good at lyrics!"

It was the closest I ever came to slugging my mother. "Listen," I hissed at her, "I've spent all this time trying to get a foothold in this industry by writing lyrics, which I hate doing, just so I could have the chance to write music, and now you want me to write lyrics for *her*?"

"Why, yes!"

"Not on your life."

So when Roger Englander asked me to write "It Takes Three to Make

....

Straw Dogs, All That Jazz, eventually *Kramer vs. Kramer.* By then he and Linda and their art collection had divorced; he got the Braques and Chagalls and all that.

Music" soon thereafter, I naturally asked Linda to provide the music for my words. What can I say? I didn't dislike Linda—that came later. Mostly, I wanted to please my mother, who was, as far as affection goes, a leaky bucket, never filled.

Linda wrote the song, which showed promise. Then I went one step further. It occurred to me that this concept could be turned into a tidy little twenty-minute musical sketch for kids, with a section devoted to each of the three elements: the composer, the orchestra, and the audience. So I wrote that, too, including the script and the lyrics for six songs, two in each category. Linda set five of them, but when she couldn't figure out the sixth, I set it myself. To be honest, she needed more practice. There was nothing original about her writing. It was too reminiscent, too secondhand, too—what's the right word?—Rodgersy.

But Tommy the Ick loved it, and scheduled the mini-musical, the overall title truncated to *Three to Make Music*, for a concert at Hunter that Christmas. Roger apparently loved it, too, because he demanded 10 percent of whatever we subsequently made from it, arguing that it was his idea. Well, 10 percent of nothing was fine with me, but that's not how it turned out. I don't know how I had the nerve, but once the piece was accepted for performance I marched over to Mary Martin and Dick Halliday's apartment with the manuscript in hand to see if Mary might be willing to perform it at the premiere.

Mary Martin was then one of Broadway's two biggest stars, the other being Ethel Merman. Having helped make *South Pacific* such a monster hit, and soon to do the same with *The Sound of Music*, she had long been close to Daddy—though not in *that* way, as far as I know. In fact, there were rumors she was a lesbian; Dick, her second husband, was one of the gayest people I ever met in my life, which is saying something. In any case, she was a riveting performer, charming and ageless; not many people could pull off playing the postulant Maria, who is supposed to be twenty-two, at forty-five. Offstage, she was always fun and good-humored and worked terribly hard, but was a little bit saccharine, as if covering something; you never really knew what she was thinking. That was apparently part of the marital deal. There was a saying about the

1958: Mary (background, standing) and Linda (at the piano), at work on
Three to Make Music with Mary Martin. Martin was "always fun and
good-humored" but "a little bit saccharine."

Hallidays: Mary makes the bullets, Dick fires them. I could believe it.
Dick was a nasty piece of work, and an alcoholic, with all the concomitant
ailments, including long bony fingers that shook.

At the time, Dick told me, they were planning an ambitious eighty-
seven-city concert tour, from September 1958 through March 1959. At
each stop Mary would perform a kiddie matinee called *Magic with Mary
Martin* and an adult evening show called *Music with Mary Martin*. At the
end of the tour, on Easter Sunday, both would be broadcast live on NBC
and recorded by RCA Victor. Remember, this was in the days when a
Broadway star of that caliber was automatically a pop star and could
make the economics of so much exposure work.

And possibly make my economics work, too. I played them *Three to
Make Music* and, despite my awful croaky voice, they said yes to the Little
Orchestra concert.

Not only that, but they—that is, Dick, waving his bony fingers in the
air—had what he called a marvelous idea. *Magic with Mary Martin* was
supposed to include three segments, two of which were already in place:
a chunk of Mary's huge TV hit *Peter Pan*, and a chunk of Daddy and

Ockie's huge TV hit *Cinderella*. But they had no plan for the third chunk, and *Three to Make Music* might just be the thing. Could I get it ready in time? Their one and only tryout would be in Rochester in late spring; it was now, I pointed out, early spring.

I could and did. Also, at their request, I went to Rochester to see the result. Daddy, ever the watchful keeper of his own flame, went, too, to see what they were doing with *Cinderella*. Which was, in brief, a bad job. The songs were fine, but the staging and the book adaptation were inept, confusing, and no damn good. I muttered to Daddy that I thought I knew how to fix it. He grunted.

That evening, home in New York, I got a phone call from Mr. Bony Fingers. My father had told him I knew how to fix *Cinderella*. Would I like to try? Sure. It wasn't very hard, really, because the problem was just that she was doing it solo. She needed someone to bounce off of. I rewrote the script, if you could call it a script, and everyone called it a big success, which apparently meant they didn't have to pay me. Not even train fare to and from Rochester. Never mind. I made a good impression and had a good time.

Sometimes, despite my father's creed, underselling yourself is a good tactic. In any case, Dick Halliday soon came back to me to rewrite the grown-up concert, too. There wasn't much to rewrite in that one, just interstitial material, but I did compose a horrid piece of music, to someone else's horrid lyric, for Mary to sing as her Christian creed.*

This time, at least, the job came with money: the thrilling fee of six thousand dollars. It wasn't just the sum that excited me; the sum was a key that turned a particular lock. A year earlier, in 1957, I'd auditioned for Steve's agent, Flora Roberts, one of the biggest, and I do mean biggest, in the business.† She was short and round, as if she'd been squashed; she

....

* The hymnlike song included the lyric "I would be brave / For there is much to dare!"

† Flora Roberts (1921–1998) was eclectic in her business and her tastes. Over the years, aside from Sondheim, she represented the composer

wore big red hats, hung around racetracks, and talked like a truck driver. She could have starred in *Guys and Dolls*, and not as Adelaide.

After I auditioned, she said she loved what she heard but couldn't sell children's songs: "Come back when you write other things." Which I promptly did. Odd how ecstatic all writers are when they land someone who will take 10 percent of their earnings. Daddy, naturally, was appalled. "What are you doing with that fat agent!" he howled. "You just need a lawyer."

"*You* just need a lawyer," I said. "*I* need someone to find me good work."

As usual, he was right, at least about Flora, whom I soon came to dislike for her laziness on my behalf. Many years later, we were sharing a room with two twin beds at Arthur's house in Quogue when I woke up to find her asleep on the floor in a pair of polyester panties, gleaming in the moonlight like a beached whale. Later Steve explained that she'd thrown her back out. "Why didn't she throw out the rest?" I asked.

Over the next year I really earned that six thousand, flying all over the country to keep tabs on the show as it toured. (This cured me of my fear of flying.) But on the late March day of the dress rehearsal for the broadcast, Halliday fired me. Maybe he understood that the show was tanking, and he needed a scapegoat.* He shouted that I was not giving Mary, *his* Mary, my full attention: All I cared about was my growing pile of other projects.

He rehired me a day later, but how right he was.

. . . .

Maury Yeston, the playwright Tina Howe, the director Susan Stroman, and the lighting designer Jennifer Tipton. She trained to be an opera singer but also owned a racehorse.

* Everyone, including the star, had the flu, and the reviews were poor. The *Herald Tribune* said that the music "wasn't of the melodic variety." The *Times* said that the telecast "dragged rather noticeably." It may well be that Mary, who hated the show, was the one who told the critic it dragged. But by then it had dragged itself all over the country and all the way to the bank, thus qualifying it as an unqualified success.

25.

I HAD CONFIDENCE

'd been writing for Marshall Barer at Little Golden for three years or more, with dozens of ditties to my name, when he said to me, in April of 1958, "Come to Tamiment this summer and write for grown-ups. And *be* a grown-up."

This was not entirely disinterested advice. Dean Fuller, his collaborator in several of his eight previous seasons there, was unavailable because he had a newish baby at home. Marshall, desperate for a replacement composer, and probably having run through a few better options, must have been in a panic by the time he asked me, because the season started in June. He pitched it to me as excellent training: I'd work fast, have my music played every week by a sixteen-piece orchestra, and get instant, incontrovertible feedback. "The audience doesn't pay extra for the shows," he explained. "So if they don't like it they walk right out." What a comforting notion.

Tamiment was a hundred miles' drive from New York City, on the fringe of the Pocono Mountains, near Stroudsburg, Pennsylvania. Originally a socialist summer camp, and later a retreat for the ladies' garment workers union, it was by the time I heard of it an inexpensive resort for office types: secretaries who hoped, in the one short week they could afford to be there, to identify and pin down a marital partner; men who were simply hoping to get laid. Most of the guests probably went home without having achieved either goal, but in the meantime, from Sunday afternoon to Sunday morning, they had free access to a Robert Trent

1958: Jay Thompson, Mary, Marshall Barer, and Moe Hack outside the
Tamiment Playhouse. "Where else were wannabes supposed to
become bigwigs before turning into has-beens?"

Jones golf course, tennis courts, a lake for swimming and boating, and,
on Saturday night, a new musical comedy or revue, very professionally
produced and performed at the Tamiment Playhouse.

The show would then be repeated on Sunday evening for the new
arrivals, who always received it more enthusiastically than the departing
audience because they had not yet worn all their best clothes and were
still full of marital-sexual excitement.

For the staff, it was more of a nursery: a talent incubator in which
they hoped to hatch themselves. Where else were wannabes supposed to
become bigwigs before turning into has-beens? The names of the stars
that had perfected their polish at Tamiment, or at a similar joint called
Green Mansions in the Adirondacks, were shared back in New York like
talismans.* But the reality on the ground was a bit grubbier. Like most

* Tamiment: Neil Simon, Jerry Bock, Jonathan Tunick, Herbert Ross,
Jerome Robbins, Barbara Cook, Danny Kaye, Sid Caesar, Imogene
Coca. Green Mansions: Clifford Odets, Harold Clurman, Lee Strasberg,

incubators, Tamiment was a hothouse. The artists, though the word is too grand, got a twelve-week crash course in whatever it was they did: write, compose, act, sing, dance, direct, orchestrate, design, play in the pit. The writers, especially, worked like demons. For the first six weeks they put together a brand-new revue every week; the second six consisted of plucking from the first all the bits that worked and recombining them into new and supposedly better ones. Or if some of the writers happened to be interested in cranking out a book show, and if Moe Hack, the barky, crusty, cigar-smoking sweetheart who ran the place, thought it was a good idea, they would be free to go ahead and try it.*

It seemed like heaven, if you were single, or a married guy who thought nothing of leaving his wife back home to tend the brood. But I had no wife, and no husband, either, just three little kids in the care of a Peruvian nanny named Vicky, who was barely bigger than they were. What was I supposed to do with them?

"Bring 'em," said Marshall.

"But where would we live?" Obviously, I couldn't billet my tribe in the barracks where the writers were housed communally.

"I'll find a place for you," said Marshall.

"And I don't even have a car," I protested.

"Get one!" ordered Marshall.

I was scared out of my wits but said I'd think about it. Then I made a date with Daddy to see what I thought.

Daddy often ate lunch at the manly Barberry Room, a posh nosh near his office in the MCA Building that featured candy-striped curtains, vegetation scattered on the tablecloths, and a mural of a satyr entertaining four bosomy nymphs. Usually when I joined him, his opening shot was

....

Sheldon Harnick, Stella Adler, Charles Strouse, Elia Kazan. There was a lot of overlap as well.

* Monroe B. Hack (1898–1993) was a onetime Broadway director and lighting designer who took over as the producer of the Tamiment Playhouse in the late 1940s and ran it until it shut down in 1960. In 1976, the building was razed.

"Why are you so mean to your mother?"—a query pre-programmed into him by Herself—but this time I got started right away with Tamiment and ran his ear off before letting him have a word. When I finally finished, he said, as he had so often, "Are you asking me or telling me?"

I was telling him, I decided. But not everything. I omitted the salary, which was six hundred dollars for the whole summer; he'd have screamed, and rightly so. A bird couldn't live on that.

But I would manage it. Marshall found me a nice four-bedroom cottage for very little money, right down the hill from Tamiment's main buildings and near a rushing river. (The whole place was a floodplain; by the following year the house was gone.) He even saw to it that an upright piano was waiting in the living room. And Steve, now flush from *West Side Story*, sold me his old car for a dollar. I had no excuses left, so once Moe Hack officially hired me, off we went like the Joads in early June: twenty-seven-year-old me; the kids, ages five, four, and two; and the Peruvian nanny—all of us scratching westward thanks to Steve's itchy fake-fur upholstery.

My von Trapp–like cheerfulness in the face of uncertainty soon crashed, though. The whole first half of the season was, for me, demoralizing. Everybody was more experienced than I. Everybody was, I felt sure, more talented. Everybody was certainly more at ease. At the Wednesday afternoon meetings to plan material for the coming week, when Moe would fire questions at us—"Who's got an opening number?"—the guys would leap up to be recognized like know-it-alls in math class. If they were all little red hens, I was the chicken, silently clucking *Not I*. "Who's got a comedy song?" More leaping; more ideas. "Who's got a sketch?" Woody Allen always did.

At twenty-two, Woody looked about twelve but was already the inventive weirdo he would become famous as a decade later. His wife, Harlene, who made extra money typing scripts for the office, was even nerdier, but only inadvertently funny. She looked, and sounded, a bit like Olive Oyl, with reddish hair, freckles, and a bad case of adenoids. Woody, whenever he wasn't working on his sketches—his best that summer was about a man-eating cake—was either sitting on a wooden chair on the porch outside the barracks, practicing his clarinet, or inside with her, practicing sex, possibly from a manual. He was doing better, it seemed, with the clarinet.*

At least my kids were having fun. Every morning I drove Kimmy and the nanny to Moe's wife's cabin, to spend the day lolling, and Tod and Nina up the hill to the Sandyville day camp, which they loved except when Tod had mumps. Then it was back down the hill to our cozy sylvan bower, where I would spend eight hours plinking out tunes to accompany Marshall's lyrics. These were revue songs, with titles like "Waiting to Waltz with You," "Miss Nobody," and "Hire a Guy You Can Blame," fitted to the talents of particular performers with no aim of serving a larger story.† "Miss Nobody," for instance, with its super-high tessitura, was written for a thin little girl named Elizabeth Lands, who couldn't walk across the stage without falling on her face but was a knockout and had an incredible four-octave range like Yma Sumac.‡

Music did not pour out of my fingers; the process was more like wringing a slightly damp washcloth. With Marshall's lyric propped up on the piano desk, precisely divided into bar lines as a road map, I would begin with some sort of accompaniment or vamp or series of consecutive chords, then sing a melody that matched the lyric and went with the accompaniment, then adjust the accompaniment to service the melody, which began to dictate the harmony, until I had a decent front strain that satisfied me and, more important, satisfied Marshall, who wouldn't stop hanging over my shoulder until he liked what he'd heard. Then he'd leave

....

* The Allens divorced in 1962, soon after Woody, in his stand-up act, started calling Harlene "Quasimodo."

† Unknown to Mary at the time, many of Barer's lyrics were retreads of ones he had already tried out on other composers, including Fuller; whoever wrote the most popular tune got to keep it. It was, she said, like finding out your husband is a bigamist.

‡ Born Zoila Augusta Emperatriz Chávarri del Castillo, Yma Sumac (1922–2008) was a Peruvian coloratura soprano renowned for her crazy voice and reversible stage name.

me to clean it up and inch it forward while he took a long walk on the golf course to puzzle out the lyrics for the bridge.* Back to me, back to the golf course, back and forth we went, until the song was finished.

Even when I did that successfully, I had another problem. My abandoned Wellesley education had taught me the rudiments of formal manuscript making, but what the Tamiment orchestrators needed, and fast, because the first orchestra readings for Saturday's shows were on Friday, was a plain old lead sheet.† I had no idea how to make one. Daddy had ear-trained me, not eye-trained me. As a result, I kept naming my notes wrong, calling for fourths when I meant fifths, and vice versa. This made the orchestrations sound upside down. I could just imagine the guys saying, "Get a load of Dick Rodgers's daughter, who can't even make a lead sheet."

Actually, the orchestra men, kept like circus animals in a tent apart from the rest of us, were the merriest people at Tamiment. They weren't competitive the way the writers were. They just sat there with a great big tub filled with ice and beer; you tossed your twenty-five cents in and had a good time. And I had the best time with them. Especially the trumpeter.

Elsewhere at Tamiment, I felt patronized. It didn't help that Marshall tried to dispel my parental paranoia by preemptively introducing me to one and all as "Mary Rodgers—you know, Dorothy's daughter?" Between that and the chord symbols, it was enough to drive me to drink.

Or pills, anyway.

"What's that you're taking?" Marshall asked, when he saw me swallowing one.

"Valium," I told him.

"*Valium!*" he screamed. "Why *Valium?*"

....

* Barer later said that 85 percent of the words in *The Princess and the Pea* were written on that green.

† A typical lead sheet consists of the melody, the lyric, and the harmony written as chord symbols. Mary only knew how to write full piano accompaniments, which slowed down the process.

"I asked the doctor for something to help me write."

"And he gave you *Valium?*" said Marshall. "Here. Try this."

He handed me a pretty little green-and-white-speckled spansule. Bingo! I wrote two songs in one day, and, whether because of the Dexamyl* or the songs, felt happier than I'd ever been. It completely freed me up. Whatever inhibitions I had about playing in front of Marshall or feeling creative and being able to express it were suddenly gone.

The story of me and pills—and, much more dramatically, Marshall and pills—can wait for later; what matters now is that the two songs I was so elated to have written so quickly and easily, one of them a comedy number called "Shy," weren't any better received than anything else I wrote in the first half of the season. And if you think I was depressed by that, you should have seen Marshall. I would find him in a major funk in his bunk, head in hands, eyes closed, forlornly listening to the tape player blast out *The Emperor's New Clothes*, a musical he and Dean had done the previous season to great acclaim, as he kept reminding me. I didn't need reminding; it was abundantly clear what a disappointment I was. I was no emperor, barely a princess, but I was the one with no clothes.

From great funks sometimes come great ideas. Marshall had for a couple of years been nursing the notion of turning the Hans Christian Andersen fairy tale "The Princess and the Pea" into a musical burlesque for his friend Nancy Walker. Nancy, a terrific comedian, liked the idea but was too big a star by then to be summer-slumming at Tamiment.† Nor was good old reliable Dean around, but since Marshall was stuck

....

* The "tired housewife" pill, introduced in 1950, was a cocktail of an amphetamine, to raise mood, and a barbiturate, to keep the amphetamine in check.

† Nancy Walker (1922–1992) had been a Broadway name at least since singing "I Can Cook Too" in *On the Town* fourteen years earlier. Later, she played Ida Morgenstern, the world's second most self-dramatizing mother, on *The Mary Tyler Moore Show* and *Rhoda*, and achieved even greater fame as Rosie, the waitress in commercials for Bounty paper towels who sang the praises of the "quicker picker-upper."

with me anyway, he figured it was worth a try. Did I like the idea? he asked.

As it happens, I did, very much, but it wouldn't have mattered if I hated it. I did what I was told. At Tamiment, even Marshall did what he was told. Moe said we could write this "pea musical" on the condition that it would accommodate his nine principal players with big roles. *Nine big roles?* Moe had hired these players at a premium, he said, and he wanted his money's worth. Furthermore, the principal players would be very unhappy otherwise, and none of us wanted that, did we?

The deal struck, Moe scheduled the show for August 16 and 17. It was now late July.

With only three weeks, Marshall couldn't possibly manage the book by himself while also writing the lyrics. To speed the story along he enlisted Jay Thompson,* who had until then been providing the revues with material that didn't succeed any better than ours. Also, to save time, we custom-cast the show on the cart-before-the-horse Moe Hack plan, before a word, or at least a note, was written. There was, for instance, a wonderful girl, Yvonne Othon, who was perfect for the lead, Princess Winifred: appealingly funny-looking, very funny-acting, and the right age—twenty. But there was a significant drawback: She wasn't one of Moe's principal players. Meanwhile, Moe wanted to know what we were going to do for Evelyn Russell, who at thirty-one was deemed too ancient to be the Princess but *was* a principal player. Okay, okay, we'd cast Evelyn as the Queen: an unpleasant, overbearing lady we just made up, who is overly fond of her son the Prince and never stops talking. We would give her many, many, *many* lines and maybe even her own song. And to seal the deal, even though the Princess was (along with the Pea) the title character, we would cut her one big number; we'd been planning to have her sing "Shy," the song that hadn't worked earlier in the summer. That was

---

* Jay Thompson (1927–2014) was a musicologist, composer, and lyricist, and a gentle, gay, overweight, sweet, self-effacing gent from Myrtle Beach.

just as well because it was a tough, belty tune and Yvonne couldn't sing a note. She was a dancer.*

Lenny Maxwell, a comedian and a schlub, would be Prince Dauntless, the sad sack who wants to get married but his mother won't let him; since he had limited singing chops, we'd only write him the kind of dopey songs any doofus could sing.† We created the part of the Wizard for a guy who, I had reason to know offstage, was spooky; he was practically doing wizard things to me in bed. Meanwhile, Milt Kamen, by virtue of his age (thirty-seven) and credits (he'd worked with Sid Caesar), was considered by Moe, and by Milt, to be the most important of the principal players, but he too had a couple of drawbacks: He couldn't sing on key and couldn't memorize lines. He claimed, though, to be an excellent mime, so Marshall and Jay invented the mute King to function as counterpoint to the incessantly chatty Queen. Marshall brilliantly figured out a way to make his lyrics rhyme even though they were silent: They rhymed by implication.

In this way, one role at a time, we wrote the show backward from our laundry list of constraints: a dance specialty for the good male dancer who played the Jester, a real ballad for the best singer, even a pantomime role for Marshall's lover, Ian, who moved beautifully but, well, fill in the blank. Soon all personnel problems were solved except what to do with Elizabeth Lands. You remember, the gorgeous but klutzy Yma Sumac type? When Joe Layton, the choreographer, and Jack Sydow, the director, started teaching all the ladies of the court—who were meant to be pregnant, according to Marshall's story—how to walk with their hands clasped under their boobs, tummies out, leaning almost diagonally backward, Liz kept tipping over. Pigeon-toed? Knock-kneed? We never discov-

---

* After her Tamiment season, Yvonne Othon played the role of Anybodys in the London production of *West Side Story* and then Consuelo in the movie.

† His big love song wasn't even a ballad; it could be sung perfectly well by a tin-eared ten-year-old, and often has been.

ered what exactly, but she was a moving violation. Thus was born the Nightingale of Samarkand, who was lowered in a cage during the bed scene while shrilling an insane modal tune to keep the Princess awake.

Do not seek to know how the musical theater sausage is made.

With the casting complete, now came the songwriting, which, oddly enough—maybe because it was a real musical with a plot and identifiable characters instead of a series of unmoored tunes sung by anybody—I was looking forward to. Medieval music? I had a fairly confident notion of what a Mary version of that should sound like, and I already knew from listening to Daddy on the subject of *The King and I* that it wasn't necessary or even advisable to reproduce the exact sounds of the locale and the period. So no square notes or Gregorian chants. Just the flavor would be fine, with whole-tone scales sprinkled liberally throughout.* The joke would come, as it did in the script, from juxtaposing the antique with the contemporary, or as contemporary as I got in 1958. One song, called "Quiet," was a spoken-word fugue, so perhaps I was anticipating rap.

Of the dozen songs we wrote for the show at Tamiment, only one gave me terrible trouble, a dance number for the Jester called "Very Soft Shoes." The problem was the rhythm; if you're writing a song called "Very Soft Shoes," it had better be a soft-shoe. For days, I wrote and rewrote it, with Marshall shouting "Like this! Like this!" while tippy-tapping madly around the tiny closet off the main theater lobby where both of us were sweating bullets and smoking nonstop. Finally, after eleven tries, he okayed the result. Not only did I get quite a good song out of it, but I also got over what was left, post-Dexamyl, of my fear of being eavesdropped on while writing: a very good fear to get over if you're a composer.

Marshall had so much to teach me. Most of it he had taught him-

----

* If you want to dig up the Broadway cast album, you can best hear Mary's fifteenth-century stylings in the prologue ("Many Moons Ago") and in "Opening for a Princess"—which was built on a typically clever Marshall pun, as, for that matter, was "Shy."

self. Born in Brooklyn, the son of a man who owned a window-washing business in West Palm Beach, he got himself educated—he had a mind like lightning—and began his career as a graphic designer at *Esquire*. The lyric writing eventually took over, but he remained highly sophisticated visually, drawing magnificent sketches for costumes, sets, and musical numbers that gave the people he was working with, be they designers themselves or directors or collaborators, inspiration and a deeper sense of what he had in mind. Like any good songwriter, he didn't write anything without knowing how it could be staged, how it should look. His demanding eye did not restrict itself to the theatrical, though; at one point, he insisted I should wear more lavender and pink. But perhaps that was more of a political statement.

He was a big believer in big statements, political, visual, or otherwise. At an apartment he later rented on St. Lukes Place, same block as Arthur's, I once attended a party whose decorations included thirty variously sized and shaped erect plaster penises, sheathed in Reynolds Wrap, protruding from every surface of the upright piano. He had also laminated an empty closet on all six surfaces with mirrors, into which he would entice addled guests to enjoy the Greenwich Village equivalent of a fun house. He once even fabricated a new exterior for his secondhand Mercedes by gluing blue denim over every inch of its body, then leaving it out in the rain until it dried taut and fit like a glove. From that point on, he said, he never had to wash his car.

It would be a while before I could argue with such a man. That summer I only crossed him once, when he gave me an idiotic lyric he titled "Song of Love." It was for the Prince to sing to the Princess, backed up by the ladies and gentlemen of the court, about halfway through the show; the chorus began "I'm in love with a girl named Fred" and went downhill from there. I complained bitterly as I was writing it: It was just plain stupid. It would never work. It was going to be a disaster. After our one week of rehearsal, at the Friday dress before Saturday's opening, I was even more convinced. I told Marshall we absolutely had to yank the thing immediately and come up with something better. He told me I was crazy, and to please shut up.

My kids came to that dress rehearsal and liked it, but seeing them there pulled me up short: They were like creatures from another world. I'd been in a cocoon for three weeks, laying eyeballs on them only in the early morning or when they were asleep. Men did that all the time; it was expected, rewarded even. Did that make it right? I don't know. Without Jerry there to criticize my mothering, I'm afraid no one did. I do know that even before we opened *The Princess and the Pea*, long before everything that followed, I was changed by the joyful, insane, somewhat pharmaceutically enhanced emergency of writing it. I was no longer a mother who dabbled in songwriting but a writer with kids. I knew how to do it. I had confidence.

Just not in that song.

Cut to Saturday night. The end of the week for the guests, most of whom had had a nice time but not quite as nice as they'd hoped. I stood alone, very anxious, in the back of the house on one side, Marshall alone on the other. Considering that the show was built on a baby-shoe shoestring—the budget, I've been told, was $250—it looked pretty good, but as a piece of writing it felt very rough. And then the horrible number, sounding tinny and echoey to me in that sixteen-hundred-seat barn, started. All of a sudden Marshall appeared out of nowhere and grabbed me by the arm. "Hey!" he shouted in a hoarse whisper. "This is unbelievable!"

"What is?" I asked.

"Nobody's leaving," he squeaked, then checked his watch. "By now they've usually left in droves."

We were a hit, and not just because sixteen hundred people hadn't run screaming from the playhouse; they were screaming with laughter instead. And Marshall was right: "Song of Love" was the high point of what would have been the first act if we had one, and worked equally well in New York when we did.

After the Sunday night show, which was, as Marshall also predicted, even better received, Moe agreed to give us a repeat performance on a hot Wednesday ten days later so that we could invite friends, family, agents, and television producers—it never occurred to us to invite the-

Tamiment Playhouse

PRESENTS

A NEW MUSICAL

Book, Lyrics by Marshall Barer and Jay Thompson
Music by Mary Rodgers

MONROE B. HACK . . . . *Producer-Director*

Direction	Jack Sydow
Choreography	Joe Layton
Sets	William Bohnert
Costumes	Joseph Codori
Musical Direction	Milton Greene
Orchestrations	Jay Brower
Vocal Arrangements, Dance Music	Jay Thompson

THE CAST
(In Order of Appearance)

Mother	Maureen Bailey
Pantomime Prince	Ian Guthrie
Pantomime Queen	Kay Herman
Pantomime Princess	Hlenka Devon
Wizard	David Gold
King Sextimus	Milt Kamen
Lady Gosling	Elizabeth Lands
Minstrel	John Smolko
Jester	Sylvia Tysick
Prince Dauntless	Lenny Maxwell
Queen Aggravain	Evelyn Russell
Sir Studmount	Ralston Hill
Lady Lapin	Buzz Halliday
Lady Ermintrude	Hlenka Devon
Lady Minkus	Kay Herman
Sir Tyte, the White	Ian Guthrie
Sir Luce, the Puce	Claude Underwood
Attendants	Paula Hack, Arnold Soboloff
Princess Winifred	Yvonne Othon
Lady Glinda	Maureen Bailey
The Nightingale of Samarkand	Elizabeth Lands
Mistress Much	Cynthia Taylor

THE AND THE

The Time: Long Ago   The Place: Far Away

SYNOPSIS OF MUSICAL NUMBERS

Prologue: (In the Nursery)
"Many Moons Ago" .... Mother and Company
Scene I: (Throne Room of the Castle)
"Argument" .... Wizard
"Mamalogue" .... Queen Aggravain
"Ladies-in-Waiting" .... Knights and Ladies
Scene II: (A Corridor in the Castle)
"The Minstrel, the Jester and I" .... Minstrel,
Jester and King Sextimus
Scene III:(Courtyear)
"Titlesong" .... Lady Glinda
"Song of Love" .... Prince Dauntless, Princess
Winifred, Knights, Ladies and Attendants
Scene IV: (The Wizard's Chamber)
Scene V: (The Main Hall)
"This is My Knight" .... Lady Glinda, Minstrel,
Knights, Ladies and Attendants
Scene VI: (A Corridor)
"Quiet" .... Knights and Ladies
Scene VII:(Bedchamber)
"Lullaby" .... The Nightingale of Samarkand

Scene VIII:(A Corridor)
"Very Soft Shoes" .... Jester and Court
Scene IX: (Banquet Hall)
"I Wonder Why She Couldn't Sleep" .... Queen,
Wizard, Knights and Ladies
"Finale" .... Company

Entire Production Staged
Under the Supervision of
MONROE B. HACK

Stage Manager, Technical Director	George Thorn
Assistant to the Producer	Paula Hack
Assistant to the Choreographer	John Smolko
Assistant to the Musical Director	Myron Levite
Assistant to the Scenic Designer	George Roland
Assistants to the Costume Designer	Cynthia Taylor, Marty Thorn
Technical Assistants	Robert Diehl, Lew Goren, Roger Volkstadt
Stage Electrician	Harry Greenberg
Production Secretary	Harlene Allen
Rehearsal Pianist	William Goldenberg
Graphic Arts	George Roland

1958: At Tamiment, *Once Upon a Mattress* was still a one-act called
The Princess and the Pea. "Nobody's leaving," Marshall squeaked,
then checked his watch. "By now they've usually left in droves."

atrical producers.* Of the forty New York guests invited, maybe fifteen came, including Steve and Sheldon, the designers Jean and Bill Eckart, a bunch of Marshall's and Jay's pals, my pained-looking parents, and a guy who introduced himself as Louis d'Almeida.† I was too busy giving the party—arranging for food and liquor, my usual role in life—to pay much attention. But through the din I heard that Louis, whose credentials amounted to having a mother who was a baroness and a father who was a Warburg, albeit one known as Piggy, thought our show would make a great vehicle for his friend Rosalind Russell. Would Marshall, Jay, and I sign a letter of agreement giving him the rights to produce the show on Broadway? Well, sure, why not? There was no money involved, but since the whole venture sounded highly improbable (he'd never produced anything) we figured we had nothing to lose. On the same principle, but with even less forethought, we had already given Moe Hack 10 percent of all future royalties in case the show ever made it to New York. Who reads contracts?

And that was that. My work at Tamiment was basically done, but with the kids now off with Jerry for a couple of weeks in Quogue, I stayed and hung out with the musicians a while longer, tossing my quarters into the tub of ice and fishing up beers.

....

* The authors' ambition for the material at the time was to turn it into one of the sixty- or ninety-minute television musicals then beginning to become popular; *Aladdin*, by Cole Porter and S. J. Perelman, had been broadcast by CBS that February. A theatrical future seemed unlikely. There had been only one previous Tamiment-to-Broadway transfer, *The Straw Hat Revue*, which had played at the Ambassador for just two months back in 1939 despite featuring Imogene Coca and the as-yet-little-known Danny Kaye, Alfred Drake, and Jerome Robbins.

† Louis d'Almeida (born 1934) was one of three highly cultured Buenos Aires–raised brothers Mary would eventually get to know two of.

26.

FAIR GAME

At the end of the season, we all trooped home to resume our normal lives. Mine hadn't really been normal for a while. However rocky, marriage had been a road. Now I was off the map, a single mother long before it was a common and dignified thing to be. In the eight months since the divorce, and for three more years of what I would later call the interregnum, my main extracurricular activity was what it had been as far back as Brearley: looking for husband material. Already by the end of that Tamiment summer I'd blown through the better part of one or two prospects, with more to come.

Number one was an old familiar figure: Hal. Shortly after my divorce, he took up with me again, or I with him, and the first thing he said to me, when we went out to dinner, was, "I'm a millionaire now. Are you more interested than you were ten years ago?"

He was half joking—not about being a millionaire. In fact, he took me to Alfred Vanderbilt's house on the North Shore of Long Island for the weekend, the kind of place where an officious maid comes up to your room and, much to your discomfort if you are sloppy with your underthings, unpacks your bag.* Also the kind of place where, at a very

---

* Alfred Gwynne Vanderbilt Jr. (1912–1999) was a grandson of Cornelius II and a great-great grandson of the Commodore, founder of the

circa 1960: Hal Prince in his Rockefeller Center office.
"Hal was born clasping a list of people he wanted to meet."

fancy Sunday lunch complete with crystal and ten-ton silver, the servants brought in this incredibly soft, squishy, overdone brisket and I thought: *Why do these people not know how to cook brisket?* The answer: Because it was venison—which I'd never had before or since. The weekend was like that overall: squishy and gamy. When I first got into bed there, Hal came bouncing in, but he smelled like a dirty washcloth. How long had I not noticed this? I, who was born in a perfumed linen closet, could never marry someone like that. And I wouldn't have been right for him anyway, as we both knew. Luckily, he found the woman who was, Judy Chaplin,* about two minutes later; she was smart and tough, which he needed. Early in their marriage, I said to her, "You are one of the brightest people I know, and you read more than almost anyone I've ever met; why don't

....

fortune. He looked a bit like Jimmy Stewart and enjoyed the ladies almost as much as the horses.

* The daughter of the songwriter Saul Chaplin, Judith Chaplin Prince (born 1940) is a classically trained pianist.

you do something with it?" She snapped back: "Just because your father is famous and you feel you have to work to justify your existence, you think everyone does." Touché.

At Alfred Vanderbilt's that weekend I also met the guy who, if I were ever to be murdered, would probably be involved. He was Cord Meyer,* glamorous and mysterious, with John Lindsay hair, horn-rimmed glasses, and a glass left eye, the result of a grenade wound he suffered during the Battle of Guam in World War II. He presented himself at Alfred's as the founder of the United World Federalists, a liberal world-government and disarmament organization, but was actually, I later learned, working for the CIA. Much was covert about Cord. When we met, he was recently divorced from Mary Pinchot,† with whom he'd had three kids; even more recently he'd been dumped by a nice Jewish girl who promptly disappeared to England. About women and everything else, Cord had that blasé St. Paul's–Yale thing down, but along with his patrician air came patrician arrogance. Between trips to South America, possibly fomenting revolution, he'd occasionally have his secretary in Washington call me on a Friday and say, "Mr. Meyer is going to be in New York tonight and wants to have dinner with you at such-and-such a time and place," assuming I had no other plans.

Our first date was at 21.‡ We sat at the bar and he said the most extraordinary things, as if he were in a noir movie, with the smoke from his cigarette billowing up into his dead eye and causing it to tear. One

....

* Some people later thought (incorrectly) that Cord Meyer Jr. (1920–2001) was Deep Throat. Others have suggested he was involved in the assassination of JFK. Really? Both?

† Mary Pinchot Meyer, who later had an affair with JFK, was murdered in 1964. The crime remains unsolved.

‡ The 21 Club, named for its address on West Fifty-second Street, was the self-consciously upper-crust hangout of its time. A line of lawn jockeys, painted white as if that would make them inoffensive, guarded (and still guards) the entrance.

was: "My parents always made me feel ashamed." He didn't mean, as I naturally assumed, that they made him feel ashamed of himself; I'd have sympathized. He meant that they made him feel ashamed of *them*.

The point is that he didn't quite see anyone else as real, a failing strangely common among idealists. Taking me home in a cab after that first date, he tried to kiss me, not even bothering to ask. I said, somewhat hypocritically myself, "Listen, what do you think I am?" and mentioned the Jewish girl who'd exiled herself to England as an example of what I was not about to get messed up in. He looked at me strangely as if it had never occurred to him that I was anything at all. But now I'd made the game interesting, and even though he didn't really want me, nor I him, we began an on-and-off flirtation that punctuated the rest of the interregnum. It became a real affair only after he'd trotted me out to parties given by his friends, as though I were a dog being inspected for a show. I guess I passed, because he then became much more aggressive, almost abusive, about sex: *I want it now, right on the living room floor.* One night, the closest I've ever come to being raped, I had to hiss, "Cut it out or I'll scream and the nurse will come"—which, come to think of it, he might have liked.

Why are so many men so awful? Or at least the ones who came flocking to me? You'd have to conclude that I was part of the problem. When you find out that your husband is certifiably gay, it makes you feel so unfeminine: There must be something wrong with you, as a woman, to have married someone so categorically uninterested. You set out to disprove it. But it was more than that. I was terribly lonely, and also, for all my flailing gestures of independence, helpless. Around that time there was a play called *Fair Game*, a comedy on Broadway about a divorced young woman who is beset by men who assume she's available.* I remember seeing it and thinking, *That's me.* Except that the girl in the play wakes up way earlier than I did to the fact that she doesn't have to have sex with someone just because they buy her a meal. I still thought I had

....

* *Fair Game*, by Sam Locke, played the Longacre Theatre from November 1957 through May 1958. Susan, the divorcée in the play, is all of twenty-one.

to sing for my supper.* With what other currency could I repay a man's interest, his affection, the surprise and pleasure of his wanting me, or even just a favor? When a writer named Ira Wallach† made a pass at me at Flora Roberts's house, and said, after the party, "Can I drop you home?" I tried to quash the quid pro quo: "Thanks, but you live in Brooklyn and I live way up on Seventy-second Street; why would you want to do that?"

"I thought it would be nice?"

"Well, I'm not going to sleep with you."

At the time, having dropped Sandor Rado, I was seeing a gay lady shrink who said, "Why on earth would you say a thing like that?" The answer was something more complicated than preemption. It wasn't so much "I don't want to feel I was unfair to someone who was nice to me" as "I don't want to owe anyone anything."

The funny thing is that a few weeks later I compromised: I did go to bed with Ira, but in somebody else's apartment. In midtown.

Between Flora and the theater, he and I at least had something to talk about. Cord barely acknowledged my family, let alone my career. While I was working on the New York version of *Once Upon a Mattress*, he once said to me, "Can't you just hire someone to tell you whether it's going to be a hit? It's such a waste of time if it's not." I wanted to slug him, but even then I thought I'd better hold on to him in case. It's not like I had a lot of perfect proto-husbands available. If a guy was smart, he was obnoxious; if he was kind, he was wimpy; if he was attractive, he was domineering; if he was artistic, he was gay. What was a young divorcée looking for someone smart, kind, attractive, and artistic to do?

So when Tamiment was over, and Marshall said he wanted to marry me, I took it seriously.

....

* "Sing for Your Supper" is a 1938 Rodgers and Hart song from *The Boys from Syracuse*, full of bird images that double as filthy double entendres about this sort of expectation: "So, little swallow, swallow now."

† Ira Wallach (1913–1995) was at the time turning out comedy sketches for stage revues with instantly forgettable titles like *Once Over Lightly* and *Dig We Must*. Earlier, he'd written a novel called *Absence of a Cello*.

Have I completely lost you yet? Wait. Marshall was crazy, and yes, he had Ian, a big blond Radio City dancer he obviously adored. But Marshall was at least three of the things on my list. He was very good-looking, incredibly smart, and, even though he was more interested in his own visions of what was pleasurable than in what was pleasurable for me, fun in bed.* And he loved the kids, which was a kind of kindness; more important, they loved him back. Or so I assumed from the way they teased and tricked him. They would do things like bring him a sandwich made of white bread and mayonnaise with a great big daddy longlegs squashed in the middle.

Eventually, after a lot of experimentation I'm not going to detail—except to say that its outward expression was that I started wearing a lot of lavender and pink—I understood that if I kept on going with Marshall I was going to end up like that spider. It's not that he wasn't serious: At one point, he brought me down to Florida to meet his mother and his sister and two nieces. But Ian was with us, and Marshall was restless, and when we later returned to New York, he asked me: "Were you under the impression that I was going to stop having sex with men if we got married?" When I said yes, he laughed. "Well, of course not!"

He at least was honest, which was a step up from Jerry. I wondered whether, based on that honesty, I could make a go of an arrangement like the one he was apparently suggesting. Probably not, but couldn't he change? Oddly, my lesbian shrink thought it possible. Daddy, not so much. When he learned what was going on with Marshall, he called me into his study, just as he had when I set the organdy curtains on fire. "Why don't you go all the way and just marry Truman Capote?" he said.

....

* Anaïs Nin certainly thought so. In her 1947 diary she describes their meeting ("I saw a small, slender young man, with hair over his eyes, extending the softest and most boneless hand I had ever held, like a baby's nestling in mine") and their subsequent affair. ("Marshall's body is completely lax, loose. When he lies down, he seems to spill onto the couch, no rigidities.") She was forty-four; he, twenty-four.

"Marshall isn't Truman."

"It doesn't matter. Those marriages don't work."

"What do you mean by 'those' marriages?" I asked.

He reeled them off: Mary Martin and Dick Halliday. Cole and Linda Porter. Lenny and Felicia. Oddly, all of those marriages *did* work, in some way. But then he added: "Your own."

I was in no mood to be lectured. When he concluded our interview by saying "I'm not going to let you do this," I'm afraid I was merely teenager-surly. "What are you going to do, kidnap me?" I snorted.

Instead he sicced Ralph Colin on me. Ralph, the family's legal fixer and my divorce chaperone, didn't threaten me—or rather, he did, but with something unknown. *Untold consequences*, I suppose. It was the only time in my entire life my father strong-armed me before the fact; usually that was Mummy's department. And, of course, he was right. I was simply naïve to think that if Marshall married me he would stop being gay, or that if he didn't stop being gay I could be happy with him as a husband. Yet I apparently didn't have it out of my system quite yet.

Stupid as it sounds, I do not judge myself too harshly. I was, to look at it one way, self-deceiving, but to look at it another way, daring. To live a different life from most of the women I knew was not a bad idea in itself, it was just difficult. It meant, for me at least, finding a different kind of man from most of the men that most of those women married. I had in common with gay guys, though they had no choice, the inclination to escape convention. I thought then and have often thought ever since: Screw all that. You only have one life. There is no god. There is no punishment for things you shouldn't have to be punished for anyway. You may have to be discreet a lot and lie occasionally. But if you don't try to shape your world to your life instead of the other way around, what good have you done for anyone? And if it takes some time to make it happen—for me it still took a couple more years—so be it. Where else do you have to be?

I declined Marshall's proposal, as much for his sake as for mine. He was too exuberantly wayward to be trapped in any marriage, let alone a straight one. Between the pills and his ferocious neurotic energy, he would have been too much for me, anyway, though those same things

circa 1985: Marshall Barer. "The best living lyricist
and the worst living houseguest."

sometimes made him a terrific collaborator. When he died, in 1998,[*]
a friend eulogized him as "the best living lyricist and the worst living
houseguest," which was at least half right. He moved at some point to
Venice, California, and whenever he was in New York, sometimes for
long stretches, he'd stay with whatever friends he could mooch space
from until one of us kicked him out. You'd find him cooking up a succulent hunk of mammoth on the stove but later find the pans, archaeolog-
ically encrusted, festering in the sink. Adam, by then in his thirties, said
you could knit a sweater with the pubic hairs he left on the bathroom
floor. Not that he bathed much; you could write your name in the dirt on
him. And he dressed bizarrely; he would wear a large straw hat packed
with other bits of his clothing. Eventually I understood that this was not
just idiosyncrasy but a sort of madness: a mad focus on only what he
liked. Nothing else got in.

....

[*] Of liver cancer, likely from his heavy drug use—not, as Ian did in 1987,
from complications of AIDS.

Most of the rest of us have to focus also on what we don't like; Marshall powered through that stuff, blustering it into submission. I'm sure he thought my father's objections would just melt away, but he hadn't counted on mine. He was shocked and then furious when I said no. I at first thought I'd be losing a writing partner forever, and probably a career, let alone a fun person to be around, but his desire to work outstripped everything else and we were soon back at it.

That was a useful lesson for me as a woman. I said no to a man's plan for me, in favor of trying to scratch out my own, and, look, he was angry, but he didn't bolt. Maybe I didn't have to sing for my supper.

27.

CHIP OFF THE OLD
BLOCKBUSTER

Among those who came to see *The Princess and the Pea* on August 27 at Tamiment were, as I said, Jean and Bill Eckart, the great husband-and-wife design team.[*] Well, it doesn't matter how great you are as a husband-and-wife set design team, you're still quite low on the totem pole, and they wanted to climb higher. Apparently, they thought our show might be their ticket up, so one evening that fall they took Marshall and me to dinner at the Forum of the Twelve Caesars.[†] Did we think we could expand what was only an hour and fifteen minutes at Tamiment into a full-length musical?

Jean always spoke in a very quiet voice, hardly loud enough to hear even with her mouth an inch away from your ear. It's a wonderful way

....

[*] William (1920–2000) and Jean (1921–1993) Eckart were a full-service package, offering sets, costumes, and lights, or any combination thereof. They would go on to design the original productions of *Fiorello!*, *She Loves Me*, *Anyone Can Whistle*, and *Mame*, among many others.

[†] A bizarrely opulent restaurant in Rockefeller Center, with theme dishes like Lobster Jupiter and Oysters of Hercules. The waiters wore purple toga-like uniforms.

to get attention. "We're thinking of becoming producers, and so if you would consider it"—and that's when Marshall interrupted: "Yes."

I can't remember what his thinking was, but his thinking was always "yes." *Yes. Yes. Yes, of course.* And I didn't disagree. My theory ever since Brearley was this: When people ask you if you know how to do something, you say you do, even if you don't. I don't remember very much of what I learned at Brearley, but I did learn that. So Marshall said, "Yes," and I said I knew how to do it, and there we were, hands all shaken, except for, oops, we'd forgotten Louis d'Almeida.

You remember, the guy who got us to sign a contract allowing him to produce any future Broadway version of *Pea*, with Rosalind Russell dangling as bait? When I nervously told him about the Eckarts' offer he immediately bowed out. "I'm not going to hold you to that, it's ridiculous. Nobody knows who I am." There are honorable people on the planet.*

The Eckarts sensibly said that we'd have to have a bigger director than Jack Sydow, who'd staged the show at Tamiment.† The man they had in mind was George Abbott, for whom they'd recently designed *Damn Yankees* and the movie of *The Pajama Game*. "Don't you think Mr. Abbott would be a great director for us?" Jean cooed. "Yes!" we answered, though in truth we had no idea whether he would be or not. In 1958 he turned seventy-one, ancient by our standards, and despite his unparalleled track

....

* A decade later, d'Almeida was charged with second-degree manslaughter in the death of a twenty-year-old "acquaintance." The charge was knocked down to criminally negligent homicide, and he was sentenced to five years' probation.

† As a consolation, Jack, who was vaguely related to the actor Max von Sydow, was hired as the New York production's assistant director because he knew how to stage the "mattress romp" near the end of the show. It's very specific and if it doesn't work, as it didn't in the recent Broadway revival, the second act deflates. Jack also took over as stage manager for a while and understudied several roles—something that would never happen today, but back in the theater's Wild West years was not so unusual.

record of hits starting in 1926,* he was a formidably cold fish, conde-
scending to youth. Less so to me, perhaps, than to others: I'd known him
since I was six, when he lived on Long Island near Mummy and Daddy
around the time I spent the summer there looking at the gardener's tool. I
was allowed to call him George; to everyone else he was Mr. Abbott. Still,
I was nervous when we auditioned the Tamiment version of the score for
him in the huge, two-story living room of the Eckarts' converted carriage
house in Washington Mews, explaining that we knew the show needed
expanding but were sure we could accomplish that in no time.

"How much time is no time?" he asked when we finished. He actually
looked at his watch.

Mr. Inflexible had without fail to be in his summer home, which was
then in the Catskills, by the middle of May, so the show would have to
open before then. Counting backward, he ticked off the timetable: opening night around May 11, one week of previews before that, four weeks
of rehearsal before that, four weeks of casting and preproduction before
that. Where did that bring us? To early March. It was now nearly the end
of January. Could we write the full-length version, and could Jean and Bill
find a theater and raise the money, in, let's see, six weeks' time?

Definitely, we assured him, lying through our chattering teeth.

Fine, said George, calling our bluff. I'll see you in six weeks.

But he did have another condition. He wanted to call the show *Once
Upon a Mattress*. We knew that *The Princess and the Pea* wouldn't fly, but
this idea seemed even worse: dreadful and dumb and totally misleading.
People would think it was a sex farce—and, later, when I would tell cabdrivers the title on the way to the theater, in the days when cabdrivers
followed such things, they all thought it was a stripper show. I've often
wondered how many customers we lost because nobody could figure out
from the title what kind of show it actually was: too dirty or too clean.

George listened very nicely to our concerns and said, "Okay, but
that's the title."

---

* Among them, in an astonishing burst between 1935 and 1940, were four by
Rodgers and Hart: *Jumbo, On Your Toes, The Boys from Syracuse,* and *Pal Joey.*

Foaming at the mouth, I went to my father, who was, as you've seen, a stickler not just about music but words.* I was sure he would understand that *Once Upon a Mattress* was a smarmy, overeager idea. Remember, Daddy was the one who taught me to get rid of any gimmicks in my writing: no exclamation points or italics or shouting, unless there was no other way for people to derive the proper feeling—or the name of a state was involved. He detested vague or inaccurate language, as do I: At Kimmy's second wedding, when the groom got up and made a speech about being so grateful for how cordial everyone had been to "Kim and I," out of my mouth flew "me!"—perhaps disproving his point.

But when I told Daddy about *Once Upon a Mattress* and how we all thought it was not a hit title, he uttered this Zen koan: "A hit title is the title of a hit."

Which is to say, George's name meant more than the show's. Sure enough, the minute they had Abbott on board, the Eckarts were able to persuade Norris Houghton and T. Edward Hambleton, the producers and owners of the Phoenix Theatre,† that instead of letting their twelve-hundred-seat off-Broadway house stand empty after their regular subscription season ended in April—which was tantamount to leaving a 747 on the tarmac all summer—they should co-produce *Mattress* and lend them the space. They, too, said yes. Even I invested once I knew George was directing. In any case, with both him and the Phoenix in hand, Bill and Jean quickly raised the hundred-thousand-dollar capitalization and set about designing the show.‡

....

* In that radio bit with Charlie McCarthy, the dummy said, "After all, none of us are human," and Rodgers immediately cut in with "is human."

† The Phoenix, on Second Avenue at Twelfth Street, opened as the Yiddish Art Theater in 1926; later, as Club 181, it offered drag shows; and even later, as the Eden, it housed *Oh! Calcutta!* and *Grease*. Now it's the Village East Cinema. But in its heyday, it was a beacon of serious work; *Once Upon a Mattress*, which did not fall into that category, was a rental.

‡ *Once Upon a Mattress* was so well produced that the Eckarts spent only

That just left writing it. It's a good thing the Eckarts' living room was so huge, because when we were all working there, we made quite a crowd, not even counting the three standard poodles wandering about. Every morning at nine, with Jean and Bill listening from their studio on the balcony level and tossing down suggestions now and again, Jay Thompson and Marshall and I—and eventually Dean Fuller, whose child had been born by then—gathered there to pound out what amounted to a completely new book, with major new characters, major new subplots, and major new gaping holes for songs. A typical day's plan would go like this: *Mary, you figure out section 9A, which is an in-one scene between the Queen and the King. Dean is going to take 10A and someone else is going to take 10B. Marshall—where's Marshall? Probably has his head in the fridge.* We parceled out the work that way, and then at the end of the day, which was two in the morning, we'd all get together to see if we had anything. Throughout, Jean and Bill fed and martinied us liberally, which is why when the show started previewing and they gave us money I was absolutely floored. I had never heard of a cash advance, just an edible or drinkable one.

It was exhausting, thrilling, euphoric. And, of course, all-consuming. Sometimes we ran so late that I spent the night at Marshall's place, talking ideas as we drifted off. (This was during Our Peculiar Experiment.) But even when he put me in a cab—which he often hailed by lying down in an intersection—I would speed up Third Avenue, or any avenue, freezing cold and filled with excitement and panic. Panic because, as the book began to take shape, I was also trying to write the new songs, quietly, so as not to wake the kids, whom I now almost never saw. I don't know how they survived: some combination of nannies, babysitters, and God knows what.[*] Why they love me, I'll never know.

....

ninety thousand dollars of the hundred thousand they raised. Partly that was due to the lovely modesty of their sets, which were lightweight and colorful and easy to move.

[*] As a kind of consolation prize, when the first TV production of *Mattress*

The music came more easily than it had at Tamiment; I was getting more fluent. But fluency isn't enough. It may tell you that you can write something but not whether what you write will serve the purpose. For that, most composers, Daddy included, must wait for an audience, if only the audience of their collaborators. You'd think it would be obvious right from the start; people later say it must have been. But it rarely is. We had, for instance, to beef up the role of the Princess hugely,* not only because she was meant to be the star of the show and had no songs but because we had a star, Nancy Walker, set to play her and sing them. It's always easier to write when you know whom you're writing for, so I didn't have much trouble finding a voice for the two new numbers that—along with "Shy," which we planned to restore—would form the backbone of her musical track. But if "The Swamps of Home" was "obviously" a great comedy number, and if "Happily Ever After" was "obviously" a show-stopper, no one told me when I wrote and rewrote and rewrote and re-wrote them, mostly in blood. Voice is one thing; effectiveness is another.

And I couldn't always tell the difference. I loved the odd and wrong stuff just as much as what later became popular. We had a real humdinger of a song for the chorus of knights, called "Brotherhood," that I thought was terrific; it was so long that you could dangle page one of the manu-script from the balcony and watch it unflap all the way down to the or-chestra floor. George was sure it would drag the show but said, "I'll give it a chance for one night, and if it doesn't work then out it goes." Out it went. "This is no damn good," he'd say on many other occasions. "Write another one." To him it was like throwing salt over your left shoulder. To us it was another night, or several, of no sleep. So many songs got cut that we gave George, for an opening night gift, a large wastebasket decou-paged inside and out with the rejected sheet music.

The songs that remained were, maybe as a result, all pretty solid. I

....

was shot in 1964, Nina and Kim, along with Linda's son, Peter, were al-lowed to play extras in the prologue. Which was cut. That's showbiz.

* While also beefing up her name from Winifred to Winnifred.

1959: Mary and Richard Rodgers. "I decided never to play him my music again."

found I was able to give my own spin to traditional forms like the love duet and the charm number. A lyric for the new ingénues called "Yesterday I Loved You"* required only—only!—a Rodgersy midtempo 4/4 tune for the A sections, but for the bridge I suddenly switched gears. I was so pleased with it that I played it for Daddy, who curled his nose and said, "Why did you do that in the bridge?"

"I don't know, I thought it sounded good?" Actually, I was really proud of the unexpected change of key and rhythm, especially because it gave the song, and the scene, a sense of propulsion.

"Well, I wouldn't have done that."

Which is when I decided never to play him my music again.

George especially loved the new number for the Queen, "Sensitivity,"

....

* This turned out to be one of Marshall's trunk lyrics; he'd used it, with music by a different composer, in a revue called *Walk Tall* that toured Texas in 1953 and 1954.

which wasn't even supposed to be in the show until Jane White, who played the role in New York, said, "Why don't I have a real song? I need a song!" And I loved it, too, because it's just a waltz in the bridge but 5/4 in the A section, even though the musicians always said it was really 5/8. I don't think Daddy ever wrote a song in 5/4 *or* 5/8. And we all liked "Normandy," even though it nearly killed me to write it. I remember that after Marshall gave me the lyric and I looked at it for a while, I finally said: "I know what you want, you want a Jule Styne song!" And that's what it is, except for the bridge, which I couldn't figure out until Marshall, who was really a genius at knowing what kind of number was needed at what moment, told me it should be like *Songs of the Auvergne.* Songs of the what?* But he gave me the record, and I listened to it, and boy, did I love the harmonies them Frogs used.

I don't know how many new songs I wrote that February and March— dozens? But eight or nine made it into the show, along with four or five we kept intact or adapted from the twelve at Tamiment. Of all of these, and possibly of all the songs I wrote in my whole career, the number we added for the King, called "Man to Man Talk," is probably my favorite. Not because of the tune, which is fine, or the performance by Jack Gilford, whom we hired to replace Milt Kamen and was brilliant. No, it's the situation that makes it so good: the mute father trying to teach his child about love. It made all my gay friends cry. And if I ever cried it might make me cry, too, now that I think about it. *The mute father trying to teach his child about love.* In the song, at least, he's successful.

....

* The series of folksongs collected and arranged by the French composer and musicologist Joseph Canteloube under the title *Chants d'Auvergne* became a favorite of opera divas and their fans from the 1930s onward.

28.

WHAT'S MY MOTIVATION?

Exactly six weeks after George started his stopwatch, we auditioned the new, enlarged version of the show for him.

With no acknowledgment of what we considered a miraculous achievement, he nodded briefly and set about scheduling our first production meeting. It was at that meeting, with thirty people (and the three poodles) crammed into the Eckarts' living room, that we faced our biggest and most unexpected headache: casting. We writers were all counting on Nancy for the lead, of course; she'd loved the tapes Marshall had brought her and, after a two-year absence from the New York stage,[*] was eager to get back in the saddle.

But at the end of that first meeting, George said, "How many people here think Nancy Walker is the right person for this role?" All hands shot up.

"I have to disagree," he said. "I've worked with Nancy. She's wonderful. But I don't want to work with an established star; I'd much rather create a new one."

....

[*] Nancy Walker's most recent appearance had been as a police officer in *Copper and Brass*, a one-month flop in 1957. Her husband, David Craig, wrote the lyrics and co-wrote the book with Ellen Violett, who later became a good friend of the Guettels. The Eckarts designed the sets and lights; Burt Shevelove, called in as director in Philadelphia, tried but failed to save it.

1959: Mary, with Joe Bova singing and Dean Fuller watching, perform
the new *Mattress* score for George Abbott. "I said I'd direct this show
and I will. But I won't like it."

Dead silence.

Finally, Marshall leapt to his dirty little feet and exploded in a fit of nonstop stuttering, spluttering, expostulating, foaming, and arm-flinging. In
short, he was absolutely ghastly: another thing he was a genius at. When
he subsided, George—cool, reasonable, but implacable—addressed the
group. "All right. If this is what you want, you can have Nancy. But it
won't be any fun for me. I said I'd direct this show and I will. But I won't
like it. Let me know what you decide." And with that, he left the meeting.

Later that night, Jean called me at home. "Listen," she said, which between her infinitesimal voice and the shouts of my neglected kids clamoring for my attention wasn't very easy to do. "I just heard from George. He doesn't want Nancy. But it's worse than that. He doesn't want Marshall. He said, 'Who is that bad-tempered brat who made such a scene this afternoon? Because I don't want him in a meeting ever again.'"

"But he's the lyricist!"

"I told him that. But he said, 'I don't care who he is. He's unpleasant and I don't want to see him again.'"

"We can't possibly do the show without Marshall," I cried.

"Then, Mary," Jean concluded, "you have to do something. He has to give up Nancy and he has to apologize to George or we're going down the tubes. Is that clear?"

I did manage to do something with Marshall, but it wasn't easy and it wasn't fun. For many years, Marshall had harbored his dream of Nancy cavorting around on top of a bed with twenty mattresses; now he was going to have to abandon the dream, disappoint Nancy—which both of us dreaded—and worst of all, have to spend the next several weeks making nice to a man he already hated. I told him he didn't have any choice. I was only twenty-eight, I might have other opportunities, but he was thirty-nine. He'd spent the last ten years knocking around Broadway and not making it. This could be his last chance. Did he really want to blow it?

After several hours of human bing-bang between us—"You're an effing coward!" "You're a stubborn bastard and you're going to shoot yourself in the foot!" "This whole thing was my idea in the first place, and you're sabotaging it!" and so forth—he finally agreed to swallow his pride and say he was sorry to Mr. Abbott. George accepted the apology with grace and cautioned Marshall not to behave like that ever again. Marshall gave his promise, which he broke many times during the rehearsal period. When that happened, George would issue a stern "That's enough, Marshall," and the battle usually ended before it began.

Now we had to find a new star. Having paid a call on Nancy, having begged her forgiveness—which she, though saddened, generously gave—we began the search for a suitable Princess. A lot of people were good at one thing but not another; it's a very hard part to cast. You need a real clown with a great voice, someone with a huge personality but immediately likable, and there aren't many performers like that, as we unfortunately found out in the 1996 revival, when Sarah Jessica Parker got one of those four things right.*

We finally were on the verge of signing Pat Carroll, another Tamiment alumna,† but days before rehearsals were to start, I was down at Marshall's apartment, bashing away on the piano, when the phone rang. It was Jean, whispering that there had been a change of plans. Luckily, Pat Carroll hadn't been signed yet, because they'd heard about this funny woman called Carol Burnett, who had been a guest on *The Garry Moore Show* and was now garnering all kinds of cabaret acclaim with a song called "I Made a Fool of Myself over John Foster Dulles."‡ I reported this latest turn of events to Marshall and waited for the temper tantrum, but it turned out that Marshall was mad for Carol Burnett. They'd been at Tamiment together in 1956: She was brilliant, she was perfect, why hadn't he thought of her himself?

Marshall called her where she was living in some cruddy apartment with her husband at the time, Don Saroyan, a nephew of William, not a good marriage. "I already know your work," he told her, "but could you come sing for Mary?"

She showed up at Marshall's within the hour, looking terrific: long-legged, great figure, huge smile, flawless skin, glorious red hair. She sang and, as I have said many times, could have been heard in Brooklyn. But it wasn't just the volume that made her voice incredible—and in fact her range wasn't that enormous. It was her flexibility. She could break sud-

----

* Parker was immediately likable.

† She was probably too old anyway, but Pat Carroll (1927–2022) was certainly versatile enough to handle the part. In her long career since, she has pretty much run the gamut, voicing Ursula the sea witch in *The Little Mermaid* and succeeding in traditionally male roles like Falstaff and King Lear.

‡ If you don't know who Carol Burnett (born 1933) is, you're definitely not reading this book.

denly from melody into her hilarious hog-calling hoots, which didn't have any particular note in them but suggested immense fun and eagerness and strength and health. For me there was no question that she was exactly right, but there was one problem: She was too attractive. Our Princess was supposed to look like a bedraggled blob. "What's the ugliest, most repulsive piece of wardrobe in your closet?" we asked. Carol said she had a really icky, olive brown suit that didn't fit very well. We told her to show up at ten o'clock on Friday morning at the Phoenix Theatre—and *wear that suit.*

Friday, there we were: George; the Eckarts; Marshall; me; the other writers; Hal Hastings, the music director; and Judy Abbott, the casting director. Does her name look familiar? When George was a very young and ambitious actor, very nearly in the nineteenth century, he married his high school English teacher; she bore him one daughter—Judy—then eight years later inconveniently died of breast cancer, leaving him with this child he didn't know what to do with. He dumped her on his wife's family in Rochester and saw her in New York City exactly once a year, on her birthday. How do I know all this? Judy told me. She also told me that on one of these annual birthday jaunts George met her at the train station with a beautiful girlfriend in tow. George was famous for having beautiful girlfriends, especially if they were good dancers and he could whisk them off to Cuba for a spin around the dance floor; with the exception of the raven-haired, ivory-skinned, super-beautiful Mary Sinclair, to whom he was married for all of five years, he tired of them quickly, but they were delicious dishes while they lasted. Anyway, this particular girlfriend was charming all day to little Judy, who on her long, lonely train ride back to Rochester received a telegram reiterating the Happy Birthday wishes and signed "Daddy." Yeah, right. She had never called her father "Daddy" in her life.[*] The telegram was from the girlfriend.

....

[*] Like her mother, Judy Abbott (1922–1984) died of breast cancer. She predeceased her father by eleven years; he stubbornly hung in until he was 107.

1959: Carol Burnett as Princess Winnifred, trying to get some sleep while the Nightingale of Samarkand shrills "an insane modal tune."

Anyway, Judy walked onto the stage and said to her father, "Mr. Abbott, this is Miss Carol Burnett." There wasn't any question; Carol went home with the part. And George had the satisfaction of creating a new star. They didn't call him "the apprentice's sorcerer" for nothing.

The only other casting trouble we had was with the imperious non-stop-talking Queen. We couldn't find anyone good enough until one day at the auditions Judy announced, "Mr. Abbott, this is Miss Jane White," and out she came. Jane was very imposing and very bright, with absolutely beautiful diction for the role—she'd gone to Smith and done plenty of Shakespeare. And she sang just swell. But as she gathered her things to leave, George said, none too quietly, "I'm not casting her; we can't have a Negro queen in a medieval kingdom."

"But with makeup, Mr. Abbott?" Judy said.

"No! It's not the color, it's the features! She'd stick out like a sore thumb! Forget it—and thank you, Miss White."

I sat there with my jaw dropping lower and lower toward the floor, but otherwise immobile.

Marshall was up in a flash, though. He made it to the stage door in time to catch the crestfallen Jane before she caught a cab. He asked her if she had heard of Marcus Blechman, because Marcus Blechman was not only a brilliant theatrical photographer but also a brilliant makeup artist. He could make Jane up to look white, and then she could come back and audition again, how would that be?

"I have to think," Jane said. "You know who my father was." And of course everyone knew he was Walter White.* "It's . . . problematic."

Hideous as this was, we wanted her very much for the role and she wanted to do it. So Marshall sent her to Blechman to devise a whiteface that would look natural under the theater's work light, and however difficult that must have been for her, the worst part, she said, was driving downtown in the taxi that way, five days later.

Nevertheless, she made it to the theater, where Judy once again said, "Mr. Abbott, this is Miss Jane White." He took one look at her and shouted, "I told you no Black queen in a medieval musical!"

"Shut up, George," someone said, and it must have been me because I was the only one who called him that. "Just listen."

George found her irresistible this time, and I guess "white enough," and gave in.

In the end, Jane was terrific; she played the part over and over. But that was a mixed blessing. When the second television version was being shot in 1972 in Los Angeles, because that's where Carol lived at the time, the New York contingent was all staying in a crummy motel, where, one evening, we had a drink before dinner. I said, "So, Jane, what else are you working on?"—and she burst into tears. No matter what she did, she said, it was the wrong time in history. "When I first did *Mattress*, I was

---

* Walter White (1893–1955) was a towering figure in the civil rights movement, and head of the NAACP from 1931 until his death.

too Black. Now nobody wants me because I'm not Black *enough*."* Jane finally married Alfredo Viazzi and they ran two wonderful Italian restaurants in the Village.

I guess there was one other casting problem, in a way: Joe Bova, whom we hired as Prince Dauntless, was a moron. Playing opposite him, Carol never knew from one night to the next what the arrogant, undisciplined little shit was going to do. He was worth it, though, if only because he was the instigation for one of the most famous ripostes in theater history. At one point he stopped a rehearsal to ask, as he made a cross that Abbott had blocked: "What's my motivation?"

Abbott snapped back: "Your paycheck."

And yet Joe Bova later married Judy Abbott! Judy had a hard time with husbands, which is no wonder, given her father. She had previously been married to Tom Ewell, who was gay; she found him two days after their wedding with his head in the oven. She removed his head—he wasn't dead, just a little singed. After Joe, she married Dick Clark, but not even the Dick Clark of *American Bandstand*.

Anyway, future son-in-law or not, Joe Bova was no match for George. George knew how to run a rehearsal. If an actor—say, Robert Rounseville as the Minstrel—was no good, he just kept cutting his part until he quit. This was exasperating if you had written lots of material for his voice, but George wasn't interested in niceties like that. He was a man of many firm and fast opinions. To Dean and Jay, huddled together in a couple of orchestra seats: "Fellows, I need a line to get the chorus off the stage." They'd confer hastily, but not hastily enough. "Never mind," says George, "I have one. You there in the front with the blond hair, you say, 'Ladies, we have to go get our dancing shoes!' and all of you exit downstage right. Got that?"

Dean and Jay would lock eyes, then roll them to the chandelier. "Mr. Abbott, how about—"

"That'll be fine for now, you can fix it later," he'd tell them. Later, of course, never came.

....

* Nontraditional (or color-blind) casting is more common now but was almost unheard of then, at least among whites.

Once Upon a Mattress opened at the Phoenix on May 11, 1959, just in time for George's vacation. My parents and sister came downtown for the premiere; I think they were pleased, but my mother didn't say anything other than "Darling this is wonderful, congratulations"—the sort of thing that just fell out of her mouth without thinking, like "Gesundheit." It didn't matter because the reviews, though not all raves, were good—and great for me and Carol. Walter Kerr called me a "genuine new talent" and a "chip off the old blockbuster." I was startled and pleased. I wasn't my father, but I thought: *I have a life here.*

Though I also didn't. The theater is like a little disease; it keeps dying, and if you're not careful, you die with it. We opened, with no advance, in what was not yet civilized enough to be called the East Village, just as the regular theater season was ending and the New York summer was in your face like a damp drunk. You know what I did to help *Mattress* along? We extended and extended as we kept making money, but the Phoenix had another booking coming in November: *Lysistrata.* So to get some publicity we faked a strike. We painted huge placards down in the cellar, and Jane White marched right off the stage one night after a per-formance and out into Second Avenue, leading the company with signs saying things like *Bolster Our Fourposter* and *Our Kingdom for a House.* Jane got pneumonia, but we actually made enough noise in the press with that fit of simulated pique to book a Broadway theater, the Alvin, where we opened on November 25.

And then, in order to make sure people *came* to the Alvin—early on, the coat attendant told me he didn't have high hopes—I took a bunch of show cards and went up and down every single street in the Broad-way district, walking into every bar and restaurant and candy store. I told whoever was behind the counter who I was, said that our show finally had a home, and asked if they would they put our card in their window. To a man they said yes. They must have thought it was a hoot: Richard Rodgers's daughter—I introduced myself as such because it was good for business and I was shameless—tromping around in her sneakers, handing out show cards. Later, when *Mattress* moved from the Alvin to the Winter Garden to the Cort to the St. James, all within a year, we called it "the most moving musical in town."

1959: Mary (right) and Carol Burnett move a mattress into the Alvin Theatre, one day before the opening of "the most moving musical in town."

The initial production ran for 460 performances. It might have run even longer, but when Carol left after a year and was replaced by Ann B. Davis, later famous as the bossy maid on *The Brady Bunch*, business dropped through the floor.* Despite that, and despite the enormous cost of the four moves, the Eckarts and their investors not only recouped their investment, but turned a 100 percent profit.

You know who also did well by *Mattress*? Moe Hack.

....

* The show closed on July 2, 1960. A thirty-week national tour, headlined by Dody Goodman as Winnifred and Buster Keaton as the King, began on September 1.

None of us ever resented a nickel of his cut. We owed him as much for making us create nine principal parts for his Tamiment "stars." (Nine principal parts mean eighteen proud parents of nine high school students.) The Eckarts, too, deserve everything they made, not only for feeding us as we wrote but also for forcing us, through their understanding of design, to structure the show sensibly and economically. Almost anyone can produce *Once Upon a Mattress*, and almost everyone has. Which is why, year after year, decade after decade, it returns the most money I've ever made as a writer.[*] Some people have a medley of their hits; I have a medley of one.

---

[*] *Mattress* was among the most popular musicals licensed by the Rodgers & Hammerstein Office, now part of Concord Theatricals. At the time of Mary's death, her royalties, though they had been drifting downward, were still well more than a hundred thousand dollars a year.

29.

WAY DOWN DEEP I'M DEMURE

O nce Upon a Mattress wasn't actually my Broadway debut; it was my Broadway debut featuring humans. Earlier in that incredible year of 1959, a show called *Davy Jones' Locker* opened for a limited run at the Morosco, featuring the Bil Baird Marionettes. William Baird and his less-credited wife, Cora, were leading puppeteers of the time,* and it was not any sort of comedown or embarrassment, especially for me, who said yes to everything, to work on one of their shows. For *Davy Jones' Locker* I wrote eight or nine songs, both music and lyrics, all pretty good.† One, called "Sugar and Spice," was sung by a mermaid:

> *Oh, a girl can get lonesome*
> *Swimming round and round.*
> *And I wish I could own some*
> *Little piece of ground*
> *To stand on with the feet that aren't there.*

....

* Later, they designed and performed the "Lonely Goatherd" sequence in the movie version of *The Sound of Music*.

† The *Times* called the score "vivacious," and *Variety*, "okay tune-wise and clever with the lyric." The faint praise of "mildly pleasant" in the *Daily News* was made up for by the *Herald Tribune*: "Her songs . . . establish her in her own right."

No autobiography in that, surely.

Though marionettes were very popular at the time, I found them a bit creepy, especially at the Bairds' combination home, studio, and theater on West Seventy-first, where I composed the score while Bil's blind mother sat rocking away in a rocking chair, like something out of Wyeth or Hitchcock. She kept saying, "I'm Bil Baird's mother; I'm blind, you know." The Bairds stored all their marionettes on a separate floor, like a morgue; you'd pull out a big drawer and in there would be Peter Pan or Pinocchio, dead.*

As I kept telling myself, you can learn something from anything. Working to solve a specific problem related to the situation at hand, you are also exploring broader questions of craft. For instance: I realized while writing *Davy Jones' Locker* that you don't want to give marionettes any long notes to sing because they're wooden: with their mouths stuck wide open they look like they have tetanus. And, unlike Ethel Merman, they can't make facial expressions to distract you. You're better off writing up-tempo numbers with shorter note values; their clackity jaws can bounce up and down all they like. This insight, small as it sounds, turned out to be useful later, not only in writing for certain wooden humans, but also in thinking about how the art of songwriting is mostly the art of threading the needle of limitations; the narrower the limitations, the better. You just have to find the right ones, which is easier in specific genres. For instance: Children's books require morality. Comedies need jokes.

With *Davy Jones* and Mary Martin and *Mattress* all hitting in the first half of 1959, people told me I was "on the verge." Surely a composer with so much concentrated success would soon be offered a new Broadway musical. Daddy, whose reference point was *The Garrick Gaieties* in 1925, expected me to be off and running because he had been, but the offers kept not pouring in. In fact, the only big offer I got in 1959 came from

....

* In 1973, that Pinocchio, or one just like it, starred in another Baird musical Mary wrote, this time with Sheldon Harnick providing the lyrics. Meanwhile, *Davy Jones' Locker* kept returning, as many as six times over the years, even after the Bairds both died, which made it even creepier.

him. During rehearsals for *The Sound of Music* that fall, Ockie, suffering from what he thought was an ulcer, was given a diagnosis of terminal stomach cancer—or rather, his family was given the diagnosis. Astonishingly, they didn't tell Ockie, but being a practical bunch they did tell Daddy, figuring he might have to develop a Plan B. Daddy told me about it and said, "If he dies before we're done, maybe you'd be interested in completing the lyrics."

I was just floored. Floored that he would ask me and also that he thought I was good enough—because he'd never suggested as much before. I took a look at what they'd already written and remember thinking that "Do-Re-Mi" was just silly. "Do, a deer"? "Fa, a long, long way to run"? What is that? Of course, what else are you supposed to do with the spelling of those notes, but Jesus. Anyway, Ockie lived long enough that my services were not required; the last lyric he wrote was "Edelweiss."[*]

The projects I tried to start up on my own universally stalled. I read an advance copy of a comic novel called *The Street of the Laughing Camel* and immediately asked Flora, my fabulous new agent who had not yet done anything for me, to inquire about the rights. (She forgot, and David Merrick got them.) A project that went a lot further before dying involved the composer Marc Blitzstein.[†] I'd met Marc through the Eckarts, and got to know him more through Lenny, who had conducted his labor musical *The Cradle Will Rock* at Harvard and championed him at the Philharmonic. Marc was also one of Steve's Killer Bees, as I called them: vicious anagram players who could turn *harmonicas* into *maraschino*.

At a party at Jerry Bock's house, Marc told me he had been approached

....

[*] Hammerstein died the following August, at sixty-five. The two new songs written for the 1965 film—"I Have Confidence" and "Something Good"—have lyrics by Rodgers himself. As a lyricist, he was square and arid but not bad. He certainly knows how to set the phrase "my wicked, miserable past" perfectly.

[†] High-minded Marc Blitzstein (1905–1964) wrote socially conscious musicals (such as *The Cradle Will Rock* and *Juno*) and operas (such as *Regina*, based on *The Little Foxes*).

by E. B. White's agent about making an animated musical out of *Charlotte's Web*. I'd loved *Charlotte's Web* ever since it was published in 1952 and had read it to my kids often. Marc, knowing me as a Queen of Kiddie Shows, thought perhaps I could write the screenplay. (Naturally he'd be doing the songs.) I had mixed feelings about that: I wanted to write my own songs and I wasn't a big fan of his. Daddy, I knew, was outright contemptuous. On the taxi ride home from seeing *Juno*, which had opened that March, he and Mummy ripped the score apart for what we all felt were its prosaic lyrics and unmelodiousness. "Maybe the driver could sing 'We Have Reached Our Destination,' to similar effect," Daddy sneered.

Their distaste for Marc, which was part of their distaste for that entire set of gay men,* naturally endeared him to me, and of course I said yes. I would have said yes to almost anything. He was brusque and sharp but wonderful to work with. Once a week for several months in the fall of 1959 he would come to my doorstep at eight in the morning, just after the children who went to school had gone to school, and we'd kick around ideas. He made it very clear that he wanted this musical to be tough and ugly and real even though it was animated—no Disney attitudes. From our conversations we put together a rough scenario with song placements, and when we felt we'd accomplished enough and knew where we were going, we presented our ideas to Mr. White. His agent set up the meeting at the Algonquin; we sat in that lobby lounge where you rang a school bell to get another drink. Let's just say the bell rang often. White was pleasant but above it all—and, it seemed, a bit confused.

"How are you going to manage to put a spider on the stage?" he asked.

Marc and I looked at each other. We said we weren't planning to put a spider onstage; we were planning to put it in an animated movie.

White thought that made sense but said, "You know, I would never give the movie rights for *Charlotte's Web* to anyone, because it's my favorite property."

....

* Though he had a wife, Blitzstein was gay; five years after Mary worked with him on *Charlotte's Web*, he was murdered in Martinique by some sailors he tried to pick up.

Oh. The agent had never checked with him.[*]

At the time, I had just returned from a second summer at Tamiment. Daddy was appalled by the idea of my going again: Now that I'd had a hit show in New York, it looked like a step back after two steps forward. But with Marshall begging me, and with my head full of neatly edited memories of the previous year, I said yes.

There were the usual one-off songs for revues, but this time we went in knowing we wanted to write another book musical. Moe Hack, with his cut of *Once Upon a Mattress* jingling in his pocket, was all too glad to let us. The source was one I had tried to adapt with Steve seven years earlier: "The Lady, or the Tiger?"—only this time, the Stockton story[†] would be set within an outer one about a network producing a musical version of it. The writers of the outer musical also played characters in the inner one. We called it *The Happy Medium* until Marshall came up with *A Little Night Music*.[‡]

It was a complicated idea, but we figured that by applying the previous summer's methods we could get it done in the few weeks allotted. Just as before, early in the morning, Marshall would give me a snippet of lyric for the verse of a new song, then leave for the golf course to work out the rest. But soon he started not coming back, which meant, for me,

---

[*] "Which comes first, generally, the words or the music?" an interviewer asks the songwriting team in *Merrily We Roll Along*. The lyricist answers: "Generally, the contract." That could be Richard Rodgers talking about the trap of putting the artistic cart before the business horse, and yet both his daughter and his grandson fell into the trap at some point in their careers by getting to work before getting the rights.

[†] In a kingdom where a suspect is deemed innocent if he chooses the door behind which an unknown lady is pledged to marry him, or guilty if he chooses the one behind which a tiger waits to eat him, a princess must lose her lover whichever door he picks.

[‡] Barer was furious, fourteen years later, when Sondheim "stole" the title for a much better show of his own.

the whole day was shot. What was I supposed to do? I was getting faster, and after an hour I had nothing more to set.

We stumbled along that way until eventually Marshall collapsed: He couldn't or wouldn't write any more. He was having one of his periodic pill-induced nosedives. I had seen before and would see again how dangerous any drug could be if you took too much. Or even, sometimes, too little. Around that time, with my father's mood still so dark, I told my mother about Dexamyl and she suggested I give him one. He immediately had a personality change like I'd never seen in anybody: "You want to hear this new thing I'm working on?" he said, leaping toward the piano. He was so up I didn't know what to do, except never to give him another.

I never overdid it myself: I would use just enough to let a bit of creativity pop out of a brain cell. It would go "boop!" and I loved that. But you really had to respect the power of something that could fell a giant like Marshall, leaving him—as sometimes happened in the city—lying on his waterbed with the lights off and his television on low and wondering aloud when it would all be over.

Somehow we got the show up; Marshall liked to say it emptied the theater.* That wasn't true, but it wasn't good, even though it starred Dorothy Loudon. To not be good with Dorothy Loudon, a show has to be pretty bad.

Luckily there were other writers at Tamiment to work with when Marshall ground to a halt. One I hit it off with was Fred Ebb, then in his pre–John Kander days.† We wrote a few songs, including a good one

---

* *The Happy Medium*, set "in and around Studio 60" of the MBH TV studios in New York City "tonight," played on the weekend of August 22, 1959. (Parts of it had been performed earlier in the summer.) Luckily, titles aren't copyrightable, because the songs listed in the program included not just "A Little Night Music," but "Good Thing Going," and even "Soliloquy."

† Fred Ebb (1928–2004) earned a spot in Mary's top drawer with his wit, perfect scansion, and always accurate rhymes. In 1962, he paired up with

called "Two Steps Forward, One Step Back," which, again, was not at all
autobiographical, even though I just used the phrase ten seconds ago to
describe my life at the time.

Because Fred was easy to work with and completely sane, we began
that fall to talk about a book musical I'd first broached with Marshall,
who was neither. It was based on an article about a nineteen-year-old
boy I read around then in *Life* magazine—which, coincidentally, Fred had
also read, and thought would make a good musical, too.* In it, the boy,
from the Lower East Side, was accidentally approved for a Carte Blanche
card, which was then a new thing, especially to me, who was so naïve
that I didn't even know I had a Social Security number.† Anyway, the boy
proceeded to go hog wild on a monthlong toot from the Waldorf to
Montreal to Vegas to Havana, picking up girlfriends and buying up bau-
bles. In the full-spread photo, he was shown beaming proudly, with all his
purchases arrayed around him: clothing, liquor, a cocker spaniel puppy.
Another photo showed his family, looking delighted.

That's what I found astonishing: Far from being punished, he was rewarded. Carte Blanche paid the merchants and absorbed the loss. It turns
out that all credit card companies expect to be taken to the cleaners for
a certain amount. It's called "breakage"—the loss you can't repair. And
later I heard that the magazine had paid the family a huge amount of
money for the story. So where's the morality?

I thought we could do a really cheerful musical with a nice sour

....

the also-top-drawer composer John Kander (born 1927); together they
went on to write sixteen major shows, including *Cabaret* and *Chicago*.

* "My $10,000 Credit Card Binge," supposedly by the boy, Joseph R. Mi-
raglia, but sounding like an "as told to" job, appeared in the issue of October 26, 1959.

† Hilton Hotels first offered the Carte Blanche credit card ("your key to
every luxury Hilton has to offer") in 1958. Other credit cards existed by
then, but the idea was still relatively novel.

1960: Marshall Barer, Hal Prince, and Mary. *Carte Blanche* was supposed to be
"a really cheerful musical with a nice sour ending."

ending, a bad-boy *Pal Joey* story in which there is no punishment for
the kid except—we added this part—that the girl he romances with
his ill-got gains dumps him when she finds out the truth. That's *his*
breakage.

Fred and I took the idea, which we called *Carte Blanche* and imagined
for Tony Perkins, to Hal. He liked it, but because he didn't know Fred's
work—no one did yet—he asked us to write a few trial songs together. After we auditioned them, Hal said he didn't think Fred was good enough.[*]

Though Fred very graciously bowed out, it's as if the mark of Cain
were now on the project. You can't imagine the number of people who
were at some point involved or approached.

Marshall sniffed a success and came back to do the lyrics. We got

---

[*] He must have changed his mind by the time *Cabaret* came about.

the Hacketts* to take a stab at the book, but they pulled out because they hated the wry ending. I think Michael Stewart† had a go. Hal even approached, and was screamed off the phone by, S. J. Perelman, who himself had a screw-up son, or maybe better to say a son he screwed up, recently residing in a reformatory. And when George Abbott joined the project, scheduling it on his watch for fall, he too found the ending unpleasant and brought in Martin Charnin. Furthermore, he thought it would be better to change the hero to a heroine. He suggested Carol Burnett.

You can see where this is heading: It was losing its bite and gradually slipping away. Too gradually, because I worked on that sucker, much like a marriage, way longer than I should have. In March of 1960, at Hal's instruction, I even took a research trip to Puerto Rico. (We'd moved the Havana scenes to San Juan because by then Castro had seized power.) This was the first "vacation" I'd taken as a single person, and I was scared, though Hal joined me a few days after I arrived. We both loved it. He even suggested we buy a house to share there: me, him . . . and his mother. No, thank you.

Hal and I were still in a holding pattern, so to speak, and I was see-ing Cord Meyer periodically, at the insistence of his secretary. Around that time, I also started my nicest affair, with a guy in his forties who was so great in bed I'm not even going to tell you his name be-yond Jack. Jack had a classy, proper, and—if he was to be believed—not terribly sexually responsive wife in Boston, but his work as an ed-itor brought him to New York, and to me, most weekdays. Though I

....

* The married team of Albert Hackett and Frances Goodrich wrote, among many other successful things, the screenplay for *The Thin Man* and the stage adaptation of *The Diary of Anne Frank*, which won them a Pulitzer Prize.

† Michael Stewart, né Myron Stuart Rubin (1924–1987), was by then writ-ing the book for *Bye, Bye Birdie* and would soon write *Hello, Dolly!* In be-tween, he worked, for a time, on Mary's Biggest Flop.

teased him about this *Captain's Paradise* arrangement,[*] neither of us ever dreamed of breaking up his marriage. We just had a very good time.

Still, like Winnifred in *Once Upon a Mattress*, I grabbed at every guy I could, to see if maybe he was the one.[†] Before heading to Puerto Rico to conduct the *Carte Blanche* research,[‡] Flora said I had to call up her friend, a Black psychiatrist, when I got there. I did, he was marvelous, and I went to bed with him, too.[§]

Oh, don't look at me that way. Now everyone hooks up on apps, and Instagrams their hickeys. But I was discreet, and not just because I was afraid of being cut off if Mummy found out. I was discreet because what I was doing, however poorly, I was doing to educate and enjoy myself, not to shock others. In a way I was writing my obit: "a woman who tried everything." I damn well didn't want anyone else writing it for me.

....

[*] In the 1953 movie *The Captain's Paradise*, Alec Guinness runs a passenger ship between Gibraltar and Morocco. In Gibraltar he has a respectable wife; in Morocco, Yvonne De Carlo.

[†] From Marshall's lyric for "Shy": "I'm going fishing for a mate. / I'm going to look in every brook. / But how much longer must I wait / With bated breath and hook?"

[‡] *Carte Blanche* was scheduled to open on Broadway—at the Shubert Theatre, no less—in the fall of 1960. Then in early 1961. Then in May of 1961. Then in fall again. Then never.

[§] "The people are wonderful," Mary told an AP reporter writing about her research trip. "I loved them."

30.

THE BREAKAGE

The 1960 Tony Awards* were given out in the Grand Ballroom of the old Astor Hotel in Times Square, not in a real theater as they are today. We sat at round tables, jammed together, and though an orchestra played snippets of Broadway tunes as winners snaked their way to the dais, there were no performances from the season's shows, no medleys or in memoriams, no close-ups of nominees chewing their nails. The ceremony wasn't a Broadway marketing extravaganza but an industry function: a dressier but duller version of an undertakers' dinner. Most of the acceptances were just quick thank-yous, fifteen seconds at most. The whole thing took an hour.

I suppose I went with Marshall, but whomever I went with, the whole thing felt as if I'd fallen into my address book and couldn't get up. I knew all the younger set scrabbling around in the game, and I had the additional, dubious distinction of having grown up on the laps of a lot of the elders. So the Best Musical category was, for me, a monument to incestuousness. Everyone I knew was piled into that one bed.†

....

* The ceremony honoring the season that had begun in May of 1959 was held on Sunday, April 24, 1960. It was broadcast locally on CBS, with Eddie Albert hosting.

† There were no categories for Best Music, Best Lyrics, or Best Book in those days. On the other hand, there was a category for Best Stage

That included Hal, who, when *Carte Blanche* failed to arrive that season, produced *Fiorello!* instead. With him were Mr. Abbott, who directed it and co-wrote the book, Jerry Bock and Sheldon Harnick, who wrote the songs, and the Eckarts, who designed it. Also nominated was *Gypsy*, meaning Steve and Arthur and that masher Jule Styne must have been there. Over at the *Take Me Along** table was Jackie Gleason, who would soon be my employer, though I didn't know it yet. The remaining two nominated shows were *Once Upon a Mattress*—with me and Marshall and Jay and Dean and the Eckarts and Mr. Abbott again and Carol—and, oh yes, *The Sound of Music*. I was literally competing with Daddy. Except that, as usual, there was no competition.

My recent patroness, Mary Martin—wearing, I kid you not, a hoop skirt—had already won the Best Actress award for playing the well-preserved postulant Maria in the show, beating not only Carol in *Mattress* but Ethel Merman in *Gypsy*.† I assumed that Daddy, as producer and composer, would win the big prize as well, which would make things a lot easier for me with Mummy on the phone the next day. So I was as surprised as anyone when Celeste Holm, announcing the winner, said, "And wait till you hear this: It's a tie!"

It would make a better story if the tie had been a father-daughter one, but no, the first winner named was *Fiorello!* Tall, lordly George spoke for the show, complaining about the staging of the awards ceremony itself. The path to the dais was a mess, he said.

That was true, as I would soon find out. After the *Fiorello!* troupe collected its medallions, Celeste announced *The Sound of Music* as the other winner. None of the producers or songwriters, or producer-

....

Technician. That year it went to John Walters, the chief carpenter for *The Miracle Worker*. He was unavailable, so naturally the award was accepted on his behalf by Julie Newmar in a tiara and knee-length chinchilla.

* This was the unlikely musical, with a score by Bob Merrill, based on *Ah, Wilderness* by Eugene O'Neill.

† "You can't buck a nun," Ethel said philosophically.

songwriters, were there to pick up the prize. Daddy and Mummy were in Italy, vacationing; Ockie was in Bucks County, dying; the co-producer Leland Hayward was who knows where; and Dick Halliday, Mary Martin's long-fingered husband, was supposedly in Brazil. So three of us kids—Ockie's son Jimmy, Mary's son Larry Hagman, and I*—went to the dais to accept the award, along with the book writers, Howard Lindsay and Russel Crouse.

Who knows what I would have said? It was a very weird situation. I have no doubt that Daddy and Ockie, despite "Do-Re-Mi," deserved the award over me, if not over *Gypsy*. But there was something sad and pro forma about it, like acknowledging an ancestor's grave, especially knowing as we did that there would be no more H in the R&H shows.† I was worried about R's future, and the fact that Daddy had put me on standby cut two ways. I was proud but also queasy; I was trying to get further away, not closer. But I knew he was terrified of his gifts fading, which in my opinion was in fact beginning to happen. Not yet in the melody but in the foursquare rhythms. "Climb ev'ry mountain." "The hills are alive." It's like he was composing on an organ.

Not that I would have said anything like that. However snide I am in private, I know the limits when a microphone's in front of me. And then I step over them just a bit.

As it turned out, only Russel spoke, which was fine with me. But why did I let myself be photographed—and televised—wearing those nerd glasses? So I could see deeply into Celeste Holm's décolletage? In other publicity photos of the period I look pretty good: I'm finally slim, I've

....

* Yes, Larry Hagman of later *Dallas* fame. As for Leland Hayward's kids, they were in no shape. Their mother, Margaret Sullavan, had died that New Year's Day of a barbiturate overdose. Two of the three kids would themselves be suicides; the third, Brooke, wrote the family memoir *Haywire*.

† Not until Rodgers paired up with Sheldon Harnick on *Rex*, fifteen years later.

perfected my black-and-pearls style, my eyes are clear, my skin unlined.*
But at the Tony Awards, with the men all in tuxes and the women mostly
in shoulderless gowns and big jewelry, I seemed determined to mouse it
up in a meek floral tea dress.

In that room I was someone's daughter, and I guess I dressed the part.

But I was someone's mother outside it. None of the twenty-two other
writers nominated were—mothers, I mean. Only two were women.† Back
then there were barely any female writers on Broadway at all, let alone
composers; besides me, you could count the women who had produced
scores for Broadway book musicals on the ring finger of your left hand:
Kay Swift.‡ A few months later, *Irma La Douce* would introduce, and say
farewell to, Marguerite Monnot, who had made a name writing for Piaf
but was never heard from on Broadway again.§ I guess Ann Ronell, June
Carroll (Leonard Sillman's sister), and Mary Cohan (George M. Cohan's
daughter) contributed songs to revues, but Carroll and Cohan didn't

....

* On the other hand, you can frequently see in these photos where the
lines would come from. One of Mary at the piano that year, with six-
year-old Tod, five-year-old Nina, and three-year-old Kim looking on wor-
shipfully as their mother "composes," features packs of Parliaments and
Winstons in the foreground. And this was a staged shot!

† Neither Lillian Hellman, nominated for *Toys in the Attic*, nor Lorraine
Hansberry, nominated for *A Raisin in the Sun*, had children. But one of
the previous year's winners—Dorothy Fields, who wrote the lyrics and
co-wrote the book for *Redhead*—had two.

‡ Kay Swift (1897–1993) wrote the music for the 1930 musical *Fine and
Dandy*. She was also George Gershwin's lover. Oscar Levant introduced
them at parties as "George Gershwin and the future Miss Kay Swift"—
though he used that line about many couples who were never going
to wed.

§ With its jolly whores and penguin ballet, *Irma La Douce* is a creepy
stinker.

write whole shows and there is some doubt about what, in fact, they did write.[*]

But wait. You say I'm being sexist. You're right.

I'm discrediting those women exactly the same way people discredited me. *Maybe she couldn't really write anything. Maybe her fill-in-the-blank male relative did it for her.*

I wasn't a very enlightened feminist, not much of a solidarity type, since I couldn't yet see around the corner of my own situation. Which is forgivable, the way I think it's forgivable that gay men of that era stayed in the closet. And anyway, forgivable or not, I don't forgive myself, because it wasn't just a bad way of thinking, it was a bad way of acting. This trait of mine is what later made me such a prime sidekick for Arthur's malice: I was so eager not to be his victim that instead I became his accomplice. My real thinking went deep underground while I took the course of least resistance. I behaved like my own worst enemies. I was, at least a little, an antifeminist woman, an anti-Semitic Jew, a snob bohemian. I would have been an excellent snitch in Vichy France, had I not been ten years old and living on the Upper East Side at the time.

Later I would go out of my way to support women artists. And at the time there were a number of women lyricists I knew and at least pretended to root for: Betty Comden, Carolyn Leigh. But I shied away from them as collaborators, including even the best of them, Dorothy Fields,[†] who sought me out right after *Mattress*. I ought to have leapt

....

[*] Between 1934 and 1968, Leonard Sillman (1908–1982) honchoed a series of New Faces revues that gave dozens of writers and performers, including Henry Fonda, Imogene Coca, Eartha Kitt, Paul Lynde, Maggie Smith, and Madeline Kahn, a Broadway start. George M. Cohan was George M. Cohan.

[†] Dorothy Fields (1905–1974) was a top-drawer lyricist who, in addition to *Redhead*, had written with Jerome Kern ("The Way You Look Tonight") and would later hitch up with Cy Coleman (*Sweet Charity*). Her father, Lew Fields, once a great vaudeville comic, produced many of Rodgers

at the chance to work with her! Not only was she a fine lyricist but the Fieldses were Rodgers-approved. Is that why I ducked? Or was it just that, shamefully, I thought men were superior, not only to her but to me?

And this, too: Collaboration—in the musical theater sense, not the Vichy sense—is so much like a romance, however dysfunctional, that I didn't want to share it with women. Maybe I would have been better off if I'd swung both ways in song and in life. But the one time I worked with a woman lyricist, years later, it was no fun. The erotic part of song-writing, the way you mate words and music, is for me very heterosexual. Even though I did it best with gay men.

Which reminds me that for a blink of time around the Tony Awards that year I had music of mine playing in two Broadway theaters. A song Marshall and I wrote at Tamiment was included in *From A to Z*, a dead-on-arrival revue starring Hermione Gingold. The song was called "Hire a Man."*

Which also reminds me, this was around the time I got engaged.

I'd been going out with a very nice guy called Paul Heller, who'd been an assistant set designer at Westport the summer before Steve and I arrived. I'm not sure how we met, or re-met, but Paul was a sweetheart and I knew I couldn't go on forever the way I had been. As I cleared the decks, he was the last man standing. (Well, the last but one.) Hal and

....

and Hart's early hits, for which her brother Herbert wrote many of the books. Her brother Joseph co-wrote the books for *Wonderful Town*, *Gentlemen Prefer Blondes*, and *Flower Drum Song*.

* *From A to Z* opened on April 20 and closed on May 7. The letters of the alphabet were matched with twenty-six sketches and songs by a ton of newcomers, including Woody Allen and Jerry Herman. "Hire a Man," with a lyric satirizing big business that Barer had shopped around heavily among his composer friends until Mary bit, was pretty good. But the critics didn't like anything about *From A to Z* much, including Gingold. Richard Rodgers didn't like it, either; the first act ended with a spoof called "The Sound of Schmaltz," in which Gingold played the nanny to the Klaptrap Family Singers.

I were now just colleagues; my weekday captain's paradise with Boston Jack had run its course. I even managed to put a full stop to the madness with Marshall, or at least a semicolon. And, screwing up my courage, I finally called Cord to say we couldn't see each anymore, no matter what his secretary felt.

"Why not?" he asked.

"I've found someone I'm very involved with," I said.

"Oh, and I suppose you don't care that I now have cancer of the lip?" I didn't, in fact.

Anyway, just after *Mattress* closed on Broadway in July and before I left for England in August to rehearse the London production, Paul gave me a very pretty little pearl ring to signify our engagement.

I didn't tell my parents, and Marshall was too busy with his own problems to notice the problem on my finger. He was so depressed by the closing of *Mattress* and the problems with *Carte Blanche* that even though we'd landed a job writing songs for a television special, he was pretty much commuting to Dr. Feelgood's every morning and shooting up at home every night. I mean the genuine, original Dr. Feelgood,[*] whose crazy office was down the block from me on East Seventy-second Street. His shots, which even Jack Kennedy bent over for, were supposedly "miracle tissue regenerators," and why not? They were a concoction of amphetamines, vitamins, painkillers, and human placenta. As far as I know they only killed one person: the Kennedy photographer Mark Shaw, whose ex, Pat Suzuki, starred in *Flower Drum Song*. Another addict was Alan Jay Lerner, who infuriated Daddy when they tried to work together, soon after Ockie's death, on *I Picked a Daisy*. When it turned out that Alan was too crazy to work—on the rare occasions he showed up, he had ten Band-Aids on ten fingers because he chewed his cuticles to the point of infection—Daddy dropped the project like the bomb that it was.[†]

....

[*] After years reigning supreme with his syringe as "Dr. Feelgood" and "Miracle Max," Max Jacobson (1900–1979) lost his medical license in 1975.

[†] With Burton Lane taking over, it eventually became *On a Clear Day You Can See Forever*.

But if Marshall was too blitzed to notice my engagement, Steve wasn't. For him, no one I got involved with was ever good enough. Paul was too dumb or too square or too old or too unambitious or too this or too that—I don't remember which.

Actually, he wasn't any of those things.* The only thing wrong with Paul wasn't something wrong with him, it was something wrong with me. I was twenty-nine. I could hear the party-game music winding down and all I wanted was a good-enough chair.

People get married for worse reasons. But also for better ones.

Having stashed the kids in the Hamptons with the Peruvian nanny for the summer, I flew across the Atlantic fuming, with Steve's comments in my ears. Did he want me never to marry again? Never to have more children? (Maybe not—everyone thought I had enough.) And what was he offering as an alternative? If nobody else was good enough, that was his fault, for being so excellent.

I was still fuming when I arrived at my old friend Ginny Ryan's—the sister of my gamester pal Johnny, and the daughter of the social-climbing Nin.† Ginny had married David Ogilvy, a Scottish laird and heir to the earldom of Airlie. Seventy thousand acres gives you room to think, and sheep provide the right chewing-it-over mood. In a room in the castle that came with the earldom I felt properly Romantic as I wrote Steve what I elegantly called a shit-or-get-off-the-pot letter.

What can I say? I'd always loved him. He either had to love me back or finally let me go.

....

* Certainly not unambitious. Paul Heller (1927–2020) soon became successful in Hollywood, producing *David and Lisa* in 1962 and dozens more later, including *My Left Foot*.

† Though a native of New Jersey, Virginia Fortune Ryan (born 1933) wound up a Lady of the Bedchamber in service to Queen Elizabeth II.

31.

EAST SIDE STORY

Within seconds of my arrival in London for *Mattress* rehearsals in August 1960, Ockie, back in Doylestown, died. In his honor, marquees were blacked out on Broadway, where *The Sound of Music* was ten months into its run, and on the West End, too, where it would open the following spring.

Daddy's tribute to Ockie was to move on as fast as he could. I don't blame him. He was only fifty-eight. He was always afraid that, like a shark, his talent would suffocate if he didn't keep exercising it. I don't mean that he didn't feel genuine loss after seventeen years of a successful collaboration. But Ockie wasn't the "dear friend" Daddy described him as later—no one was—and certainly not irreplaceable. (No one was that, either.) Quite the opposite: He'd long since started sniffing out possible new lyricists to work with, including not just me, a pill to be taken in case of emergency only, but Alan Jay Lerner* and others. In the end, he settled on himself, and started work on *No Strings* almost immediately.

Or maybe even sooner. In *Musical Stages* Daddy says he began writing

---

* Fritz Loewe had said he would retire after *Camelot* opened that December, and did, leaving Lerner free to play the field with Burton Lane, Charles Strouse, André Previn, and Leonard Bernstein. Playing the field was Lerner's pattern; he was also married eight times, which seems less like romance than roulette.

No Strings after seeing Diahann Carroll sing "Goody Goody" on the Jack Paar show in April 1961. But rehearsals for *No Strings* began that December. Even for the great Richard Rodgers, especially writing both music and lyrics, that would have been astonishingly fast—and the musical's book, by Samuel Taylor, also had to be written, from scratch. I suspect that Daddy had the idea in mind before Ockie died. He certainly had Diahann in mind. He'd been perving on her ever since she auditioned for *Flower Drum Song* in 1958. I don't know whether their rumored affair really happened, but if it didn't it wouldn't have been for his lack of trying. In rehearsal photographs for *No Strings* he's got his hands all over her.

Anyway, when the news of Ockie's death broke, and in those days it really was news, I was the only member of either family—the Rodgerses or the Hammersteins—in London.

That put me in the peculiar position of doing interviews there that combined eulogy and, because *Mattress* was set to open in September, self-promotion. Not that the British press wanted eulogies. They were really very seamy, trying to turn anything into a scandal.* They wanted to know about Oscar's marital misdemeanors, or how he and Daddy didn't really get along.

I could have said plenty about all of that. Though Steve would later describe Daddy as a man with "infinite talent but limited soul" and Ockie as the opposite,† the truth was more complicated. Ockie was no saint, even aside from that long-term affair with Temple Texas. The world rightly knew him as a gifted and generous thinker, a compassionate teacher and taskmaster. More than any other major artist in the commercial theater of the day, he was all conscience, all principle. And he was more than kind to me.

....

* Perhaps it was not useful (though it remains highly enjoyable) that Mary gave an interview in which she called London critics "frustrated literary talents" and the upper class in general "sick, inbred, and narrow-minded." Helpfully diagnosing the city's other problems, she added: "There are so many sick marriages and so few psychiatrists."

† In *Newsweek*, no less, in 1973.

1961: Mary, in the last year of the "interregnum." "The three and three-quarter years between my marriages . . . were the most crowded of my life."

But a saint? I don't think he was even much of a father. I now believe—though the Hammerstein children apparently don't—that it was not benign neglect he treated them with; it was plain old garden-variety neglect, with a dash of malice sprinkled on top. His son Bill* once confided in me the story of how Ockie took him to the pond behind the house to teach him to skate. He was doing just fine until Ockie stuck his cane out, deliberately tripping him. Was that meant as some kind of lesson in how to take a fall?

Despite his liberal bona fides, he treated the world the same way. Another time, Bill was walking down the street with Ockie when, a few feet ahead of them, a boy on a bicycle crashed to the ground. Bill tried to see

------

* William Hammerstein (1918–2001) was Oscar Hammerstein's son with his pre-Dorothy wife, Myra Finn. A theatrical producer and director in his own right, Bill spent the last decades of his life helping to maintain his father's artistic properties.

if the boy needed help, but Ockie, not wanting to get involved, pulled Bill across the street.

Carefully taught? You're telling me.*

I'd witnessed enough of Ockie's behavior to know that he and Daddy, however different their demeanors, were absolutely alike in the way they indulged, prioritized, and protected their talent. Maybe you have to be at least a partial monster to clear the path to do great work.

I didn't say any of that to the British press. Possibly I considered how monstrous my own life might look if summarized by a few tawdry anecdotes and subjected to unsympathetic scrutiny. For instance, I was at the time (a) trying to disentangle myself from my various postmarital lovers; (b) hoping for a response from Steve to my Hail Mary letter from Scotland; and (c) for no good reason having a London affair with Jerry Whyte, the production supervisor for *Mattress* there. Yes, the same Jerry Whyte who was Daddy's abettor and procurer. He had a magnificent room at the Savoy that overlooked the Thames. Like him, it smelled of horses.

But you'll want to know about (b). In the letter I'd said I would be back in New York for a few days in early September to tape a TV show for which Marshall and I had written a couple of songs.† Trying to be

....

* Though sometimes criticized as a preachy indictment of racism, "You've Got to Be Carefully Taught," a song from *South Pacific*, is something subtler: an indictment of parents who train their children to hate people who are different. In 1953, in response to the national tour then playing Atlanta, the Georgia state legislature introduced a bill to ban entertainment, like *South Pacific*, whose underlying philosophy was "inspired by Moscow." One state representative said that the song threatened the American way of life by encouraging miscegenation. Despite this pressure, Rodgers and Hammerstein wouldn't cut it—and if you license *South Pacific* legally, neither can you.

† "No Place Like Home" was an hour-long revue starring Carol Burnett, Rosemary Clooney, José Ferrer, and Dick Van Dyke. It aired on NBC on Thanksgiving afternoon. *TV Guide* described it as a "spoof of domestic

casual, but actually feeling preemptively hostile, I wrote something like: "If you're still interested, get in touch with me then. You know how to do that."

I didn't expect him to. I was sure I had scared him off for good. Meanwhile, I rehearsed my show about the second-rate princess who is desperate for a husband.

But when I got to New York for the NBC taping, Steve called and said, "Let's talk."

I didn't talk much; he did. He showed me the new place he'd just bought for $115,000 thanks to the movie deal for *Gypsy*, which promptly fell through, but then came together again. It was a town house on East Forty-ninth Street in Turtle Bay Gardens, next door to Katharine Hepburn.[*] "This is where we could live," he explained, showing me the bottom two floors, which were then a duplex. "And there's plenty of room upstairs for your kids," he added, pointing through the ceiling toward the triplex he was then renting to the singer Anita Ellis[†] and her not very nice husband, a neurologist and big-game hunter.

He never used the M-word and neither did I. But that's what it was intended to be: a marriage, at least of the trial variety. We gave ourselves a year, to start when I got back from London again, after *Mattress* opened.

....

man's foibles." In one Rodgers-Barer song, about having a baby, Barer brilliantly rhymed "alchemy" and "talcumy."

[*] Sondheim once heard Hepburn banging furiously out back where their private gardens joined the communal one; when he went to investigate, he found her barefoot and red-faced, complaining that he was keeping her up all night with his composing. She later told Rex Reed that Steve was "a most disagreeable person" because he complained when smoke from her fireplace infiltrated his house.

[†] Anita Ellis (1920–2015) was a pop singer before she went into analysis— and a jazz singer when she emerged. Her brother was Larry Kert (1930–1991), who starred in *West Side Story* and later took over the role of Bobby in *Company* from Dean Jones.

I know what you are saying: *Mary, don't!*

Had I not just freed myself from this sort of thing with my first husband? Well, no. I was a patsy in that marriage. Here I would be—what? A co-conspirator? The follier half of a folie à deux?

And what would Steve be? Even if I loved him, and I did, what was in it for him?

But his shrink—the one whose door Steve had rigged to play "One for My Baby"—was pushing him to have a "normal" relationship, and perhaps not having to push too hard. Together, I thought, she and Steve would fix his problem, and together, I thought, he and I would fix mine.

So I clamped my ears shut to the hurricane bells ringing everywhere[*] and decided I would give it a go. But the omens along the way were immediately unfavorable. First omen: Paul Heller. When I gave him back his little pearl ring, explaining that I was taking a flier with Steve instead of a sure thing with him, he looked at me funny and said I was totally out of my mind. Even I knew enough not to write that off as jealousy.

Second omen: London, where *Mattress* opened to seventeen—count 'em, seventeen—horrifying reviews.[†] Turns out that not everyone is Carol Burnett, and the person who most wasn't Carol was Jane Connell.[‡] She was working very hard to eke out laughs Carol got with an eyebrow. And maybe, too, the Brits didn't appreciate our humor.

Third omen: When I called Steve in New York to commiserate, and to tell him my flight information so he could meet me at the airport,

....

[*] Some of them were real: Hurricane Donna struck Long Island on September 12. The Coast Guard rounded everyone up, including Mary's children, who had been left in the care of a nanny in a rented house on Dune Road in Quogue.

[†] "Funny only in spots," trumpeted the *Daily Telegraph*. But the *Daily Express* raved: "Although this may be good enough for New York, it would be very far from halfway good enough for London even as a pantomime."

[‡] Jane Connell (1925–2013) fared better as Agnes Gooch in *Mame* a few years later.

he said, "Meet you at the *airport?*" as if I'd asked him to eat the leg of a piano.

His plan was that I should haul myself to Manhattan. There I was to join him at a party being given for Antonio de Almeida, a conductor whose brother Louis d'Almeida—for some reason spelled differently—was the producer who'd let us out of the contract to produce *Mattress* after Tamiment.*

So that's what I did. I cabbed home from the airport, fixed my hair, and met up with Steve. Once he got me to the door of the party, though, he promptly vanished, which was not in my lexicon as the behavior of someone who liked you as a friend, let alone someone who was sort of supposed to be getting experimentally married to you.

I'll give myself this: I never moved into that house in Turtle Bay with the big-game hunter upstairs and Hepburn next door and the ghost of Maxwell Perkins—Hemingway's editor, who once owned it—in the floorboards. But I didn't give up, either. Instead, on occasion, in a cab or after dinner, Steve would say, "Do you want to stay over?" and I'd say, "Sure," even if I wasn't.

I don't know what the hell he thought I was doing there. Even though he was thirty, I don't think Steve had the foggiest idea what people who love each other did. Which begs the question: *Did* we love each other?

Can one beg an answer? He wasn't in love with me, certainly, and I wasn't really physically attracted to him. I just loved him, thoroughly enough for nothing else to matter. Do you not believe in that? Have you never seen *Carousel?*†

So we would get into the same bed, side by side, frozen with fear. We just lay there. We didn't discuss anything; we didn't do anything. If we touched, it was en passant.

....

* The third brother is the painter George d'Almeida.

† Or, for that matter, *Passion.* The 1994 Sondheim–James Lapine musical, based on the movie *Passione d'Amore,* is about a homely, sickly spinster who nevertheless gets a handsome young captain to fall in love with her. For whatever reason, Mary did not like the show.

The whole thing was wildly uncomfortable. I guess eventually we went to sleep. And I can't think how I got up and got dressed and got home before the kids woke up the next morning—because I didn't want them to know I hadn't been home. It was so humiliating. I can't believe either of us put ourselves through that.

And yet it kept happening.

Was there anything satisfying about the arrangement? Nothing. It was too fraught with what I assume was revulsion on his part, if not on mine. Like a lot of women, certainly of that era, I was responsive to guys' advances if they knew what they were doing, but, willing as I was, I was never the aggressor. We just kept reoccupying this strange purgatory. All the guilt of sinning with none of the pleasure.

At some point I finally said: Look, Steve, I have three children who expect to see me in the morning, so these last-minute invitations to spend the night are difficult. We have to set things up ahead of time, make specific plans.

He replied that it was often impossible to reach me—which was true; that's why he bought me for my thirtieth birthday, that same winter, an additional phone line. Not only that, but, shades of Daddy, he wrote— and performed at my birthday party in January—a song called "Mommy on the Telephone" whose tune included the touch-tone pitches of the new number: LEhigh 5–5539.* The lyric made me seem more like a zoo-keeper than a mother: "Tod has hidden Mommy's Frigidaire. / Nina hid her extra hair. / Kimmy hid herself and forgot just where." That was pretty accurate.

But the new line didn't help. Instead of calling to make specific plans to spend the night together, he stopped inviting me entirely. I would call him instead, and that's when he began to be resentful. One side of his mind must have known it wasn't my fault, but the other side must have said, "Holy shit, get her off my back!" For him, with his crazy mother,

---

* Mary turned thirty on January 11, 1961. Touch-tone service was introduced in the United States in 1963. Perhaps there were prototypes?

there was nothing worse than someone wanting to have a hold of you when you didn't want to be held.

What I wanted wasn't his concern—nor, apparently, that of his shrink. As I understood it, from a remove, I was a bit of a pawn in their psychiatric gamesmanship. They were working through what love could be in his life, a process that would take many more years.* For now, for all I knew, he was celibate, even outside our "marriage."

But if I was a pawn, I wasn't just Steve's. Marshall, my work husband, was in full undermining mode. Sometime that fall he decided to disabuse me of whatever illusions I still harbored about Steve's heterosexual potential. "Guess who was at the gayest of gay parties I went to last night?" he said one day while we were working.

His motive was transparent: to punish me for not choosing him. If I was going to marry a gay guy, he felt, why not the one who *wanted* to be married, who loved kids and could get it up for a girl if necessary?

But he wasn't lying about Steve. To prove it to myself I pulled a little trick. On nights I wasn't staying over, I'd call him after going to the theater or dinner together. If he didn't answer—if the service picked up after the requisite number of rings—I knew he had just dropped me off and gone on his way.

The service always picked up.

I didn't confront him. I just said, "Steve, this isn't working, is it?"

And he said, "No, it's not." Not meanly. Merely an observation.

I'm not sure he would have known how to call it off himself. He was probably looking for a kind way to unhook the fish. That's me all over: The fish did it for him.

....

* And at least one more woman: Lee Remick. He adored her, but if push had come to shove, the results would have been the same. Luckily for both of them, it didn't.

32.

WILL NOT ENDURE

'm not a crier, as I've said and you'll see. But I was thirty, and for more than half my life all I'd wanted was to marry that boy who beat me at chess. I'd been involved with other very talented men, like Dean Fuller, but those relationships were really just about sex and friendship. Anyway, I never felt the same about anyone who wasn't a musician, and only top-drawer musicians at that. It goes right back to my father, of course, which is so Freudian it's stupid. But artistic people have a certain magic if they're any good. And Steve was good. Who better? I now see, it's so obvious, I was trying to glom on to someone whose gift I could be proud of, in a way I couldn't really be proud on my own. Because unfortunately I had an ear for the best and wasn't deceived by my merely pleasant abilities, which I am not putting down. But knowing what I knew, feeling how I felt, who, after Steve, could ever be enough? Something was going to have to give, and clearly that something was me. I fell apart. Pathetic, really.

Later I understood that the failure of the "marriage" was a good thing wrapped in a bad thing. But at the time, my infatuation—no, it was more than that, let's say it plainly: It was the love of my life—kept me from crediting not only the huge incompatibilities between us but also the little ones that, in the end, probably matter more than things like sex if daily happiness is part of what you're after. Like sleeping habits. I thought we both got up at the same time: me very early, Steve very early. But it turns out not. In all those years that I'd call him as soon as the kids were at school, or wherever they went, he politely never pointed out that he preferred to sleep in. And to stay up all hours. When I was heading to bed so I'd be ready for the dawn birdcall of children, he was just getting started; only after a great late dinner and hours of games, after everyone went home, did he start work.*

In so many ways he was much more bohemian than I. He dressed badly—even his ties looked rumpled—while I now wore clothes Mummy couldn't argue with. (A lot of them were in fact hers, adapted.) His parents were divorced, which counted as debonair in those days. (I only wished mine were.†) He was way more adventurous, and not just in his harmonies. One birthday, knowing I've always loved pocket watches, he gave me a beautiful Victorian one. I assumed it wasn't ever going to work—and if I'd opened the case, I wouldn't have known what to do anyway—so I never tried to set it. But Adam discovered it years later, jimmied it right open, and found a nice little packet of cocaine hidden in the works. Steve just assumed that I was as much into experimenting with drugs as he was; it was part of his game mentality to try everything. I suppose if he'd managed to squeeze some Dexamyl back there, that might have been different; I prefer my drugs prescription.

Not that I was some dull wifey without a husband. But my unconventionality was, in a way, conventional. I was a dogged worker who didn't consider any assignment beneath her, as men too often do. After three years I was still assisting on Lenny's Young People's Concerts for five hundred dollars an episode. Meanwhile I was writing a television revue with

---

* At this particular moment he was working on something called *Roman Comedy*, a musical based on Plautus with a book by Burt Shevelove and Larry Gelbart. A year later, produced by Hal, it was *A Funny Thing Happened on the Way to the Forum*, and a hit.

† But that's not really true. They were surely more useful psychologically as a bogeycouple than they would have been separately.

Martin Charnin and Woody Allen for U.S. Steel.* Marty I'd known since
West Side Story;† Steve had heard some of the lyrics he was beginning to
write for revues around town and recommended him to me when Marshall was away on one of his peeve binges. And when old Arthur Shimkin
of Golden Records contacted me just as I was falling apart to ask if I'd like
to set some of Shakespeare's lyrics for a recording by Maurice Evans,‡ I
of course said yes, despite his description of them as songs for the fools
and fairies. Too close to home?

I would have expected to be past Golden Records by then. But when
you take what you can get and do your best, it can't be dishonorable.
Maurice was really quite good intoning highlights from famous Shakespeare scenes, and we got singers like Jane White to warble my settings,
which were also really quite good. Looking at the manuscripts today I
notice two things. One: My notation is beginning to seem more human
and less like the work of an epileptic spider. Two: Even though it took
me way too long to work them out with my slow hands, the harmonies
are more adventurous than I thought.§ I especially like this madrigal, "O
Mistress Mine," from *Twelfth Night*: "Youth's a stuff will not endure." It
helps to have a great lyricist, and a dead one.¶

....

* *The United States Steel Hour* (1953–1963) was a Golden Age of Television
anthology series that drew a lot of material and talent from Broadway.

† Martin Charnin (1934–2019) played Big Deal, one of the lesser Jets, in
the original cast.

‡ Maurice Evans (1901–1989) was a classical English actor who popu-
larized Shakespeare for American audiences in the days when that was
considered possible on television. Later, when it wasn't, he played Saman-
tha's father on *Bewitched* and Dr. Zaius in *Planet of the Apes*.

§ Here's a third: As was always the case in Mary's settings, the scansion of
the lyrics is immaculate, no syllable ever forced by the exigencies of the
music to sit on the wrong beat.

¶ *Introduction to Shakespeare* includes incidental music for *A Midsummer*

1961: Martin Charnin and Mary (left), and, in the back corner,
Woody Allen, at a casting session for their *United States Steel Hour* revue.
"We went wild and wrote the most outrageous, countercultural,
taboo material we could think of."

The *Steel Hour* was not beneath anyone. It was considered high-class
even if, at that moment, its producers were looking for a lowly revue.
Flora, my agent but not for much longer, explained that we would be
paid ten thousand dollars, whether they used what we wrote or not.
That was a huge sum at a time when tickets on Broadway topped out at
something like nine dollars. At least I think it was a huge sum, but you
know about me and my zeroes: I'm still no good at them, in any sense
of the word, which is bad for the bankbook but good for charities. Even

Night's Dream plus half a dozen settings from *The Tempest*, *As You Like It*,
and *Twelfth Night*. No heirs complained about the slightly adapted diction
and spelling of "Oh Mistress Mine," a delightful song that wound up in
the 1993 revue *Hey, Love*.

though an aptitude for math is always said to correlate with an aptitude for music, Daddy and I and Adam all hated it—three composers in a row.

Anyway, we went wild and wrote the most outrageous, countercultural, taboo material we could think of, things no commercial producer would let us do. I remember they wanted us to mention U.S. Steel in some of the sketches or lyrics, and we did, but maybe not flatteringly. There was also a song, I think, about cigarettes causing cancer.* When we auditioned the results for a room of stiffs and suits, they just about turned into ash themselves. So they paid us the promised money and home we went.

But what was at home, aside from three children who didn't give a rat's ass, nor should they, about whether I was happy, as long as I showed up? They had by now gotten used to having their daddy a short walk away. No one else was satisfied with the situation. You can't imagine the pressure, internal and external, to remarry. The internal was bad enough. I knew I had to do something about my life; I couldn't sit around and sob until I was ninety and dead. But I was infuriated by what that life had turned into. My anger was much more hopeless than the kind I'd felt as a child; as a child I assumed life would be better the minute I got out from under my parents' oppositional thumbs. But once I *was* out, I could no longer *get* out. You couldn't get out of your life, except, like Grandpa Ben, via the terrace.

With his usual delicacy Daddy said, "There must be somebody who wants to marry someone with three children," as if I were a warty ogre. His idea was that there's a lid for every pot, but I wasn't interested in someone who would consent to be with me so we could boil a chicken together. I wanted someone I wanted to be with, and that was much more difficult to find.

....

* The surgeon general's report on smoking would not come out for three more years, but the writing was on the wall. Or at least the nicotine stains were.

"There are no men in New York!" I complained to Burt on the phone.

"There's Henry Guettel."

"Henry Guettel is a bore."

For the first time in our friendship, Burt raised his voice at me. "Henry Guettel is *not* a bore!" he boomed.

Around that time, I began to run into Judy Abbott at the playground. As you can imagine, I hated the playground. Fun for kids but soul-crushing for proper adults. Anyway, Judy, who in the course of her three bad marriages had adopted two kids before getting pregnant with a third, must have noticed this because, one day, she said to me, "What's the matter, don't you like your children?" Which was a stupid, though in her case understandable, conclusion to draw because her father didn't like her. When she was dying expensively twenty years later and asked him for help with the bills, he said, "Why can't you be like all my other friends who have cancer?" He liked people to die bravely, pecuniously, and silently.

Anyway, she thought that my bringing work to the park—I probably had music paper in the stroller or lyrics in my purse—was a sign of bad mothering. Especially when, she always assumed, I didn't "need" the money that work would earn.

What I needed, she said, was a good husband.

"You're one to talk," I answered. She was the type who could be snappish but who, if you snapped back, would promptly burst into tears. Then, before you could apologize, she'd upshift to bossy. But that didn't mean she was wrong.

"You have to get off your ass," she said. "Men don't grow on trees." She suggested I give a big party.

So I gave a big party I don't remember anything about.

"Try again!"

I gave a smaller party this time. The men weren't growing there either. But while the maid was cleaning up after, the doorbell rang. It was Henry Guettel.

We interrupt this program for a bulletin. I'm so glad to have reached this point in the story. It's like finding your way home in a song, after the bridge.* I know I set out to shock everyone with the truth, but it's tire-some, isn't it? And kind of grandiose, don't you think?†

We take that under advisement and move forward. Even though mov-ing forward eventually means heading downhill. I mean, look, we have just barely introduced Hank and yet, fifty-two years later, as we speak, it's the end of 2013 and he's gone. As for me, between my weight and my arthritis, I have visions of ending up as asparagus. Spoiler alert! Youth's a stuff will not endure.

But it will be lovely to get to know Hank again. The three and three-quarter years between my marriages, from January 1958 to Octo-ber 1961, were the most crowded of my life: crowded with work that fi-nally went somewhere, and crowded with affairs that, all but one, didn't. I will leave it to others to judge my achievement in both areas—but it's

....

* The bridge, or release, of a standard song usually moves into a differ-ent, contrasting tonality; once there, it may have trouble wiggling its way back.

† No, Mary, I don't, and I'm going to come out of this footnote closet to say so. You're too hard on yourself, or hard on yourself for the wrong things. We were talking earlier about Jane Austen. In 1961, exactly 150 years after *Sense and Sensibility* was published, not much about the crush-ing need for a woman to be married had changed. In some ways, for a woman like you, born into a world of privilege, the enhanced expectation of personal satisfaction only made it worse. Why shouldn't you, like Aus-ten's young women, want the marriage of minds your upbringing and gifts had prepared you to appreciate? You may have been racing around in a cab instead of on the moors, but like Elinor Dashwood you knew what you wanted—just not where to find it. You were on a scavenger hunt!

Dignity before maturity is the real grandiosity, and a form of fore-closing on yourself. Perhaps abjuring it will look clumsy to some. It looked that way, you say, to your parents, who wanted you demure. But "demure"—shy!—is something a woman of ambition cannot afford to be. To be demure is to accept the idea that one's gifts are not for opening. What kind of heroine would you be if you complied?

true: No one can say I didn't do everything I could, opening every door and flying through it even if I immediately fell into a pit or just smacked my face on another door. For some reason, maybe the energy released into the universe by my divorce, everything I did at that time led to more things to do, and the chaos of my career to that point began to look a lot more orderly, with a clear direction.

That too would turn out to be an illusion, but it was a highly useful one for a while.

Anyway: The doorbell rang.

PART III

33.

AREN'T WE ALL?

t wasn't entirely a surprise. I'd met Hank—though some historians disagree—the previous winter at a pre-Christmas cocktail party on far West Seventy-second Street, almost in the river, in the large apartment that John Kander was then sharing with the Goldman brothers for pennies a month.* I knew Johnny as a brilliant rehearsal pianist; I had in fact asked him to come to Tamiment when the guy who was supposed to play for *Mattress* turned out to be a drunk who slept in his car, sometimes while driving it. Johnny said thanks, but he finally had a job in New York and felt he should stay for that; it was *Gypsy*.

I knew the Goldmans, too, and had even dated Bill, which was a mistake. They and Johnny had all gone to Oberlin, and before that, as boys, to camp in Wisconsin, and were now scraping around the edges of the-

---

* William Goldman (1931–2018) wrote novels, plays, screenplays, and *The Season*, a classic if homophobic portrait of a year in the theater industry. Adam Guettel would later work with him on adapting Goldman's screenplay for *The Princess Bride* into a musical, but the project fell apart. James Goldman (1927–1998) was a screenwriter and playwright as well; his book for *Follies* had the immense good fortune to be attached to one of the great musical theater scores. The monthly rent on the nine-room apartment the brothers shared with Kander was $275.

1931: Henry Arthur Guettel, age three. "Very Finzi-Contini."

atrical New York, writing musicals in various combinations.* Johnny was probably the most talented of them, though he didn't seem to know it, because he was certainly the most modest. Was the modesty something to do with his having grown up in Kansas City, in a segregated community of rich Prairie Jews, with their own country clubs and stores and card parties but the gentiles all around them? (The Goldmans were from Chicago.) Anyway, who should it turn out was Johnny's childhood pal but Henry Guettel, known universally as Hank, who had recently returned to New York from an unsuccessful marriage in Arizona. En masse, they

---

* One of them, *A Family Affair*, which made it to Broadway for two months in 1962, provided Hal Prince with his first directing credit; he took over when the previous director was fired out of town.

suggested I come by and meet him, and I did and we did and I don't remember anything about it. How's that for flattering?

We next met on January 30, 1961; I know the exact date because it was
Hal's birthday as well as FDR's. (Hal turned thirty-three.) Hal gave himself a party at his mother's place on the Upper East Side because he was
for some reason in between apartments. And because no world is smaller
than the theater, there was Hank, who had gone to Penn with Hal. I am
told—again I have no recollection—that I sat on the floor talking, very
boringly, about the genius of Steve. And about how I didn't like Steve's
mother or Hal's or mine.

For unfathomable reasons, Hank decided to invite me out to dinner
anyway. We went to some not very good French restaurant for a date
I unfortunately do remember; I thought he was supremely uninterest-
ing, and no doubt he me. Admittedly, there were points in his favor: He
was quite handsome, with clear blue eyes, and he spontaneously ordered
"my" drink, a dry Rob Roy, which is like a Manhattan but with Scotch
instead of rye. I'm not sure this qualifies as another of my parenting tips,
but you must always order it dry, otherwise they bring you one made
with sweet vermouth, which is disgusting.

Despite our similar taste in drinks, he was one of the few people in
those years I didn't invite back up to my apartment to "pay for dinner."
Nor did he ask to be paid.

Not sure whether that constituted gentlemanliness or squeamishness,
I decided not to decide. But a few weeks later, after Burt squalled, I did
invite Hank to my second snag-a-man party. He said he wouldn't be able
to make it because of work but asked if he could drop by toward the end.
That's usually just a polite dodge, so when the doorbell rang after dessert,
I thought: *Now that's interesting. Someone who actually does what he says he's
going to do. Someone who shows up.*

This time, I didn't flap my lips. Instead, I drew him out, because I'm
pretty sure I'd already told him way too much of my own story. Maybe
that's why I'd found him boring over dinner at the French restaurant—
because I bored myself.

His story, matrimonially at least, was arguably worse and thus more interesting than mine. He married his first wife, Miriam, in 1948, right after he came to New York to be an actor; they were both twenty.* In 1951 they had a daughter named Laurie; just two or three years later they divorced. The bitter decree—it had been Hank's wish to end the marriage, not Miriam's—left him paying through the nose and with restricted visitation: Laurie could not visit him, only he her. But we'd see plenty of Laurie later.

Next, after his stint in the army,† came Annie, a terrific redhead four years older than Hank who went around in the same theatrical circles, acting, assisting, building résumés, and just scraping by.‡ He was crazy about her for all the right reasons but, like Miriam, she had this unfortunate fault of drinking too much, which was bearable in a friend but not in a spouse. Nor was being a spouse bearable to Annie, apparently: At thirty-four, she'd already been divorced twice.§ And though she didn't run out on Hank until 1960, their marriage probably ended almost as soon as it started, in 1958, when they were living in Arizona and she delivered a stillborn son. The baby was to be named Christopher or even Henry; is it too Freudian to suggest that some of Hank died with him?¶

....

* Miriam Broud (1927–1980) was raised in the same close-knit Jewish community of Kansas City as the Guettels; members of their families wound up in the same Jewish cemetery.

† From 1954 to 1956, Pfc. Henry Guettel served as a clerk in the 6021st Personnel Center Troop Information and Education Office at Fort Lewis, Washington. While there, he directed a production of *Mister Roberts*.

‡ Ann Lilienthal (1924–1966) grew up on Park Avenue, the daughter of a prominent stockbroker.

§ Her first husband was Thomas Ewing Noyes, a stage manager turned producer; her second was the actor Tom Tryon, whom she'd met in summer stock.

¶ The certificate of fetal death, dated September 8, 1958, lists the child's

circa 1939: Hank, scion of the Palace Clothing clan. "The Guettels . . . each
did as they pleased and expected others to do the same."

In any case, he and Annie were separated by the time I came into the
picture—he back in New York and she still in Arizona with their basset
hound named Butts. It turned out not to be a very bright-line separation,
though; we'd see plenty of Annie later as well.

All of this was explained matter-of-factly; I thought I was dry, but
Hank was dryer. (We would be delicious as Rob Roys.) It was the Midwest-
erner in him, and something else. Johnny Kander's family may have been
wealthy—they were in eggs and poultry—but the Guettels *acted* wealthy,
without all the neurotic strings that accompanied money among, to pick
a random example, the Rodgerses.

Unfortunately, this stringless wealth came without much attachment
of the good kind, either. His father, a lovely man, inherited the Palace
Clothing Company,* a wildly successful chain of haberdasheries he

....

name as "Inf. Boy Guettel," but at least one other document gives the name
as Henry.

* Palace Clothing was founded in 1888 by Hank's grandfather and namesake, Henry Arthur Guettel (1866–1921). The Kansas City flagship, one

seemed to enjoy running into the ground. (The job fell to him because his older brother, Eddie the Crook, was otherwise engaged.) He loved polo, looked good in jodhpurs, had his own plane and farm and mustache, and when he died left almost no money, having gaily frittered it away. In the meantime, the family was running on fumes. Guess what? It turns out you can get pretty far on fumes.

But one didn't talk of such downsides among the Guettels. In retrospect they seem very Finzi-Contini: attractive, drifting, doomed.* They each did as they pleased and expected others to do the same and it was all Jim-dandy as long as you didn't rub anyone's nose in it. Hank loves to talk about a man from their set named Herbert Woolf,† a "courtesy uncle" who ran Woolf Brothers, a competing luxury goods department store chain. This Woolf lived like a country squire, even owning a racehorse that won the Derby in I don't know what year.‡ Only later did I learn that he'd had an affair with Sylvia, Hank's very pretty, very tiny, big-blue-eyed blond mother—Woolf did, that is, not the horse. This did not seem to affect his standing among the Guettels; they adored him.

They adored Hank, too, but paid him no attention, which sounds lovely to someone like me, for whom the opposite was true, until you see how liberality and laissez-faire can add up to negligence. Hank had no guidance of any sort, intellectual or financial. When his wonderful sister,

....

of eight eventual branches, is on the National Register of Historic Places. Hank's father, Arthur Abraham Guettel (1896–1969), became president of the company upon his father's death and ran it until it closed in 1964.

* *The Garden of the Finzi-Continis*, a 1962 novel by Giorgio Bassani that was turned into a 1970 film by Vittorio De Sica, concerns a fictional Ferrarese Jewish family in the years before World War II. For all their beauty and tennis skills, things don't end well.

† Herbert M. Woolf (1880–1964) was said to be a cousin of Leonard and Virginia.

‡ Woolf's Thoroughbred Lawrin, ridden by Eddie Arcaro, won the Kentucky Derby in 1938.

1949: Hank's headshot at about twenty-one, shortly after
he moved to New York to be an actor. "He had a moment's hope
with a Broadway show that lasted a whole month."

Suzy, got polio in her first week at Bennington in 1940, they decided to
spend their winters in Florida so she could swim her way back to health.*
Hank, who was five years younger and still in middle school, loved that:
sitting under the palms doing his homework, except that he didn't do any
homework. Work in that family was always left for the next generation.
All he was really taught was how to be gracious and generous and gentle-
manly. Which explains how, when he later became a producer, he wound
up compulsively overpaying actors.

He had tried to be an actor himself and knew from a few seasons
of summer stock just how tough it was. After graduating from Penn,
where his parents had dumped him at sixteen at the entirely unsuitable

* It didn't work. Suzanne Guettel Suskin (1922–1970) remained sickly and
died at age forty-seven.

Wharton School because they expected him to return to Kansas City to run the business, he confounded them by moving to New York to live the actor's life.

Although promptly encumbered with a wife and a kid, he had a moment's hope with a Broadway show that lasted a whole month.* But he quickly saw that he wasn't going to make his way doing walk-ons, and he settled into a series of backstage jobs like talent agenting and stage managing and producing road companies.

When we got to know each other, he was thirty-three and a booker for Morty Gottlieb's operation, arranging tours of recently successful Broadway shows. He was no meteor, but I quickly began to sense there was nevertheless something shining about him. As we began going out that spring, I thought: *This is possible.* He had all of the second-husbandly qualifications I'd come up with, which were: someone responsive, someone as bright as or brighter (in some aspects, if not all) than I was, and, most important, someone with a terrific sense of humor.

That was all true of Hank, just not in the way I expected. One very nice day, maybe in May, he toodled me around Central Park in a friend's car, which he had borrowed for his upcoming drive to Chicago, where he was producing the summer season at the Edgewater Beach Playhouse.† I remember we had the radio on, and I was explaining how one could tell the difference between Mozart and Haydn. Which was very pompous, especially because I soon found out that he knew much more about mu-

....

* *Now I Lay Me Down to Sleep* was an adaptation of a novel by Ludwig Bemelmans, of *Madeline* fame, that ran for a month in 1950 and starred Fredric March and Florence Eldridge. Along with Annie's first husband, Thomas Noyes, Hank was one of the stage managers; he also played "Aristide, the General's Chauffeur" and "Third Indian."

† The Edgewater Beach Playhouse, at the time located within the huge and pink Edgewater Beach Hotel on Lake Michigan, was basically a summer stock joint not unlike Westport, with stars dropping in for short runs, sometimes filled out by locals.

sic than I did; he could tell the difference in four bars without waiting for whatever my dead giveaway was, and could name what the piece was, too. But he was very patient and never shamed me for my pretension and ambition, which left me feeling something I wasn't used to feeling about men: grateful.

Also, and I suppose this is another husbandly qualification, the sex was fun. It was always on my living room floor—I don't know why. My favorite carpet? Or maybe because my bedroom was too close to the kids'. And maybe, too, the danger was exciting, in part because it wasn't very dangerous except that you might wind up banging your head on a sofa leg. Hank once said, "What about your children?" and I answered, "If they come out in the middle of the night, good for them. They'll just have to know that's the way I am."

I wasn't being flip. Kids, early on, should get used to the idea that sex, like everything else adults do, is something to know about, learn, and discuss. I bought them a Kama Sutra and taught them about birth control and everything else. When Alec, in his teens, told me that he and his girlfriend at the time, whom we called Cupcake, were considering having sex, we sent them into some drugstore to buy condoms; if they weren't mature enough to do that, they weren't mature enough to do the other. (The clerk said, "Oh sure—but, hey, you kids aren't going to do this in the street, are you?") And because there are all too many men who have no idea, I took it upon myself to describe to the boys what women liked in bed. Respect, sure, but get down there and get to work.

Wait, where was I?

As summer and his departure for Chicago approached, Hank and I were getting serious. He took me one night to a wonderful big apartment he said he wanted to lease, on the top floor of a building in the theater district. It had a terrace that could be closed in, he said, and wouldn't it be a ball? I thought it sounded iffy and expensive for a single man, until I realized he was showing it to me with a different purpose in mind: We were finally talking about marriage. I say "finally," but it was very fast. Five months from boring each other to "we." And I thought: *Let's go for this one.*

Naturally, that's when he told me that Annie wasn't completely out of the picture. She had just written him a letter from Arizona saying she knew about me and that was all very well, but she wanted to try to patch up the marriage. She suggested meeting him in Chicago, which was interesting because Hank and I had already made a plan that I would meet him there. On the same dates, as it happened.

What do they say: History repeats itself, the second time as farce?* This was two farces, one onstage and one off. At the theater, the Edgewater was presenting a season of B-list retreads, including Jan de Hartog's *The Fourposter*, starring Steve Allen and Jayne Meadows, and Eve Arden in *The Marriage-Go-Round*. In between, for two weeks in early July, when Annie and I would be there, came Mae West on the first leg of a national tour of her play *Sextette*,† supposedly bound for Broadway.‡ West played Marlo Manners, an international sex symbol recently wedded to a knight. The story, if you could call it that, featured the new couple's attempts to consummate their marriage amid interruptions from many ex- and would-be lovers staying at the same hotel.§

In her late sixties, Mae West¶ was still a beautiful woman, tiny, waspwaisted, unpretentious. She traveled with her bodybuilder boyfriend,

....

* Marx—Karl, not Groucho—did say something like that, though he was referring to Napoleon III.

† *The Fourposter*, *Sextette*, and *The Marriage-Go-Round*: Do you smell a theme?

‡ *Sextette* never made it to Broadway, but a film version was released in 1978, when West was in her mid-eighties. It is a classic camp bomb.

§ In the movie, these include the "United States Athletic Team," whose sport seems to consist of setting up double entendres. "I'm a polevaulter," one jock says. Marlo replies: "Mmm, aren't we all?"

¶ Mae West (1893–1980) had been appearing professionally in plays, many of them her own, since at least 1911, but *Sextette*, written in 1959, was her last stage role.

Paul Novak, and spent some time each day hanging upside down in her closet. If only her co-star, a handsome Australian actor named Alan Marshal, had taken the same good care of himself. The day after opening, during the Saturday evening performance, he had a heart attack onstage. He finished the play, but it finished him: He was found dead in his bed at the hotel the next day.

I had my own health routine at the time, involving the lesbian shrink, vitamin B$_2$ shots, cigarettes, Rob Roys, and speed. We considered all this chic then; before Hank left for Chicago, he'd had Cartier make me a little gold Dexamyl charm. They got it wrong, though: They made me the pill version called a purple heart, with a groove in it for dividing, if you were so inclined. I favored the spansule version called a Christmas tree.

You laugh, but it was thanks to that Dexamyl and my B$_2$ shots, with which I duly jabbed him, that Hank memorized Alan's role as Mae's husband in one day and played it for paying customers until a replacement could be found.

That was the onstage farce. Offstage, with elements of the same script, there was the farce with Annie. When I'd told my interesting gay lady shrink that both the not-quite-ex and I were going to be visiting Hank at the same time, she said, "What's the matter with you, don't you know what to do?" And for the first time, I did. I said to Hank, "Annie walked out on you. That's dirty pool. You just tell her to come later, after I leave," and he very meekly did. Also, as a precaution, when I got to the hotel I went to the desk and ever so politely asked to switch my friend Annie's room, for her comfort of course, to the other end of the enormous hotel when she came. The other end from Hank.

My plane left and hers arrived and Hank moved her room back to his side of the hotel. "It's only fair," he told me on the phone. He didn't want to humiliate her, and he had to give her a chance.

So Finzi-Contini! The Guettels would have given Göring a chance.

Not that Annie was in any way evil; she was adorable. She was just doing what I imagine any woman in her late thirties might do if, facing a third divorce with no children, she wanted to rescue her last chance at a traditional life. And it seemed to me that Hank and I would both be better off if he faced this challenge—or was it a temptation?—and beat it back once and for all. I trusted him, which was also a new feeling; if I hadn't, I wouldn't have left. Even so, I think he rather enjoyed my agonizing as I waited those three days back in New York. On the phone he'd talk about everything but the marital reunion. Finally he got around to telling me what he'd told Annie: It was too late for her. Which was news she took rather too literally, as she then proceeded to drink herself to death.[*] When what Hank meant was only this: that he and I had come too far.

....

[*] Four years after Annie and Hank divorced, in 1961, she married one more time, briefly; her death in Malibu in 1966 has been reported as a suicide.

34.

MARS LANDING

I was working that summer on *Feathertop*, a title I now realize would make a good companion piece to *Mattress*. *Feathertop*, with lyrics by Martin Charnin, was a one-hour television musical based on a Hawthorne short story about a scarecrow, but there wasn't much Hawthorne left by the time the book writer, a guy named John Marsh, was finished with it.* He moved the setting from New England to New Orleans, where a witch (Cathleen Nesbitt), seeking revenge against the governor (Hans Conried), brings a scarecrow to life as a fancy gentleman (Hugh O'Brian) to seduce the governor's daughter (Jane Powell). It's *that* kind of story. Marsh had earlier been involved with the recording session of "Tickle the Trolley Mouse," the horrible title song I wrote for the proposed children's show with Shari Lewis, so I should have known it would be saccharine. In my defense, that was during the period when I would basically do anything. And that period has been my whole life.

Sponsored by the confectioner Mars, *Feathertop* aired on ABC two weeks before Halloween† along with commercials about how candy is so

....

* Nathaniel Hawthorne's "Feathertop: A Moralized Legend" was published in two parts in 1852. Much more cynical than the mini-musical turned out to be, it concludes that there are plenty of actual scarecrows in the world; we call them people.

† On October 19, 1961, at 8:30 p.m.

healthy for kids. In fact, the sponsor very kindly sent me a gigantic box of Mars Bars that summer, which landed on my doorstep when no one was there because I'd stuffed all the kids at camp while I was gallivanting. Poor little Kimmy: She'd been told she looked like me, so she spent all day, I was told, looking in the mirror to be closer to what she missed. Pathetic! It's super-cruelty to put a little person, five years old, into camp. My sister had gone to camp at four, with a nanny yet; for my parents it was a life of "now you see her, now you don't." I wish I'd been able to avoid repeating some of their mistakes, but doing what I was trying to do, I didn't think I had other choices. Selfish? Probably.*

Feathertop was shot in Los Angeles; the creative team stayed at the Chateau Marmont. Marty was there with his marvelous soon-to-be second wife Genii Prior, whom he'd met when they were both in *West Side Story*.† Genii is a superb human being, half Jewish and half Filipina; fortunately, by the time Marty wanted to divorce her, he'd already written *Annie*, so she cashed in. In 1961, though, they were premaritally happy. So was I, and not just premaritally. I had never been to California as a grown-up and I thought it was just a blast. The moment I saw oranges on an orange tree, memories of my early childhood there rushed back, this time accompanied by the pleasure of having survived it instead of the dread of wondering whether I would.

Feathertop itself was less joyful. Of the four leads, only Powell had any sense of rhythm, but she yowled all over the scale as if hoping the right

....

* But lots of letters were written. Several included chapters of a serialized story, and one, this poem: "Imagine lazy Mummy, / Lying by the water, / Resting on her tummy, / Writing to her daughter, / Soaking up the sunshine that trickles through the trees, / Blowing big, fat smoke rings, (a ring around the breeze!)"

† Genii Prior Charnin (born 1932) was a replacement Estella—one of the Shark girls—in the original production. She and Charnin married in 1962 after Charnin divorced his first wife, Lynn Ross, who was, bizarrely, the original Estella.

notes would somehow poke out from the blur. O'Brian, then a huge star just coming off a long run as Wyatt Earp on television,* couldn't hear rhythm at all. During the taping of "Perfect Strangers," a nice gavotte I wrote for him and Powell, Marty had to get down on his hands and knees—and Marty is quite tall—so he could whack O'Brian's shins to force him onto the beat. Nesbitt didn't know what she was doing either, but she was pleasant and became a friend; Conried sounded like a dog sneezing.

The seven songs I wrote didn't stand much of a chance, but Hank was in the wings, metaphorically, which took the edge off my disappointment. Maybe our romance was even more enjoyable because I had to remain somewhat mysterious about it. Two impediments to our marriage remained: that Hank wasn't divorced and that he hadn't met my parents. My parents I dreaded more than the divorce; after all I had put them through with men, I wanted to be sure about Hank before I brought them another burnt offering. So when I went to Chicago to see him, I lied and told them I was going for a meeting with the *Feathertop* sponsors; Mars fortuitously had offices there. Mummy didn't believe me, of course; no one in her right mind goes to Chicago in the summer to see a sponsor.

By August we finished working on *Feathertop* and I headed home. Unlike Steve when I returned from London the previous fall, Hank, who was back in New York after the Edgewater season, planned to meet me at the airport. In fact, he wouldn't think of *not* meeting me. But the flight was delayed on the runway in Los Angeles, and I was so upset about his possibly having to wait for me, or his possibly deciding *not* to wait for me, that I said to a clump of crew members, "There's a bomb on the plane." I don't know what got into me. I immediately realized what an asinine thing I'd done and ran after them saying, "No, I was just kidding." One of them said, "Thanks for telling us now, lady, we were just about to cancel the flight."

My psychotic outburst only delayed us further. But Hank did wait.

....

* Hugh O'Brian (1925–2016) starred in *The Life and Legend of Wyatt Earp* from 1955 to 1961. The show had aired its final episode that June.

And when he got me home to East Seventy-second Street, I found the box of Mars Bars waiting, too, all melted into one *big* Mars Bar.

By the end of the summer, we knew we could no longer put off the pilgrimage to Rockmeadow. Hank handled himself perfectly, as he always did with my parents, and the proof was that Daddy had no opinion of him, or none he would share. High praise.

Mummy found Hank very charming and appropriate but had three questions afterward. The first was: "Is he Jewish?" Like most of us, she had not heard of Plains Jews and was delighted to find Hank an example of the hitherto unknown variety.

The second question was: "Does he have a good job?"

"He will," I said, which she accepted, tentatively—as did I. I figured he'd get one soon enough.

The third question was the one that really mattered to Mummy: "Does he like his parents?" She believed this to be a bellwether of whether he would like mine, which understandably was a chief concern. She felt that Jerry, who hated his father, also hated her: QED. Of course, Jerry's father was a pig.

"He adores his parents," I said, perhaps overstating a feeling that was more assumed than demonstrated. We had her blessing.

The legal system's blessing was not so forthcoming. Divorces still took forever in those days and could turn even relatively sane couples into calculating adversaries—as I knew. So now that Annie had agreed to end their marriage, she and Hank decided to get a Mexican "quickie," just as she had done with Tom Tryon before marrying Hank.* This time, though, Hank would fly to Juarez with me instead of her, not get sick on tequila, and, to save money and time, have a wedding in Mexico City a day or two later.

....

* Mexican courts, unlike those in the United States, did not require both parties to be present to obtain a divorce. And until 1970, when the laws changed, they were also not very strict about jurisdiction. You could get a residency certificate in the morning and the divorce immediately thereafter.

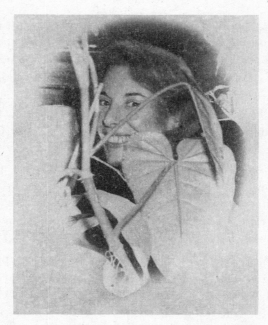

1961: The bride-to-be at a restaurant in a Mexico City hotel,
"hidden in the fronds of a big plant."

Now this is what you call a tale. Hal saw us off at the airport that October, all the while talking rapturously about Judy Chaplin, whom he'd
just met in Europe and would marry the next year. That was a relief;
we never spoke again about what had transpired—I almost said
"perspired"—between us.

On the flight to Juarez, also heading there for a divorce, was a girl
called Pam Bookman, whose younger sister, Nancy, I knew. We told her
our plans for the trip, and she said, "If you're going to Mexico City and
don't know anyone there, I've got two great friends you should call."

After the divorce, which really was as easy as advertised, we got to
Mexico City on a Wednesday and stayed in a very posh hotel; there's
a wonderful photo of us hidden in the fronds of a big plant in the
restaurant.

The next morning, October 12, we called the embassy to find out how
and where to get married, but no one answered, which we thought was

very peculiar. And so, with nothing better to do, we tried Pam Bookman's friends, whose names were Rita Tillett and Octavio Señoret.* They were very cordial, explaining over the phone that the embassy was probably closed because of Columbus Day; Columbus discovered them as much as he discovered us, they said.† Then they invited us for lunch at what must have been the best restaurant in Mexico City, with an inland waterway stocked with real swans. If you pointed at one, they would take it to the kitchen and cook it for you.‡

Rita was one of the prettiest women I'd ever seen in my life, and very blond, with her hair pulled back in a chignon. Octavio was great-looking, too, though we found out when we got back to New York and asked his countrywoman Felicia Bernstein about him that he had something of a violent reputation.§ Even compared with our cosmopolitan ways, their manner was sophisticated and effortlessly blasé. Rita had a son by her previous husband; the custody arrangement was that she kept him for seven years and then her ex-husband kept him for seven years. Or so she said. She also had two children with Octavio, a baby and a toddler, both gorgeous, too.

Over lunch, we explained why we were in Mexico and asked if they knew any judges. Well, yes, they said, they knew *all* the judges, but they didn't think a courtroom wedding sounded like much fun. "Why don't we give you a wedding at our house?" they suggested, even though we had to leave on Sunday and it was already Thursday. But we didn't really have any other plan, so we put it in their hands.

....

* Rita Butterlin (born 1931) was married four times, first to textile artist Jim Tillett, with whom she made fabulous sarongs; then, from 1959 to 1963, to the Chilean actor and producer Octavio Señoret Guevara.

† Or as little. In Mexico, Columbus Day is known as Día de la Raza and is observed on October 12.

‡ A joke, but one of the few times Mary seems to have been taken aback by luxury.

§ In 1990, in Los Angeles, he killed himself with a gunshot to the heart.

1961: Hank and Mary at their wedding, which was attended
by strangers and presided over by a panel of Mexican judges.

The next night, to scare up a guest list and a bridal party for Saturday,
they took us apartment hopping and introduced us to all the glamorous
expats. I can't remember whom we hopped into the apartments of, other
than the *Time* magazine correspondent there, but somewhere we stumbled across Budd Schulberg.* He knew Hank distantly, and his second
wife, Victoria, knew us quite well after her tenth drink. Budd agreed to
be best man and Vickee perforce my matron of honor.

....

* Seymour "Budd" Schulberg (1914–2009) wrote books and movies. In
1951 he named names before the House Un-American Activities Committee but by 1961 had rehabilitated himself with the screenplays for *On
the Waterfront* and *A Face in the Crowd*. Hits will do that.

So on Saturday I went to another posh hotel to get my hair done, and Hank called me at the salon asking for Mrs. Guettel just for fun, and after I changed into a navy-blue wool suit that my mother had given me, Budd and Vickee drove us at the appointed time to Rita and Octavio's unbelievable town house, on Mexico City's equivalent of Fifth Avenue. As we arrived, there was Rita standing out on the street looking a little disturbed. It seems that after inviting scores of people to the wedding, her stove broke. Her staff, which was huge, had to go to the neighbors', cook everything, and bring it back. It was all incredibly generous and weird. We were suddenly and literally the toast of Mexico City society, on an invitation extended by people we'd never heard of before. They'd lined up not one but three judges for us, all seated at a carved wooden table two rooms from where the music was playing. As this tribunal married us, completely in Spanish including the *sí*'s, the orchestra coincidentally but marvelously struck up "The Gentleman Is a Dope."*

I don't remember the party, which was huge, except that Vickee got so drunk she fell down a flight of stairs yet wasn't hurt because her body had turned to rubber from so many similar falls. I felt like I had fallen *up* a flight of stairs, or like Cinderella enjoying a ball not meant for her, with midnight approaching. In this case, midnight meant the next morning, when we had to leave for New York so I could get to work on time for the next Young People's Concert.† So we hugged our hosts goodbye and said thanks for the lovely wedding and barely slept a couple of hours before getting on the plane and wondering what had just happened to us besides my becoming Mrs. Henry Guettel.

There is a postscript to this story, involving a midnight call from Octa-

---

* From Rodgers and Hammerstein's *Allegro* (1947): "The gentleman's eyes are blue, / But little do they see."

† Mary Rodgers Beaty and Henry Arthur Guettel were married on Saturday, October 14, 1961. "What Is Impressionism?"—in which Bernstein discussed Debussy, Ravel, and the whole-tone scale—was taped the same day at Carnegie Hall, according to a typescript of the telecast. Perhaps the Guettels' flight crossed the International Date Line, backward?

1963: Aboard the RMS *Queen Elizabeth*, Kim, Tod, and Nina Beaty
say goodbye to Hank and Mary, leaving on a belated honeymoon.

vio in jail, a dinner with Dick Avedon, a photo shoot with Raquel Welch
(whom Dick called "the rudest trash ever"), and Rita's fourth husband,
who looked exactly like Hemingway. The punch line is a washer-dryer.
I'm not going to tell it, though, because Hank and I don't come off very
well, even compared to Raquel Welch.

Where was I?

Back home, my kids adjusted quickly to the new domestic arrangement. They had already met Hank and liked him, so it wasn't much of a
stretch to have him around full-time. Still, every now and again they were
surprised, and would give me odd looks, when he suddenly got Germanic
about table manners. (He wasn't terribly sensitive to the psychology of
children, having had no model for that; at least I had the model of my
own mistreatment.) And I wasn't sure I liked his attempts to discipline

them, especially on such petty matters. Keep in mind that he was my husband, not their father. They already had a father; Jerry still came faithfully every Wednesday and took them for two weeks every summer. On the other hand, you have to give Hank credit for putting up with my odd ménage, and for accepting without much gulping that managing it was now his problem.

Credit the kids, too, for adjusting, in their own way. One day right after we got back from Mexico, while drying off from a shower, Hank found the bathroom door cracked open with three little heads stuck through it, checking out his equipment.

They weren't the only ones. I liked being married and, as of that December, loved being pregnant again.

I'd been through enough men to know that Hank, who was funny and kind and terribly smart, was what I needed. I never was interested in marrying for money and material security; I was much too idealistic to let that get in the way. And we had a lot of things in common superficially, being from different neighborhoods of the same social stratum. Later I wished he'd had more drive; when we got married, I called him "Mumbles" because he was so shy and unsure of himself around people who were neither. He'd start out a sentence in a nice, big, booming voice and by the end you couldn't hear what he was saying. His confidence ran down. But at the time I wasn't ambitious for him. If I had been, we probably wouldn't have ended up together. And though I found him plenty attractive, my attitude about a man, most of the time, is that it's what he does rather than how he looks that matters. Hank both looked and did more than fine. He fit my bill.

And what was the alternative? I was much more afraid of being alone for the rest of my life than of missing out on some crazy orgasm of genius and sex that was never going to happen. The small things really do add up to more, at least in memory. When I remember great sex, I can't actually feel it, but when I remember shared jokes, I find myself smiling or even laughing again. One of our earliest jokes was a little secret code we arranged for that surprisingly frequent situation when someone we couldn't recall having met before greeted us super-effusively at a party. "Mary! Hank! So great to see you again! Shirley and I were hoping you'd

1963: Mary and Hank aboard their honeymoon cruise.
"The Nick and Nora Charles of Central Park West."

be here!" Afterward, or even right there, mouthing it over the shoulder of a mystifying bear hug, one of us would say to the other: "N.A.C." Which meant "not a clue."

If funny, smart, and responsive were my requirements, I got something more in the bargain: someone who got me. After all, Hank must have had his own bill, too, which I fit as he fit mine, with whatever compromises that entailed. It sounds mechanical, but really those checklist traits are a reasonable way to choose someone—for a second marriage or later. It's only too sad for a first.

35

NO DON'T!

M atthew* was a gorgeous newborn, all blond fuzz and blue eyes, with pink-and-white skin like Hank's.

It was another easy childbirth; what can I say, I'm a contented cow. But twelve hours after we brought him home, I noticed that his diaper was still dry. Not that I was concerned; I was just thinking how great I was to have produced an abstemious urinator. Mummy would be proud.

It was lucky the au pair insisted on calling the pediatrician, because something really was wrong. As it turned out, Uncle Morty, after his usual cocktail hour delivery, had botched the circumcision; he clipped a little too much and left it to get infected. Neither he nor anyone else at Lenox Hill, where he was the director of gynecology and obstetrics, bothered to tell us.

Not only did I finally have what the family considered just cause to fire him, but my mother, who was magnificent at dudgeon, reported him to the hospital. After that, he performed no more deliveries or circumcisions. At sixty-four, he became a consultant, but not to me. And though Matthew was soon fine, thinking about it still gives me a gridge in my crotch.

At the time, we had just finished moving across town to the Majestic—

....

* Matthew Rodgers Guettel was born on September 12, 1962.

1963: Mary with Matthew, "all blond fuzz and blue eyes."

not the ocean liner or the theater but the co-op at 115 Central Park West. The building, home to theater people, bohemians, and Jews—often all three at once—suited me well with its louche reputation. Five years earlier, the gangster Frank Costello, who lived there then, was shot in the lobby.* When I heard we had to be interviewed by the board, I asked, in my snarky way, "Did Costello have to be interviewed, too?" I was told no: The building wasn't a co-op then.

Remember that in the early 1960s the Wild West Side was still a place where good girls dared not venture. You've heard the term "needle park"? We had a literal one: Drugs were openly sold alfresco in the greenish median of that bow-tie intersection at Seventy-first and Broadway. The whole neighborhood was littered with hypodermics and, for some

---

* Other than a ruined suit and a hole in his hat, Costello was fine. That building was very well run.

reason, covered with soot. To buy anything legal was nearly impossible: There were no drugstores or bookstores or shops for flowers or gifts. Well, there was one little Japanese place where the kids used to find us odd-lot birthday presents. Alec, when he was very little, got Hank three handkerchiefs embroidered with the initial B. There's not a B in his name anywhere.

Mummy objected to the move, of course, but with my fourth baby on the way, even she understood that the East Side apartment was one bedroom shy. The realtor kept telling us to buy on the West Side while it was still a bargain: "Once that Lincoln Center thing gets finished, you'll never be able to afford it." And she was right; how else do you think we were able to get a nine-room, four-bath apartment at the Majestic for $47,500? It was dark and only on the fourth floor, but even accounting for inflation, it would still be a steal today.*

An added advantage was that its location kept Mummy at bay; neither she nor my children's East Side schoolmates liked to cross the park for a visit. I may have enhanced that effect, as far as my mother was concerned, by painting the whole place white; I didn't have time to worry over colors. Mummy was appalled and would frown at the walls. The painters were also critical. "You don't maybe want a drop of red?" they asked. No. A gravid lady never does.

The imminent Matthew was not the only reason I was in such a hurry. Much as I loved being pregnant, there was a lot I wanted to do in 1962— and over the next six years with their three more pregnancies—that did not involve stirrups. Turns out, you wind up with your ass in the air either way.

Which of my failures do you want first? Marty Charnin alone can account for several. Only one was the kind of disaster that makes a mushroom cloud; most were the small almosts or mehs that slowly poison your confidence. If only you could tell rottenness in advance, the way you can spot a mushy banana. But all new ideas look identically great before they're peeled.

....

* About four hundred thousand in current dollars; large units at the Majestic today sell for ten times as much.

Marty and I had bunches of them. At the time, we were working in a nice suite of offices that Marty's publisher, Buddy Morris, had on West Fifty-fourth Street, near the Warwick Hotel and the Museum of Modern Art.* Also buzzing around Buddy's was Mike Nichols, who was supposedly writing something there during the brief period between his superstardom as a comic dialogist with Elaine May and his superstardom as a film director.†

He did not seem to work much, though, so one day, when we crossed paths idling in the hallway, I told him about a story I'd come across—like *Carte Blanche*—while leafing through *Life*.‡ It was about Gamble Benedict, a nineteen-year-old Remington typewriter heiress being raised by her grandmother, a Park Avenue dragon named Mrs. Henry Harper Benedict. As the tale went, Gamble fell in love with her grandmother's Romanian chauffeur, a man named Andrei Porumbeanu. The dragon of course forbade the relationship, so of course the couple eloped, and of course Andrei turned out to be a con man, a drunk, and a multiple philanderer. In real life, this ended in a tabloid divorce a few years later, but in my fictional twist, to complicate the second act, Gamble chooses to stay married even after she realizes Andrei's true character. She's using him, too.

....

* Edmund "Buddy" Morris (1906–1996) was a major music publisher—not in Chappell's league but canny enough to sign up composers like Cy Coleman, Jerry Herman, and Charles Strouse when they were novices, and then cash in on them when they weren't. In those days, as in the Tin Pan Alley era, being a music publisher also meant providing workspace for motley composers, lyricists, and book writers who could not afford their own or just preferred the college dorm atmosphere.

† Mike Nichols (1931–2014) had his first Broadway hit (*An Evening with Mike Nichols and Elaine May*) in 1960 and his first Hollywood hit (*Who's Afraid of Virginia Woolf?*) just six years later.

‡ *Life* magazine was a bountiful source of ideas for excellent musicals never to be made. "The Elopers: Gamble and Andrei" appeared on the cover of the April 18, 1960, issue.

Mike loved the idea and suggested we meet at Buddy's offices every morning at eleven to work on turning it into a musical. But whenever we did meet, after twenty or thirty minutes he'd say, "Is anybody hungry?" We'd spend twenty more minutes ordering Chinese, gossip while eating it, and then he'd say, "I have to go now." We never got any further with that musical than "Is anybody hungry?"

Hank used to meet me at Buddy's at the end of what passed for work, and we'd go for a drink at the Warwick before heading home. The opposite of Jerry, he supported my work spiritually if not financially.* He didn't complain, as everyone else did, about how much time my scratching at staves was taking from the children; even I thought it was nearly unconscionable. Instead, he'd strategize how to get more bang for my work. One of the biggest things in my way, we agreed, was Flora. She was a terrific agent for top male talent but didn't seem to have much time for this mid-tier female who needed her more. Still, I abhorred confrontation, so when I decided to fire her I could only do it by inviting her to lunch at the Majestic. Over shrimp salad I delicately said, "It's not that you're not a great agent. I just don't think you're the right agent for me."

"Funny, I was about to tell you the same thing," she brayed back. "You're not the right client."

Agenting is less like marriage than foster care: You keep getting passed along. After Flora, Charlie Baker, the top theater agent at the William Morris Agency, took me on briefly. He was lovely, queer as Dick's hatband, and had a penthouse apartment on the East Side where we went for dinner and he drank a great deal while talking about the miracle of liver regrowth. Then he died of cirrhosis anyway. Before that happened, he turned me over to a colleague who swore up and down that, if I signed, he wouldn't disappear or die or dump me but proceeded to do two of those things two weeks later. I hung on with some other subagent at William

---

* Between 1962 and 1964, Hank had a series of steady but not especially lucrative producing gigs, including the second national tour of *Camelot*, the third national tour of *The Sound of Music*, and a bus-and-truck tour of *Oliver*.

Morris until, once again feeling lost in the shuffle, I deposited myself on the West Fifty-seventh Street doorstep of Robby Lantz, who I somehow neglected to notice at the time was a slimy charmer and a rotten shit.*

That was later. Now, after firing Flora, I let myself be represented by Marty's agent, Abe Newborn, who got us into some soul-sapping deals. One of them found me, three months pregnant, composing in the empty ballroom of a fancy Florida hotel, where Marty and I were being put up to write a series of twenty-minute musicals for Jackie Gleason.† The first of these mini-musicals was a spoof of *The Untouchables* called *The Retouchables*, complicatedly featuring Jackie as his Reginald Van Gleason character playing crimefighter Eliot Flesh.‡ There wasn't a second.

While working for Gleason, we met our next disaster: the team of Weinstock and Gilbert, who wrote skits for him.§ Their claim to fame was being two of the writers credited with the book of *How to Succeed in Business Without Really Trying*; the third was Abe Burrows, but only

....

* Born in Berlin, Robert Lantz (1914–2007) had a very classy client list, including Lenny, Elizabeth Taylor, and—as will become relevant—Carson McCullers.

† With various incarnations of his self-named variety show and his maudlin domestic comedy *The Honeymooners*, Jackie Gleason (1916–1987) was one of the biggest television stars of the 1950s and 1960s. He also appeared on Broadway and in movies. The songwriters met him just once, while auditioning in his trailer on a golf course.

‡ "The Retouchables" aired on September 29, 1962, as the opening sketch on the premiere of *The Jackie Gleason Show: The American Scene Magazine.* Later in the same episode, Gleason and Art Carney, in a *Honeymooners* sketch, built a bomb shelter.

§ Jack Weinstock (1907–1969) was a doctor, but unfortunately not the play kind. (He was a urologist.) Willie Gilbert (1916–1980) was his patient and, later, improbably, his collaborator. One of them performed an emergency appendectomy on the other.

Burrows got the Pulitzer Prize.* That was a good call by the Pulitzers:
Everyone knew that Burrows had done the real work of making the odd
source material—a satire of self-help books by Shepherd Mead—into a
musical, while Weinstock and Gilbert were just hacks lucky enough to
have their names on the rights. But who were Marty and I to be picky
when they came to us with what they described as an original idea for
a new musical?† We said yes at once, but my newborn agent Newborn
then had to sell us to the producers, Fryer and Carr.‡ Me he depicted as a
bargain, telling them I didn't need a big salary because I had a rich father.
I said, "I beg your pardon! I don't get any of that money." It was one of
the few times I stood up for myself, for which brazenness I was rewarded
with my rightful chunk of what turned out to be almost nothing.

   Hot Spot, as the idea came to be called, stunk up a year of my life,
and in some ways a good deal more. It was supposed to be an ensemble
comedy about idealistic Peace Corps workers fabricating a Communist
threat on a South Seas island so the United States would send money and
make everyone happy. Maybe I should have seen the writing on the wall
when I saw the writing on the script; Weinstock and Gilbert had named
the island D'hum, which might have worked later in *The Mad Show* but
was too juvenile for the attempt at sophisticated satire at hand.

   There were plenty more laugh-begging names to come. Gabriel Snap-
per. Sumner Tubb Jr.§ When Fryer and Carr told us we'd have to have a

....

* The prize also went to Frank Loesser, who wrote the excellent score.

† Others said that its plot was suspiciously close to that of a 1949 Ealing
comedy called *Whiskey Galore!*—which was known in the United States
as *Tight Little Island.*

‡ Robert Fryer (1920–2000), often in league with Lawrence Carr (1917–
1969), had already produced the hits *Wonderful Town* and *Auntie Mame,*
and would later add *Sweet Charity, Mame, Chicago,* and *Sweeney Todd* to
his credits.

§ Sumner Tubb Jr. was played by George Furth, born with a funny
name of his own: George Schweinfurth. He later became Sondheim's

star because they couldn't sell the story to their theater party ladies without one, we promoted one of the Peace Corps workers to leader of the pack and gave her the ridiculous name Dulcie Hopwinder. Later it was changed to Sally, which is almost a joke in itself, like the one about John Shitson. You know: Unable to stand it anymore, he changes his name to Alex Shitson. People are always fixing the wrong problem.

Anyway, a funny name and new material aren't enough to make a star role. For that, you need an actual star. The one that Fryer and Carr, as well as our director, Morton Da Costa, elected to go for was Judy Holliday,* who had been bona fide brilliant in *Born Yesterday* and *Bells Are Ringing*. In some ways she was a good fit for the reconceived lead, a lovable hygiene teacher who before landing in D'hum has already made a mess of three previous Peace Corps assignments by getting involved, like Ella Peterson the phone service operator in *Bells Are Ringing*, in other people's problems. But Holliday was now past forty; Hopwinder should have been in her twenties. And there was another problem that had to be addressed: Holliday's health. Two years earlier, in 1960, she'd had a mastectomy after a diagnosis of metastatic breast cancer. When we went to meet her in her apartment at the Dakota—across the street from mine at the Majestic—she told us she'd totally recovered; somehow the sight of her mother, who was wearing a sheer nightgown that did nothing to hide the glory of her great big floppy boobs, seemed to confirm it.

But a few months later, as we were rewriting the show, Judy came to see Marty and me to say she'd had a recurrence. She needed treatment but made us swear not to let on. When she then informed Fryer and Carr that she was backing out, without being willing to tell them why, they were beside themselves. Fryer, who had a terrible temper, turned red in

....

collaborator on *Company* and *Merrily We Roll Along* and was, according to Mary, a pain in the ass all around.

* Judy Holliday (1921–1965) was born Judith Tuvim. (The Yiddish word *yontoyvim* means "holidays"—hence the stage name.) She was one of the great comic actresses, typically playing women whose dizziness conceals, yet also proves, a deep intelligence.

the face the moment she left the room and said, "That woman is a cunt!" To which I could say nothing in her defense except, "Well, she must have problems."

Everything ground to a halt as we started auditioning for a new star. We looked everywhere; nothing doing. Finally, we went to hear this girl, Barbra Streisand, who had just finished her first Broadway show[*] and was singing at the Blue Angel. We thought she was perfect: the right age—she was just twenty-one—and a once-in-a-lifetime comic with a once-in-a-lifetime voice.

After her set, we went backstage to find this gawky woman gobbling a peach, her hair still braided up like a challah. Her debut album, cleverly called *The Barbra Streisand Album*, was about to be released, and it was clear she'd be a huge star in about ten minutes. Even so, when we asked if she'd learn a couple of songs and audition them for the producers and director, she said, "Sure!" as if we'd offered her another peach. A few days later, she sang the bejesus out of them. After which, Tec—that's what everyone called Da Costa because he was born Morton Tecosky— immediately said, "Don't be silly, she's too ugly."

It would have been best to kill the show right there, but few in show-biz are strong enough to swallow the cyanide. You don't die until you're buried. And lo and behold, it was at this moment—we were at a Howard Johnson's, crying into our coffee—that Judy called with revitalizing news. "I'm fine, I'm fine, they've given me a clean bill of health. Come right up with the papers!" So after a stop at Fryer and Carr's, we trooped off to the Dakota, where she signed the contract and celebrated the good news.

Which wasn't true.

Later I came to think she'd lied from the start. She wanted to work

....

[*] Barbra Streisand (born 1942) was nominated for a Tony Award as Best Featured Actress in a Musical for *I Can Get It for You Wholesale*, which closed in December 1962. (She lost to Phyllis Newman.) She began her three-week stint at the Blue Angel, with Stiller and Meara also on the bill, in January. Arthur Laurents directed both the musical and her club act and forever after claimed to have invented her.

1963: Judy Holliday in *Hot Spot*. "She indulged in ordinary diva
behavior, too, including helping herself to other people's songs."

no matter what, which as someone who felt the same way I understand.
But there was also a rumor that she had immense tax debts to pay off.
Her life was not so happy even aside from the illness; her longtime boyfriend, who was out cheating on her every night, was Gerry Mulligan, of
saxophone fame, which I think is why so many unnecessary saxophones
wound up in the *Hot Spot* score. And maybe she had no idea how bad the
situation would get.

Whatever the reason, she was grumpy and needy and tired in rehearsal. She didn't look or smell good; she wore wigs but never washed
them. She indulged in ordinary diva behavior, too, including helping herself to other people's songs. Mary Louise Wilson, whom we'd hired to
play Dulcie's, or Sally's, right-hand woman, found most of hers hijacked;
Judy wound up with something like ten. It unbalanced the show, but because there *was* no show without Judy, we were at her mercy.

The reviews of the Washington tryout were awful.* Another highlight of the run there was the freezing cold night one of the chorus girls got sick and I went to her hotel room to see if I could help. Though she was indeed languishing under a pile of quilts I pretty quickly realized that she wasn't sick, she was drunk, and that what had caused her to drink was that she'd just been jilted—by my father.

She was just the canary in the coal mine. Tec soon fled in the middle of the night through a secret tunnel that led to New York Hospital. Various other directors then dropped in and dropped out—even Arthur was approached—but we got to Philadelphia still without one.† We finally landed up with Herbie Ross, who brought the show, uncredited, into New York.‡ In the meantime, everyone got axed but me and Rouben Ter-Arutunian, who did the sets. (They couldn't fire him because they couldn't spell his name or pronounce it.) I wish they did ax me—I would have been delighted to offer my neck—but instead they fired Marty. And guess who arrived to rescue the lyrics?

Steve.

There wasn't much even Steve could do by then. The blame for that—and, as far as I'm concerned, for everything—falls on Weinstock and Gilbert. They had been so bruised and angry about the Pulitzer snub that they had a non-interpolation clause written into their contract for *Hot Spot*, which meant that when the show was in terrible trouble, we couldn't bring in any book writers to fix it. Even so, some arrived secretly,

....

* *Hot Spot* played the National Theater in Washington, D.C., from February 4 through 23, 1963, opening on February 5 to reviews featuring socko lines like: "With three weeks here and further convalescence in Philadelphia, *Hot Spot* may survive in a season of negligible competition."

† The Philadelphia engagement, at the Shubert, was from February 27 to March 16.

‡ Ominously, no director or choreographer is listed in the *Playbill* for the Broadway production.

rolled up in rugs, I guess. Herb Gardner and Larry Gelbart were said to have rolled in, and Michael Stewart, but they must have rolled right back out again, because I never saw them.* I did find Comden and Green trying to hide themselves in a Philadelphia elevator one night. They were not very hidable.

Philadelphia is where Steve wrote the supposed "additional" lyrics for two songs, both sung by Judy: a new opening number called "Don't Laugh" and a new second-act opener called "That's Good—That's Bad." In reality, his lyrics were barely additional; they were almost the whole thing. For "Don't Laugh" I wrote the chorus, setting some of Marty's old lyrics, but Steve wrote both music and lyrics for the very long verse, which frames the situation and makes the song. The result sounds like pure Steve to me, even the part I wrote; that's how generous a teacher and collaborator he was. And dramatist: the way he places pauses in the melody to set up jokes, the way the jokes are really character statements. "Show me a hundred lighters, I'll show you the one that won't," Sally sings, describing her genius for bad luck. And then, closing the couplet with wry self-awareness: "Show me a priceless vase—No, don't!"† It's so funny and charming, it suggests a far better show than the one we then delivered.

Which isn't to say I didn't write some good numbers.‡ It's just that

....

* Gelbart was smart to tell *Variety* that although he had in fact written new material for *Hot Spot*, he had also withdrawn it.

† Musically, "Don't Laugh" sounds almost as if it might have come from Steve's score for *A Funny Thing Happened on the Way to the Forum*, which opened in May 1962 and was still running.

‡ The best songs include "Hey Love," which is still performed in cabarets, if they still exist, and which became (with a comma added) the title of a revue of Mary's songs years later. Also "Gabie" and "A Far, Far Better Thing." All of them were written for Holliday's character, which is to say for Holliday.

1963: Judy Holliday, cover girl for the short-lived *Hot Spot*.
"A bunch of nitwits had let Our Lady of Comedy down."

writing some good numbers could never fill what was quickly becoming—
like *Spider-Man* but without the aerial trauma—the season's punching bag.
For one thing, it was, at the time, the most expensive show ever, with a
capitalization of $350,000.* That we were booked into one of Broad-
way's most prominent theaters† didn't help. When Fryer and Carr kept
delaying the opening to squeeze money out of the show before word of
mouth killed it, the vultures started cawing.

And everyone knows what it means if, when you finally do open, it's
on a Friday: It means you hope it's true that no one reads the papers on
Saturday.

I read them Friday night on the fire stairs at Sardi's. The reviews were
across-the-board terrible, of course; Howard Taubman's in *The Times* began "It's a shame" and went downhill from there. The general idea was

---

* Now that's nothing: about three million dollars. The capitalization for
Spider-Man: Turn Off the Dark, which began previews in 2010, was said to
be seventy-five million.

† The Majestic, which had become available when *I Picked a Daisy*, the
Richard Rodgers–Alan Jay Lerner musical about reincarnation, failed to
materialize.

that a bunch of nitwits had let Our Lady of Comedy down. I was not spared, nor should I have been.* I undoubtedly wasn't doing the best work I could.

The humiliation stung for a while, though I didn't lose friends and no one spat at me in the street. Maybe that's because Hank and I took off for Europe immediately after the opening for a Lick Your Wounds tour. Soon after we got back, the show shut down; and not long after that, so did poor Judy. "You can only live through one or two Hot Spots in your life," she told the press.† I would prove her wrong.

---

* Taubman's review of the April 19, 1963, opening allowed that Hot Spot had "some agreeable songs." Other critics did not allow.

† Hot Spot closed on May 25, 1963. Judy Holliday died on June 7, 1965. She was forty-three.

36.

WHAT, ME WORRY?

I n Merriewold Park* during the summer of 1963 I realized that, for the fifth time in eleven years, I was pregnant. You'd think that at thirty-two I would no longer be surprised; the evidence of my fecundity was zooming around the house. Tod was ten, Nina nine, Kimmy seven, and Matthew—more like creeping than zooming—nine months.

Hank agreed that it was too soon in our marriage to have another child, and especially too soon after Matthew was born. I'd done that once, with Tod and Nina, fifteen months apart, and it wasn't good for either of them. It's like the subway when trains are spaced too closely—or so I'm told: The first one gets crammed, so the next is deserted.

Hank was also about to change jobs. He had just been named the producing general manager of the newly established Music Theater of Lincoln Center, which in an amazing coincidence was headed by Daddy.†

....

* Merriewold Park was a summer getaway community in the Catskills, near Monticello, New York. The Guettels rented a house there for one summer and later bought a different one nearby.

† Music Theater of Lincoln Center was established in 1963, with Richard Rodgers as its president and producing director. His first season, which started the following July, featured hit revivals of *The King and I* and *The Merry Widow* at what was then the brand-new New York State Theater. (We will not say what it is now.) He continued at Lincoln Center until

1965: Adam, Matthew, Kim, Nina, Tod. "The evidence of my fecundity
was zooming around the house."

And of course I had my own new jobs, dozens of them, piling up on the
piano. Big or piddling, successes or fizzles, they took all the time I didn't
spend traffic-copping the menagerie.

Not that I needed excuses to get an abortion. I was not yet three
months pregnant, and the fetus, I read, was the size of a strawberry. Neither Hank nor I had any moral qualms about it. But it was not possible
in New York then, nor in the rest of the country, to get a safe, legal pro-
cedure.* I asked around and was given the name of a Cuban doctor who
had escaped Battista and worked in Miami. Not even Miami Beach.

....

1969. Hank, glad for the unspoken nepotism but also uncomfortable with
it, left sooner.

* Some states already permitted abortion in cases of rape or maternal
danger. But under other circumstances it would not become legal in New
York State until 1970, and not in the entire country until 1973.

Linda, with whom I was having one of my periodic cessations of hostility, came with me for the adventure of it. She had a lot more money to spend than I did. Her husband, Danny, had by now left his big job at ABC to join David Susskind's production company.* I liked Danny, as I've said: He was outrageous and a climber and very smart. Linda, who had very little else on her mind at the time, having given up music completely and not yet discovered the glamour of social work, thought I was sleeping with him. Even I was too prim for that. He did put his hand on my knee under their table in Pound Ridge once, but I just removed it and he understood.

Anyway, I felt like Linda's poorer cousin; she would open her closet and it would be double-hung with beautiful linen blouses. They had more Giacomettis than you could shake a stick at, and most of them looked like sticks to begin with.

So we stayed at the Fontainebleau. On the prescribed day, I went as instructed to a pay phone and called the number I'd been given. The voice on the phone then told me to go, alone, to a certain address where a person would meet me at a certain corner; I was to stay a hundred yards behind as that person led me to the abortion facility. It was all very cloak and dagger, cash in my poice, but when I got to the secret location, it was just a tidy, clean office with normal nurses, anesthesia, and a perfectly lovely English-speaking obstetrician.

Afterward, back at the hotel with Linda, I had a dry Rob Roy, a shrimp cocktail, a sirloin steak, a baked potato with sour cream and chives, and a salad with Roquefort dressing.

I wonder if I was trying to refill myself for the strawberry I'd expelled. Not that I was ashamed; when I signed the *Ms.* abortion statement years

....

* At Susskind's Talent Associates, Daniel Melnick would eventually help create highly successful shows, including *Get Smart*. But he would first get tangled up in producing a Broadway musical, *Kelly*, that was a bigger flop even than *Hot Spot*, closing immediately upon its Broadway opening on February 16, 1965. He lost his entire investment, some of it borrowed from his father-in-law.

later, I wanted to do it as publicly as possible, so I signed it as Mary Rodgers instead of Mary Rodgers Guettel.* Since then I have helped some young women who couldn't afford it pay for abortions they needed. Politically, I'm a full believer. But as a personal matter, I knew I wanted more children someday, and I'd already been so fortunate in that department it seemed like tempting fate. You shouldn't trust young luck—a lesson the theater was always drumming into me.

And yet there I was, a year later, summer of 1964, pregnant again. That fall, in his column, Leonard Lyons had me "racing the stork" to finish my "new musical" before my fifth child arrived. The stork won by a mile.

The musical was *Miss Moffat*, based on *The Corn Is Green*, by Emlyn Williams.† The Eckarts brought the play to me and Marshall, suggesting that the semiautobiographical story about a nearly illiterate Welsh boy saved by a determined English schoolteacher would have to be Americanized. The Welsh boy, Marshall and I decided, would become Black; for the impoverished late-nineteenth-century coal miners he lived among we would substitute sharecroppers in the Jim Crow South. But after we asked Ossie Davis, who knew that world from personal experience, to write the book, Emlyn said no, he wanted first crack at it.‡ "And if at the end of a year I haven't done something you find satisfactory," he said, "you should feel free to fire me."

....

* "We Have Had Abortions," which appeared in the Spring 1972 issue of *Ms.* magazine, was undersigned by fifty-three women, among them Billie Jean King, Susan Sontag, Anaïs Nin, Gloria Steinem, and Nora Ephron. Ephron hadn't in fact had an abortion but signed for solidarity. Some people assumed that Mary, likewise, had never had an abortion, as if a woman with lots of children could not possibly need one.

† Ethel Barrymore starred as Miss Moffat in the 1940 Broadway premiere of the 1938 play; Bette Davis starred in the 1945 Warner Bros. movie.

‡ The actor, writer, and activist Ossie Davis (1917–2005) grew up in Georgia under the ever-present threat of racist violence by the Ku Klux Klan.

We laughed nervously and set to work on the songs.

When Emlyn returned some months later, script in hand, he insisted on reading the entire thing aloud, in a hotel suite Jean and Bill rented for the purpose. It was unspeakably bad and acutely discomfiting. His horrifying attempts at Black dialect sounded as if they'd been lifted from Stepin Fetchit movies: "Who be that person jumpin' through the corn husks?"* The structure, character development, and overall tone were just as bad.

Thank God for Jean; when Emlyn, having finally finished reciting the second act, asked proudly, "What do you think?" we all sat there slack-jawed until she had the guts to whisper, "I'm so sorry, this just doesn't work."

"In that case, I won't give you the rights," he huffed. "Anyway, I'd much rather write with Richard Rodgers than with his daughter." But Daddy was loyal when Emlyn had the nerve to ask him. "It's not my project," he answered. "It's Mary's."

Actually, it wasn't either of ours now. Into the piano bench went the songs I'd written, there to molder with all the rest. But the story isn't entirely unhappy because, years later, we learned that Emlyn had given the musical rights to Albert Hague,† a neighbor of mine at the Majestic. Hague's version actually made it as far as Philadelphia but laid a huge egg there and promptly died.‡ I am not ashamed to say that, *chez moi*, a lot

....

* Not a real line from Williams's libretto. But according to *Opera News*, this is: "I'm gonna be drinkin' ch-ch-ch-cham-cham-wiiiiiiiiiiine."

† Albert Hague (1920–2001) wrote the music for Broadway musicals including the Amish-themed *Plain and Fancy*, the Gwen Verdon vehicle *Redhead*, and, with lyrics by Allan Sherman, *The Fig Leaves Are Falling*. Later he played the music teacher Benjamin Shorofsky on *Fame*.

‡ Bette Davis, re-creating her film role, starred in *Miss Moffat*, with music by Hague, lyrics by Williams, and a book by Williams and Joshua Logan, who also directed. The production began a supposedly pre-Broadway tour in Philadelphia on October 7, 1974, but closed there eleven days

circa 1980: Mary, at a gala in her honor, joined by Arthur Laurents and
Stephen Sondheim. "Here's to us! Who's like us? Damn few."

of giddy schadenfreuding ensued. I have always taken comfort in other
people's failures being even worse than mine.

Though it would be a while before *Miss Moffat* got buried in the piano
bench, Adam Arthur Guettel was born that December. The "Arthur" part
requires an explanation, because the horrible Mr. Laurents later called
himself Adam's godfather and middle-namesake. Neither claim is true.
Jews don't have godfathers anyway, and if they did, Adam's would have
been Hank's father, Arthur Guettel. Also, how many godfathers, short of
the kind in mobster movies, would do to their godson what Arthur did to
Adam with *The Light in the Piazza*?*

....

later, when Davis dropped out. "I'm too big a star to be giving a poor
performance, which I'm now doing," she said. The Broadway production
was canceled. So was the cast recording, though there's a bootleg. Davis
wound up suing Logan for libel. Good fun!

* At one point, Arthur Laurents was going to write the book for the musical. Let's just say, without getting into the contractual shenanigans, that

To be fair, the Arthurs of this world don't thrive in a vacuum. Those of us who wind up their victims have usually been their enablers first.

My life should have taught me by then that trying to paper over problems instead of exposing them never works for long. But I was very stubborn, refusing yet again to pack up my marbles and go home; I wouldn't reach that stage until later. I was too scared of insulting people or of getting them mad at me. Which is not a surprise, since I spent my entire childhood with everyone mad at me. All two of them. No wonder as an adult I sought to correct for that. I had the idealistic peacekeeper's notion that if you forced two people into one room with a common goal, whatever resentments they harbored would eventually subside. Maybe that's not a peacekeeper's notion but a woman's notion, or just a me notion: If I could endure so much bullshit for the sake of a higher goal, why could men endure so little?

Piazza was a classic case. Shortly after I read the Elizabeth Spencer novella,* I took it to Daddy; I was trying to get him going again after Ockie's death. I knew he liked stories, set in exotic locales, that test love against apparently impossible oppositions. *Piazza*—in which a pretty American girl with the mental capacity of a child goes with her mother to Florence, where her deficits disappear in translation and she finds adult love she might never have found back home—had both. But Daddy said it was not for him: He didn't want anything to do with what he called mental illness, having trafficked in it himself. Many years later, when I suggested the same story to Adam, he loved it and was specifically drawn to that aspect; somehow he identified with Clara, the defective daughter.

....

it didn't end well—though the show, with Craig Lucas eventually writing the book, certainly did. It opened on Broadway on April 18, 2005, ran for more than a year, and won six Tony Awards, including Best Score.

* The novella appeared in the June 18, 1960, issue of *The New Yorker*. In 1962, MGM released a film version starring Olivia de Havilland as the mother and Yvette Mimieux as the daughter.

You may ask why I recommended this material to my father and my son but not to myself. Let me know when you have an answer.*

Anyway, it took forty-five years for that idea to pan out. Others moved faster, which wasn't always better. Soon after Daddy rejected *Piazza*, Arthur, with my prompting, brought him another story about an American woman who, unlikely to find a man at home, finds one in Italy. This was Arthur's play *The Time of the Cuckoo*,† a perfect solution to Daddy's *Piazza* problem because its leading character, named Leona Samish, isn't brain-damaged but a spinster. (Which at the time meant thirtyish.) Venice, where she falls into a canal and then in love, seemed as exotic as Florence, and even more musically suggestive.

My agenda wasn't just to get Daddy working but also to sell him on Steve, and vice versa. Steve, understandably, didn't want to collaborate with Richard Rodgers; aside from his personal misgivings, he rightly thought he had come too far to write lyrics again for another man's music. But Ockie had apparently instructed him, before dying, to work with Daddy if he could, and so for that reason, as well as friendship for me, Steve consented.

The result—which opened in 1965 under the title *Do I Hear a Waltz?*—was what I called a "Why?" musical: perfectly competent but lacking the spark that comes from having a specific passion for writing it.‡ I

....

* Perhaps it was that Mary felt insufficiently connected to the mother, who is after all the lead, and instead identified, like Adam, with the daughter. She'd certainly lived through a Clara moment: When Mary was eight, her grandmother May took her and cousin Judy Crichton to the Statue of Liberty, where, as Mary leaned out of the torch, which you can't do now, her hat—a gray felt one with a smooth crown and a little brim and a gray grosgrain ribbon—blew off, just as happens to Clara, except no one caught it.

† Shirley Booth starred in its 1952 Broadway premiere; the 1955 movie, called *Summertime*, starred Katharine Hepburn.

‡ Mary had defined the "Why?" phenomenon without yet naming it in

don't mean a motivation; everyone had a motivation. Arthur wanted to squeeze more money out of that dried sponge of a story; Steve wanted to honor Ockie's wishes (and mine); Daddy wanted to write lovely music regardless of what it was about. And the music *is* lovely, if square, with those eight-bar phrases Dr. Sirmay would approve even if Steve's lyrics sometimes scanned best at seven. But the real problem was that no one ever solved the riddle of how to make an emotionally frozen woman like Leona sing. Steve's idea that she should not do so until the end, when she has a breakthrough, must have seemed as unappealing to the composer as it seemed insane to the producer. Daddy was both.

This "Why?" musical was also the start of a protracted "Why?" moment for me—and by protracted I mean for decades. Why did I keep trying to make things happen that didn't want to happen on their own? Why was work such a struggle? My career in musical theater seemed to fit me like one of my mother's dresses, the kind that needed so much retailoring it hardly seemed worth it. Sometimes I wanted to rip the thing off. I sure wished I hadn't pushed everyone into *Do I Hear a Waltz?* My comeuppance for meddling was that Daddy wound up loathing Steve even more than he already did,* and Steve and Arthur loathed him right back.

One of Steve's lyrics, for a song called "We're Gonna Be All Right," about a couple on the skids, captured the damp rancor of the forced collaboration:

....

1961, telling a Broadway reporter, perhaps a bit too revealingly: "You must have something to say in a show. This business of doing it automatically, the way some women have a baby every two years, is just no good." Sondheim's definition, in *Finishing the Hat*, is: "A perfectly respectable show, based on a perfectly respectable source, that has no reason for being." He also points out the irony of Mary's having helped push him into writing exactly the kind of show she'd identified.

* "The more we worked on the show, the more estranged I became from both writers," Richard Rodgers wrote in *Musical Stages*. "Any suggestions I made were promptly rejected, as if by prearrangement."

1965: Richard Rodgers, Stephen Sondheim, and Arthur Laurents
during rehearsals for *Do I Hear a Waltz?*—the original "Why?" musical.

All is well
Least as far as their friends can tell
Please excuse the peculiar smell
Mildew
Will do
Harm.

Daddy, who liked the lyric enough to hug Steve upon reading it,
showed it to Mummy, who sniffed a satire hitting too close to home.*

---

* Dorothy Rodgers had recently published her first book, *My Favorite
Things*, in which she told people how to decorate their apartments and
serve aspic. That her marriage was just as cold and gelatinous may be
indicated by this story, probably apocryphal, about a glamorous sports

Daddy backpedaled with a vengeance. "What is this shit?" he snarled the next day at lunch with the creative team. Out it went.*

Was the cynicism she couldn't tolerate—about marriage, about anything—exactly what I was drawn to in my own work? At any rate I was afraid of sentimentality, which is what you keep hitting when you aim for romantic and don't have the craft to stick a bull's-eye. Satire is safer, and my music, not just because of the lyricists I worked with, was at that point mostly satirical. It was commentary. Which is not necessarily a bad thing. One of my favorite songs, unfortunately now disappeared, was something Marshall and I wrote for *That Was the Week That Was*.† The show was a kind of pre–*Saturday Night Live* recap of whatever awful things were happening then, but in our song, called "That Was the Week That Wasn't," we did the opposite. We listed all the awful things happening, but then, with the title refrain, declared that they had not—including, at the end of the song, the deaths of Goodman, Cheney, and Schwerner in Mississippi.‡ It was like having an anvil dropped on your chest, an effect enhanced by the jaunty waltz tune: whimsical and charming and sour and deadly.

But you do enough of one kind of thing and it's all anyone can see. Robby Lantz had evidently identified me as the silly romp girl, so he attached me and Marshall to a project he was packaging called *The Mad Show*. The title referred to the spoofy, raspberrying *Mad* magazine, which had given us the rights to make a musical revue based on its contents,

....

car Dick bought. Eager to take his wife for a first spin in it, he got frustrated when he couldn't locate the ignition, and kept poking around the dashboard with his key. "If it had hair around it, you'd find it," she said.

* The replacement lyric passed the Dorothy Rodgers test: It was dull.

† An American version of a British comedy show, *That Was the Week That Was* ran on NBC from January 1964 to May 1965.

‡ The three young civil rights workers were shot to death by Klansmen on June 21, 1964; "That Was the Week That Wasn't," sung by Phyllis Newman, aired on July 10, the final episode of the season.

with the condition that its publisher, Bill Gaines, could toss out any material he didn't like. But the title was also a kind of curse, describing the process of writing it, in which everyone was apparently possessed with the spirit of that leering imp and idiot icon Alfred E. Neuman.

I know now that the best way to write a show is with all the major players locked in one room, or at least in one city. You need the constant sweaty contact, to ensure you are all making the same thing from the same ingredients. You might think that would be less important in a revue, which is by its nature disjointed, but a revue actually requires at least as much tonal discipline as a "book show" because it has no narrative through line to pull it taut. Not only that but, in keeping with *Mad*'s youthful outlook, we had hired a cast of goofball unknowns, and though they were all brilliant and had good-to-great careers later—Linda Lavin, Jo Anne Worley, Paul Sand, Richard Libertini, MacIntyre Dixon—we had no star magic to hold the mayonnaise together.

Nevertheless, everyone instantly retired to different noncommunicating worlds, much like the snotty kids whose attitudes we were echoing and mocking. Marshall and I worked at the Majestic, writing songs that thumbed their noses, if songs have noses, at anything we considered square, including hipness.* Stan Hart and Larry Siegel, who wrote the sketches, went somewhere else; we never saw them. Our neophyte director, Steven Vinaver,† who had a British accent even though he'd graduated from Bronx High School of Science, left New York to polish his *r*'s in London, and did not return until just before Bill Gaines decided to exercise his option.

So picture this. In a nasty, hot little attic room above the New The-

---

* "Well It Ain't" parodied a mumbly, tune-wrecking folksinger like Bob Dylan: "You think it's easy singing about misery and how the world is up a creek / When you're making over four thousand dollars a week? / Well, it ain't."

† Sometimes credited under his own name, and sometimes as Alfred E. Neuman, Steven Vinaver (1936–1968) died of pancreatic cancer the summer after *The Mad Show* closed. He was thirty-one.

atre on East Fifty-fourth, long since torn down to make room for the Citicorp building, we grubby writers gathered to audition the material for the suits: Gaines and his *Mad* mag flunkies; Columbia Records execs (they had, sound unseen, agreed to produce the album) and theirs. Vinaver looked halfway businesslike in tweed, and Stan, Larry, and I at least presentable, but—

Oh god. Did I mention that Marshall and I weren't getting along while writing the show? Depending on which drugs he was taking that day, he'd yell at me about my music or snarl if I dared to criticize his lyrics. I eventually decided I was sick of arguing with him, and would set absolutely everything he gave me, no matter how bad it was. But it was a tough slog and of course it was dangerous to have him in the house anyway, he made such a mess of everywhere he went.

Anyway, back at the audition, there's Marshall, wearing pointy boots, jeans, a shirt festooned with yesterday's tuna fish sandwich, and a fringed leather jacket. He is foaming at the mouth from an overdose of Tums, squinting at his coffee-stained, unpaginated sheaf of lyrics, putting on his distance glasses, taking off his distance glasses, losing his distance glasses, which are resting in his hand. He stumbles through the entire score, at the end of which:

Silence. Bill Gaines rises. Reminds the room of his right to toss out any material he doesn't like. And what doesn't he like? Everything. He doesn't like everything. Couple of tunes, maybe, but otherwise, forget it. Unless we can come up with better material pronto.

Rehearsals are scheduled to start on Monday. It's Friday. What, me worry?

That night, Marshall shows up at my apartment to announce he's leaving immediately for Palm Beach. He slams the door behind him so fiercely the paint flakes off.

Like I said, I was never one to quit in a huff. I was barely one to proceed in a huff. I just didn't huff. I got to work, drafting Vinaver to write the lyrics for a couple of new songs, which were quite good; Larry Siegel to cover another; and even Steve to chip in.

Steve's chip was pseudonymous: In the official songwriting credits he goes by Esteban Ria Nido.* But boy, that Esteban was terrific. It was he who suggested, in keeping with the *Mad* attitude, a spoof of a currently popular song. Among the most popular in the mid-1960s was "The Girl from Ipanema," a bossa nova with lyrics about a man in love with a willowy woman who barely even knows he exists.† Our version would be gender-flipped: a woman in love with a willowy man who barely even knows she exists—because he's gay. I'm pretty sure that part was my idea because, well, how could it not be?

As for the music itself, when I listen to it now, and I often do because it has become a cabaret standard, it all sounds like Steve. Maybe I wrote the front strain, the bossa nova, and then he cleaned it up or dirtied it up; I know I couldn't have done all those wonderful key changes in the bridge in the little time we had. And there's no question most of the lyrics are his: "Why does he say he's Castilian? / Why are his trousers vermilion? / Why do his friends call him Lillian?" Who else gets three jokes to rhyme?

But we did come up with the kicker together, in which the boy from Tacarembo la Tumbe del Fuego Santa Malipas Zatatecas la Junta del Sol y Cruz—a made-up mouthful of a name—turns out to be heading to a town with an even longer one: Llanfair-pwllgwyngyll-gogery-chwyrn-drobwll-llan-tysilio-gogo-goch. That town, in Wales, is real; we called the first Welsh person we could think of, Sybil Burton, Richard Burton's ex, from two extensions in my apartment, scribbling down her pronunciation phonetically so we could teach it to Linda Lavin later.

Later meaning the next day; after the nonstop work weekend, with four new songs, and as many sketches, we started rehearsal. Marshall

....

* That is, "Stephen Sondheim" in Spanish via butchered German. In the show's program, he went with a different nom de plume: "Nom de Plume."

† "The Girl from Ipanema," with music by Antônio Carlos Jobim and lyrics by Vinícius de Moraes, became an international hit in 1964 when performed by the saxophonist Stan Getz and sung, in Portuguese and English, by the guitarist João Gilberto and his then-wife, Astrud Gilberto.

reappeared, rested and cheerful and lacking any apologies. When Bill Gaines arrived after a week away, and heard the revised show performed by the excellent cast instead of a nutcase with a mouthful of Tums, he allowed it to go on. And even though we opened in the middle of poor Mayor Lindsay's transit strike and I had to walk crosstown to the theater, we got terrific reviews and ran for twenty months.*

It was nice to have hit the sweet spot of the zeitgeist: anarchic, unpretentious, and adolescent. (I mean the show, not the creative team.) That it never returned much money didn't bother me until I noticed that my checks kept going down even as the houses went up. I finally said to Robby Lantz, "What's with the royalties?" It turned out the theater owner, who was also one of the producers, and who later went to work in the circus, was ripping us off. Lantz said, "Darling, what do you want me to do? Sue him?" And I said, "Yes!" But Robby represented that guy, too. Always being on everybody's side, he was, effectively, on no one's but his own.

---

* *The Mad Show* opened at the New Theatre on East Fifty-fourth Street on January 9, 1966, and closed on September 10, 1967. The strike by transport workers against the New York City Transit Authority started on January 1, 1966, the first day of John V. Lindsay's first term as mayor. (It ended on January 13.) In the *Times*, dour Stanley Kauffmann gave *The Mad Show* a qualified rave ("it is always amusing") and *Life* magazine called it "a carnival of caterwauling idiots"—which was a compliment.

37.

THE BOY FROM

One hundred miles northwest of the Upper West Side, with twenty-five hundred acres of forest and a sixty-acre lake, Merriewold was supposed to be a refuge: a healthy place for kids to spend the summer outdoors without gulping mouthfuls of soot.* Also, for me, a refuge from my parents, the city, and the world.

But how much refuge could any place be in that messed-up decade? Merriewold, in hindsight, offered no sanctuary, healthwise or otherwise. If you knew where to look, it even told you so: At the entrance there was an enormous Japanese gatehouse imported from the St. Louis Exposition of 1904—but no gateman.

We'd come at the urging of Judy Abbott, who was part of the artsy sub-enclave there, along with Neil and Leba Sedaka, Freddie and Myrna Gershon, Cousin Brucie, and Agnes de Mille.† Agnes's family had been

....

* Hard to remember now that in the mid-1960s New York's air was considered the most polluted in the country. A two-week major "smog event" in January and February of 1963, when Matthew was four months old, resulted in 647 "excess deaths" over the next few months among New Yorkers exposed to it.

† Neil Sedaka (born 1939) is the singer-songwriter most famous for "Breaking Up Is Hard to Do." Freddie Gershon (born 1939) is the longtime head of Music Theater International, the licensing agency for hundreds

among the founders of the colony in 1891, back when it was a hideaway for the moneyed Wasp intelligentsia, with black-tie dinners in the club-house.* But after World War II, the fanciest people either died or left. The clubhouse shut down and the wrong type moved in—and by wrong type I mean us. But not only us.

After renting there in 1963, we bought a house in 1965. Compared to Long Island or Connecticut it was incredibly cheap, only fourteen thousand dollars for fourteen rooms. Even so, my parents wouldn't help because Merriewold was too far from them in Connecticut: a whole two hours away. More generally, Mummy found the Catskills déclassé, and that was even before I showed her the business card the septic-tank man gave me: "Your shit is our bread and butter." Instead, George Abbott loaned us six thousand dollars and we scrounged the rest from royalties and sofa cushions. I bought a nice-shaped brown grand piano from my dressmaker and stationed myself at it while the kids went to day camp. Hank came up for weekends by bus.

It didn't take long to realize that except for our motley bunch, Merriewold was a sinkhole of bigotry, filled with Catholic Republicans whose kids shrieked "kike" and "faggot." The casual—and formal—racism was the worst I'd seen anywhere, a seething hatred not only of Black people (there were none) but of anyone who might be assumed to support them.

That was us, of course. After Martin Luther King Jr. was killed in April 1968, Judy and I got all the New York City kids together to say this

....

of Broadway titles. Cousin Brucie is Bruce Morrow (born 1935), the radio host and disc jockey. Aside from her classic ballets, Agnes de Mille (1905–1993) was the choreographer for many Broadway shows, including *Oklahoma!* and *Carousel*—and *Allegro*, which she also directed.

* Among the amenities touted to "selected owners" in a 1927 advertisement in the *Brooklyn Daily Eagle* were a golf course, "a stable of beautiful saddle horses," and a "large clubhouse furnishing excellent meals and rooms for guests, thereby solving the servant problem."

racial shit has got to stop. Our idea was to integrate the place. There was no point trying to get a Black couple to buy a house in that atmosphere, but why not at least have some Black kids spend the summer?

I hear you muttering over there! Yes, it now smells of Lenny-style liberalism, however well-intentioned and ham-handed, or like when we schoolgirls tried to integrate Brearley. At the time, though, it just seemed like a small start a few people could make. Or, rather, one person, because only Judy's daughter Susannah was willing to take up the cause. That summer she brought a Black friend from school to stay with her, and though the other Merriewold kids for the most part accepted her, their parents were furious. One refused to screen the weekly film at the lakeside clubhouse if the girl was in attendance.

Now, Agnes had an ornate old show curtain in her attic somewhere, which gave us the idea of keeping everyone out of the bushes and off pot by putting on musicals. Judy directed shows like *Bye Bye Birdie* and *Fiorello!*, featuring just the kids and an upright piano and Agnes's curtain strung between plywood walls they put up to enclose the pavilion by the lake. The shows were great fun until, one night during the summer of our integration experiment, vandals ripped down Agnes's curtain and spray-painted *Resurection City* on the plywood. Leaving aside the indignity of the misspelling, we took it as a racist and anti-Semitic threat.*

The state police met us at the palace gate. They were brush-cut Republicans and probably anti-Black themselves, but they took the complaint, asking whether we had any idea who did this. We had several, in fact, but suspected one family in particular, which consisted almost too perfectly of a drunk father who was later shot to death by one of his four sons while defending his abused mother. The cops wouldn't make

....

* Resurrection City was the name of a fifteen-acre encampment of tents and shanties set up that summer in Washington, D.C., to protest economic injustice. Organized by the Poor People's Campaign, it was so big it had its own zip code and mayor, Jesse Jackson.

an arrest but, much to our surprise, said they could drive into the family's driveway and scare them good, which they did.

I know it seems like we were playing with people's lives. You could reasonably ask how much good we did, or could ever have done, for the world, let alone for Susannah's Black friend. Was anyone changed for the better by the experience? A few years later, when one of the racist girls in the community had an affair with and got pregnant by a Black kitchen worker in her school, was that a sign of borders being breached? And when her family wouldn't let her bring up the baby, was that a sign of the opposite? Eventually, I came to think of the experiment as a well-meaning disaster in an era full of them.

Two other disasters had already transpired. Back in the late spring of 1966, while I was starting work on a musical version of *The Member of the Wedding* (disaster no. 1), Matthew, who was three, stopped breathing (disaster no. 2).

His asthma—or, rather, his "croup with asthmatic breathing," as the doctors called it—had started when he wasn't even a year old. The next two years were terrifying, as we were on constant lookout for signs of a cold that could provoke an attack. Quite quickly we discovered that whatever it was the doctor shot him up with to calm him down—this was when doctors made house calls—sped him up instead. The only thing that helped was taking him into a steaming hot shower or to the hospital. I spent a lot of time in both.

But this attack in the spring of 1966 was worse: He was choking to death. I remember his naked terror, and my own. We raced him to New York Hospital, where they tried to resolve the situation with steroids and antibiotics. He cried when he saw the pills but cried worse when he saw the shots. I said, "Matthew, they won't have to give you the shots if you'll eat everything they ask you to." He nodded yes, yes—he couldn't talk—but he just couldn't swallow. So with Burt Shevelove at his bedside trying to entertain him with funny faces, the nurse shot him up. To no avail; finally, they had to do a tracheotomy.

That ended the emergency, but over the next months, as he got very chubby from the ongoing steroids, we lived every day with the feeling that it might happen again. I remember thinking to myself: What will we do if he dies? And if he doesn't die, how long can we live like this? The doctors said he might grow out of it, but not until he was six at least. I didn't think I could last that long.

So although it was scary to leave the city, we figured that for his sake, and ours, and the other kids', too, it made sense to go to Merriewold that summer. I remember thinking how much better the air would be for him there—and also that we could use those months to have his bedroom at the Majestic redone, getting rid of anything that might harbor dust. Now, of course, I realize that our cigarettes were part of the problem—not just ours but everyone's. Even in the woods with the windows open, we all lived in smokehouses.

Did I mention I smoked a lot? Right now, as I sit here croaking, you could call what happened karma.

We moved up to Merriewold at the end of the school year, with a nurse named Gerry to monitor Matthew and a wonderful English au pair named Lulu to mind the four others.

At first, Matthew thrived. He was so funny, sunny, and charming; he would stand up on a table and conduct the entire camp with a stick.

But one morning in late August, while Hank was in Los Angeles on business, I woke up around six o'clock thinking I was dreaming about a train thumping down the tracks. I soon realized it was Matthew running down the hall—and into me; I just caught him as he collapsed on the light blue carpet of the bedroom. He wasn't breathing. He'd wet his little lightweight pajamas, which was a bad sign for a boy who was thoroughly house trained; my god, he was almost four. I didn't know how to do artificial resuscitation, and anyway I was thinking it was hopeless—and if it was hopeless anyway I wanted it to be truly hopeless, because even though there were a lot of Catholic people up there, including once upon a time myself, I had no intention of letting him be a vegetable for the rest of his life.

I yelled for Tod, who was almost fourteen, to call the doctor, a guy named Gus Gavis who spent his summers in the Catskills, which he said was better than dealing with spoiled mothers freaking out their kids in the city.

But Tod was so nervous he dialed the wrong number.

It wouldn't have made any difference. After I redialed and Gavis said he was on his way, we all stood there staring, not knowing what to do. Matthew was still on the light blue bedroom carpet in his wet pajamas. I kept my eye on the tracheotomy wound, which by then was beginning to heal; no movement. He lay there in those cotton pajamas, looking like himself but just . . . gone.

I said to Tod, as simply as I could, "He's going to die." And Tod said, "You always think you know everything about medicine!"

Kimmy, who was ten, was so frantic she left the house. She thought they were going to take Matthew away and she couldn't bear to see that, so she went on a long walk and came back just in time to see him being taken away.

By then Gavis had arrived; so had a couple of other Merriewold doctors, one of them a lung specialist, and even the police. I didn't want my son's body brutalized. I said: "I don't think there's anything you can do, and there's nothing I want you to do if it's too late." Five or ten minutes had gone by and, you could see on their faces, it was.

I went downstairs, sat in the kitchen, and called Hank. It was still very early in California, maybe four in the morning, and he didn't answer his phone at first. I thought: This is cute, he's out playing around, and he's got this dead son here. But two seconds later he woke and saw the light flashing and he knew. The airline arranged to fly him back to LaGuardia immediately, and then by private plane to Monticello, so he arrived at the house late that afternoon.

It was a Sunday. Everything bad always happens on a Sunday. People kept coming around, in their Sunday clothes, bearing food, which was a good thing because I didn't have anything to feed them. I was not literally sedated but I felt like a dead planet moving through far space. At one point during the day I stumbled and did something to my right big toenail—I forgot to put shoes on—that caused it to get blacker and blacker and blacker, as if it were having my feelings for me. The next day Judy would have to drive me to a doctor, who drilled a hole in it to let the pressure out.

Somehow, I took care of responsibilities. I called Steve, I called Hal, I called my other friends, I called Frank Campbell.* I suppose I called the *Times* or got someone else to.† And then I finally had to call my parents. My father answered the phone in Connecticut, and since he never listened to half of what you said anyway, I'd decided to come right out and announce it clearly: "Listen, Daddy, Matthew died."

And he said, "Yeah, that's fine."

And I said, "Daddy, no, you're not listening to me! Matthew died!" With exclamation points. At which point he let out this horrible cry of pain.

That was the kind of incident that let you know he had some feeling. But it was not so much a human feeling as an animal shriek, like he must have emitted when his father lanced his index finger a lifetime earlier. Not so my mother. Her enamel never cracked. She picked up the phone and said, in her "kind" voice, "Well, darling, I guess you'll have to bring everyone down to New York to our apartment."

"I'm not uprooting them to be with you," I answered. "If you want to be with us, drive up here." Which they did. Probably just long enough for a few drinks.

What I held in mind as I moved through the day—and for that matter through my life as a parent—was to be the opposite of her. To be not selfish, not self-dramatizing, not confusing what happened to my child with what happened to me. I think I even had myself convinced. It wasn't until the very end of the evening, when I got around to taking a bath, and I realized I was wearing what I'd slapped on that morning—a T-shirt and a pair of white pants with an irregular blue plaid—that finally, with the door closed behind me, I cried.

Not much, though. I never saw what that would do.

My first responsibility was to my kids: to get them together and feel-

....

* All the best people were buried (or cremated) by the Frank E. Campbell Funeral Chapel, on Madison Avenue at Eighty-first Street.

† RODGERS'S GRANDSON DIES was the headline on the short item naming pulmonary edema as the cause of death.

ing better if possible. The worst off was Nina, who was twelve and had spent the night at a friend's house. I had to drive over and say, "Matthew has died." What comfort could I offer? I told her, as I told all of them, to do exactly what she felt like doing. Do you want to scream? Scream. Do you need to watch TV? Watch TV. Do you feel like playing volleyball? Then do it. Tod did. I wasn't about to make them sit around and just stare at the walls or observe any ridiculous funereal behavior. I even sent the older ones to see the Beatles at Shea Stadium with the parents of some of their friends two days later; I thought they should not be denied that experience, especially at that moment.[*]

There was no funeral. There was a cremation, but we're a great family for not knowing where anyone's ashes are. Years later, after Daddy died, I realized I didn't know where his were, either. And later my mother's. Even Frank Campbell didn't know. They're all probably somewhere in my living room, camouflaged.

People seemed, and have seemed ever since, dissatisfied with my grief and my management of my kids'. What can I say? Lose your own child and see how it feels. For me, grief was too complicated an emotion to have, at least at first. I felt simpler, sharper things, unpredictable stings and slaps, like someone invisible was trying to hurt me.

At the same time, someone quite visible was trying not to. By the evening of the day Matthew died, Adam, all of twenty months old, had suddenly turned into a clown. While the adults and older kids were glumming through some form of dinner in the great big living room, he came downstairs in his Dr. Dentons and suddenly started entertaining us. Previously in his short life he hadn't done much or said much, he'd been picky and morose, but now he became a complete extrovert, singing and dancing and laughing. Maybe it was that we were finally paying attention to him; when Matthew was always getting sick, no one had the bandwidth.

....

[*] The Beatles concert at Shea on August 23, 1966, was one of the last on their final tour, coinciding with the release of *Revolver* that month.

How families reconfigure after a death is something I wound up thinking a lot about. That fall, Adam's personality continued to change. He started to eat more regularly, or irregularly, depending on your point of view. Previously, feeding him was a nightmare; now we used a system called "cafeteria eating" I'd read about in psych classes at Wellesley. We would cut up food—bacon and cucumber and fruit—in little bowls and place them on the floor; he'd go around nibbling from the bowls, like a cat, having a grand time. As far as I know, he's grown out of it.

It was also when I think his musical gift arrived, or let's say was unwrapped, as if his brother had left it for him as a keepsake.* One day when Lulu the au pair was getting him ready for a walk in Central Park, I heard her singing "The 59th Street Bridge Song"—a song I loved.† *Slow down, you move too fast.* After a chorus I suddenly realized it wasn't Lulu, it was Adam, note perfect. I thought, *My god, what kind of ear does that child have?*

For him, his brother's death was some kind of aperture. But for me, the fallout was disfiguring.‡ Returning to the city, we had to face Matthew's room, newly redone and perfectly dustproof. I found myself in a rage: I had five kids a month ago and now I've got four? I even lied about it sometimes, saying, when strangers casually asked, that I had five. I felt

....

* The corporate name under which Adam publishes his work is Matthew Music.

† "The 59th Street Bridge Song (Feelin' Groovy)," by Paul Simon, was released on the Simon and Garfunkel album *Parsley, Sage, Rosemary and Thyme* on October 10, 1966.

‡ That November, Mary had the first of three back surgeries, a spinal fusion. It was the result not only of having had five kids but also of the day, when she was twelve, that Josh Logan taught her how to go sledding in the Connecticut hills in a mini-toboggan called a Connecticut Jumper. The sled hit an outcropping of rock, and boom!

swindled: How dare this happen! It was so unfair, and I didn't even have God to blame.

I did have myself, though: Why had I taken Matthew to a party the night before and let him have a little cake, which he wasn't supposed to have? Why had I smoked so much around him? God was silent on those points, but all the monkey letters pouring in kept speaking for him. Jean Kerr wrote, "God must have loved him very much to have taken him." And I thought: *If God loved him so much, why didn't he leave him where he was? He was doing just fine.*

After the winter I began to revert to type. Get on with it. Solve things, don't just feel them. This was when I started going uptown to Columbia to observe work being done there on neonatal pulmonary procedures and hyaline membrane disease,* which they would create in a sheep and then try to cure. I thought maybe I could find some paramedical work, possibly involving breathing monitors, but after three years of observation it occurred to me that I wasn't cut out to be a medical technician and I could never now become a doctor. I didn't even have a college degree, and if I did it would have been in music.

Meanwhile, another problem was becoming apparent. As the other kids, one by one, peeled off to boarding school, Adam was left more and more alone, just as he was blooming. Fishing around for a solution, at first we thought of Pearl Buck's orphanage; Alice Hammerstein had adopted kids there, so why shouldn't we?† There were so many children that needed a home, and we had a home that needed a child.

Then, in the middle of 1967, I got pregnant. We discussed abortion

....

* Hyaline membrane disease, now called respiratory distress syndrome, compromises the lung function of premature newborns.

† In 1949, along with the Hammersteins and the *South Pacific* author James Michener, the Nobel laureate Pearl S. Buck (1892–1973) established an adoption agency called the Welcome House to find homes for American-born Eurasian children, many the offspring of GIs.

and adoption again, but I figured why undo one baby just to take another? As always, being pregnant cheered me up, though my mother charmingly said, "You must be out of your mind." She thought I had enough children, dead or not; to have another—voluntarily!—was insanity.

I guess I was insane.*

....

* Alexander Burton Guettel, called Alec, whose middle name honored Burt Shevelove, was born on April 17, 1968.

38.

SOME BOMBS

All rancid charm and Berlinisher bubbles after the success of *The Mad Show*, Robby called in early 1966 with an irresistible offer. "Would you and Marshall be interested in making a musical out of *The Member of the Wedding*? You can have any producer and director you like."

"Yes, we would," I answered instantly and plurally.

It was not just a huge opportunity; it was a beautiful one. I had sobbed through the play's premiere in 1950.* What affected me most was the loneliness and tomboy anger of Frankie; she was one pissed-off little character, left out, bossed around, passionate in a world determined to crush oddballs.† I never once thought of her connection to me because the details were so different, based as they were on McCullers's own childhood

....

* The stage adaptation of the autobiographical novel by Carson McCullers (1917–1967) opened that year on Broadway, starring Julie Harris, Ethel Waters, and Brandon de Wilde. Harris received an Academy Award nomination for the 1952 movie version.

† Over the course of an end-of-summer weekend, motherless twelve-year-old Frankie, cared for by her family's Black maid, Berenice, and befriended only by her six-year-old cousin, John Henry, dreams of joining the honeymoon of her adult brother and his new bride as a way of escaping her solitude and finding "the we of me."

in Georgia. But part of the reason I have always been drawn to writing about kids, and to having them, too, is that I knew that feeling all too well. Childhood is the most miserable punishment ever exacted upon anybody; you're just fucking stuck there with no control over your life until you're eighteen. I was barely a year older than that when I saw the play; the memory of walking around the reservoir with my sister one Sunday and muttering "three more years, three more years" was still fresh. "Three more years and *what*?" she asked, because she was younger and had chosen a different way of dealing with the parental dilemma. You could be headstrong but disliked or a worm but praised—and I was the headstrong one.

Headstrong if naïve. McCullers was Robby's client, and his pal Floria Lasky was her lawyer, so it was all a tightly tied-up package, another of his prime triangulations except with four sides. The only slight hitch, he said, was that we had to get McCullers's blessing in person, and though she was definitely interested she was also very ill.

So sometime that spring, Robby hired a car and we were driven to South Nyack to her great big horrible house.* Though she was only forty-nine, she'd already had a stroke; she was living in a small room on the ground floor with nurses fussing about. They should have fussed a little more: She was a mess, the ugliest thing I'd ever seen, with scrambled teeth and short, greasy hair. When we arrived, she was lying in bed drinking Maker's Mark, with an enema bag festooned over a shower rod in full view.

Whether she was drunk or not, she certainly wasn't interested in what I had to say about our approach to the project. All she wanted to do was talk about the party that the play's producers had thrown after the 1950 Broadway opening, and ask, like a demented child, whether we'd be having a party as nice as that one. I said, "Well, first we have to write the musical," but she kept on asking about the food and liquor.

....

* McCullers's home, twenty-five miles north of New York City, was listed on the National Register of Horrible Places—sorry, Historic Places—in 2006.

So much for her blessing; Dracula could have obtained it if he promised a buffet and an open bar at Joe Allen.*

Over the next months, she would call me practically every day and ask, "Well, Miss Mary, how is everything coming along?" After I grumbled to Robby about the constant interruption, he tried to explain to her that we couldn't even start writing until the contracts were signed—which wasn't quite true. In fact, Marshall and I wrote most of the songs without a contract that summer and fall, a period of time punctuated but somehow not interrupted by Matthew's death.

I don't mean that the work wasn't influenced by it; how could it not be? I just didn't sense the connection even as I found myself making unsettled harmonies, strange rhythms, and abrasive clusters: things I wouldn't previously have dared to do. One song I wrote at my friend Sally Brown's piano—I was always looking for friends with pianos in homes that didn't have five people asking for lunch—gave me chills as I pawed my way through it.† It was as if by working myself into Frankie's story I was working myself out of mine.

Maybe it was just that the material demanded a very different treatment, and Marshall's poetic, non-jokey lyrics modeled that for me. Or maybe I was getting better with age. I remember thinking I was finally experiencing the kind of freedom that Daddy must have felt when working on *Carousel*. Everything about that show led him to write differently;

....

* Aside from its bar and burgers, Joe Allen, the theater district bistro on West Forty-sixth Street, is best known for the posters of Broadway flops that line its walls, lending even mediocrity a kind of immortality. For the Guettels, it became a favorite pre- and post-curtain haunt.

† The song is "Something Known," a hushed ballad sung by Berenice near the end of the show. Barer's lyric derives from a line Berenice speaks in the play: "Yes, that is the way it is when you are in love. A thing known and not spoken." Structurally, the procession of stately chords recalls the hymnlike cadences of "You'll Never Walk Alone"—but the yearning, rangy melody is bracingly original and full of surprises.

1966: The first page of Mary's manuscript for "Something Known" from
The Member of the Wedding. Her notation improved to the point that it
eventually looked "less like the work of an epileptic spider."

everything about this one, including who I was when it came to me, led
me to write differently, too.

It's a good thing Marshall and I were working so well on our own,
figuring out where the musical moments needed to be and what they
should feel like, because we had a lot of trouble finding an actual book
writer. It certainly wasn't going to be McCullers, even though the deal we
finally signed gave her, in addition to a .5 percent royalty for the underlying rights, a 2 percent royalty for the libretto. Marshall and I were allotted
2 percent each, and everyone else would have to scrape what they could

from the rest of the pool. I think I got an advance of $1,250, which was the last penny I made from *Wedding* during three years of work.

If the show was cursed, as I came to think, there were at least three witches doing the cursing. Remember Robby Lantz's promise that we could have any producer and director we wanted? We wanted Hal, and so the day before he was leaving New York in October of 1966 for the pre-Broadway tryout of *Cabaret* in Boston, we auditioned what we'd written of the *Wedding* score for him. He loved it and said he would postpone his trip by a day in order that we might play it again, for Joe Stein, who he thought would be a great book writer.* Joe would not have been my choice, but what the hell? The second meeting went as well as the first and Hal agreed to produce and direct. When I left his office, I flew to the nearest phone booth, called Robby, and pretty much shouted, "Hal wants to do it!"

"But darling," he oozed, "we can't give it to Hal, he's too inexperienced."

I got furious, but you know how I get furious: not enough. "But you said . . . !"

"What makes you think he can direct this? He can't. He's never directed anything."†

"But you said . . . !"

"Maybe I did, but this is not possible." He hung up, not violently but with a click of finality.

No one else—by which I mean Marshall—had the guts to tell Hal, so I was the lucky messenger; he didn't talk to me for two years. I wouldn't have talked to me, either.

....

* Among the many books that Joseph Stein (1912–2010) wrote for Broadway musicals, *Fiddler on the Roof*, based on the Sholem Aleichem stories, was by far the most successful.

† Prince had in fact directed four Broadway shows by then: *A Family Affair*, *She Loves Me*, *Baker Street*, and *It's a Bird . . . It's a Plane . . . It's Superman*. What Lantz probably meant is that none of them was a hit, unlike *The Pajama Game*, *Damn Yankees*, *West Side Story*, *Fiorello*, and *Fiddler on the Roof*—shows Prince had produced but not directed.

That probably should have been our cue to decamp, but we loved the material too much. I mean that literally: We loved it *too much*, which is a mistake, because you'll put up with anything, including things you shouldn't, when you're in love. And sure enough, Robby soon called to say, "Don't despair: I have the perfect producer for you," presenting us with the fait unaccompli of Ted Mann, a no-talent shit, just awful, and, big surprise, Floria's client.* He agreed to produce the show because he really wanted to direct it, but Robby didn't tell us that part. The deal was signed, and the production was announced in the papers with McCullers named as the book writer—which was absurd because she was nearly dead and a few months later would be dead the rest of the way.†

That gave Ted cover to hire a real book writer, only instead he hired James Leo Herlihy, a sweet guy who had written the novel *Midnight Cowboy* and would later kill himself. As I discovered when I went to San Francisco to work with him in 1967, too late to experience the Summer of Love, but the Winter of Love was adorable, too, he could plot till the cows came home. But we already had a plot. The rest of what a musical book writer has to do—structure the scenes to lead to the songs, create characters who have reasons to sing—he couldn't. He knew it and bowed out.

Next, Joe Hardy, who had just directed the off-Broadway version of *House of Flowers*, came aboard, supposedly to write the book and direct.‡

....

* Like Prince, Theodore Mann (1924–2012) started his career as a stage manager and producer before crossing over into directing. When he did cross over, he met with acclaim. He was also the co-founder of Circle in the Square Theatre, a mainstay of the early off-Broadway movement.

† A March 1967 *New York Times* item, naming no director, reported that the production would come to Broadway "early next year"; McCullers died in September.

‡ Despite a top-drawer score, the Harold Arlen–Truman Capote musical was a notorious flop on Broadway in 1954. The off-Broadway reworking, which opened on January 28, 1968, was also a flop, if less notorious.

I can hardly untangle the mess now but, after a year or so, the following things happened: (1) Ted fired Joe; (2) Marshall and I quit in protest, withdrawing our nearly full score; (3) Ted fired himself; and (4) the whole thing landed back in Robby's hands. At which point, with the amazing nerve only a true machinator can muster, he wrote me to say that, far from a roadblock, this was an opportunity, and I was now free to play the score for Harold Prince "or any other first-rate producer"!

This time I really did collect my marbles and go home.* I fired Robby, or tried to, but he pointed out that we had no contract.

---

* But that was not actually the end of the musical version of *The Member of the Wedding*. When the rights reverted to the McCullers estate, Mann commissioned a new score from George Wood, an actor, cabaret pianist, and songwriter who, under the stage name G. Wood, was an original member of Mann's Circle in the Square company. Lantz attempted to reinstate the Rodgers-Barer score by arranging to have it performed for McCullers's sister, Rita Smith, but she either declined to hear it or, as another version of this story suggests, listened to it with Julie Harris and didn't like it. In any case, Smith awarded the rights to Wood. Wood's version of the show, called *F. Jasmine Addams*, produced and directed by Mann, was announced for Broadway but instead opened, after twenty-two previews, at Mann's Circle in the Square Downtown in October 1971. Clive Barnes, in the *Times*, called the score "thin and unmemorable." The show lasted five days; the schadenfreude lasted a good deal longer.

39.

THE RAKE'S PROGRESS

Maybe I should have kept fighting, especially because everyone now tells me it was my best musical work, the first stirrings of a "mature" voice.* But back then, after three years of wasted work, I came to the conclusion that I couldn't spend the rest of my life like this. I didn't have the emotional stamina to tilt at windmills, which in the theater turn out to be not figments but actually rather aggressive, or the financial wherewithal to support my family when our only new source of income was a series of little one-offs like the shows I wrote for TheaterWorks.†

It is rude for the rich to cry poor. But touch any family, at whatever level, and you're likely to find people operating at the edge of their wealth, and often well past it. That was us, and *The Member of the Wedding* was not our only or even our biggest financial headache. Our biggest, which became a heartache, was developing concurrently. It began in January of 1967, when Hank resigned as general manager of Daddy's Lincoln Cen-

....

* The fifteen or so Rodgers-Barer songs for *The Member of the Wedding* can be performed individually, as a few of them sometimes are in concerts and revues. But they can never be performed in the context of the show.

† The first, *Young Mark Twain*, with lyrics by John Allen, was part of the 1966–1967 season of TheaterWorks/USA, a company that produces original musicals for children and families.

ter enterprise to start work for the American National Opera Company. It would prove to be his own special windmill.

He got involved with the new company through the set designer Oliver Smith.* Funny, handsome, and warm, Smith lived in Brooklyn Heights, in a funny, handsome, and warm yellow house whose "garden" apartment—that is, in the basement—he rented to Truman Capote. This was just a couple of blocks from the site of February House, where, in 1940 and 1941, McCullers had written most of *The Member of the Wedding* while rooming with an unlikely and rotating crew of bohemians including W. H. Auden, Benjamin Britten, Jane Bowles, Kurt Weill, Gypsy Rose Lee, and, tending the furnace, Oliver himself.† When we visited him in the Heights, the idea of all that creative ferment and louche living appealed to me, a lady with five children, in a road-you-didn't-take way.

Though we must have seemed square, Oliver and his partner, Jack Brown, a lighting designer, loved us—and Oliver especially loved Hank. Together they had tried to produce Alice Childress's play *Wedding Band* on Broadway in 1964.‡ Seeing our lack of funds accumulate over the next few years, Oliver and Jack were always trying to get us to move to the Heights, where grand old brownstones could be had for a penny, and which, Oliver told us, he knew how to decorate beautifully on the cheap.

....

* Oliver Smith (1918–1994) designed dozens of films, operas, ballets, and Broadway musicals, winning Tony Awards for nine of them, including *My Fair Lady*, *West Side Story*, and *The Sound of Music*.

† The mock-Tudor brownstone at 7 Middagh Street was called February House because many of its tenants (including McCullers, Auden, Bowles, and Smith) had birthdays in that month. The house was razed in 1945 to make room for the Brooklyn-Queens Expressway.

‡ Alice Childress's *Wedding Band: A Love/Hate Story in Black and White*, about an interracial love affair in South Carolina in 1918, was optioned seven times for Broadway, but none of the would-be producers could raise enough money from skittish investors to put it on. It was finally staged off-Broadway at the Public Theater in 1972.

Which was clearly true. The first time we went to dinner at his house, we looked down at the carpet and thought, hmm, that looks familiar. He had lifted it straight off the set of *The Sound of Music* when the Broadway production closed.

Knowing that Hank was seeking work that amounted to more than being Daddy's deputy, Oliver started talking up the new project for which he was designing the sets. The American National Opera Company was the brainchild of Sarah Caldwell,* but as brainchildren go it was a breech birth. Maybe not artistically; the idea was admirable. Caldwell envisioned a high-culture road show—a hipper version of the Met's failed version†— that would tour the country with both classic and adventurous operas, like those she'd done in Boston, performed by stylish singers in modern productions accompanied by a top-flight orchestra.

But financially the idea began life already upside down.‡

Not that Hank would have known. He was by upbringing and nature disinclined to discuss money, and a soft touch if forced. When he was producing musicals at Lincoln Center, an actor would come to him saying, "Mr. Guettel, I can't possibly live on three hundred dollars a week, I have a wife and children." And he'd reply, "Well, of course you can't, who could, why not let's give you four hundred instead?"

....

* Sarah Caldwell (1924–2006) parlayed her success at the Opera Company of Boston, where she not only conducted but often directed the productions, into a national career as an impresario and ambassador for opera. In 1976, she became the first woman to conduct at the Metropolitan Opera.

† The Metropolitan Opera National Company began its first season in the fall of 1965; it folded in 1967, just before Caldwell's company launched.

‡ Initial funding came from the newly established National Council on the Arts, in the form of an astonishing $350,000 grant—worth $2.7 million in 2020. But by the time the company reached the Brooklyn Academy of Music with its first three productions, in October 1967, Caldwell was already telling the press that she'd need another $500,000 to keep going.

But he didn't come a cropper in any serious way until he was married to me, because there was more to come a cropper with. To begin with, he was blinded by Caldwell, who was smart and talked a good game but had a reputation for never paying bills and for using people like paper towels. You didn't have to look very far—but he just didn't look at all, or chose to ignore what he saw—to find the bodies littered in the path of her smelly destruction. And that's all I'm going to say about her and her noisome black crepe dresses, except that, trust me, you couldn't get within forty feet of the orchestra pit.

If Hank, as a matter of dignity, wasn't looking, I wasn't looking, either. My zero problem and my parent problem combined to make me an innumerate ostrich. We were so irresponsible we had to have an accountant pay our bills because we didn't know how to balance a checkbook and didn't want to be bothered.

And, to be honest, I was just relieved that—thanks to Oliver, and also Lenny, who recommended him to Sarah—Hank had a job he finally found dignified. Managing Director of the American National Opera Company sounded like the kind of position a Henry Guettel should have. Dinner table talk now tended toward Tosca and Lulu instead of Tuptim and Laurey. I was living the dream. Well, somebody's dream. And, anyway, I was still in my own fool's paradise with *Wedding*.

I don't think I noticed anything wrong until March of 1968, when, a hundred months pregnant with Alec, I went with Hank and the Chapins on a vacation to Young Island in the Grenadines. Like the first stirrings of a flu, the trouble was at first barely noticeable: merely a matter of Hank's spending an awful lot of time on the phone back to the States.

That was the fuse; the bomb came the Tuesday after Memorial Day, when I returned to the city from Merriewold to a call from our accountant—who also, significantly, was my parents'. "We have a serious problem," he said. "There's no more money and you haven't paid our bill and the apartment maintenance is three months overdue."

Did you ever think that if an ostrich does lift her head out of the sand, her eyes will be full of grit? She still won't be able to see.

So I believed Hank when he told me we had no money because American National Opera, in financial distress, had not been paying his salary. Horrified and terrified and angry, yet instinctively knowing it was really both of our faults, I called his mother, still living very nicely in Kansas City. I said we were desperate and asked for a loan, but she was very cold and claimed not to know what I could possibly be talking about. Later I learned that Hank's father had by then run through their fortune.

That left me with no choice but to tell my parents, a humiliating nightmare for Hank, and not very nice for me, either. Almost immediately they set up a meeting at 730 Park, where, in the library, with a prominent view of the pianos in the living room, the four of us tensely sat: Daddy, Mummy, the accountant, and me.

Do you detect someone missing? Hank, having been told they would summon him later, was sent to wait on a bench in Central Park.

The accountant led the meeting, which he'd planned like a prosecution. After going through our endless unpaid bills while Mummy tutted, he smoothly asked me whether Hank had any outstanding loans. I said no, but it turned out he did, and that's when I learned the part of the story that he had kept from me for months.

American National Opera had been touring *Falstaff*, *Tosca*, *The Rake's Progress*, and *Carmen*, among others, with the usual backstage dramas (technical flubs, missed flights, mixed reviews) but also some unusual ones. When the company landed in Santa Fe, or maybe it was Dallas, the airline wouldn't let the costumes off the plane because the home office hadn't paid the freight bills. At the Dorothy Chandler Pavilion in Los Angeles, while Sarah hid behind a backdrop, Hank had to fight with a sheriff who was threatening to impound the scenery over a creditor's claim. When that leg of the tour ended, artists who could not cash their paychecks were left stranded at LAX.

In each of those cases, when the show would not go on otherwise, and even when it was merely a matter of disgruntled artists, he'd "solved" the problem with our American Express card, expecting to be reimbursed. When even that wasn't enough to keep the company going, he'd borrowed the rest from a bank, assured by Sarah that he'd be repaid by the Boston office. But the Boston office, as everyone but him knew, never repaid anything, and because he was the general manager, he was held personally responsible. Furthermore, despite Sarah's assurances, which he diligently failed to investigate, the company had not paid its taxes.

For the American National Opera Company, the solution was relatively simple: Its lawyers filed for bankruptcy a couple of weeks later. Sarah was soon back in Boston conducting and collecting honorary degrees.

For us it was not so easy. We were now flat broke and hugely in debt. We owed well over one hundred thousand dollars, at the time a shocking number, even for the non-zero-challenged.* Carte Blanche it wasn't.

As was always the case when I misbehaved as a child, I found myself in the teeth of an emotional bear trap. I could succumb in shame or wriggle my way toward some scrap of dignity. If I succumbed, I died quickly, but if I wriggled, I suffered more. In this case, I wriggled briefly. I said, "Listen, we don't need money. We don't have to live the way we do. We can move to Rockland County and send the kids to public school and buy a simple house."

My mother was appalled. "That's not possible!" she exclaimed. "The house would need to be air-conditioned!"

That was the problem?

"And what about a dishwasher? You can't live like pigs!"†

It was then I recalled that, a few years before, she'd tried to give us one for Merriewold on our anniversary. I said, "I don't need a dishwasher, I need a water softener, because the water is so hard I can't clean the kids' hair." But she wouldn't get us that: It was too "downstairs" to brag about to her friends.

Would I never escape from the struggle in which money bought, if not obedience, then the next best thing, guilt? For a moment, thinking of

....

* The equivalent of nearly one million dollars today.

† *The House in My Head*, Dorothy Rodgers's book about building and decorating her new home in Fairfield, had recently been published. In it, you could learn all you wanted about the wonders of automatic dishwashers, then still a novelty—and also about the delightful serendipity when your color scheme matches your Picasso.

circa 1970: "I'd been through enough men to know that Hank,
who was funny and kind and terribly smart, was what I needed."

Oliver Smith and Truman Capote and February House and artists who
made do without dishwashers, I imagined moving to the country and
telling my parents to go screw. That whiff of freedom was very unbal-
ancing and very exciting, but I was easily enough talked out of it when
Daddy, who refused to participate in the struggle, simply if cruelly cut
through it.

"Do you love this fellow?" he asked. Never mind that "this fellow" was
my husband of almost seven years by then; he was now relegated to the
position of petty thief, like the Romanian chauffeur in *The Elopers*.

I said yes without having to think. There was no question. I didn't
need to add that I wished he'd been more responsible, or that I'd been
more responsible myself.

"Okay," Daddy said. Mummy nodded. And that was it. They would
cover the whole debt. As I've said, however terrible they were about small
things, about big things they were wonderful.

Or he was. There was a certain amount of nose rubbing from my
mother; later, when I wanted to buy an empty-nest apartment after the

kids were grown,* she refused to lend me the money, citing what Hank
had done so many years before. She did agree to be my guarantor when
I borrowed the money from the bank instead; I still owe four hundred
dollars on that loan—I mean four hundred thousand.

But for the rest of his life my father never brought up the subject
again.

He was even kind when Hank, left humming on that bench for an
hour, was summoned to have his fate explained to him. After the litany
of debts and the announcement of the bailout, when Hank said, "I'll find
a way to pay back every last nickel," Daddy, even though he must have
been thinking, *That's a likely prospect*, had the decency to say nothing.

Eventually Hank did pay it back, though it took his own parents'
deaths.†

The episode didn't end up changing our lives right away, though of
course Hank had to find a new job‡—as, in effect, did I. We also had to
economize, which turned out to be hard; certain traits are too deeply in-
grained to respond even to humiliation. As Jerry Beaty taught me, cutting
back doesn't just mean buying fewer bottles of Scotch, it means buying
less-good bottles of Scotch. Which was not Hank's way. One night that
summer, he said, "By the way, I traded in the bus"—we had a Volkswagen
bus—"for a Porsche."

"What's a Porsche?" I asked.

"It's a great kind of car and will only cost us a hundred bucks more."

What I didn't understand was that he meant it would cost us a hundred bucks more every month for the rest of our lives. Had he learned
nothing? I told him he really had to go to a shrink, because I already had

....

* In 1989, the Guettels moved to a three-bedroom apartment on the fif-
teenth floor of the Beresford, on Central Park West, where they lived for
the rest of their lives.

† Arthur Guettel died in 1969; Sylvia Guettel in 1971.

‡ From 1969 to 1972, Henry Guettel was an associate at Kaplan-Veidt, a
talent agency.

five children and didn't need a sixth. He did go, and from that point on he was a completely responsible businessperson.

But something in our world—in the larger world, too, because this was 1968—was falling apart, wearing down. You could almost hear the grinding. I was a thirty-seven-year-old mother of five who had written a bunch of musicals—some hits, some bombs, some never-to-be-produced—but all of that was wiped out now. In musical theater you're only as good as your last failure. I was back at zero, which was not so terrible except for feeling old. If you'd given birth six times in sixteen years, you'd feel old, too.

Could a person start over on a different footing? I hated the prospect of leaving the theater behind—and I never did leave it completely—but trying to be more financially responsible made me think about being more responsible with my talent as well. It was not so great that I could afford to waste so much of it. I suppose if someone had come along with a wonderful idea and a good lyricist, I would have dropped anything and done it. But that didn't happen, and I couldn't interest anyone in my pet projects, either. It was time to move on, the way a singer moves on. You don't say to a diva who's lost her voice, "Why aren't you doing major roles anymore?" You already know why.

40.

TWO MINDS

didn't really think of myself as shipwrecked, but the proverbial message in a bottle washed up anyway on the shores of Central Park West. Actually, it was a letter from Ursula Nordstrom, who I later learned liked to find fresh blood for her children's-book empire* by making contact—sans agent, sans introduction—out of the blue. Or not quite out of the blue, in my case: Maurice Sendak, her most celebrated author, had suggested she ask Steve whether he wanted to write a children's book: a bizarre idea, but something I'd love to have seen. Steve said no thanks, instead recommending me.

Steve was always recommending someone for something; though he was already known and respected, and about to be beatified by his masterpieces of the 1970s, he still knew what creative frustration felt like. Even just asking for your opinion, he offered an ego boost by proxy. In 1969, when he was writing *Company* and my main contribution to the arts

....

* Ursula Nordstrom (1910–1988) became director of Harper Books for Boys and Girls, a department of Harper & Brothers, in 1940. By the time she fully retired, or was pushed aside, in 1980, she was acknowledged as the doyenne of the field, having published many of the great mid-century children's authors.

involved sitting on the board of the Episcopal School,* he called to say he could use my input. *Company*, he explained, was in essence a series of sketches involving a bachelor, his three girlfriends, and the five couples he third-wheels with. The theme was marriage: its pros and cons. Since he had no experience (he said) with either and I had plenty, he asked me to Turtle Bay to spew out everything I'd learned in two tries.†

It would have looked to an outsider like analysis in reverse: Steve lying on the couch, taking notes on one of those yellow legal pads he used, somehow not falling asleep as I sat in a chair nearby talking nonstop. I told him that even a good marriage is not always great, which is something I would still say to someone this very minute. That to make up for the rough patches you have to be both challenged and entertained, so you need a spouse who's both smart and funny. That if you find that combination, you'd better stick with it, because everything else will eventually wear off. That if the big things are right, the fights will mostly be over small things. That compromise is essential because marriage itself is a compromise: being trapped and not wanting to let go.

When I listen to *Company*, which I love, I flatter myself that I can hear some of those ideas, honed razor-sharp, in the ambivalence of "Sorry/Grateful."‡ In the jabby wit of "The Little Things You Do Together."§

....

* Despite its name, the Episcopal School was nondenominational, and many of the toddlers enrolled there were Jewish.

† "I figured it was the least she could do after steering me into *Do I Hear a Waltz?*," Sondheim wrote in *Finishing the Hat*.

‡ "You don't live for her, / You do live with her. / You're scared she's starting to drift away— / And scared she'll stay."

§ "It's not talk of God and the decade ahead that / Allows you to get through the worst. / It's 'I do' and 'You don't' and 'Nobody said that' / and 'Who brought the subject up first?'"

1979: Mary with Stephen Sondheim at the recording session of *Sweeney Todd: The Demon Barber of Fleet Street.* "Scary, brilliant, and gorgeous, yes, but also fun."

In the paradoxes of "Being Alive."* What I still can't hear, after all these years, is the specific tip of the hat Steve hid in a countermelody in the title song: "Hank and Mary get into town tomorrow." There's so much going on chorally at that point that I don't notice it unless somebody actually punches me and says, "Here it is." It's like the cocaine in the watch case: the gift that's invisible, or in this case inaudible, to the person it was intended for.

I don't know why Steve ever trusted my ear after that, but he did. He continued to play his songs for me, hot off the piano: a double pleasure because they were so good and because he wanted me to think so. And I always attended his recording sessions.

In the case of *Company,* I was there semi-officially, having been hired for a hundred dollars to serve as a glorified liaison between the theater folk

---

* "Someone who, like it or not, / Will want you to share / A little a lot."

making the album and the documentary folk filming it. I knew both sides: Hal and Steve from the show and, from the producers, my cousin Judy and my brother-in-law, Danny.* Unfortunately, I also knew Barbara Barrie,† the female Arthur Laurents, who spent the morning trying to incite the cast not to perform because they were being underpaid. And then there was Elaine Stritch, who had once stayed with us interminably at the Majestic; she'd come home, slam the door, shout, "Tea, please!" and flounce to her room with her yappy dog. Sure enough, she brought the yappy dog to the recording studio, along with an assistant, a filthy bucket hat, and a picnic basket filled with chicken and champagne. She started drinking midday and was soon loudly insisting on the eleven o'clock spot, which doesn't exist in a recording session unless you're so impossible and sly that you make it so. Anyway, by the actual eleven o'clock she was drunk out of her gourd, which made for great takes of her botching "The Ladies Who Lunch" way into the wee hours. But nicely coifed and made up a day or two later, she had her full senses, or as many of them as she needed, and she sang it right. There wasn't anything more fabulous than that.

By then, my new career had been launched. Or I guess I should say my new careers, because the book thing and the board thing began simultaneously. Actually, the board thing had a false start even earlier, when Matthew was about to enter nursery school at Episcopal in 1966. He didn't wind up going, of course—he died. Two years later, though, the headmistress, a wonderful woman named Priscilla Houghton, a member of the Steuben Glass family, came across the park to check out her next prospect: Adam. She had a cup of tea while sitting on the toilet seat as he

....

* D. A. Pennebaker's *Company: Original Cast Album* was shot in May 1970 and opened the New York Film Festival that September. Judith Crichton, who came up with the idea, was the producer; Daniel Melnick, the executive producer. Mary is credited as assistant to the producer.

† Barbara Barrie (born 1931) played Sarah, the karate-kicking wife, in the original cast of *Company*. She was married until his death to Jay Harnick, the founder of TheaterWorks/USA and the brother of Sheldon.

had his bath, during which he couldn't stop talking about his itchy bottom. That's a way to impress the head of a school!

Turns out, he had worms. And I had a board seat. Or rather, a teeny chair on which I sat among all those fancy upper-class ladies discussing the school's future.

Such was the deserted island of my life when Ursula's bottle washed up on its shores in 1969—except now that I think of it, messages in bottles come seeking rescue, not offering it. That was part of her genius: making authors feel as if they were doing her a favor, rather than the other way around. In my case, she merely asked "Would you come talk to us?" as if I were a dignitary.

"Us" was not an abbreviation for "Ursula," though she responded to "Urse" and often wore a necklace with a capital "U" dangling off the cliff of her matronly bust. "Us" meant her and Charlotte Zolotow,* who in later years succeeded her, and in former years was married to the showbiz journalist Maurice Zolotow. Ursula and Charlotte ran a female fiefdom at Harper, kinder and more authentic than any male-centered enterprise I'd observed. Those qualities came from Ursula, who was sixtyish, short and plump, totally adorable, bright-eyed and a little dowdy, with a nice scrubbed face and no makeup, always in suits, very warm and sharp-tongued, an easy laugher and the kind of person who you knew right away if she liked you. All that plus being gay† made her the best possible mother figure: the kind who isn't your mother.

Had any real mother ever said to me, as Ursula did the day I showed up at her office, "Tell us who you are"?

---

* Aside from being a children's book editor, Charlotte Zolotow (1915–2013) wrote more than seventy children's books of her own.

† Nordstrom wrote one young adult novel, *The Secret Language*, a crypto-lesbian romance. Her longtime romantic partnership with Mary Griffith was less crypto, though in public she referred to Griffith as "the friend with whom I live."

I told her I was bad: that badness was the thing I enjoyed thinking about most, as a kid and even as an adult. I gleefully enumerated all the bad things I'd done or had in mind to do. Many of them involved Mummy. Others involved Sarah Caldwell, Robby Lantz, my sister, and Richard Nixon, who'd just taken office. Daddy was terrified he'd be invited to the White House and that he'd have to show up, lest shifty revenuers start looking at his taxes. This from a man who never lied about three cents, who declared his own underwear at customs.

But I also told Ursula and Charlotte—in that braying way I have—that I was, despite all appearances, shy. That the shyness is what restrained the badness, except when it didn't. That if I'd been only bad, I'd have been a monster. That if I'd been only shy, I'd have been no one.

I didn't know at the time that I'd struck a chord with Ursula, whose motto at Harper was "good books for bad children." All she said then was: "Write about that."

So I went home and wrote a story about a boy called Simon who, hearing his parents talk about a "rotten" kid they know, daydreams about doing some of the stuff I actually did: throwing things out windows, abusing a younger sister, wrapping gross food in a napkin and stuffing it behind the radiator. For some reason, I didn't have Simon, in his fantasy, steal trading cards from his schoolmates' lockers, or tell them that if they were nice they could borrow his "key to heaven," which was actually just a trinket that had come with some fancy chocolates. Yes, I had done those things, but who would believe it in fiction?

I wrote the whole thing very quickly and without consulting Ursula or Charlotte further; I'd only ever had collaborators and didn't know what editors were for. I put no more thought into the writing than I'd put into writing stories for my kids at camp, but no less, either. I knew what I wanted to do, which was to show how a child's freedom of imagination is vital to the development of morality. And I knew how to do it, though I wound up thinking there was too much dialogue in the book, which I'd padded slightly to reach the very modest length I'd been told was acceptable for kids three to six, or for their parents. Then I simply turned it in, and Ursula published it with barely an edit but with illustrations she didn't love by my friend Steven Kellogg.* When I dropped by a bookstore on Lexington Avenue that fall, in that way new authors do, the clerk looked puzzled by what she must have thought was a salacious question: "Do you have *The Rotten Book?*"

"We don't *sell* rotten books," she sniffed.

The title perhaps did not help sales. But I later learned that it was a favorite among child psychiatrists.

I was not surprised, when the collection of Ursula's letters came out,† to read how much handholding, pen-prodding, and ego-massaging she had to do to squeeze manuscripts out of her authors. I was only surprised to find that I was one of the authors so heavily masseused. I'd thought, as writers go, even writers with five kids, that I was fairly fluent once I had the idea nailed down. *The Rotten Book* took just a couple of weeks to write—and before I was finished, I was already hunting for my next idea. But that took a couple of years, not to mention those encouraging letters from Ursula, to become an actual book.

I would blame Mummy except that, as always, her role was two-sided. She was both the cause of the delay and, in a way, the inspiration for the solution—which I wouldn't have had if not for the delay.

It began with a different book entirely. Mummy, already a successful author, got us a joint deal with Bob Gottlieb at Knopf to collaborate on a guide for modern women. Even if I wanted to, I couldn't afford to refuse it, and the idea, originally called *It Depends*, wasn't bad: We would update antique works like *Mrs. Beeton's Book of Household Management*‡ with prac-

....

* *The Rotten Book* was published on September 24, 1969. The dedication, to Matthew, was accompanied by Kellogg's drawing of a bird flying off with a worm.

† Among the letters in *Dear Genius: The Letters of Ursula Nordstrom*, published in 1998, several are addressed to Mary Rodgers. "Bless you, dear author," ends one from June 1969. "We love you. We need you."

‡ First published in book form in 1861, *Mrs. Beeton's* is still in print.

circa 1972: Mary and Dorothy. "She had an orderly life with
no children underfoot; I was basically Mother Hubbard."

tical information on everything from plumbing to husbands—but told
from our different points of view. The differences were not just genera-
tional, though Mummy was sixtyish and I was not yet forty. They were
also attitudinal. She was East Side; I was West Side. She had an orderly
life with no children underfoot; I was basically Mother Hubbard. She was
grand; I was anti-grand.

Despite that, our working relationship was good. She was unfailingly
respectful of me as a writer, perhaps understanding that I provided a useful contrast to her very correct but not wildly imaginative style. She had
such a highly developed and serene sense of taste that you could mistake
it for originality, but she didn't have any fun with words. They were like
pieces of furniture to her, to be put in the right place and left there. When
she told a joke, it was someone else's.

To emphasize the contrast between us instead of watering it down,
we had to find a way of collaborating while remaining distinct. Writing
together directly would have left us with what Steve called a "muddle

in the middle.”* After trying a few ideas, we finally came up with one I referred to, in my half of the book's introduction, as a "dualogue": a text that's continuous but "in which we interrupt each other, frequently in some chapters, less frequently in others, with comments, embellishments, occasional gentle gibes, and a few arguments." To distinguish between our voices, though a deaf dog could have done it, we had the bright idea of printing her portions in black and mine in brown.

The book, with Daddy's cute title, was published in 1970.† I guess it was a success; we were soon asked to turn it into a radio show and a monthly column for *McCall's*.‡ It even led, a few years later, to a television commercial for Cool Whip; the caption said I was "Mary Rodgers, Author," but should have said "Mary Rodgers, Fraud."§

But when I pick up *A Word to the Wives* now, I find myself intermittently embarrassed, not by what Mummy wrote, which was her truth, but by what I wrote, which wasn't. Even when I'm funny, I'm too ac-

....

* From *Sunday in the Park with George*: "What's the muddle / In the middle? / That's the puddle / Where the poodle / Did the piddle."

† Reviews of *A Word to the Wives* appreciated its humor but also pointed out that its assumptions of privilege and ideas about women's roles were not as far from Mrs. Beeton as one might expect more than a century later.

‡ The radio program was syndicated nationally in 1971 and 1972; the *McCall's* column, retitled "Of Two Minds," ran from February 1971 through September 1978. The column started out with provocative real questions like "What sleeping arrangements should we offer my nephew who is bringing his fiancée for the weekend?" but quickly devolved into tedious fake ones, obviously written by the editors, like "How do I tell my sister I don't want to make Thanksgiving dinner this year?"

§ The ad, which aired in 1973, features Mary, pretending to be a housewife, serving Hank and Adam and Alec strawberry shortcake with a dollop of Cool Whip on top. "My family, quite honestly, has come to expect the best," she purrs.

commodating. As I've said, I would have been a great Vichyssoise, or whatever you call French collaborators, because as a writing collaborator I wanted only to keep the peace. Our piquant little disagreements* were for show; mostly, you'd think that I warmly accepted the wisdom of Mummy's ways, with only slight modifications for modern times. But actually, I was outraged by her ways—her motherly ways, at least. In private I mocked her mercilessly.† I'm not saying that was nice or even fair; mocking her was a way of mocking the part of me that wanted to be like her despite everything.

The odd thing is that while we were writing the book in 1969 our relationship improved. She was happy having us bound by a joint contract, and I felt valued for my real abilities—not for the way I imperfectly emulated hers. With my guard thus down, I agreed to accompany her on a two-week trip to the Soviet Union and Finland that summer, when the older kids were away at camp and we had an au pair for the little ones.‡ I'm not sure who took care of Hank.

I didn't intend the trip as research for the new book I was writing for Ursula, though it turned out that way. I went because I knew that with Mummy it would be first-class travel, which after so many kids I was good and ready for. The idea of deep baths and big beds with breakfast in them was enough to make me temporarily forget how it always felt after a few idle hours alone with her, when disapproval slumped into te-

....

* A feature in the *Times* listed some of them: "whether children should have an allowance (Dorothy, yes; Mary, no); whether wives should make doctors' appointments for husbands (Dorothy, no; Mary, yes), and whether a visiting child who becomes ill should be sent home (Dorothy, no; Mary, yes)."

† Later, when Dorothy was dependent on oxygen, Mary made the "Granny" signal to let everyone know when she called: two fingers just under the nostrils, representing her cannulas.

‡ Tod was sixteen; Nina, fifteen; Kim, thirteen; Adam, four; Alec, fifteen months.

diousness. And I'd forgotten how it felt when she was up and at 'em at seven in the morning, rapping on the door of the connecting rooms she always booked and not waiting for an answer before sashaying in with her peignoir flowing, ready to start the day when I wasn't ready to start anything but a cup of coffee.

At the time I told myself that she just hated being alone, that she wanted someone to talk with or, failing that, talk at. But it was really more complicated, if you could separate the mothering from the companioning. As a mother, she was driven mad by the things I did that she wouldn't have done the same way. She carped at what I was wearing. She sighed at the way I ran through my allowance barefoot. But she desperately wanted me as a companion; she especially thought I was fun to travel with. These were the little clues I missed my whole life, until the end of hers: the clues that she enjoyed having me around. What she'd told me so long ago was exactly backward. She didn't love me but— surprise!—she liked me.

But could I like her? On the trip that summer I watched how a woman entirely defined by wifeliness operated in the absence of a husband. (Daddy had refused to come.*) She was both tougher and more frivolous than any man would dare to be. On the first leg of the trip, while we flew to London, some of her Vuitton luggage flew to Barbados; what could she do but head directly to Harvey Nichols and replenish her entire wardrobe? (Even so, she whined about it for the rest of the trip, the way she once whined about the waste of her trousseau.) When we got to Moscow, the room she had booked for herself, where Roosevelt and Churchill and Stalin had supposedly met during World War II, proved unavailable

....

* He was working with Martin Charnin (lyrics) and Peter Stone (book) on *Two by Two*, the Noah's ark musical based on Clifford Odets's play *The Flowering Peach*. It opened in November 1970, starring an out-of-control Danny Kaye, who turned it into his own club act, including curtain speeches that began "I'm glad you're here, but I'm glad the authors aren't."

until she browbeat the desk staff sufficiently. I got the room next door, I guess where their bodyguards bunked.*

I think Mummy thought of herself as a semiofficial cultural ambassador deserving a certain degree of deference. She dropped "Mrs. Richard Rodgers" all over the place, and in filling out her visa form wrote grandly that the purpose of her trip was to pay a call on the beautiful churches, as if she were also a beautiful church. I wrote that the purpose of *my* trip was to visit the Pavlov Physiological Society in Leningrad, which, like everything else they didn't want us to see, turned out to be either closed or "under repair." Instead, they said I could visit a mental hospital.

Needless to say, I leapt at the chance, even though Mummy worried I'd be committed. So there I was at the mental hospital one day, attending a fascinating seminar on alcohol recidivism, listening to it in English on headphones, when I vaguely heard a commotion at the back of the room. Dressed up in her best mink, Mummy had crashed the conference for no other reason than to find me. She was distraught until one of the American doctors in attendance recognized her from Daddy's stay at Payne Whitney twelve years earlier.

Her saving grace was that she could laugh at herself; she didn't mind how she looked to others as long as she got what she wanted. She knew when to make a scene but also, unlike me, when not to. At lunch one day, when her glass of wine broke off at the stem, the waitress ran up shrieking, "You pay! You pay!" And I shrieked back, "She do *not* pay! She do *not* pay!" Mummy shushed me and put on her best dragon smile. She didn't pay.

I began to understand—and even, to my surprise, envy—the way she turned her dependency into immense, steely competence. On our last night in Leningrad, after a private viewing of the jewels at the Hermitage, with our bags all packed for the next day's flight to visit our retired maid Elna in Helsinki, we were awakened by a call from Danny Melnick

....

* There's no evidence that the three Allied leaders ever met in Moscow during the war.

saying there was something wrong, not very specific, with Daddy.* First thing in the morning, determined to rebook our flights, Mummy raced, with me in tow, to the lobby of the hotel where the travel agents' offices were located. But no one was there; the lobby was dead. As Mummy started rapping on desks, we realized that it was July 20, the day of the moon landing, which all Russia was watching, presumably enviously, behind closed doors. With the attention on space, it was as if the earth had shut down.

We knew there was just one flight a week from Moscow to New York, and it left later that day. All I can tell you is that she got us to Moscow, got us to London, got us to JFK. And that having quit smoking three years earlier, she bummed some cigarettes off me en route. It was one of the few signs of breakage of discipline I'd ever seen in her.

Back in New York two days later, we went straight from the airport to the hospital. Daddy had had a heart attack, we were told, but it couldn't have been too serious; he looked just fine. I wondered whether, subconsciously, it was even a ruse; he tended to get really sick only when Mummy was away. Upon her arrival, as doctors watched the return of the moon mission on one screen and his heartbeat on another, he said, verging on tears, "I didn't think I'd ever see you again," which gratified her.

Maybe she wasn't so weak. Maybe everyone else was.

---

* In *Musical Stages*, Richard Rodgers writes improbably that it was only "with the help of Mayor Lindsay" that the call got put through.

41.

DINGUE DINGUE DINGUE

The idea for the book I at first called *Annabel*—but that later, under the title *Freaky Friday*, turned into a mini-empire and a twenty years' occupation—came from several directions at once. Nina and Kim were in the full splendor of teen girlhood, vexing but enviable; sometimes I wanted to kill them and sometimes I wanted to be them. I imagine they felt the same way about me, because however much better a time they were having than I'd had, and despite my nutso liberal ways, I was still, to my astonishment, an authority figure. How had I become my own mother?

Which made me think of a funny comment Mummy once made: "I woke up this morning and looked in the mirror and I swear to God I saw my mother's face"—meaning not just the wrinkles but the worries that caused them.

And that, in turn, made me remember that when I was fourteen, I'd read and loved a novel called *Turnabout*, by Thorne Smith, in which a husband and wife switch bodies and the husband gets pregnant.* Vicious

* Thorne Smith (1892–1934) was the author, most famously, of the *Topper* novels, which became successful films starring Cary Grant and Constance Bennett and, later, the two-season television series written, in part, by the young Stephen Sondheim. *Turnabout*, published in 1931, was made into a 1940 film and a six-episode television series in 1979.

and hilarious, it was something I thought I could emulate in children's fiction—not, as in *The Rotten Book*, for toddlers but for teens. In those days there weren't many, if any, really smart, funny books for that age group; they were all like Judy Blume or *by* Judy Blume. You know: dead serious about your period.

As it happened, Ursula felt she'd made a mistake in pushing me toward early readers. Whether for that reason or because she was squeamish, she rejected another kids' picture book I wrote, called *George*, about a four-year-old boy, rather like Alec when he was that age, who gets so interested in his various activities that he wets his pants all the time. But she loved my idea of a book for older kids and badgered me to start writing it—even before *The Rotten Book* was published and even without a contract.* By the time Mummy and I went to the Soviet Union in July 1969, I'd turned in thirty pages and an outline for the rest, which were good as far as they went. Ursula wrote saying that she and Charlotte and even their office assistant were "in hysterics" over it, and that I was to plunge forward, take care of my health, and "forget children and husband," which was not even a joke. But whatever she said, I knew I was stuck—as would be my pattern ever after—at the spot where the excitement of my first impulse crashed into the dead end of my ability to carry it out.

A lunch with Ursula quickly unstuck me. "I'm not very visual," I said, "so I'm not very good at writing that kind of stuff."

"Then don't," she replied.

"What I really have fun with is dialogue."

"So do that. Have fun. Fun is what you *should* be having. That's how the reader will, too"—thus giving me permission to write snappy ripostes instead of long, boring, Tennyson-like descriptions.

Not that I was composing an ode, but I was so much more interested in the action than the atmosphere, which I learned would take care of

----

* No contracts were signed until 1971, by which point the book was nearly finished. Harper & Row agreed to pay Mary Rodgers Guettel, "writing as Mary Rodgers," an advance of $2,500, half on signing, half on acceptance of the manuscript.

itself once the action was clear. That clarity took a long time to achieve, interrupted as it was—but also informed—by working on *A Word to the Wives* with Mummy. I kept getting snarled in the implications of the simple idea, which was that thirteen-year-old Annabel Andrews wakes up one Friday to discover her consciousness now housed in the thirty-five-year-old body of her mother, Ellen. But what, you may ask, has happened to Ellen's consciousness? Is it in Annabel's body? If so, would they not recognize each other right away and, in so doing, snuff out the plot? It took forever to work around that one. Also, Ursula kept worrying, how could we avoid the suggestion that Annabel, in her mother's body, might wind up in a sexual situation with her father?* Solving that problem was easier: I simply had the parents sleep, as Hank and I did except when we didn't, in separate beds.

The key to moving ahead with the story was accepting that although it's a two-way exchange, I was more interested in Annabel's consciousness than in Ellen's. After all, smart adults remember what it means to be a kid, but kids have no idea what it means to be an adult. That freed me up to let Ellen disappear until the denouement. Meanwhile, as Annabel stumbles through her mother's day—ruining the laundry; forgetting to meet her younger brother at the bus; flubbing an encounter at school with the principal—she begins to understand the burdens of parenthood, which include the burdens of being responsible for headstrong children. But I also wanted to show that not every impulse an impulsive teenager has is wrong; Annabel fires the cleaning woman, Mrs. Schmauss, whose name I found in a phone book, for making racist remarks about the "colored." Ellen would have been too timid to do that.†

I enjoyed working out the details, and the way the secondary characters fit into the story and furthered its themes. Plotting was like a treasure

....

* As Nordstrom admitted in her letters, this was a fixation of hers; she was always typing "father" when she meant to type "husband." That slip finds its way into Annabel's story.

† Even though Mrs. Schmauss's racist remarks do not go unpunished, they were the subject of many angry letters to the author.

hunt combined with a game of anagrams, bending possibilities this way and that. The real problem wasn't the outline but the writing, something I found almost impossible in the middle of our household chaos. Eventually, I pulled an Ellen: I disappeared until the denouement. I left Hank and the kids in the apartment with an assortment of help and went to Merriewold for up to three weeks at a time throughout the fall of 1969 and into the following year.

As most writers know, the physical helps; every time I'd get up to go to the john I'd have to tear back to the typewriter because I'd be filled with ideas. An even better source of inspiration was walking. I'd get up early, watch the *Today* show over breakfast and cigarettes, then head out into the woods with a pencil and a spiral notebook. Every sentence I'd write, good or bad, I'd transcribe when I got back to the house, then try to connect into cogent thoughts. That was my eight-to-noon shift, the most productive, after which I took a lunch break. Then it was back to the typewriter from one to five, reworking the morning stuff, then dinner break, then a third shift from six to ten, when I'd plot for the next day. Twelve hours of writing all told.

It was an exhausting and possibly dangerous routine; I would come back from my walks and wonder why I couldn't seem to make my fingers move. I was an inch away from frostbite. But there would also be that miraculous moment when I'd realize, *Oh! It's going to work!*—which made even frostbite seem worthwhile. Or there wouldn't be that moment, which was awful.

But it's not as if I had a choice. Like it or not, and I mostly liked it, hacking my way through the vines of fiction was what life insisted I do next. I wanted creative occupation, I needed to make money, and at a time when people were desperate to get into publishing, the best editor in the country was giving me marching orders. Was it as fulfilling as writing music? Depends on what kind of fulfillment you seek. Writing music is fun while you're doing it and also when you're done; writing words is fun only when you're done. It's much more of a chore, as even Steve, the greatest lyricist ever, says. Words aren't pin-downable, the way notes are. And there are so many more of them.

Plus, I felt guilty, at least a little. I was operating at the extremes of what it meant to be a working mother—and I thought I should be capable of that. I thought the world should, too. My politics told me I could leave the kids with Hank just the way most husbands, including my own father, felt they could leave their kids with their wives. But in 1970 it wasn't yet a two-way street, not like today when you see men in the park toting the diaper pack and nursing their twins. Back then, even good guys like Hank, who understood about feeding and clothes and colds, didn't do certain things a mother did. Forget about playdates. Forget about birthday gifts for other kids; I think he sent Adam to parties with bottles of wine. It was enough that the ordinary upkeep kept up, even if not as well as it would had I been there. I couldn't exactly harangue Hank during my daily check-ins by phone; that would have been to harangue myself.

Anyway, for haranguing, I already had Mummy, who in letters complaining about my unmotherliness and undaughterliness helpfully pointed out that she had invented the Johnny Mop—and the Turn and Learn storybooks, just then patented—at home. Well, goody for you; my storybook was different. Being at Merriewold was not a way of avoiding my responsibilities but, at that moment, the only way I could meet them.

By spring I was ready to send what I'd written to the Ur-mother, who suggested we have lunch to discuss revisions. I marked off three weeks in my calendar to make whatever changes she might have in mind, but we were finished with those before dessert. All she said was that in a book likely to be a classic—whaaaaat?—you don't want to date yourself with references that will become anachronistic over time. And indeed, though we took out three such references, people do still write me to ask what Nok Hockey is. The only thing we didn't solve by the end of lunch was the title; Ursula felt that *Annabel* was too bland for a bestseller. (Whaaaat?) When we returned to her office at Harper & Row, we wandered around the juvenile floor asking people for ideas. At one point we considered *Funky Friday* but decided it was too close to *Fucky Friday*, which, come to think of it, might have been a blockbuster. *Freaky Friday* seemed like its tamer sister.

Tamer or not, the book was a hit, as Ursula had predicted.* Be careful of hits! They are nicer, of course, than bombs, but require so much more aftercare. This one kept me occupied—with two sequels, two musical adaptations, three movies, innumerable "Freaky" festivals, several bannings, and various foreign editions†—for the next twenty years.

I didn't mind. I was making good money for the first time since *Once Upon a Mattress* opened ten years earlier, and though I was trying to write a novel with more adult themes, too,‡ I had plenty more to say about parents and children. In the first sequel, *A Billion for Boris*,§ I wanted to write about how children can be so reactionary: more conformist than their liberal parents or more offbeat than their conservative ones, as the case may be. Luckily, I'd already suggested in *Freaky Friday* that Boris, the boy who lives upstairs from Annabel, has a problem with his divorcée mother's unconventionality, so I could flesh her out in the

....

* Dedicated to "Nina, Kimmy, and Ma," *Freaky Friday*, with a cover illustration by Edward Gorey, was published by Harper & Row in April 1972. Among many honors, it received a Notable Children's Book citation from the American Library Association, a Library of Congress children's book award, and, most unexpectedly, a Christopher medal for books that "affirm the highest values of the human spirit." It has never been out of print.

† Among others, the German *Verrückter Freitag*, the Spanish *Un viernes de locos*, and the French *Un vendredi dingue dingue dingue*.

‡ *The Year of the Daley Diaries* was about coeducation at a school very much like Exeter, where Kim had enrolled in the fall of 1971 as part of the first group of sixty girls who boarded. The abandoned manuscript includes a prologue and diary entries written by various students as homework for an English class taught by Maggie Daley.

§ *A Billion for Boris* (in some later editions titled *ESP TV*) was published in November 1974, two and a half years after (and double the length of) *Freaky Friday*. It is dedicated to "my small sons, Adam and Alec, without whom I was finally able to finish it."

sequel as a rotten housekeeper, a distracted single parent, and a "muddleheaded, self-indulgent" writer barely scraping by. "I spent my entire childhood with a mother to whom food and furnishings mattered terribly," this mother, named Sascha, says, "and I swore, when I grew up, that I wouldn't let them matter to me." I did not have to research that character one whit—or her mother, who, just like mine, tried to pin you down for July in December.

But where Sascha sees a bohemian lifestyle, Boris sees just chaos and failure. The phone is always being disconnected for lack of payment. He's about to be kicked out of private school because the tuition hasn't been paid in two years. So when his broken TV magically starts showing the next day's programming, he uses its advance information to win piles of money on horses at OTB.* He pays the phone bill, pays the tuition, and pays for Sascha to go to a shrink. All of which infuriates her. "Has it never passed through that conservative, Naugahyde-bound, mingy little mind of yours that I already *am* happy?" she says. "I *like* the way I am."

A book you're writing is like a possibly haunted house. As I crept along with the story, I had a sickening sense that something was wrong, but I wasn't sure what or where it was—and was uneager, on a deadline, to go hunting for it. Eventually, though, I came to a full stop, realizing, in a kind of seizure, that I was letting Boris get away with murder. Although Annabel, reappearing from *Freaky Friday*, insists on doing some good with the magic,† Boris, in my first draft, just made a fortune and spent it, like the boy in *Carte Blanche*. Worse, the book as a result seemed to endorse the idea that Sascha was some kind of loser for struggling honorably while her son lucked into an easy way out.

You can't do that in books for children; there has to be an implicit morality to counter the freedom of imagination you're championing.

....

* Off-track betting was legalized in New York City in 1970.

† *A Billion for Boris* is written in the form of a dossier that Annabel compiles for an ESP research center. Unlike Boris, she uses her foreknowledge wisely, to help a young journalist get great scoops, thus ameliorating if not preventing future disasters.

You have to let kids know you don't get something for nothing—a theme I'm apparently hung up on. After a lot of rewriting, I had Boris lose all the ill-gotten gains that magic had deposited on him, and I had Sascha finally stick up for herself. "We've always survived, haven't we?" she says. "Maybe not your way—but your way is not my way." This bit of biblical borrowing was my defense of all artists whose children would rather they be rich than happy, would rather they attend the PTA meeting than decamp to Merriewold to write a book.

Which is not to say—as I sense you are itching to—that *A Billion for Boris* is a defense or apology. I never felt I was working through issues in my writing so much as taking advantage of things that I knew so I could write well. People want to make these biographical connections, but the connections are often wrong, beside the point, or backward. It's a way of trying to turn differences into defects, which are easier to swallow. I used to get it all the time about having so many children. Women of my class and background typically had just two, maybe three if they were old-fashioned, so my having six minus one had to be proof of extreme privilege or a sign of my rebellion against it. But I don't think it had anything to do with privilege. Yes, I wanted to show my mother that I could be a better mother, or at least a more plenteous one, than she was. But the real reason I did it was because I loved it, which in babies or books is the only reason, if not always reason enough.

Anyway, my children wound up good people despite my time away and their unconventional upbringing. Yes, there were lots of crises, and as soon as we'd smooth one over, another would pop up, like a game of Whac-A-Mole. But knowing that crises can be dealt with is better than not having them, and who knows but that they benefited from learning that lesson early?

After the success of *A Billion for Boris*—not a self-perpetuating monster hit like *Freaky Friday* but with a tiny tail of its own*—I took a break

....

* A movie version, under the inflated title *Billions for Boris*, was released in 1984—and apparently never found again.

circa 1978: Hank and Mary with Alec (left) and Adam.
Life with five children was "like a game of Whac-A-Mole."

from magical children's books. When I returned a decade later it was because Harper & Row wanted a trilogy and because I'd figured out something else I wanted to say. By then I'd begun my unplanned ascent up the
ladder of board memberships at educational institutions. I'd spent a lot of
time watching boys and girls wrangling with what were mostly the boys'
problems about coeducation. And I'd watched plenty of men on boards,
who weren't very much better than the boys.

At the same time, Hank was continuing his unplanned ascent up a film-world ladder that was more like a conveyor belt, all moves essentially horizontal.* He had the talent for advancement but not, as I've said, the interest. Or maybe I mean: not the personality. Which was more than fine with me, who'd never wanted alpha men anyway. But other people sometimes misjudged Hank as a fizzle, whereas anything I succeeded at was considered a wonderful miracle. Did people just expect so little of Richard Rodgers's daughter? No one ever said to me: Pick one thing and excel, if you please! I never got criticized for changing venues. But Hank did, implicitly, even though in the end we both achieved at about the same level in our fields. The difference was sexism, destructive not just to women, as we know, but more insidiously to men.

And that's the point of the third book in the trilogy, *Summer Switch*, which with my usual acuity I at first called *Ape Face*. In this one, it's the father and son who change places, at Port Authority Bus Terminal. There, Ape Face—Annabel's brother Ben, now twelve—is about to get on a bus for Camp Soonawissakit, a sports camp he doesn't want to attend; after dropping him off, his father, Bill, a film executive, is headed to the airport to fly off for a meeting at Galaxy Pictures in California, which he also doesn't want to attend. After they switch, Ben (in Bill's body) turns out to be a better fit for the movie business than Bill; Bill (in Ben's body) a better fit for the simpler pleasures of jock camaraderie than Ben.†

Summer Switch is complicated to read because, unlike *Freaky Friday*, it follows both father and child, in alternating chapters.‡ But it's funny and

....

* From 1972 through 1982, Henry Guettel worked in the movies, first for the art-house distributor Cinema 5, then for Columbia Pictures, and finally as a senior vice president for East Coast production at Twentieth Century Fox.

† Published in November 1982, *Summer Switch* bears the dedication "For Hank and for Tod"—thus completing the circle of dedications to husband, mother, and all six children, living and dead. Nothing for Daddy, though: "He didn't need it."

‡ It was even harder to understand when it was crammed into an hour-long

I like what it says. I remember as a girl thinking: *Thank God I'm not a man.* They have to grow up and support everyone and be top banana, but by definition there can only be one top banana. On the other hand, there can be any number of kind and gentle second bananas, or third bananas—a whole bunch of bananas—which is what I wanted men like this father to be proud of. Or at least not be unproud of because they aren't heads of companies. Only rarely would I run into a man, a copyist or arranger, say, who was completely content with his moderate success. Short of the geniuses who actually manage to shine, they are always the best guys to be around.

But as it turns out, most of you poor men grow up with a fear of exactly that contentment: the one fear I was spared. I didn't expect to be my father—who could? I never dreamed of equaling Steve. I wasn't jealous, or do I mean envious, of Adam's talent as it emerged—how could I be? It was enough, with all of them, to have had a front-row seat.

....

ABC Afterschool Special that aired on September 19, 1984. Robert Klein played Bill; Scott Schwartz played Ben.

42.

ENEMAS FOR ELEPHANTS

t's a mortifying genre, this self-hagiography humbly disguised as an "and then I wrote" memoir. And now we come to the most mortifying part of it. So I'm only going to give you the highlight reel. The time: the mid-1970s through the mid-1980s. The setting: Hollywood—not the place but the disease.

Around 1975, the Walt Disney Company hired me to write a movie version of *Freaky Friday*.

It was released in 1977, starring Jodie Foster as Annabel and Barbara Harris as Ellen. Though I am credited as the sole screenwriter, I have to tell you, to salvage my honor, that it's not entirely true. After I wrote my draft, which was already compromised because I was forced to add a waterskiing climax, the company handed it to two in-house hacks to "polish." That meant cramming in typical Disney shit of that era like a car-chase sequence and a sexy-secretary subplot. When I finally read the hacks' polish, I threw it across the room, just like in a movie. And then they had the nerve to appeal to the Writers Guild for full credit, which I fought and won. But what did I win? Full credit for the blame. Even though the movie was a hit, I moped around embarrassed about it for years.* Everything I swore not to let happen in writing a movie, all the sexism and sitcomery, happened.

....

* The moping continued at least into 1980, when Ursula Nordstrom,

1977: "Even though the movie was a hit, I moped around embarrassed about it for years."

The 1995 and 2003 remakes were better, even though they too were Disney productions; my ditzy movie agent at the time had apparently chained me in perpetuity to the studio named for the recently frozen Re-

....

awaiting the manuscript of *Summer Switch*, wrote: "Please don't avoid me or anyone at Harper because of the 'dumb-assed movies.'"

publican.* The first, for television,† starring Shelley Long and Gaby Hoff-
mann, was good enough, even if they decided to explain the switch by
introducing a magic amulet. (Why explain it at all?) The second, starring
Jamie Lee Curtis and Lindsay Lohan in roles turned down by Annette
Bening and Kelly Osbourne, was a big hit eight years later.‡ I thought
it was swell. Almost everything was changed (the amulet became a fortune cookie), but for the first time on film the characters seemed real
despite the unreal goings-on, and plucky instead of whiny. A lot of that
comes from Curtis. Have you ever met someone who, after one minute
together, you somehow know that anyone who likes you would also like
her? And if not, not? She was one of those people for me.

But that Hollywood ending was long in the future when I started
writing screenplays; however degrading the sexy secretary was, I still had
lower to hang my head. For low-head-hanging, I doubt you could improve on *The Devil and Max Devlin*, which began as a Hammer Films horror flick called *The Fairytale Man* but somehow got sold to Disney. When
Disney later found it moldering on a shelf, probably the shelf beneath
Walt's head, they naturally asked me, the author of a successful screenplay about vaguely supernatural events, to resuscitate it. And because it
was a *Faust* knockoff, and I love *Faust*, I said I'd take it on. But the creepy
original was not what you'd call a good match for my sensibility—or for
the studio's.§ Disney wanted something that played like a comedy, to star
Elliott Gould and Bill Cosby. Uh-oh.

....

* The agent was Shirley Bernstein, Lenny's sister. The recently frozen
Republican was Walt Disney himself, rumored to have been preserved
cryogenically since his death in 1966.

† It aired on ABC in May 1995.

‡ The 2003 *Freaky Friday*, directed by Mark Waters, who would direct
Mean Girls the following year, earned $160 million worldwide.

§ The original, by the British screenwriter Jimmy Sangster, best known
for horror films, was supposed to be a vehicle for Vincent Price, playing a
dead actor who served as the Devil's collector of children's souls.

In my version, the Faust character, played by Gould, is Max Devlin, a Los Angeles slumlord killed by a bus and sent to hell after tripping on a blind woman's cane. The Devil's ambassador, Barney Satin, played by Cosby, proposes a deal: In exchange for being sent back to Earth, Max has to enlist three young innocents to take his place. One is a high school super-nerd, one a boy whose father has died, and one a nineteen-year-old aspiring pop star.

Disney demanded the addition of the aspiring pop star—in the original, the character had been an aspiring actor—because the suits wanted songs in the movie. But who, they wondered, should they get to write them? When I pointed out that I was a composer, they were totally surprised, never having heard of a woman who writes music. Magnanimously, they allowed me and Sheldon Harnick, with whom I quickly wrote two numbers, to fly to California to audition, along with a very sweet and good pianist who developed a kidney stone while he was playing and had to be taken (by me) to the hospital, where he was in agony well into the middle of the night. Anyway, the suits listened and said, "But these are Broadway songs." Yes.*

"Well, we don't think Broadway songs are right for a movie."

At which point Sheldon, who was already very famous from *Fiddler*, slunk out of the room humiliated. The movie wound up with a pair of acutely non-Broadway songs by Marvin Hamlisch instead.

Sheldon's slink should have been my cue. (Have you noticed how I'm always missing my cue?) In the typical Disney style of that era, everything had to be dumbed down as far as possible so as not to trouble anyone's brain with a new or elevated thought. The little boy's story had to end with his mother's marrying Devlin. The nerd needed to become a sports whiz. Even then, when I suggested tennis, a sport I know and love, it was dismissed as too girly. Soccer? Too European. Which is how I wound up one day at a motocross racetrack outside Los Angeles—a terrible dusty

---

* The songs—"Free" and "Topanga Canyon"—were indeed "Broadway" songs, meaning that they are craftier and more complicated than pop songs.

place filled with toothless kids—doing "research" and looking somewhat out of place in a sweater set. Also how I wound up talking to Cosby for four hours about the "meaning" of his role. Boy, did he have theories. But so did I: that he was the most arrogant, pompous pain in the ass I'd ever met.

I never saw the finished movie, though I think Hank and Alec did.[*] Unforgivably, the reviews did not congratulate me for sneaking the first curse words ever into a Disney movie: *damn* and *son-of-a-bitch*—that second one only partway. But they were not otherwise inaccurate. The *Times* called it "neither the worst nor, certainly, the best" of *Faust* adaptations. *People* was more pointed: "If there's a Purgatory for movies, this one belongs there."[†]

If there's a purgatory for movies? That's all there is. During my Hollywood decade, I worked all told on five stories or screenplays, each resulting in a movie worse than the one before, or no movie at all. I think I hit bottom after an *ABC Weekend Special*[‡] and an Encyclopedia Brown mystery, based on the boy-detective series, I didn't have the heart to finish. Here's how insignificant writers are in the film ecology: I offered to return the Encyclopedia Brown advance, but they wouldn't even take it. I realized, like Daddy before me, that writing for Hollywood is writing on water. With a book, assuming you can sell it, you are the absolute ruler

....

[*] *The Devil and Max Devlin*—with the terrible tagline "Their main goal is swiping soul"—opened on March 6, 1981. It was a bomb.

[†] Years later, Jimmy Sangster offered an even more damning review. "My only consolation in the affair (apart from the money) was the fact that I got to share a screen credit with the daughter of Richard Rodgers," he told the author of a history of Hammer Films. "Would that his daughter had been as good a screenwriter as her father was a musician."

[‡] Mary Rodgers is credited with the idea for *Columbus Circle*, a television movie about five children who play a practical joke on a neighbor. It aired as part of the ABC anthology series on November 23, 1985.

of your lands and domains; with a movie, as everyone who tries to do it must learn, you are merely cannon fodder.

Why submit to the degradation? It's like Daddy's joke about the guy at the circus hired to give enemas to elephants. Someone says: "Such a terrible job! Why don't you find another line of work?" To which he answers: "What, and give up show business?"

My time at the back end of the elephant certainly put the difficulties of writing for the theater in perspective. Musicals, which I'd walked away from in 1968, began to look a lot more alluring. And though they did not exactly come chasing me thereafter, I met a few halfway over the next ten years, offering songs for hire as requested.

One request came through Ursula, who in a letter attaching a review of *Freaky Friday* in March 1972 mentioned having met Marlo Thomas.* Marlo, she wrote, was "very caught up with Women's Lib (which I know you are not particularly) and she has been upset by some of the 'sexist literature' being fed to children." Marlo had asked Ursula to ask me if I would be willing to meet with her about a project she was hatching to respond to that problem. We did meet, and Marlo explained her idea of creating an album of songs and stories that would help undo gender stereotypes baked into children's culture. Released that November, the album and accompanying illustrated book were called *Free to Be . . . You and Me*—and, later, so was the animated television special adapted from it.†

I wound up writing the music for two songs used on the recording. The first, based on a children's book by Charlotte—to whom Ursula,

---

* A daughter of the comedian Danny Thomas, Marlo Thomas (born 1937) became famous in 1966 as the star of *That Girl*, a proto-feminist series about a single woman working and dating in Manhattan. Significantly, she never marries her boyfriend.

† The *Free to Be* album eventually went diamond, selling ten million copies. The television special won Emmy and Peabody awards. The book reached number one on the *Times* bestseller list.

1972: Marlo Thomas, Jack Cassidy, Mary, and the producer
Carole Hart celebrating *Free to Be . . . You and Me.*

around that time, was handing over the reins at Harper & Row—was
"William's Doll," about a boy who is teased because he wants one. Sheldon wrote the lyric, and Marlo sang it with Alan Alda.* The other was
"Girl Land," with a lyric by Bruce Hart, a *Sesame Street* songwriter who
turned us, briefly, into the second coming of Rodgers and Hart. Alas,
he was no kin to Larry in any sense; he was one of those "time/fine"

---

* For the animated special that aired in March 1974, "William's Doll"
was retitled "William Wants a Doll." In both versions, William's wish
is granted but also made less threatening by the reassurance that having
it will help him be a good father someday. It was advanced, but not that
advanced.

rhymers, which for me is like spitting at Jesus on the cross.[*] "Girl Land" is about the closing of a circus sideshow in which traditional femininity reigns and "good little girls pick up after boys." I guess I did the same thing, picking up a motif from Victor Herbert's "Toyland" and setting it to calliope harmonies—very creepy and effective, especially the way Jack Cassidy and Shirley Jones sang it. Lots of former kids tell me even today that they are scared of it, as they should be. Sexism is a nightmare.

I say that now, but at the time I tended to laugh it off. I am ashamed to admit that I found performative feminism too often unconvincing. Marlo always referred to herself as "me and my boyfriend Herb Gardner,"[†] smushed into one word—which for a liberated woman was a strange thing to add to every sentence. If I wasn't particularly "caught up" in women's lib, as Ursula noted, it was partly because I'm not, as the Brits say, clubbable. When you have an artist father and a steel trap mother, you grow up in what feels like a vacuum, where your successes are your own and your failures are, too. Which is why, for so long, I didn't think of myself as having been kept down by the patriarchy—even by my own patriarch, who, unpleasable as he was, expected the highest level of achievement from me. Or to put it the other way: He would have been just as disappointed in me if I had been a boy. Our family motto—you could have put it on his tombstone—was "Just get on with it." So I just did feminism; I didn't talk it. I worked straight through that entire era, switching gears if I got stymied, racing around like a loony in jeans while all the other mothers at Adam's schools wore Peck & Peck suits and had cocker spaniels on the end of a leash. It never occurred to me that their lives weren't what they wanted, any more than mine was, or who was at fault if so.

Now I wonder. Did I wind up writing so much and so long for chil-

....

[*] In "Girl Land" he pairs "eighty" and "lady," which is passable, and "are" and "before," which isn't.

[†] Herb Gardner (1934–2003) was a cartoonist and playwright, the author of *A Thousand Clowns* and *I'm Not Rappaport*.

dren* because that's what women in my field were mostly consigned to doing? Probably. And yet I loved that work—when it worked—and am not sure I would have had as much success, or any, with what were considered men's genres. Even now that I see how sexism operated in my professional life, I'm loath to pin my regrets on any donkey but me. If I could have been, I would have been, as Rose says in *Gypsy*. Maybe I should have been a bubble dancer after all.

If I'd been less focused on men, I might have rethought my assumptions sooner. What jump-started that process for me was *Working*, the musical Stephen Schwartz was putting together based on Studs Terkel's 1974 book of interviews with everyday wage earners.† I knew and loved Studs, and loved the book, so when Schwartz asked me, through Shirley Bernstein, to participate, I immediately said yes.

The musical was to be a kind of proletariat *La Ronde*, each character's song or monologue linking to the next. Schwartz, also directing, farmed out most of the songs; I was assigned to write several of them with Susan Birkenhead, whom Shirley introduced me to and who became, amazingly, my first woman lyricist since college.‡ One song was "Nobody Tells Me How," in which a teacher nearing retirement despairs over the decayed state of educational methods and standards.§ Another, "Terry's Song," followed one of her students, who after high school goes

---

* By 1973, when she wrote *Pinocchio* for the Bil Baird Marionettes, even Alec was too old for it.

† Studs Terkel (1912–2008) was a radio broadcaster and an oral historian whose classic book *Working: People Talk About What They Do All Day and How They Feel About What They Do* was published in 1974.

‡ Susan Birkenhead (born 1935) later wrote the excellent lyrics for the Broadway musical *Jelly's Last Jam*.

§ "But nobody teaches them spelling today, / Who has the time between weaving and play?"

through stewardess training, which is worse.* "Terry's Song" was cut, which is why it never acquired a proper title, but it and the other have superb lyrics: perfectly formed, smart, with an undercurrent of emotion and yet not mushy. My music wasn't bad, either.

I didn't mind that "Terry's Song" was cut; even shows in good shape have to throw out good material, and this show, which tried out in Chicago in late 1977, wasn't. What got me furious was that Schwartz, the little pisher,† fiddled with my music for a third song, about a housewife; I showed up at rehearsal one day to find the pianist playing an accompaniment that was totally different from the one I wrote. Unbelievably, Schwartz had changed my harmonies and refused to change them back— which was not only rude and unprofessional but also prohibited by my contract. There was quite a big scene, and I threatened to yank all my songs from the show, but Susan, who was still writing for *Captain Kangaroo* at the time, had never had a Broadway credit. I couldn't deprive her. And what were a few of my harmonies worth anyway? So I yanked only the one Schwartz had mauled.‡

But it gnawed at me, and I began to ask: Would Schwartz have pulled that stunt on one of the guy composers—like James Taylor? I doubt it. Yet the way he treated me was no worse than the way I treated myself. Or rather, it *was* the way I treated myself, as someone with no right even to fight for my rights. The men who took advantage of me were in some ways merely my proxies, reflecting my self-disregard in real action. That doesn't let them off the hook; I don't think I deserved to be cheated, any more than I deserved to be hit by Jerry Beaty. Is it a coincidence that

....

* "The second week started with physical fitness; / the pace was insane. / Each night we departed, as God is my witness, / in horrible pain."

† At twenty-nine, Stephen Schwartz (born 1948) already had three Broadway musicals to his credit and had worked with Leonard Bernstein on the lyrics for *Mass*. Later he wrote the score for *Wicked*.

‡ That Rodgers-Birkenhead song has since disappeared. It was replaced by "Just a Housewife," by Craig Carnelia.

Susan, too, had been hit by a husband—habitually, and with much worse bruises than mine?

After *Working* flopped in New York in May 1978,[*] I retreated to the safe worlds of fiction and philanthropy. It wasn't until years later, when, after many attempts, the show got fixed,[†] that I realized I'd really missed the boat. I should have written more songs with Susan. I should have written more songs, period.

But between 1978 and whatever year it is now, I wrote just two new musicals. The first was a last-ditch attempt to work again with crazy Marshall, who did not get less crazy with time. It was he who suggested the source material. Like "The Lady, or the Tiger?"—which I'd taken two stabs at—"The Griffin and the Minor Canon" was a short story by Frank R. Stockton.[‡] This one was about a beast and a priest. The beast falls in love with a carving of himself above the door of a small-town church; the priest, though young and frightened, befriends him. The enemy is the town itself, full of selfish conservatives concerned only with maintaining their way of life. In other words, Quoglodytes.

I loved the story; like *Mattress* but more gothic, it's a fable and a love story and a satire combined, raising questions about bravery and sacrifice. In the summer of 1987, after Marshall suggested it, I sent it to Lyn Austin, founder and director of Music-Theatre Group, whose production of *Garden of Earthly Delights*, the dance theater piece by Martha Clarke,

....

[*] Though it lasted just a month on Broadway, *Working* was nominated, in a thin year, for five Tony Awards, including Best Score and Best Book, both of which it lost to *On the Twentieth Century*.

[†] A revival by the Prospect Theater Company—revised by Schwartz, directed by Gordon Greenberg, and featuring two interpolated songs by Lin-Manuel Miranda—ran at the 59E59 Theaters in December 2012.

[‡] "The Griffin and the Minor Canon" was published in 1885, a few years after "The Lady, or the Tiger?" An edition of the griffin story wonderfully illustrated by Maurice Sendak was published in 1963.

I'd seen a few years earlier and thought was terrific. When I didn't hear back, I took it to André Bishop at Playwrights Horizons, with whom I'd been talking about writing a play. The working title of that play was *Dominique*, named after Nick Dunne's daughter, who a few years earlier had been strangled to death by an ex-boyfriend.* Around the time, among our own circle, there was a spate of similar incidents: privileged girls whose less privileged boyfriends became enraged and stalky and violent when dumped. But in the play, I wanted to have the mother—of course—create the situation in which the guy kills the daughter, because she's as suspicious and paranoid as he is. I wrote reams of notes but only one scene. Save it for my "And then I didn't write" memoir.

Nothing came of that except my friendship with André, who liked me because I'd helped untangle him from a fight with Mummy over funding for *Sunday in the Park with George*.† I liked the idea of following Steve into the wilds of off-Broadway, and *Griffin* didn't seem like Broadway material anyway. At the end of 1987, the two companies—Playwrights and Music-Theatre Group—announced plans to produce the musical together the following summer in Stockbridge, Massachusetts, where Lyn started many of her shows in an adorable little nineteenth-century

....

* The actress Dominique Dunne (1959–1982) was the daughter of the journalist Dominick Dunne and Ellen Beatriz Dunne. Her ex-boyfriend, John Thomas Sweeney, a sous-chef, was convicted of voluntary manslaughter but served less than four years for killing her.

† Having served on the New York State Council on the Arts from 1963 through 1979, Dorothy Rodgers remained an honorary member until her death. In 1983, she threatened to use her influence to cut Playwrights Horizons' funding if it produced the show, arguing that Sondheim was a commercial composer who did not need public support. Maybe so, but the theater did—and, after some back-channel cajolery, and a letter from Bishop saying that, instead of interfering, Dorothy should "get down on your knees and kiss my feet"—she responded: "Point taken." The funding was maintained.

schoolhouse called Citizens Hall.* The plan was to move it to New York the following year.

By the time rehearsals started in July, all the writers but me had been swapped. Peter Parnell was supposed to write the book, but something happened and we wound up with Wendy Kesselman. Then Marshall, after snoring and farting all the way up to Stockbridge a few times, became too erratic to work with and had to be fired (by me); Ellen Fitzhugh, a wonderful lyricist whose work on *Grind* I'd admired, came aboard.† We now, inadvertently, had an all-female creative team—the designers were all women, too, though the director, also a replacement, was not—and you'd think that would have been heaven after what I'd learned on *Working*.

It was, for a moment.‡ But then the crazy started and wouldn't let up. Among the crazy-makers were an Orthodox ex-stripper, a German film crew making a documentary about my glorious return to the theater, and imaginary Nazis. Mandatory Friday night fucking was also in-

....

* Lyn Austin (1922–2000) was a Broadway producer who decamped to the avant-garde. She and her partner, Diane Wondisford, ran Music-Theatre Group from its inception, work that Wondisford continued after Austin was killed in 2000 by a taxi on Eighth Avenue.

† Years after writing the words to Larry Grossman's excellent music for *Grind*—a 1985 Broadway flop directed by Hal Prince—Ellen Fitzhugh (born 1942) provided additional lyrics for Adam Guettel's *Myths and Hymns*.

‡ From a 1988 interview with the *Times*: "I haven't felt so happily immersed in a project since working on *Once Upon a Mattress* at Tamiment in the Poconos . . . It's also been an interesting experience to collaborate with two other women. As we were working, I realized that thirty years ago, I would have felt insecure about it. At that time, I wouldn't have thought three women could do as good a job as one woman and two men. But we've had a wonderful time with each other."

volved. Ellen, whom I'd loved, escaped under cover of dark; threats flew about; the terrific cast braved on, as terrific casts do, learning and then unlearning new material every day. I don't even know how we finished; maybe we didn't. But something showed up onstage that August,* when it was so sweltering in the adorable old schoolhouse you couldn't breathe without air-conditioning and the air-conditioning drowned out the music. We could turn it off, but then the audience started getting undressed, and anyway there was no way to turn off the crashing river behind the theater. The only thing you could hear were the whimpers of the cast in their heavy medieval robes and the wonderful-horrible electronic sounds that Adam, who was twenty-three and up the road that summer at Williamstown, had created for the griffin.†

The reviews were respectful,‡ but it was obviously a work in progress that wasn't going to progress. The plan to bring it to New York was abandoned, and the songs, which were some of my best—with some great lyrics, too—went into the trunk.§

· ·

* *The Griffin and the Minor Canon*, directed by André Ernotte, ran for fifteen performances in August 1988, at the Lenox Arts Center in Stockbridge.

† For the Williamstown Theatre Festival's July 1988 production of *The Legend of Oedipus*—a two-part mashup of Euripides, Aeschylus, and Sophocles—Adam Guettel composed three hours of music in five days.

‡ *The Schenectady Gazette*: "Rodgers' music is clearly evocative of the period and the dark mood, while revealing some personality traits of the characters. It is exceptionally well executed by the small cast accompanied by dual pianos . . . There is great warmth and appeal in the production, which will be given greater stature as it progresses to a finished work."

§ A few have emerged. "Am I?"—sung by the griffin while gazing at his sculpted image—appears on *Rodgers, Rodgers & Guettel*, an album of songs written by three generations of the family and sung by Judy Kuhn. Like much of Mary's late work it is both stately and adventurous, as if

I blame the Orthodox ex-stripper.

What could I do but put a good face on it? It always seems shameful, let alone pointless, to mope. But the failure of my big return to the theater after ten years' recusal was crushing. I know because I started doing something I almost never do: listening to classical music. All my life, I've avoided it; it's so moving and intense, and makes me so sad, that there's always the chance it might make me cry. But I'd decided, for no particular reason, not to drink that year, so I didn't have my usual way of dealing with sadness: in private, with a dry Rob Roy. Instead I wept into my Bach.

. . . .

she'd at last accepted the heritage of her father (it's a waltz) while also anticipating the extreme chromaticism of her son.

43.

GIVE AND GET

Though he used recreational drugs only sparingly, and only on weekends, it was Arthur who recommended my pusher.

She lived on the second floor of a nasty brick building at Fourteenth and Broadway, where her apartment, he warned me, was perpetually underheated. With that in mind, I stuffed fifteen hundred dollars in the inside pocket of my only mink coat and took a taxi downtown. The place didn't seem so arctic to me, but Barb, as we might as well call her, was certainly sniffling.

After hellos, out came a big tray like the ones at Cartier, but instead of colorful rings it was studded with colorful pills. I pointed to ones that were especially pretty—*What's this? What's that?*—while explaining that I was looking for the least offensive, least dangerous mood-elevating medications, like Dexamyl and Daprisal, which by 1988 were no longer available.*

"The real stuff will cost more, because it's made for hospitals," Barb explained, taking out a new tray.

Whatever she gave me on my first two visits didn't do much. But on my third visit, she said, "Now I've got something I think might work."

....

* Dexamyl was discontinued in 1982 when drugs with fewer side effects and less potential for dependence came on the market. Daprisal, a painkiller that also elevated mood, likewise sank into obsolescence after its side effects became known.

"What is it?" I asked.

"I have no idea, but people like it."

She opened a little box. Inside were single pills encased in silver foil, along with a little piece of thin paper covered with microscopic directions, evidently in German.

"What's the dose?"

"As much as it takes to feel good, I guess."

That turned out to mean about three a day. I know because soon after starting that schedule my mood cleared right up, the first sign of which was realizing that Barb didn't have a cold but was on cocaine.

This didn't seem like an ideal situation. I had recently started with another dreadful new shrink—I guess I was depressed, though in my family it felt humiliating to admit it—so I handed him the directions and asked him what I was taking. He couldn't read German, either, but said he'd show his colleagues. About three weeks later he told me it was Ritalin.

Made perfect sense to me. Depression and lack of energy are conjoined twins, and if you can't do much about the former, why not attack the latter?* But shrinko, feeling we could make more progress with drugs specifically targeted at depression, sent me to Steven Roose, the Columbia psychopharmacologist. Roose saw me for fifteen minutes, immediately diagnosed dysphoria—*minor* depression, which was a relief; I didn't really plan on hanging myself—and suggested I try imipramine.†

Now why do I go into all of this? Well, for one thing, this isn't a children's book. There is no moral and I am not a role model. To my knowledge, nothing bad happened to me because of any of the drugs, legal or semi-, I took in my life—except nicotine, which was not only legal but heavily promoted. I'd never recommend nonprescription drugs for children, of course, but mine had their phases anyway and you'll have to draw your own conclusions.

....

* Ritalin, though most often used to combat attention deficit hyperactivity disorder, is a stimulant.

† Sold as Tofranil, imipramine had been around since the late 1950s.

I also bring this up because it gives me a bit of a naughty thrill when thinking of my many years in service to educational institutions. The morning after I took my first dose of imipramine, I was heading up to Exeter* for a trustees' meeting; the shrink had asked me to call him first and report how I felt. How I felt? It was like a bolt of lightning. I was suddenly so happy and energetic and baffled and amazed and thrilled and—

"Cut it in half!" he shouted.

Even so, I could hardly wait for the next dose. Which was still too strong, so he sent me back to Roose, who prescribed Prozac, then brand new.† That worked just fine, making all my worries seem small except one: Now that I was feeling so much better, might he take it away from me?

Because, let's face it, most people would have to be on Prozac, or even Ritalin, to find board membership fascinating. Which is why—even though my career as a philanthropeuse and educational do-gooder lasted longer than any of my others and mattered to me almost as much—I absolutely forbid any discussion of it in this book.

Or at least let's keep it short. My board service began, you may recall, back in 1968, at the Episcopal nursery with Adam's itchy bottom. From there, I simply paralleled my kids' progress up the educational ladder, to the Professional Children's School in 1969, Brearley in 1970, Exeter in 1977, and eventually Juilliard in 1992. Each stop was its own education.

At the Professional Children's School, which serves young performers and athletes,‡ we worked on accreditation, so the ice skaters would

....

* Phillips Exeter Academy, an hour north of Boston in Exeter, New Hampshire, is one of the oldest and wealthiest boarding schools in the United States. Though girls were first admitted in 1970, it took a number of years to graduate alumnae who could serve as trustees; until then, to diversify the roster, mothers filled the bill.

† Discovered in 1972, Prozac became generally available in the United States in January 1988.

‡ The Professional Children's School was founded in New York City in

1992: A drawing made by Kim Beaty in preparation for a portrait
commissioned by Exeter to mark Mary's eleven years of service as a trustee.
"I could only attend the meetings as a guest of the men."

be forced to learn something other than Lutzes, and the ballet kids who
didn't make it into a company still had a chance of getting into college.
That was interesting, but in the wake of the American National Opera
disaster, I'd become very aware that boards weren't supposed to just sit
there and say yes when the administration laid out plans to build a gigantic new building or start an overambitious new program. When something like that began brewing at PCS, I left.

By then I was serving on the alumnae board at Brearley, which was
just silly; we met in the library and the headmistress poured tea. The ba-

....

1914 to educate young stage actors in the local theater industry and on
the road, but over the years has expanded to serve dancers, musicians,
and others.

sic thing I learned during my do-nothing term was something I already knew in a different context: that white-glove types are no fun. When the hallways needed refreshing, and I proposed getting the parents together for a weekend paint party, you'd think I'd suggested spattering the walls with menstrual blood. And when I was on the search committee for the new head of school, who should come before us but Jean Harris, wearing, yes, little white gloves. I just knew she'd kill a diet doctor someday.

It's possible my personality was too much and my mouth too big for those boards. The other ladies all wore hats and tilted their legs just so when seated, while I folded myself into a yoga pose and stirred my coffee, when a spoon was lacking, with the stem of my glasses. Nevertheless, when Exeter—which, by the way, you will want to pronounce EX-iter, not EGG-ziter, so you don't sound like a rube—asked me to join its trustees in 1977, I was so flattered and cowed, I basically didn't speak at meetings for three years. Among so many uptight Waspy men, I was at least a double minority, and like minorities of all types anywhere began by studying the milieu and looking for an opening. Eventually my unease became my entrée: Since I was the outlier, I could speak up for the outlaid. Why were there still so few Black people on campus? How could we get more working-class students? When the other trustees were worrying "what to do" about all the Asian students applying—as a group, they were much better prepared than the whites—I said, "Well, here's an idea: You could let them in."

Sometimes you have to put a pin in people's discomfort, or even your own, to prick the conscience underneath. And this did the trick.

Another discomfort at Exeter was coeducation. To me it was not just about girls, who had been admitted since 1970 and now made up about 40 percent of the student body, but about women on faculty and in administration, whose numbers lagged. So in 1986, when Stephen Kurtz announced his intention to retire as principal the next year, I joined the search committee to find his successor. A double standard applied: Though I could not say publicly I was seeking a female candidate,* it was perfectly acceptable for one of my colleagues—a man whose dog later

* From a 1987 *New York Times* article about the search: "'We frankly didn't

buried his cell phone in the garden—to say, "There's this woman candidate, but we should interview her anyway."

We did. On a terrible, snowy late afternoon in December, at the headquarters of the headhunting firm in New York, we were introduced to Kendra O'Donnell,* who was in her fifth year chairing the board of trustees at Emma Willard, a very good, straitlaced, unsnobbish boarding school for women in Troy, New York. During her tenure, she'd increased the school's endowment somefold; don't ask me to do the math.† She had sterling academic credentials and was at the time working for the Rockefeller Brothers Fund. What more could you ask? Within two seconds we all, especially the women, but even the men, thought she was terrific, and those of us who could go to the ladies' room did so to discuss it.

But when we forwarded her name to the trustees en banc, the fights that ensued were fierce. There were five members of the board who felt women should not even be allowed to join the Century Club, where the meetings took place in the billiard parlor, let alone become Exeter's principal. (I could only attend the meetings as a guest of the men.) The five dinosaurs and some other embalmed alumni put up such resistance to hiring Kendra that we had to truck faculty down to New York to talk about why they liked her. Now Exeter, like all good schools, is the kind of place where if the faculty doesn't back what you're doing, forget it; if they do, that's half the battle. With their help, Kendra was approved in a squeaker of a vote and assumed the post in July 1987. I was asked to

....

expect to be able to find a woman,' says Mary Rodgers Guettel, a composer and Exeter trustee."

* An academic and a painter, Kendra Stearns O'Donnell (born 1944) studied English at Barnard and Columbia, was highly regarded as a teacher at Princeton, and served as a program officer at several nonprofit institutions. The *Times* also noted approvingly her "unpolished but nicely rounded nails."

† Approximately threefold, from eight million to twenty-three million dollars.

1982: Alec (about fourteen) and Adam (about seventeen). "Exeter would find you a course in purple cows if purple cows were what you wanted to study."

extend my term by one year in case she needed support as she settled in, but she was absolutely terrific right off the bat, popular with all four constituencies: trustees, alums, faculty, and, hardest of all, kids.

Though I sent two of my own kids—Kim and Adam—to Exeter, and Tod to Choate and Alec to Andover,* I can't say I'm sure that boarding school provides the best education for everyone, even if everyone could afford it.

Yes, Exeter would find you a course in purple cows if purple cows were what you wanted to study. But the petri dish environment isn't always an ideal medium for learning. What I can say is that the intensity of the experience, along with the resulting intensity of the problems, makes serving on educational boards a lot more fascinating than serving on the boards of hospitals with ladies who have a lot of diamonds. At a school you can actually make a difference, while the diamond ladies can have no effect on what goes on beyond the balls and galas at the institutions they purport to care about. Which is a good thing: Do you want a bunch of

---

* Nina stayed in New York for high school, moving from Brearley to Dalton.

social X-rays making medical policy at the Hospital for Special Surgery? They're just there to open their checkbooks.

That was probably the expectation for me at Exeter, too. Most non-profit boards are "give or get": There's an amount of money you are expected to donate or raise each year.* Whatever the "give" number was at Exeter, I couldn't afford it and so, instead, had to get it from Mummy. But after reading the school bible—the booklet that had been in use since the late eighteenth century—she said, "I'm not giving to a school like that! They say right up front that they only want Protestants."

"Mummy, that's not true anymore. They have plenty of Jewish kids."

"But are there Jewish teachers?"

There weren't.

She wasn't wrong to withhold a donation, but on the other hand how can you make change at an institution if you're not inside it? Mummy was much more frightened of what she assumed was the anti-Semitic upper crust than I was, not because she was so Jewish but because she was so isolated. All strangers were dangerous to her; most strangers were welcome to me. Anyway, I'd had much more experience of the Wasp type, including one Wasp husband, and though they sometimes made me a little nervous, they all seemed to be fine once I got to know them and puncture them. Mummy not so much, though she eventually relented and left Exeter something like a hundred thousand dollars: enough to fund their choral society and keep them touring around the country ever since.†

When my extended term ended in 1988, after eleven years, I thought I'd worked off my debt to society: the debt of having access to money I hadn't earned, and through it the power to do some little good or not.

I continued my dalliance with some other nonprofits, not looking for

....

* Some are "give and get," requiring up-front donations in addition to fundraising quotas.

† The Richard Rodgers Music Fund was established at Exeter in 1996, four years after Dorothy Rodgers's death.

another new marriage.* But a few years later, in 1991, Anna Crouse and Mary Ellin Barrett† approached me about joining the board at Juilliard.‡ I asked Mary Ellin what the give or get was and she said, "Well, I give fifty"—meaning fifty thousand a year. I couldn't do it, and Mummy was finished with paying for activities that would keep me busy anywhere besides her bedside or on the phone with her multiple times a day. When I said, "I'd love to, nothing would be more flattering, but I can't afford it," they asked me to meet anyway with the incoming chairman, Peter Jay Sharp. But the meeting kept being postponed and eventually I was asked to join the board regardless. I guess they figured I'd be good for the "give" eventually and in the meantime could at least do some "get"—or supply a few stars for the galas.

Sharp died the next April, of melanoma, which explained our postponed meetings.§ I don't know what explained the state of the board when I joined it soon thereafter. It was too small, completely unprofessional, with no terms, no rules, no expectations, and no interest. There were generous members who never showed up, and ungenerous ones who never failed to. It felt like a dining club with a dead maître d'.

....

* Modesty! Mary served, often simultaneously with her other philanthropic work, as vice president of the Young Playwrights Festival, on the council of the Dramatists Guild, and on the boards of ASCAP, Lincoln Center, the Bridgehampton Chamber Music Festival, and of course the Rodgers and Hammerstein Foundation.

† Anna Crouse (1916–2013) was the widow of the playwright Russel Crouse, who with Howard Lindsay wrote the books for *Anything Goes* and *The Sound of Music*. Mary Ellin Barrett (1926–2022) was the oldest of Irving Berlin's daughters.

‡ Founded in 1905 as the Institute of Musical Art—where a young Richard Rodgers studied for two years—the Juilliard School is one of the world's leading training programs in music, drama, and dance. Since 1969 it has been part of the Lincoln Center campus, on West Sixty-fifth Street.

§ Peter Jay Sharp, a hotelier and real estate developer who owned the Carlyle, was sixty-one.

After a year in which I worked like crazy doing all the drama stuff, including the annual benefit at the State Theater, Anna and Mary Ellin told me they'd discussed it with Joseph Polisi[*] and decided I should be chairman. Which I thought was a fascinating and desperate and completely crazy idea. Surely there was a janitor in the building more qualified. I told Joseph, whom I respected immensely, "Gee, I'm honored and flattered, but listen, I don't know *Robert's Rules of Order*, I can't do charts or budgets, I can't do fundraising, I didn't grow up around a lot of rich people—theater people may be rich one year but are just as likely to be starving the next; it's an iffy sort of existence—and I still don't know a lot of rich people, I don't hang out with CEOs or foundation heads, and most important of all, I don't do zeroes."

"We have other people to do those things," he said.

Thus in 1994 began my seven years as chairman. If my personal bookkeeping proved I couldn't read a budget—every few months I just called the stockbroker and asked, "Am I broke yet?"—I could at least improve the atmosphere. Most of the trustees didn't know anything about the actual work of the school, so I started these little show-and-tell events to remind them what they were bothering about. The students had no idea who the trustees were, either, so I introduced them in the speeches I was expected to give. At the same time, I sought to change the nature of the board: As the idiots gradually dropped off, we replaced them with better people, increasing the size to thirty-five from twenty-five. I guess the main thing I did was to warm the place up. I got to be friendly with the faculty and the kids, going out to eat with them, having them over here to play. It was a peaceful time.[†]

....

[*] Joseph W. Polisi (born 1947) was the president of the Juilliard School from 1984 to 2017. His Italian father was the principal bassoonist of the New York Philharmonic; his Jewish mother a dancer in the chorus at Radio City Music Hall.

[†] More modesty. According to the playwright Marsha Norman, Mary was "the moving force behind the most sweeping changes the school would experience until . . . well, until she resigned." Among those

1995: Mary speaking at Juilliard. "The main thing
I did was to warm the place up."

But the world was changing around us. By 2001, the idea that a board chairman might not do zeroes—obviously an unusual accommodation—had become obnoxious and insupportable to some. One of that some, lovely Bruce Kovner,* had Joseph's ear. Now keep in mind that Bruce

....

changes was the reinvigoration of the moribund Lila Acheson Wallace Playwriting Program. It is also unlikely that Juilliard students of any other era greeted the chairman of the board of trustees at convocations and commencements with spontaneous chants of "May-REE, May-REE, May-REE!"

* The investor and hedge-fund manager Bruce Kovner (born 1945) has

was persona non grata among the board members at Juilliard, confined to the lower-level Juilliard Council, in part because he had a beard and in part because he got in trouble with the Securities and Exchange Commission.* Anyway, he and Joseph came to the apartment and said they wanted me to step down.

I asked Bruce, "Are you planning to take over?"

"Do you want me to?" he replied.

Few people who are fired say that the people who fired them were wrong; they say what was wrong was the way it was done. I say it, too: The way it was done to me was wrong, but getting rid of me was right. It was time for someone more professional. Still, I wasn't lying when, at my abdication shindig, I said, "Juilliard has become—is—my self-respect, my pride." For me, it had been an unenhanced high, a true give and get experience.

Anyway, I got over my annoyance pretty quickly, because we were coming up on the complete reconstruction of Lincoln Center, involving delicate negotiations and high-level fights with the Met, and I'd never have known in a million years how to handle it. I would have sold Juilliard right down the river trying to be nice and accommodating; give the man credit, Bruce was very good at not being nice and accommodating.†

Having resigned the chairmanship, I remained on the board; recently I've threatened every six months to leave. It has been too long; board members shouldn't take up space in perpetuity—and I have not been happy, from my emerita perch, to watch the next phase of the transformation of arts philanthropy. As in our economy and politics, decision-making has become divorced from the work of working people, which includes artists, as those in power have become richer and more Republican.

....

given at least eighty million dollars to Juilliard, where he once took evening music courses.

* In 1994, Kovner's company Caxton Associates agreed to pay thirty-six million dollars to settle antitrust and securities charges.

† Kovner has been chair of Juilliard's board of trustees since 2001.

You think I'm rich? Kovner, who supported George W. Bush and Dick Cheney, is worth five billion. That's a bad fit for a school whose mission is built on liberal values, but a place like Juilliard now can't survive without moneybags that big. Bruce at least is a cultivated person: He gave the school his collection of musical manuscripts—including the marked-up printer's proof of Beethoven's Ninth Symphony, for gosh sakes—and didn't even put his name on it. But having their name on it is the only thing most of that crowd wants; they don't give a shit about the art. Even I had to put my name on something because, I was told, it looks bad if I don't encourage other people to put their names on something else. So on some floor at Juilliard there's the Mary Rodgers Guettel something; I honestly don't remember what it is—a water fountain? I don't care!* Meanwhile, Juilliard doesn't have a musical theater division, which for the country's premier musical and theatrical training program is just ridiculous. In my post-chair years, I tried to get one going; I even got Johnny Kander, Kathleen Marshall, Paul Gemignani, Jay Binder, and others to commit to three months each of teaching. But nothing happened. I was told it was too costly.

---

* The Mary Rodgers Guettel Pre-College Suite, housing the offices of Juilliard's programs for children ages eight to eighteen, was dedicated in 2010, in recognition of a million-dollar gift.

44.

I DISMEMBER MAMA

f you're lucky enough, and also unlucky enough, you eventually tack from making new things to managing the fruit of old ones. That's true of people in general (tending their assets, launching their grandkids) but especially of composers, whose gifts begin to evaporate after sixty. There are very few Bachs in history, let alone Verdis, pumping out glorious music into old age.* And Bach and Verdi didn't write for Broadway. Classical composers could write dozens of works a year, not just one every four, if that. To avoid the problem of obsolescence in our musical theater, you have to die young, like Gershwin. All the others—Berlin, Porter, Arlen—got squarer as they got older, as if their fingers had frozen in familiar positions. They couldn't find the new notes anymore, let alone the rhythms.

The real question is how hard you fight it. Daddy fought it tooth and nail, even though he was missing several of the former and one of the latter. The fear of losing his gift made him stingier with it, not freer. At first the fear was misplaced; a lot of his music for *Do I Hear a Waltz?*—which he wrote when he was sixty-two—was perfectly beautiful; even Steve

....

* Bach wrote profusely and without diminishment almost to his death at sixty-five, which was plenty old in 1750. Verdi's masterpiece *Falstaff* premiered in 1893, when the composer was seventy-nine—and there was still great work to come.

said he needn't have despaired. The rhythmic squareness, the dreaded um-chuck, was almost undetectable beneath the melodic honey. But after that, the decline became more and more evident, hastened by poor choices of material and collaborators. *Rex*, about Henry VIII, had lyrics by Sheldon Harnick and ran for less than two months in 1976;* its supposedly big "classic" Rodgers ballads—like "Away from You," sung by Henry to Anne Boleyn—laid petrified dinosaur eggs. His next and last show, *I Remember Mama*, based on the book I'd once suggested he and Ockie produce as a play, seemed more promising, at least on paper, with its nostalgic tales of a Norwegian American matriarch. But the promise proved empty onstage; despite a big star in Liv Ullmann,† it acquired the nickname, well before it opened in 1979, of *I Dismember Mama*.

That's how I think of it now: not just as Daddy's almost literal last gasp‡ but also as the dismantling of any last illusions I still had about him and Mummy. I don't mean illusions of fidelity; I never had those, even when Mummy instructed me to ignore the rumors. But I'd held on to the idea that despite his indiscretions, and her disappointment, there remained, behind the wall of their absolute secrecy and solidarity, the sturdiness of a marriage based on peculiar mutual respect. How else could it have lasted forty-nine years?

It would not last fifty. As their final anniversary passed in March 1979, Daddy was nearly dead and—I'm sure there's a joke here—in Philadelphia. Tryouts there for *Mama* weren't going well, and he asked me down to see if I could help. I showed up on a Saturday afternoon and watched

....

* Opening officially on April 25, 1976, and closing on June 5, *Rex*, which starred Nicol Williamson and featured the young Glenn Close, had the shortest initial run of any Richard Rodgers musical since *Chee-Chee* in 1928.

† A big star but in the wrong medium; Liv Ullmann (born 1938) was known for her intensely interior dramatic performances in films by Ingmar Bergman.

‡ He had a tracheotomy after a bout of laryngeal cancer in 1974.

the show that evening. It was not merely an obvious flop but the kind
that seems to be having a nervous breakdown onstage: not a "Why?"
musical but a "What the fuck?" one. With half the score hastily rewritten,
with roles eliminated and roles combined, with the cast dispirited by a
revolving door of hirings and firings, it was evident that the producers,
Alexander Cohen and his wife, Hildy Parks, were presiding over a very
expensive death spiral.

One didn't dare criticize Daddy, of course; even in better days, when
there was little to criticize, he'd clench in horror if you did not instantly
adore every note he played. Criticizing the show was just as difficult, for a
different reason: It was so misbegotten and so miscarried, I didn't then—
and still don't—know where to start. Well, okay, how about we start with
Marty Charnin, who wrote the lyrics and also directed and was strangely
partial to Ullmann even though she couldn't sing a note. Well, she could
sing maybe five. Have you ever thought about what Scandinavians sound
like when they're speaking? The range is minuscule. And it doesn't magically improve when you add music.*

We had arranged to have lunch before the matinee the next day to
discuss the situation, and by "we" I mean not only Daddy and me but also
Mummy, who was there to keep her beady eye on him and run interference with whoever might interfere. Rounding out the entourage in the
suite at the Warwick Hotel was a woman I called Nursie: a maniac and a
grand manipulator, almost a movie nutjob, like the stalker-fan in *Misery*
but with an Irish brogue. Her job was to mind Daddy's health, but she
seemed to take a liberal view of that brief.

In the middle of lunch on Sunday, my mother, like clockwork, developed a terrible migraine and went to her bedroom. This was a signal for
Daddy to go sit with her, but he didn't. Rather, he asked me to attend,
in her stead, the meeting he was supposed to have with Alex and Hildy
after the matinee. This was very flattering, and perhaps, for him, a bit of
a relief. He didn't like Mummy getting mixed up in his world: a world I
certainly understood better than she, especially in a crisis.

....

* Kirsten Flagstad notwithstanding.

"I know what it's going to be about," Daddy said. "They want to get rid of Marty."

Sure enough, later that afternoon, the doorbell to the suite rang, and into the living room walked Hildy and Alex, grim and determined. Since Marty couldn't both direct and rewrite, the idea was to relieve him of both duties. But who should do the lyrics instead? And who direct? Daddy, already a lame duck in life, just shrugged, so I suggested that if Johnny Kander was willing to relinquish Fred Ebb for a minute, he was top-notch. Alex and Hildy ignored that idea, suggesting other people much less appropriate, like Betty and Adolph. I said no to all their names and they to mine. Same thing for directors, though I didn't even dare mention Hal; he had doctored *Rex* to no avail.

The meeting went nowhere, with Daddy barely participating, and the producers left with no plan in hand.* Daddy then went into Mummy's room, where the television immediately started playing some soap opera so filled with loud screaming that I wondered how my parents could talk. After a while, I realized it was not the TV screaming, but Mummy. And the screaming went on as long as a soap opera.

Nursie, hearing the noise, came into the living room and told me they often fought like this. It was Mummy's fault, she explained: She was paranoid and impossible, and had even confessed to a plan for rigging some kind of remote-control tape recorder under the bed to capture how terrible Daddy was to her. (Actually, I could believe that.) But Daddy *wasn't* terrible, Nursie insisted: He was a saint! How could anyone abuse such a dear, sick man? It seemed she was crazy for him, and so in his pocket that for a shuddery moment I suspected he'd slept with her. Then I had a good look at her, thought about Diahann Carroll and Eva Gabor, and nixed the notion.

....

* They eventually hired the unlikely Raymond Jessel to write the additional lyrics; he would later achieve brief fame—and a spot on *America's Got Talent*—as the author of "What She's Got," also known as "The Penis Song." Cy Feuer, the theatrical and movie producer, and a longtime enemy of Richard Rodgers, took over the direction.

Nursie retreated when Daddy came out of Mummy's room, looking ashen.

"I guess she's not very happy right now," I said.

"When is she ever?" he snarled.

"But what was she yelling about?"

"That I didn't cancel the meeting," Daddy said. "And that I asked you to take her place."

Well, knock me over with a Greek drama, whydontcha? Not that it should have been a surprise. A few months earlier, when Daddy was among the first group of Kennedy Center honorees,* Mummy forbade him, despite my pleading, to let me attend the ceremony, though it would have been nothing for him to get an extra ticket.

Now in Philadelphia, sitting down at a table with me, he proceeded to talk in a way I have almost wiped out of my memory because I was so startled and horrified by his feelings. Decades' worth of fury and disgust poured out, concluding with the apt and ugly and final phrase: "I'm sick to death of her."

Is it terrible to say that his actual death, later that year—once *I Dismember Mama* had opened and closed on Broadway†—didn't feel like much of a loss? He was so miserable by then it was more of a relief. He was never going to write again, even badly, and without that I don't think he cared if he was alive or not. The only things he enjoyed besides music were wit and wine, and Mummy permitted him none of the latter. Wit he no longer bothered with because the tracheotomy had ruined his timing; by the time he swallowed the air and burped it back up to produce a sound, the bon mot was too late. He spent his last months helpless and froglike,

....

* At the gala, broadcast in December 1978, Richard Rodgers sat in a gilded box between Marian Anderson and Arthur Rubinstein, with Dorothy beaming behind him.

† *I Remember Mama* officially opened on May 31, 1979 at the Majestic Theater, where *Carousel* and *South Pacific* had triumphed in the 1940s. It closed three months later, on September 2.

blinking at the television in her dressing room, supposedly watching ball games but half the time asleep. Once, when Adam, on a visit, was playing piano in the living room, he did seem to perk up; he called out, through the wall, "Louder!" Which should have been his last word, but he still hung on. At last, I swear to god, he willed himself to die, which may be why even a complete autopsy never determined what he died of.*

Shall we wrap up the parents? Mummy lived another twelve years plus,† a lot of them spent teasing us with her imminent demise. She wasn't supposed to survive the heart attack she had in 1986 but did. Other than on her various deathbeds she was just as busy and efficient as ever, and even more controlling. Literally so, as Daddy's executor and now the solo family cashier. To the end, she kept me (and my philanthropy) on a very tight leash; the year before she died, after Hank and I dared to take a vacation cruise without her, I got a call from the accountant—still the same goddamn accountant from the American National Opera disaster. "You better look out," he said. "She's threatening to cut you out of the will."

"But why?"

"She doesn't like your lifestyle." Which meant she didn't like that it was mine.

Daddy's death had allowed her to rewrite the mortifying scene in Philadelphia (and no doubt many like it) in which she felt sidelined by him and, inadvertently, by me. It wasn't the first inkling I had that Mummy's lifelong disdain for my choices was a variation of envy. I was living a fuller life than she'd had a chance to. Even my resentments made her jealous. A few years before *I Remember Mama*, she showed me a draft of her fourth book, which was already a hot potato; Bob Gottlieb, her editor at Knopf, had given up on it, and a new editor, at Harper & Row,

....

* "After a long illness," as the newspapers reported, Richard Rodgers died at home in bed at age seventy-seven on December 30, 1979, at 10:28 in the evening, around the time the revival of *Oklahoma!* then playing the Palace was letting out.

† Dorothy Rodgers died on August 17, 1992, at age eighty-three.

who'd hated her since Horace Mann, was in despair. Hoping to help, I read the manuscript, which she called *A Personal Book* even though, as far as I could see, it was astonishingly impersonal. I urged her to be more revealing as she revised, and she took my advice with a vengeance; the finished version* is extremely revealing—but only, at least intentionally, about Linda and me. Its sour, Olympian tone is, let's say, peculiar.† People kept calling me to commiserate, as if she'd died, but no.

When I was younger, it was daring good humor to mock her as awful, inviting the response: "Oh my god, look how Mary talks about her mother!" But I wore out that record. Now I more often take pleasure in surprising people with how impressive I find her in retrospect. The device she invented to prevent kids from being trapped in discarded refrigerators? Amazing.

But the truth is that both are true: She was amazing and awful. It's just that her good qualities had little to do with parenting and her bad ones certainly did. I don't mean to settle that score, to make this my own *Personal Book*—speaking of which, have you read her preface?‡ I mean to

....

* *A Personal Book* was published in May 1977 by Harper & Row: "no more personal, really," the *Kirkus* reviewer wrote, "than the caption under a yearbook photo."

† Let's say "freakishly passive-aggressive." After 150 pages of competent autobiography, evoking the material pleasures of a pampered childhood on the highest floor of the upper middle class, *A Personal Book* takes a bizarre turn near the end, becoming a resentful diatribe against young people today, and two young people in particular. "Though much has been written of the difficult relationship between parent and child, and the special lament of children of famous parents has been given a lot of exposure," Dorothy Rodgers writes, "I don't remember hearing much about the problems famous parents have in trying to cope with their children." She proceeds to rectify that imbalance.

‡ "As children, Mary and Linda understood that their father was always

be fair, and try to understand her. One thing I understand, after all this time, is that though she was famous among a certain set, no one liked her much. Not even her "friends." One of those was Kitty Carlisle, née Catherine Conn, a woman very much in Mummy's mold: studied in Paris, married a man of the theater, became a tireless advocate for the arts. Naturally, they fought like cats, spreading stories about one another between dinner parties. Kitty told me—because Mummy sometimes deputized me to repair their ruptures—that she thought the motto on the Feiner family escutcheon should be "Mine's Better."* Her beef with Mummy went back decades. When she was newly married to Moss, she told me, she nervously invited my parents for the weekend. On Saturday morning, she asked Mummy if she'd slept well.

"Oh yes, I did manage, but I must tell you that the best place to get pillows is Bloomingdale's."

And when Kitty asked how her breakfast was, Mummy answered: "Well, it was wonderful. The thing is, when you're boiling eggs, there's this lovely way to do it."

Or that's what Kitty heard. Which I completely believe because, all my life, that's what I heard, too.

Mummy thought of herself as cunning, both in the sly sense and in the way you might speak of a color scheme. She believed she was cleverly solving problems—and often she was. She just didn't seem to understand that people dislike being treated as problems. Linda was as much a victim of this as I, though we dealt with it in different ways. Where I fought, Linda smiled, said the right things, and kept her distance. That was cunning, too, and Mummy recognized it. In *A Personal Book* she wrote that while my approach was "direct if not always wise," Linda,

....

first with me, and at times they must have felt shut out, but I think they knew, too, that they were a close second."

* There was no such escutcheon, of course, but the frontispiece of *A Personal Book* reproduced the logo Milton Greene had designed for Repairs, Inc.: a glue pot, scissors, hammer, and ruler wittily arranged as a crest.

circa 2005: Mary and Linda. "Every fifteen years or
so we have a moment of sisterly fun."

"having learned what didn't work from watching Mary, would maneuver
herself—and us—into position."

I don't like that triangulating impulse in Linda any more than I liked
it in Mummy, and we haven't been very close as adults. I'm constantly
firing her, or she me, then rehiring: rinse, repeat. Every fifteen years or
so we have a moment of sisterly fun, locked in a spa together or drinking
brandy late at night after an opening.

Once, we were at the Ritz Tower home of Mildred Hilson, a famous
Jewish Republican grand dame who looked like Barbara Bush, and for
some reason went into her private bathroom and took all the gloves out
of one drawer and mixed them up with all the handkerchiefs in another,
making a complete mess of them and giggling all the way. It's a good
thing we were totally grown, or we might have peed on them.

But we rarely had the kind of good time based on real connection,
because there was so much radioactive stuff we couldn't get near. I can
recall only one occasion when she got close to embarking on an honest
conversation, asking me what people can say when they have a relative

who is doing bad work. As in Hostilities, I wasn't sure whom she was talking about. Me? Adam? Or her own son, Peter, who was writing scores for television and film at the time?*

I answered, carefully, also as in Hostilities: "If the person is a composer, blame the lyricist."

Mostly, I felt sorry for her. She made a lot of bad choices, sometimes copying mine and usually making them worse. If I had two husbands, she had to have three. She ran through Danny Melnick, the one I liked most, after about sixteen years, engendering an ugly and costly divorce. One night while their lawyers were squabbling over the Giacomettis, I got a call from her shrink, a man named Nat Breckir.† "I can't thank you enough for being so sweet to Linda during this time," he said. Which was weird, especially considering that he was also Danny's shrink, or had been. Unethical as it sounded, could it be that something was going on between him and Linda? The next morning, when I asked her, she said, "Oh no, certainly not, what a ridiculous idea!" But three days later she called me back and admitted it was true.

Linda was thirty-six and Nat sixty-five when her divorce from Danny came through in 1971. She must have known how bad it looked to be sleeping with her superannuated divorcé shrink, because she kept the affair secret from Mummy and Daddy for something like three years. Even after they got engaged, she never seemed quite comfortable with him in public. How could she? Nat had one of those personalities that anyone not his patient or wife, or both, would immediately recognize as fraudulent. You might excuse the carved antique cane he carried; he'd had polio as a child, and one leg was shorter than the other, terminating in

....

* Aside from his film and television work, Peter Rodgers Melnick (born 1958) has written two stage musicals: *Adrift in Macao*, with Christopher Durang, and, with Bill Russell, *The Last Smoker in America*.

† Nathaniel J. Breckir (1906–1982) had a glamorous clientele, including the magazine editor Frances Lear and, briefly and secretly, her husband, Norman.

a giant black shoe. But there was no disease to excuse the Nehru jackets, the gold medallions levitating on whorls of white chest hair exposed by exorbitantly unbuttoned shirts. Need I add that he wore a cape?

Mummy took weird delight in finding him disgusting. I saw her and Daddy's jaws drop as one—and Daddy barely had a jaw to drop—when Nat and Linda, now out of the closet, arrived late for dinner one night with the rest of us at 21. "So sorry," Nat said. "We were just in bed and well, *you know!*" Then he ordered the most expensive wine, leaving Daddy to pay for it.

By then, Linda was taking courses in how the other half lives; she eventually graduated from college, the first of the Rodgers women to do so.* While she was dabbling in real life, Nat was dabbling in crime. "Darling, look at page whatever in today's *Times,*" Mummy called to tell me one morning in April 1978. And there, under an angry-looking all-caps headline, was an article listing Nat as one of an octet of conspirators who had committed Medicaid fraud.

He soon pleaded guilty and promised restitution.† But after paying back ten thousand dollars he didn't have any more money; I think he spent it all on capes. When Linda went to Mummy and Daddy to beg on his behalf, as I had once gone to beg on Hank's, they flat-out refused to help.

Lap dissolve to a few years later. Linda starts to complain that Nat has

....

* She received her bachelor's degree, with a major in social psychology, in 1977, from Empire State College, part of the State University of New York.

† A follow-up *Times* story on May 9, 1978, focused on Breckir exclusively: "One of eight doctors indicted last month for allegedly defrauding Medicaid of more than $131,000 by falsifying patient records has pleaded guilty to a reduced charge in State Supreme Court in Manhattan . . . A prison sentence will not be recommended because Dr. Breckir is 72 years old, in poor health."

been very depressed. Mummy, who knew all about depression, said, "If there are any pills around the house take them away." But according to Mummy, Linda answered, "If he wants to kill himself, let him."

He did. Maybe it was a graduation gift: Linda had received her master's degree in social work from Hunter College just a week earlier.[*]

But not to worry; even a minor heiress—Daddy was now dead—does not stay single long, unless she wants to. Two years later, in 1984, Linda married Eric Emory, a widower she met at one of those Jazz at Noon concerts given by amateur musicians and attended by women desperate enough to want them.[†] He was a percussionist; his band was called the Decades.

That marriage was happier, or at least calmer, and all traces of Nat were quickly expunged from the family history. But even though Linda and I were now both squared away with suitable long-term husbands, no grand rapprochement transpired. Our childhoods spent pitted against each other made sure of that. As some shrink we shared—not Nat!—pointed out to me or her or both of us, we each grew up thinking the other was Mummy's favorite. When the truth is that, in comparison to her actual favorite, neither of us was or ever could be.

Not to let Daddy off the hook. Like Mummy, he had no gift for friendship, which in my observation correlates pretty well with no gift for parenthood. Over the years, musicians he fired, actors he insulted—even Larry Hart's namesake nephew—liked to tell me just how cruel he was. That chorus girl in Washington wasn't thrilled with him, either. I never doubted a bad word of what anyone said.

But if you ask me what I would have changed about my childhood,

---

[*] Breckir apparently did take an overdose of pills. He hovered in a coma for three days before departing on June 15, 1982. A note was found belatedly.

[†] Born Eric Epstein, Eric Emory (1925–2014) was an investment analyst at his own boutique firm. With his first wife, who died in an accident in Acapulco in 1983, he had three children.

the first thing out of my mouth is: "to have had a loving mother." Which isn't fair, but there you have it. I could admire her, if not for anything that gets to my core and mitigates the crap. With Daddy, however cold he was, there is endless mitigation. It survives death as it survived life. I just go to an orchestra rehearsal for one of his shows and it's bliss, endless bliss, straight from him to me.

45.

A MAJOR CANON

When Adam was working on *The Light in the Piazza*, he told a writer that unlike his grandfather he aspired to be happy, "if only to be able to be kind." Forgive my saying so, but that's such a male formulation. You can be kind without being happy; women do it all the time.

But maybe it's not my place to judge. Daddy's lifelong unhappiness, and especially the misery of his last decade, was of some cosmically different order than the occasional disappointment I've felt. How can anyone with a normal-sized gift judge what it's like when an extraordinary one gets its claws in you, and then when it tears them out? Maybe he had no choice about anything as ordinary as personality or love, since his music took all of both.

I, on the other hand, had a choice and made it. From the *Member of the Wedding* fiasco of 1968 to the *Griffin and the Minor Canon* disaster of 1988, and ever after, I expected nothing from musicals, and did not pin my ego on the few small theatrical projects I undertook. Well, I suppose there was some ego involved in letting Music-Theatre Group produce a three-person revue of my work called *Hey, Love** as atonement for *Minor*

....

* Originally conceived and directed by Richard Maltby Jr., *Hey, Love: The Songs of Mary Rodgers* played for three weeks starting in March 1993 at Eighty-Eights, a piano bar in the Village. It starred Karen Mason, but

Canon. Still, it only reinforced my choice. Several great performers were involved, and I was happy that people liked my songs enough to put their expertise, time, and money* behind them. But over the course of a few years the show never quite came together as I'd hoped. Worse, it precipitated that huge blowup with Steve over my gender-flipping the song we'd written together forty years earlier. He said maybe the worst thing he could: that I had now become both my father and my mother.

Which doesn't mean I didn't enjoy working on these "extending the legacy" projects. A couple of years before the revue, Jay Harnick at Theater-Works asked me and John Forster† to write a version of *Freaky Friday* as a one-hour piece for kids. It was quite good, especially the comedy numbers, and audiences seemed to love it.‡ But I was past sixty myself by then, and could sense the squareness creeping in. So could Steve; when

....

Donna Murphy took over when it returned in May. A slightly revised version, directed and with additional lyrics by Mark Waldrop, ran for a week in Stockbridge in August 1995. Ann Morrison, who had played Mary in *Merrily We Roll Along*, starred. Finally, a major revision of the minor revisal—now called *3 of Hearts*—played forty performances at Rainbow & Stars, the cabaret atop Rockefeller Center, in September 1996, where the management screwed up the microphones on opening night and no one could hear. For that production, starring Faith Prince and directed by Waldrop, the through line about a woman in love with two men was beefed up with new lyrics. The cast recording—now reverting to the original title—was released by Varèse Sarabande in 1997.

* Not quite enough money: Mark Waldrop recalls that when the producers decided they could not afford a bass player for the Rainbow & Stars engagement, Mary said, "Oh, hell, I'll sell an earring."

† John Forster (born 1948) is both a composer and a lyricist, best known for his satirical albums and revues.

‡ The Rodgers-Forster *Freaky Friday* was first performed in October 1992; after a brief stop in New York, it toured schools, theaters, and performing arts centers around the country through April 1994.

1991: Mary at her sixtieth birthday dinner, with (from left) Mary Ann Madden, Stephen Sondheim, Jerome Robbins, Liz Smith, Hank, Elaine Stritch, Arthur Laurents, André Bishop, and Wendy Wasserstein.

he listened to the score and picked out a song he particularly liked for its unusual rhythm, I had to admit that it was the one song for which John, I can't recall why, had written the music as well as the words.

The more comfortable I got at the legacy game, the less so I got at the piano. I might eke out a song on request, like the one I did for the 1996 revival of *Once Upon a Mattress* starring Sarah Jessica Parker.* This was the production that Marshall got himself banned from, after blabbing to the press that Parker's voice needed work and that the director, Gerald Gutierrez, had staged the show "as if it were *Medea*." He wasn't wrong.

....

* The "misbegotten revival," as the *Times* review dubbed it, opened on December 19, 1996 and closed on June 1, 1997. The new song, "Goodnight, Sweet Princess," sung by Dauntless as a lullaby to Winnifred, was not entirely new. The melody comes from the verse of "Something Known," written for *The Member of the Wedding*.

But mostly I declined such offers. Another decade later, when asked to write a new number for Carol Burnett—now playing Queen Aggravain in the 2005 Disney television version—I couldn't even put my hands on the keyboard.* It made me too anxious, like going into a dark room not knowing where the light switch is. That was it for me; I never wrote a song again. And never regretted it, or almost never; those dark rooms are damned exciting.

The less I wrote, the firmer my taste was. Not that I had ever been shy with criticism of work by people I thought were talented enough to stand it, even if it turned out they were usually, like Daddy, the very ones who couldn't. After a private run-through of *Anyone Can Whistle* before it went to Philadelphia in 1964, Steve asked what I thought, and I told him honestly that it made no sense; he listened intently and asked me to share my thinking with Arthur. Uh-oh. I still have the letter Arthur wrote in response: "I hate you. The entire cast hates you. Don't come to Philadelphia." Which was not such a curse, by the way.

Eventually I learned to bite my tongue, at least when talking with friends about their precious new babes. But I rarely held back otherwise, especially regarding attempts to repackage my own work and eventually Daddy's. This may be when I got a reputation as sharp-tongued, though Mummy said I got that reputation in the cradle. It's not that I thought so highly of myself as that I knew what worked and what didn't. The third sequel to *Freaky Friday*, which forty years on I had no interest in writing, taught me a lesson. Harper & Row, by then HarperCollins, said I should pick someone else to write it if I didn't want to write it myself, and after looking around, I chose the very cute little blonde who had top credit on the screenplay for the Lindsay Lohan movie. Stupid me; it's always the last people credited who are the good ones. When this writer submitted her first treatment, it was so hopelessly bad, neither original nor funny, that I threatened to pull out of the deal. Happily, I didn't have to; the book,

....

* Instead, Ken and Mitzie Welch wrote the new song. Called "That Baby of Mine," it incorporates a chunk of "Happily Ever After," which Burnett had sung, as Winnifred, forty-six years earlier.

with the imaginative title of *Freaky Monday*, pretty much disappeared on its own.*

And by 2011, when Disney decided to make another musical of the same novel, I knew how to say no, rejecting the many, many kids who wrote songs on spec in hopes of getting the job. Eventually Disney pinned its hopes on Ryan Scott Oliver, a very young and accomplished musician who had won the Rodgers Award a few years earlier.† After listening to his songs, I had to tell him, sorry, it's not my kind of music—and not right for the show, either. Disney was annoyed, and Ryan, for whom this had been a bigger deal than I understood, was crushed. Or so I gather from a sad-slash-flattering song he wrote, called "Mary Says," after I rejected his score.‡ But the awkwardness was worth it; in the end, I wound up with a much better fit: Tom Kitt and Brian Yorkey. Their *Next to Normal* is the only show I know that includes a song about electroshock therapy, so they had me at hello.§

This business of managing one's legacy is sometimes a pleasure, mostly a pain. You don't want to live in the past, but you can't just leave it to molder in the cellar if you want it to keep making money. I never thought about that, of course, when I was young. Back in 1959, as *Mat-*

....

* *Freaky Monday*, "by Mary Rodgers with Heather Hach," was published in May 2009.

† Ryan Scott Oliver (born 1984) won the Richard Rodgers Award for Musical Theater in 2008 for his musical *Alive at Ten*. The award, endowed by Rodgers's million-dollar gift in 1978, subsidizes productions and readings of new work by young artists at nonprofit theaters.

‡ The song's final couplet: "Mary has a way with composers in their youth. / Mary changed my life, because Mary said the truth."

§ Disney's musical version of *Freaky Friday*, with a score by Kitt and Yorkey and a book by Bridget Carpenter, opened in October 2016 at the Signature Theatre in Arlington, Virginia. It has since played in several cities around the country; a television adaption premiered on the Disney Channel in August 2018. Reviews have generally been positive.

tress was first heading to Broadway, Frank Loesser called and said he had started this thing called Musical Theatre International to license shows in secondary markets and did I want the company to license mine?* Well, it's nice to be asked by Frank Loesser! So MTI represented *Mattress* for decades, until Mummy eventually asked why it had never occurred to anybody to bring it under the Rodgers and Hammerstein umbrella, and keep the fees for ourselves. We bought my way out of the MTI contract and moved my oeuvre.

There wasn't much oeuvre to mouvre: Mine was a minor canon. Daddy's canon, on the other hand, was so big and lucrative it took a company to manage it. Early on, he and Ockie set themselves up as producers of their own work (and sometimes of other people's); having retained or bought back or finagled the rights to everything they wrote, they had control over its exploitation and, unlike most musical theater artists, were able to reap the real profit.†

How to maintain that profit and protect the integrity of the eleven R&H musicals‡—as well as the non-R shows by H and the non-H shows by R§—became a complex job after Daddy's death, when there was no

....

* Loesser, along with the orchestrator Don Walker, established Music Theatre International in 1952 to license musicals for amateur and stock productions. Under the subsequent leadership of Freddie Gershon, and with Cameron Mackintosh as the majority owner, it has grown to represent more than four hundred titles.

† The business historian John Steele Gordon wrote that the Rodgers and Hammerstein empire "earned them the first great American fortune to be based on creative theatrical talent."

‡ Depending on how you count. Rodgers and Hammerstein wrote nine musicals for the stage, plus one (*State Fair*) for film, and one (*Cinderella*) for television. Two revues were subsequently fashioned from the catalog, and both *State Fair* and *Cinderella* were rejiggered for the stage.

§ The non-H shows by R include all of Rodgers and Hart, plus Rodgers's

Daddy in charge. At first, Mummy spoke for the Rodgers family; she represented herself but also me and Linda and our combined six children. Bill Hammerstein represented the rather more numerous, widespread, and chaotic family that Ockie left behind. I think there were sixteen going on seventeen of them.* Bill was a sweet and stubborn and cautious man who began as a stage manager on Rodgers and Hammerstein shows, then directed revivals but rarely first-class† ones. When he had a stroke in 1993 and left the board, his younger half brother Jamie, also a not-great director, and with a terrible temper to boot, stepped in. But while fucking his third wife after taking a slug of hash, Jamie had a fatal heart attack, or so the story goes. Bill then returned and promptly died. The job finally fell to Alice, Bill's younger sister, who had been completely ignored until then, probably for being a girl.‡

On our side, an orderly if no less fraught succession was set in motion early. Mummy wanted desperately to preserve the Rodgers legacy but wasn't interested in the details of the work; she made everyone come to her apartment at the Pierre instead of gathering at the office, even though she'd decorated it. Almost immediately upon Daddy's death, since his will directed that I eventually succeed her, she "generously" invited me to be the Rodgers family representative-in-training, meaning I attended meetings, put my two cents in, and, when I was absent once

....

six late musicals for stage and television. The non-R shows by H include his collaborations with Jerome Kern, notably *Show Boat*.

* An undercount. Oscar Hammerstein II had five children: three biological and two he acquired upon marrying Dorothy. Those five had fifteen children of their own. If you include the two matriarchs, that makes nine Rodgerses and twenty-one Hammersteins.

† "First-class" is not (only) a value judgment but a contractual category of production that usually means Broadway or London's West End.

‡ James Hammerstein died in 1999, William Hammerstein in 2001, Alice Hammerstein Mathias in 2015.

or twice over the course of many years because of my own work, got reamed out for it. There was no question of Linda's taking the role; she was actively uninterested, considered it all a pain in the ass, and would never deign to take, as Bill and I did, the agonizing four-hour ride in the blistering caboose of a train that screeched to a stop at every single town between Oklahoma City and Tulsa to hear its local high school band play "Oklahoma."* Let alone to attend the opening of the national tour of the stage version of *State Fair* at the actual Iowa State Fair, where the pigs were as big as pianos. The only thing she'd attend the opening of was a royalty check.

But the family representatives were more or less figureheads at first; the professionals told us when someone wanted to use a song in a tooth-paste ad, and on their recommendation, we either approved or didn't. In the years right after Daddy's death, that meant dealing with horrible Dick Lewine†—a real snake of a Rodgers cousin they hired as managing director on an interim basis. I couldn't wait to get him out of there, so at one of the meetings during my apprenticeship, as we were discussing people to take over permanently, I suggested Ted Chapin,‡ whose key qualification, other than being smart about theater, was that my mother

....

* The 1990 whistle-stop tour celebrated Rodgers & Hammerstein's grant-ing the state of Oklahoma the free use of the song "Oklahoma" in per-petuity. En route, Mary was offered what locals call "calf fries"—testicles, that is. "I've never been afraid to eat balls," she said.

† Richard Lewine (1910–2005) started out as a songwriter and later pro-duced musical programming for television, including the Rodgers and Hammerstein *Cinderella* and *My Name Is Barbra*.

‡ While still a college student, Theodore Steinway Chapin (born 1950) was a production assistant on *Follies*, later writing *Everything Was Possible*, the definitive gofer's-eye-view chronicle of the creation of a great Broad-way show. He was a co-founder of the Encores! series of classic musicals in concert at City Center, and chairman of the American Theater Wing from 2008 to 2012.

liked and approved of his parents. In 1981, Ted was hired on a trial basis for grooming, but it worked out pretty well because he had good hair and kept it.

Under Ted, we expanded from a glorified Tin Pan Alley office replete with shady characters chomping cigars—one of them, I think, an actual mobster—to a capital-O Organization. Ted soon realized that even with complete ownership of the properties, we were still giving other people money for work we might do more efficiently ourselves. That's when we brought the music publishing business in house and expanded the theatrical licensing business to include other shows and writers, including Irving Berlin. Ted and his team handled most of that without needing constant and generally unhelpful intervention from the families; I weighed in when asked, but my focus was elsewhere. What I cared about, besides the first-class productions of my father's shows, was developing new talent. Since we couldn't outbid Music Theatre International for the big hits anyway, we gave young writers like Michael John LaChiusa and Ricky Ian Gordon licensing and publication deals or production grants from the foundation, financed by the proceeds of *Flower Drum Song*.

The 2002 revival of *Flower Drum Song* would never have happened while Mummy was in charge. She refused all suggestions for refreshing the shows, even if that refusal meant, as in this case, that they were nearly unproducible. After she died, though, David Henry Hwang, whose plays I liked, came to us with an idea for keeping the songs—it's a very good score—but altering the book to eliminate its cultural insensitivities. Why the hell not? If the revisions didn't work, so be it. So we okayed *Flower Drum Song*, to be directed and choreographed by Robert Longbottom, though Jamie of the atom-bomb temper was furious; he had directed his own version in Las Vegas years earlier and felt he was the logical choice. True, Longbottom's production flopped,* but I think it may yet reemerge as a viable property, which it certainly wouldn't have otherwise.

Aside from that *Flower Drum Song*, the heirs have mostly been in ac-

---

* The revised *Flower Drum Song*, starring Lea Salonga, opened on Broadway on October 17, 2002, and ran for five months.

cord about these decisions; we never came to anything remotely resembling blows. Even the transition to the next generation was relatively smooth, with Alec as representative-in-waiting for the Rodgerses and Paul Jacobson and then Marc Wager for the Hammersteins.* Together we have okayed seventeen first-class productions since Daddy's death: twelve on Broadway, five in London.† Some were hits, some misses; some dull, some controversial. Luckily, my tenure began with one of the hits: the 1992 London *Carousel*, in which a big, burly Black tenor played Mr. Snow. You should have heard the howls of protest—the loudest coming all the way across the Atlantic from Mummy. By the time that production was remounted in New York in 1994, and Audra McDonald, auditioning for the role of Carrie Pipperidge, famously fainted at her final audition, Mummy was dead and I okayed the casting. My attitude is: Do the original the way the authors wrote it. After that, screw 'em. If the piece is strong enough, it won't matter; and if it isn't strong enough, it won't matter, either.

Next, the *State Fair* I'd seen in Iowa came to Broadway in 1996—not great and not a hit. It was more of a concoction, a brand extension, than a real musical, and unlikely to raise its hand again.‡

The King and I was always raising its hand. First there was the supposedly Broadway-bound 1989 tour in which Rudolf Nureyev, on his last

....

* The marketing and advertising executive Paul Jacobson (born 1953) is a grandson of Dorothy Hammerstein and her first husband, Henry Jacobson. His first cousin Marc Wager Weisgal (born 1964) is a songwriter, guitarist, and music producer.

† Since Mary's death there have been three more Broadway revivals of Rodgers and Hammerstein musicals: *The King and I* (2015), *Carousel* (2018), and *Oklahoma!* (2019).

‡ The 1995 national tour of *State Fair*, directed by James Hammerstein and Randy Skinner, opened on Broadway on March 27, 1996. It received two Tony nominations, one for Best Score, which it lost to *Rent*.

legs, was so bad we had to keep it out of New York.* Luckily a gorgeous Australian version popped up in 1991, albeit with Hayley Mills, who was charming but couldn't sing her way into a paper bag; we okayed it for Broadway in 1996 with Donna Murphy, whom I loved and thought of as my discovery.† It was a hit. The 1998 Broadway *Sound of Music*, in part because of a very bad design and in part because it was still *The Sound of Music*, wasn't. Its blandness was balanced out, the same year, by Trevor Nunn's *Oklahoma!* in London; it starred Hugh Jackman, who was so stunning, I don't remember anything else about it.‡ Have you ever been at a piano recital and when some kids play you're dying all the way through, but then that one kid plays and you sit back and don't worry? Hugh was that kid; I've never seen him not infusing an audience with confidence and joy. Unfortunately, bringing it to Broadway was a nightmare; Trevor and I had to go before Equity to ask if they would allow the British cast to transfer for a while before an American one took over. When Equity said no, the production lost momentum while we waited for Trevor, who was running the National Theatre, to become available again. That took four years—and without Hugh, the production wasn't the hit it should have been. But at least Andrea Martin was a great Aunt Eller; seeing her

....

* One review described Nureyev, who had been paid a million dollars for the engagement, as "a King who stands around like a sulky teen-ager who didn't ask to be invited to this party, and who tends to wander off when somebody tries to engage him in conversation."

† Both productions were directed by Christopher Renshaw; the Broadway version won four Tony Awards, including one for Best Revival of a Musical and one for Murphy.

‡ Mary attended the first preview of *Oklahoma!* at the National Theatre with Ted Chapin. As the cast sang the phrase "when the wind comes right behind the rain," from the title song, she turned to him (as he recalls) and said, "They're singing a D-flat instead of D-natural on the word *the*." The mistake was corrected.

perform, I regretted not hiring her when she auditioned for the 1996 revival of *Mattress*.

Though my method of choosing was based on instinct, it was no less reliable than anyone else's. We had the terrible Trevor Nunn *South Pacific* in London in 2001, but then the great Lincoln Center Theater one directed by Bart Sher in 2008. So it all evens out, except that *Pal Joey* never worked and probably never will; everyone keeps trying to fix it, but the 2008 Roundabout production proved, to me at least, that it's unfixable. The nightclub material is just filler, there's not enough plot, and the score is too familiar to register as actual storytelling. It's only fun for the costume designer.

And then I okayed another brand extension: *Cinderella*.* Or did I?

I'm not senile—yet—but I do keep conveniently forgetting how it happened. I absolutely hated it from the first workshop and tried repeatedly to stop it or get it fixed, at least until it became a hit, at which point I started to like it well enough. But it turned out that none of my machinations mattered anyway, because I no longer had the power I'd grown to enjoy when I barely knew I had it. I was a witch without a wand.

That was my own doing. I de-wanded myself. Over the course of my tenure as family representative, the deader my parents got, the more responsibility I took. I guess that's to say I climbed into things and yet, at some point, it became clear that it was time to climb out. By the early 2000s Rodgers and Hammerstein was still a lucrative business,† but once

....

* The stage version of the 1957 live television musical, billed as *Rodgers + Hammerstein's Cinderella* but substantially rewritten by Douglas Carter Beane, opened on Broadway on March 3, 2013, and ran for almost two years. It featured six interpolated songs from other Rodgers and Hammerstein scores to stretch seventy-five minutes into the requisite two hours.

† The various operations of the Rodgers and Hammerstein Organization were then earning each of the two families about seven million dollars a year.

the copyrights started expiring, how much longer would it be until the office did, too? If we were ever going to sell the assets, we couldn't wait until they weren't worth buying.

I was very hot to sell, and so was Alec. The only questions were to whom and for how much. At one meeting, Marc Wager asked me what number I was looking for and I said thirty-five dollars, which might have been a joke about my eagerness or a sign of my innumeracy.

We courted a few white knights, including Disney and Andrew Lloyd Webber, but eventually found one, the Dutch music conglomerate Imagem, that seemed like a good match and was willing to bite. Alice couldn't make up her mind, but by 2008, when Imagem made its official offer, the economy was collapsing and time was running out. As far as I was concerned, it was now or never.

It was now. We sold.*

So however heartfelt they were, my threats to shut down *Cinderella* when it showed up a few years later were idle. The sale to Imagem required that Alice and I be consulted on first-class productions—not that we be listened to.†

I have never regretted the choice. Prioritizing money over control may seem shallow, but it was never about either for me. I'd be truly shallow if my connection to Daddy's music, and my family legacy, such as it

....

* Not everything. When the $225 million deal closed in 2009, Imagem, financed by the Associated Pension Group in Holland, bought the Rodgers and Hammerstein copyrights, along with the licensing and music publishing business. It did not at that time buy the so-called "Rodgers or Hammerstein" copyrights—those pertaining to work created before and after their collaboration. In 2017, the music company Concord bought Imagem for $500 million.

† Even the right of consultation is limited: It does not pass to the next generation of heirs. The only permanently binding restriction on the properties is the one that Alice Hammerstein put on *South Pacific*: that it can never be performed without the song "Carefully Taught."

is, were a matter of contracts. I sold the copyrights, but I lost nothing. I have it all in my ears. When the wind comes right behind *the* rain.

And anyway, I still control the show I'd most like to revive: *Jumbo*.[*] At four years old, I thought that was great fun. The problem, as always in life, is finding room. Where do you keep the elephants?

---

[*] True when she said so. But Mary later sold to Imagem the rest of her father's catalog. Not, of course, Hammerstein's, which wasn't hers to sell. And not her own.

46.

N.A.C.

promised ages ago to come back to Laurie, Hank's daughter with his first wife, Miriam. After the divorce, Miriam married a Kansas City businessman named Al Bradley, with whom she had two more kids.* Laurie, raised in that family from the age of three, was ignored, beaten, and scorned like a storybook stepchild, not by her stepfather or half siblings but by her own mother—and without the Cinderella ending.

Because of the restrictive custody terms, not to mention the onerous financial ones, Hank barely saw Laurie during those years. When he did, she called him "Hank," apparently not having been told he was her father even though they looked just alike. I met her, briefly, when she was maybe eleven, and then almost never again until she came for a visit when she was eighteen and visitation restrictions no longer applied. At that point, she was supposed to be getting ready to graduate from high school but was flunking all her exams. I tried to help with her homework, but she was wild and unable to concentrate and couldn't retain anything—in my professional opinion, as a result of fetal alcohol syndrome. Well, that and maybe the phenobarbital she'd been prescribed by not even her own shrink but Miriam's. She was drugged to help the mother! We wanted to

---

* Hank and Miriam divorced around 1952; Miriam married Alvin Meyer Bradley, whose company turned scrap aluminum into granules for use in explosives, in 1954.

withdraw her from the phenobarb but were advised by a doctor that if not done properly it might cause seizures.

We felt so bad that we invited her to spend part of the summer with us at Merriewold. Actually, it was supposed to be the whole summer, but guilt only goes so far. She led all the kids—and I don't just mean mine—astray. She would persuade the waiters at the clubhouse to serve them Bloody Marys with their cheeseburgers but write them down as milkshakes. Or she'd leap into the car and drive them somewhere outside the gate and get them drunk. When caught, she'd blame anyone else, even the little boys; she was very cruel and punitive, which I'm sure was just a replay of what had been done to her. Eventually I said to Hank, "We've had enough trouble. Get her out of here now." Which he shamefacedly did.

Over the next twenty years Laurie was married five times, twice to the same man; it was that double husband, her fourth and fifth, she had to get a warrant against because he kept beating her. One of the non-beaters was a guy named Steve Carr, with whom she had a son named Tom; oddly enough, she was a very affectionate mother, when she could be.[*] But her life was a ruin, spent in and out of rehab and psychiatric hospitals. She once told me she couldn't even get her suicide attempts right, like the time she decided to kill herself on the night of the Academy Awards, so she got all gussied up in her prettiest nightgown, put on lots of makeup, took a fistful of pills, and didn't die. The kicker, she said: "It was the wrong night!"

By the time she finally did kill herself,[†] Tom had for a few years been living with Steve, a laid-back hippieish house painter, and Steve's third wife, Beverly, a very nice woman, who brought him up along with her

....

[*] Laurie Guettel married Stephen Michael Carr, the third of her husbands, in 1979. Their son, Thomas Henry Carr, the middle name given in honor of Hank, was born in 1981. About two years later, Laurie and Stephen divorced.

[†] On February 10, 1993, Laurie Cecil Guettel Bradley Bauman Worley Carr Locascio Locascio died after an overdose of Xanax. She was entombed with other members of the Guettel family in the mausoleum at Rose Hill Cemetery in Kansas City, Missouri. Tom was twelve.

children from a previous marriage. No Cinderella mistreatment there. Still, like Laurie, Tom got more and more obstreperous and irresponsible and by his late teens was flunking out of school.

This time, though, Hank had some access and sway. Seconded by Steve, he told Tom to go into the navy the minute high school was over or never get another nickel from him as long as he lived. That was the stick. The carrot, he explained, was that military service, which had helped Hank grow up in his twenties, would help Tom, too. Tom barely knew what the navy was, but just as Hank predicted, it straightened him out, or rather he straightened himself out with the help of its structure.* One year he was named the top chief petty officer on the most successful ship in the navy, the USS *Ronald Reagan*. I have no idea what that means, except the Ronald Reagan part, but we all adore him anyway; more important, Hank does.

The possibility that people can fix themselves, with help, is as wonderful to contemplate as its opposite, also true, is awful. Not everyone can do it. If Tom could, Laurie couldn't. I have often pondered what makes the difference. Recently I tried to raise the subject with Hank, but he doesn't like to dwell on such things. "N.A.C.," he said: not a clue.

I understand his reluctance, and maybe it's the wiser choice. You have to deny a lot to keep living as you're dying.† We have made plans for a cruise next year, but I know it's not going to happen.

....

* Tom served in the navy from 1999 to 2014. During boot camp, he earned his high school equivalency diploma; in 2010, he received his bachelor's degree, in justice administration, from Hawaii Pacific University.

† Hank's health began to decline seriously in 2012. In March, he fell in his bathroom. In April, doctors diagnosed endocarditis. He was too sick at the end of that month to attend a Juilliard gala honoring Mary, though he watched it online. In July, he fell again, in Quogue, fracturing his pelvis. He was frail but more stable for a few months after that, until his condition worsened again in the summer of 2013. By August he was shuttling among hospitals and rehabilitation centers in New York City and on Long Island. While staying in Quogue, he fell again, and later that month was diagnosed with leukemia. A doctor summed up his condition as "crappy."

circa 2003: Hank and Mary, cruising. "Was it a good marriage?
The answer, at a week shy of fifty-two years, is yes."

His feet are so bloated he can hardly walk, and if he stepped on a nail, he wouldn't even notice but he might start a flood. "Why aren't you wearing slippers?" I ask. "I don't *like* wearing slippers," he says. We snap at each other as if we have forever to make up. And maybe he's right. What's the point of enhancing your current misery by reexamining a lifetime of it? Three of his children died, one from each marriage: Miriam's Laurie by suicide; Annie's possible Henry, stillborn; and my Matthew, asphyxiated. It's enough to do you in, and maybe it did.

Yet that was ages ago: 1993, 1958, 1966. Hank kept working, one job after the next, through all of it. The year Laurie died was when he finally retired; he'd been the director of the Theatre Development Fund since 1982, having left Twentieth Century Fox.* Twentieth cen-

....

* The Theatre Development Fund, founded in 1968, is a not-for-profit

tury! Sometimes I feel that's where Hank still lives. As he has aged, he has become becalmed, spending hours reading, doing puzzles, and listening to beautiful music on his iPod, while I've kept on courting (and often being rejected by) excitement. Yet time is melting us together, like candle wax.

My model for aging is Larry Kramer, raging against the dying of the light. I could have done without his raging at me in particular, but you never know where your models will come from. Arthur was our connection; they'd been intimates and antagonists for decades—Arthur no doubt envious of Larry for being a real pioneer when he was just a pioneer in his own mind. The whole thing about Arthur's being blacklisted I never really believed; there are a million reasons why people don't get work in Hollywood and only some of them involve communism.* But Larry was the real deal: a game changer and a pariah—yet darling when you got to know him.

That happened for me during the summer of 1995, when he was scheduled to speak about AIDS and activism at the Bay Street Theater in Sag Harbor.† We had dinner beforehand—Larry; Arthur and Tom; Hank and I—on the second floor of a bright and cheery fish restaurant across the street from the theater. Arthur, who'd given one of these talks the previous month, asked what Larry planned to say that evening, and Larry, whom I'd met but didn't know well at the time, told us he hadn't the

....

service organization for the performing arts; its most visible outpost is the TKTS discount ticket booth, below the giant red stairway, in Times Square. Hank retired as its director at sixty-two.

* By his own account, the blacklist had little effect on Laurents's career, though at one point his passport was revoked and it took three months to get it back.

† On August 29, 1995, the playwright, novelist, and AIDS activist Larry Kramer (1935–2020) appeared as part of a speaker series at the Bay Street Theater on the wharf in Sag Harbor, not far from Quogue. Laurents had spoken there on July 25.

foggiest notion. That amazed me; how does anyone have the nerve to do that? I always wrote out my speeches.

Anyway, we had a jolly dinner, so I certainly wasn't prepared for the response when I raised my stupid hand after the talk, which was packed, and asked, "Well, what can we do?"

If you could see lava rising within a volcano, that's what Larry looked like.

"Here's Mary Rodgers, Richard Rodgers's super-rich daughter, with all the Rodgers and Hammerstein money," he screamed. "When you have all that money, why are you asking what you can do?"

Though I'd spent my whole life insisting I wasn't actually rich, I hope I managed to squelch the urge to say so then. But Arthur leapt to his little feet and shouted, "How dare you talk about my best friend Mary Rodgers like that!"

He wasn't really defending me; he was defending himself. In his talk, Larry had said that any gay author who didn't write about AIDS—an author like Arthur, for instance—was failing his community.

Whatever the fight was about at bottom, it didn't stop when the audience left; it just poured into the courtyard, with Larry and Arthur screaming and jabbing and turning bright red until people from the theater eventually pulled them apart. I stood in a corner cowering, feeling as if I'd been sucked into a huge mess without knowing how I got there. I thought I was being a nice helpful person, and the rage of God came back at me.

Larry's behavior was unconscionable, but the strange truth is, I agreed with him—once I got over the embarrassment and sting. I *hadn't* done enough. And his tantrum came to seem almost noble to me; I envied him the means of expression I had been denied as a child and had mostly denied myself ever after. He had the courage to be disliked. Most people don't want to be disliked; he didn't want to be, either. Jesus probably didn't like being disliked! Yet being disliked can be a form of self-sacrifice, something brave people swallow as a sometimes-unavoidable consequence of honesty. As long as it runs in that direction—not the other way round, as it did with Arthur, who was honest only so he could be mean—I admire those people, which is a poor second to being one.

The next time I saw Larry, a few months later, at one of Hal and Judy's Christmas Eve parties, he was so cold. I mean physically cold. This was when his liver was failing and he was waiting for a transplant.* "I just can't get warm," he said, shivering. I knew what that was like, so as soon as I got home, I looked around to see what I could find and came up with a red cashmere lap robe, which I sent him in the Village. It was as if I'd sent a little boy a puppy. Love for life! Soon, he and his partner, David Webster, were visiting us in Quogue for weekends, while Arthur, who had literally stood up for me, soon became persona non grata. Was it because, as I later realized, Arthur only stood up for me when I was wrong, as a way of buying my loyalty? Or because, thanks to Larry, I was finally less afraid of him?†

If only that fearlessness were fungible. When you feel as though death is three feet away from you, your inner Larry is useless. I've given birth six times, undergone two spinal fusions and a spinal decompression, had a dropped foot lifted after breaking a bone and the tendons in my arm reconstructed from thumb to elbow, been basted with chemo for bladder cancer, had surgery to remove an adenocarcinoma in the upper lobe of my right lung, followed six years later by surgery to remove an adenocarcinoma in the upper lobe of my left lung, leaving me with a breathing apparatus about as big as a hummingbird nest—none of which scared me the way this final aging business does. When you're thirty-six and you have a back operation, you say: I'll show them how I can recover.

....

* Though Kramer had end-stage liver disease, he had to wait years for a transplant because his long-standing (though non-progressing) HIV infection rendered him a less-than-ideal candidate. Finally, in 2001, after the Associated Press published a premature obituary, he received the liver of a forty-five-year-old Pittsburgh-area man who died after suffering a brain embolism.

† By 2009, the friendship was definitively over. In response to my request for comment for a profile of Laurents I was writing for *New York* magazine, Mary said: "Call me back when he's dead."

When you're eighty-two, well, it all seems more ominous. And this surprises me: I always thought I'd be a better sport about my own demise. And about Hank's.

I hate this part of the story.* But I'm not a good patient and I'm not a good nurse. I don't think nurses are supposed to accuse their charges of failing to recover. I wonder if Hank is deliberately not trying, preferring to die than to do things that might make him better. Which I now realize is what my mother wondered about my father, and why she was such a terrible nag. Whereas if I could figure out how to feel better, I absolutely would. I'm missing half of what's going on in this city, where I've always chosen to live because it *has* all of these wonderful things. I'm sick of canceling plans, but sometimes I don't have the energy to go into the dining room to get my datebook, let alone make a date. And if I do make a date then it takes forever to dress and do my makeup and struggle over the fucking earrings. I used to be able to get that all done, including blowing my hair dry, in three-quarters of an hour; now it takes a half hour longer, or more if there are buttons any smaller than a salad plate. And what will I put on my feeble feet? The ugly shoes I can actually shuffle along in or the nice ones that require a wheelchair? I know that's ridiculous; millions of people get around in wheelchairs, including Itzhak Perlman. But I hate the idea so much that I've never even seen the Mary Rodgers Guettel water fountain, or whatever it is, because it's on some high tor at Juilliard otherwise inaccessible to the elderly.† Who knew I'd turn out to be so vain in my decrepitude? Or that after a lifetime of dieting, I'd find myself unable to gain the weight I need no matter how much I eat? It makes you want to erase your body. I wish I wore a Mormon uniform or maybe that

....

* As Hank's health unraveled, and then her own, Mary insisted that telling the truth of her life meant telling the truth of how it was ending—even if that ending was uncomfortable and uncharacteristic. Hence, a final proposed title for this book: *Call Me Back When I'm Dead.*

† The Mary Rodgers Guettel Pre-College Suite is on the second floor, next to the elevators.

I were a hologram. You could carry my head around in a box. Failing that, I'm just relieved when I don't have to do anything in the evening, so we can eat an early supper and watch stupidvision.

Which is depressing. I went to the shrink on Monday and told him the one Zoloft I'm on wasn't doing it for me. He said: "Remember that test I gave you last year about mood and depression? I'm going to give it to you again." I went from sixty to thirty in terms of mood. To all the questions that had to do with "Are you satisfied with yourself?" I answered yes; maybe I'm lying, but I feel perfectly comfortable with what I've accomplished. It was the other questions, about optimism and engagement, whose numbers had tanked. There was one about suicide, and I thought about it very carefully before saying no, it didn't interest me, but I wouldn't mind if I just died. Ideally not at a dinner party. The idea of throwing up or bleeding all over someone's tablecloth horrifies me. So does the not knowing when it will happen and how bad it will be. I can only compare it to not knowing whether you're going into labor. Especially the first time, when you can't tell from experience if it's a labor pain or just something squirmy. Do you get yourself to the hospital or not? It's a great humiliation if you go and you're wrong.

So I asked the shrink: When you're depressed because of actual things that are depressing, are there any drugs that can make you feel better? And he said no, which was even more depressing.

But once a day I think: *You little shit, you've got a great big house, you've got people working their asses off on your behalf, you're pretty goddamn lucky compared to most people—even you over there typing! How can I be so selfish and complainy? I'm ashamed of myself. Aging is a bad deal and you should just pick yourself up and keep going.* That's what I believe. But it's not what I feel.

What I feel is disapproving and angry, as if I'd been cheated. To turn into a bad sport at the end is not good! I used to be too busy to notice how my mother's fastidiousness had gripped me, and now I'm maybe worse than she was. Imagine me, who wrote with (and slept with!) Marshall Barer, turning out to be hyperjudgmental about hygiene and decorum! The other night, at Carnegie Hall, at that incredible Daniil Trifonov recital,* we were in the first tier in a box quite close to the stage but on the wrong side if you care about looking at his hands, but actually he was so expressive that without actually seeing his hands you could see plenty. Bad shoes or not, I could access the same thrill music has always brought me. But down the row was a young girl who put her feet up and over the red velvet rail, letting them dangle over the side, and no adult stopped her. I was so outraged I could hardly concentrate. I wanted to bark at her: *How dare you treat Carnegie Hall like that? Who do you think you are?* Which is how a nasty old lady behaves. Later that night, when Hank—

Hold on a moment.

But now Hank is dead.† It's eight months later, and he's "left the building." Not the Beresford, which he left a while ago; more lately he was in a series of hospitals, finally in a place near the house in Quogue. On top of everything else wrong with his body, he had pneumonia and pretty much stopped eating. Didn't want water, didn't want morphine. Told the kids cheerfully not to bother visiting; it would be no fun for anyone. When they visited anyway, he shooed them out within ten minutes. He told one of them, I'm not sure which: "I can't see you now. I'm too busy breathing."

As the time approached, he was unperturbed but insistent, the way I'd want to be but am afraid I won't. He said he was done, reminded me not to have him resuscitated, said good night, and sent me home. When he died at four in the morning, I wasn't with him. I didn't want to be.

Was it a good marriage? I'll get back to that.

We had a memorial for him at Lincoln Center Theater, on a night the

....

* On February 5, 2013, in his Carnegie Hall recital debut, the twenty-one-year-old Russian pianist performed a bravura program of Scriabin, Liszt, and Chopin.

† Henry Arthur Guettel died, of pneumonia, on October 7, 2013, at the Westhampton Care Center on Long Island. He was eighty-five.

Newhouse was dark. Adam had gone through Hank's iPod and made a beautiful soundtrack. Tom spoke extemporaneously and hilariously.[*]

I know it will make me sound like a monster, but I felt absolutely nothing in the days and weeks after Hank died, except mild annoyance that with all the flowers and cookies I could hardly find the phone. It's like what Steve said about Burt Shevelove, that his death didn't even seem real; when people don't live near you, you tend to think they're just "away." Hank lived near me, usually right across this breakfast table, but that's what I mostly think, too: *He's just off somewhere. Back in fifteen minutes. See you at supper.* Until I remember things like setting the clocks. Who's going to do all these clocks? God, come back and do the clocks. Now the clocks will never be done.

And then, in tiny bits and pieces, like a collage, old thoughts, more like images, materialize. Funny-awful things. His performing with Mae West. His banishment to a Central Park bench while my parents decided his financial fate. His insistence on driving us all over England even though he never got the hang of the roads; he took a side mirror off every car we rented. We called him the Yankee Clipper.

Not emotional enough for you? You know I won't cry. Only one thing in this whole business has really moved me, and it hasn't been sad but joyful. As Hank got less and less, the kids got more and more. Not just Alec and Adam, but Tod, Nina, and Kim as well, who had already been through the death of a father.[†] In their attentiveness, their sweetness, their availability, they turned out to be exactly what I wanted them to be as human beings. I don't mean as professionals, though their careers as-

....

[*] The memorial was held on Monday November 25, 2013, in the Mitzi E. Newhouse Theater at Lincoln Center during the run of *Domesticated*, a play by Bruce Norris. Among the speakers was Tom Carr, resplendent in dress blues.

[†] Julian Bonar Beaty Jr. died on August 26, 2011, in Fort Lauderdale, at ninety-four.

tonish (and in Alec's case bewilder) me.* I mean as compassionate people. I can't imagine what to credit that to. Maybe they're overcompensating for me.

Beyond that, it's too much to ask a person to suffer a loss and also grieve it. On the whole, death is poorly directed. Hank, let alone George Abbott, would not have approved of the staging.

Nor of your question: "Was it a good marriage?"

The answer, at a week shy of fifty-two years, is yes. I married for love, and what I had I was lucky to have.

....

* Tod Beaty is the president of a Cambridge commercial real estate and property management firm. Nina Beaty is an artist and art therapist whose work often focuses on helping people with cancer. Kim Beaty is a painter; her work includes the official Supreme Court portrait of Ruth Bader Ginsburg. Adam Guettel's next projects include musical versions of the movies *Millions* and *Days of Wine and Roses*. Alec Guettel is an entrepreneur in the fields of renewable energy and information technology. Among them they have five children and one stepchild: Ben and Julia Beaty, Jeanine Hannoun, Mairi McCormick, and Sophie and Clara Guettel. And Tom Carr now has a son: Hank's great-grandchild, Alexander Steven Carr.

47.

ARE WE ANYWHERE?

What happens when someone dies? Nothing! Is there a better answer? I think about it because all my nurses are Catholic, and we talk about things like heaven. Some of them think it's a real, literal place, or other la-la nonsense. But heaven is just a wish while you live. Or everything you've actually lived, if you're lucky. If I'd felt luckier as a child maybe I wouldn't have needed the heaven Father Harkins promised me. By the way, I was never formally de-Catholicized; I was expecting to be excommunicated, but they didn't bother. So I'm still kosher, according to them. If it exists, maybe I'll get into heaven on a technicality.

Is heaven home? Is it just staying where you are, or, if you leave, coming back to it?* When Adam started writing songs, and I could still keep up, I would talk to him about getting back to the original key after all the harmonic wanderings. The ear likes to find its way home. The emotion, too. But he has his own ear. His songs leave home, go far afield, and, pretty often, never return; they break through into new places instead. I am listening over and over these days to demos he sent me of new things he's working on; I don't understand the way they're made, but they give me joy.

---

* In Adam Guettel's song "How Glory Goes," from *Floyd Collins*, Floyd asks similar questions: "Do we live, is it like a little town? / Do we get to look back down at who we love? / Are we above, are we everywhere, are we anywhere at all?"

2005: Adam and Mary at the opening night party for *The Light in the Piazza*.
"The ear likes to find its way home. The emotion, too."

Still, I worry for him as I don't for any of the others. He has, like Daddy, a great need to be great, but the marketplace for what he does is not what it was for what Daddy did. That's a recipe for disappointment if you care about recognition—and who doesn't? I did a terrible thing once, out of that fear, when *The Light in the Piazza* was up for eleven Tony Awards and had already won five. We were sitting in Radio City and just as they were about to announce the award for Best Musical, he turned to me—I was a row behind him, two seats over—and said, "I love you, Mom." And I said right back, "It's gonna be *Spamalot*."*

It surprises me how little I've changed from the rotten girl my mother told me I was, from the young woman who frivolously caused a bomb scare on a plane, from the New York wife who called her Midwestern

---

* It was. But Adam did receive the award for Best Score.

mother-in-law a "silly bitch," thinking she'd find it amusing. (She didn't.) I thought I was such a rebel and yet, like the songs I understand best, I've come back to the same life, or very nearly, as the one I started in. You can almost see the Lombardy and the Carlyle across the park from the Beresford. The piano my parents gave me is in the living room. As always, my sister is competing with me, this time to kick the bucket first—she says no one told her dying is such hard work.* There are Catholic helpers in the kitchen and a standard poodle at my bedside; I know that Annie, the new one, will be the last in the line that began for me with Bunthorne.

You have to face facts. This may be the last time we see each other. You cry so easily! I hoped we would finish this together, but you know what to do. Just please don't make it dull like Mummy's and Daddy's. Include everything, except what we can't. Otherwise, what's the point? We all fuck up and eventually putrefy, but at least I had fun.

And didn't you, too?†

....

* Mary won that race; Linda Rodgers Emory died on November 7, 2015.

† Mary was right about two things: I did have fun and I did not see her again. After that conversation, on April 30, 2014, she felt too unwell to meet for work. In May illness engulfed her, with all its paraphernalia: doctors' visits, house calls, home nurses, pain, pain medications, indignities, appliances, a day's improvement followed by two days' relapse. After a hospitalization midmonth, her circle quickly contracted to its innermost orbits: her children and staff and closest friends, who visited to say what they knew were likely goodbyes. When they arrived, they would find her pre-set in the dining room, in a yellow chair, so as not to be witnesses to her difficulty walking.

All the while, the daily business of being Mary Rodgers Guettel hummed along. William Baldwin Young, who had been her secretary since 1986—but often more of a governess, he and Mary joked—showed me a log he kept for one week early that June, with a mix of mundane and momentous details like these:

Monday. A gift of watches for Mary's grandchildren Clara and Sophie arrives; so do the book *My Promised Land* from Barnes & Noble, a pillow laundered by Winzer Dry Cleaning, some Miracle Care Ear Powder (for

....

the dog) from Amazon, and, from Netflix, *Tinker Tailor Soldier Spy* and *The Queen of Versailles*. Mary and Nina watch the latter and love it.

Tuesday. Mary visits her physician, who explains that her depression and lack of appetite could be a reaction to the recent withdrawal of steroids. News comes that a shirt ordered from Pure has been canceled, but the aromatherapy booties arrive. So do more gifts Mary has bought for Clara and Sophie: owl boxes. A man fixes the drain in the maid's bathroom; money is sent to the Kids Walk for Cancer; Mary has dinner with Nina, Kim, and Kim's daughter, Mairi.

Wednesday. Nina orders a short-sleeved nightshirt for Mary from Macy's and a new olive drainer for the kitchen. Deliveries include an A-line dress from Neiman Marcus and, from Falk Surgical, a Drive raised toilet seat, which Mary hates but the nurses love. Several friends come by for drinks; others come by for dinner.

Thursday. Mary is very tired from having too many friends over. Deliveries include the film *Quartet*, the book *Tigers in Red Weather*, the card game Blink, a box of toffee, the nightshirt from Macy's, and a roll-sleeve boatneck tee from Appleseed's, which Mary doesn't like and is returned. An appointment is made for a house call from the nutritionist and an office visit to the audiologist because Mary hasn't been wearing her hearing aid. Kim comes to dinner.

Friday. Mary wants to go through her email but even with help proves too "fuzzy" to do so; photo attachments from Kim and from Helen Hunt are printed out for her. People are paid. Weekend coverage is confirmed. The piano is watered.

And so it went until, in mid-June, Mary was hospitalized again. She called me from the hospital: "This time I really mean it," she barked. She was soon released and began hospice care, at home, on June 23. As soon as she was given morphine, Bill Young says, she was at peace. But Annie the poodle would no longer go near her. She died, in her own bed, around nine in the morning on June 26, 2014, with a nurse stroking her cheek and Kim holding her hand. Bill was already on the phone with the mortuary.

48.

THE YELLOW ROOM

I had come that first day to talk about Adam for the *Times Magazine*. Over tea, with Hank chiming in, Mary told me the most extraordinary things, few of which wound up in print. As the anecdotes tumbled out, it was all I could do to keep my balance on the yellow bergère, with my china cup rattling and my notebook flopping and my back to the Steinway, where silver-framed photos of "Daddy" and "Steve" and the rest supervised. On the walls hung Jo Mielziner's watercolor renderings of his set designs for *Pal Joey* and *Pipe Dream*—even though Mary told me she found his work "brown and immobile." On a music stand by the fireplace, the manuscript of Rodgers and Hart's "He Was Too Good to Me," perhaps the sweetest-saddest song ever written, sat open.

Convivial and sharp and up for anything, Hank and Mary fulfilled the playwright Paul Rudnick's description of them as the Nick and Nora Charles of Central Park West.

I had never conducted an interview with so little resistance from the interviewees. In fact, it was I who wound up resisting, worried that their stories—some hilarious, some horrendous—would turn my profile of Adam into a profile of them. Resistance proved futile, though. I stopped taking notes at some point and just listened, storing the details for personal use over dinner with Andy (then my partner, later my husband) when I got home.

That was in 2003, otherwise a low point for me. My mother, born six months before Mary, had died at the end of 2001. The daily slog of

1965: Harold Prince, Stephen Sondheim, and Mary (among others)
at one of the Guettels' famous Christmas celebrations.
"Their parties were an aristocracy of talent."

mourning had not relented. I especially missed her child-rearing advice. When Andy and I were freaking out over our younger son's toilet-training defiance, she advised us to ignore it (exactly as Mary did in her abandoned children's book *George*), since no one got married in a diaper. And if they did, she added, "they should live and be well."

Even though my mother grew up above her parents' dry goods store in North Philadelphia, and Mary at the Carlyle on East Seventy-sixth Street, they were alike in many ways. Same haircut, for one thing, at least at the end: a modified center-part pageboy. A similar serrated laugh, which was nice because I was already beginning to forget how my mother's sounded. Something deeper connected them, too: Each spent a lifetime upending the expectations of the caste she was born into. Mary's family store was grander, but, like my mother, she wanted out.

Also like me. I have to admit that part of the buzz I got on first meeting the Guettels was from the sensation of flying up, however briefly, into a higher echelon. I had twice performed in *Once Upon a Mattress*: at camp in the chorus and in high school as Dauntless. (I built my own throne from a yellow vinyl kitchen stool my mother was discarding.) Now I was being passed a plate of cookies by the woman who, with a few crazy pals, actually wrote it. The songs I eked out at the piano in my suburban Philadelphia living room in 1975 were the very ones Mary notated, with some effort, in 1959. Icons like Sondheim were her intimates and, in some cases, even better, her enemies.

That she was theater royalty—I'd also been in "Daddy's" *South Pacific* and *Oklahoma!*—ought to have made me feel like a peasant, but she and Hank acted princely in only the best ways. There was no social snobbery; their parties were an aristocracy of talent. They flipped the template of the richest people I knew, who were generous within the narrow orbit of family or in the far heavens of philanthropy but nowhere in between. I gradually learned, if rarely from Mary, about the young musicians she helped with cash, the women she ransomed out of trouble, the defunded medical researchers she re-funded, the starving artists she repeatedly fed. Toward the end of her life she was hounded by seemingly hundreds of these beneficiaries, eager to thank her in person.

I had cause to be one of them. After that first interview, as we got

2010: In Quogue, among the Quoglodytes.

to know each other better, I found myself and my family the recipients
of similar acts of noblesse oblige, similarly disowned. Restaurant checks
had a way of disappearing before Andy or I could pretend to grab for
them; if I objected, Mary would say, "When your father writes *Oklahoma!* you can pay for dinner." That was a line she used on lots of people
over the years because it acknowledged the awkwardness of the situation and swiftly walked straight through it. Hank's version was subtler,
a maneuver I called the Invisible Majordomo. When Andy and I and the
boys arrived in Quogue one day with a blown-out tire, we discovered
by the time we'd changed into bathing suits that the car was gone. It returned a few hours later, repaired, and all questions about how this was
stage-managed—recall that Hank had once been a stage manager—were
waved away.

None of this was done to wow us. Hank actively avoided acknowledgment, as if generosity were a private part you kept safely zipped up. Mary's tack, as I say, was different; she happily owned the prerogatives of wealth while disdaining the attitude that usually accompanies them. When we sat down to play Scrabble after dinner one night, I marveled over the deluxe walnut set Hank produced, with its lazy-Susan board and gilded letters. "What, do you think we live like pigs?" Mary snorted, which turned my silly awe into a joke on herself, or perhaps on her mother, who often used the same phrase.

And when, after days of drenching rains one winter, the ceiling of our Brooklyn living room caved in, she immediately asked not "How can I help?" but "How much do you need?" I could have said a thousand dollars or ten thousand dollars and the difference wouldn't have registered, but of course I said, "Nothing."

"How many zeroes is that?"

In 2009, six years after our first interview, Mary asked me to tea again. Same chair, same hilarity. But this time, for the first time, it was she who wanted something from me. For a decade at least, everyone she knew had been pushing her to write her memoirs, she said, and now she had gotten herself entangled in a contract. The problem: She'd started a few times, didn't like the results, and didn't know how or whether to keep going.

Her ambivalence was densely layered. She did not think she "deserved" a memoir: Why should anyone want to hear about the daddy (and mummy) issues of a second-drawer composer and children's-book author whose greatest contribution to art, she said, was being a midwife to it? Perhaps as a result of that attitude, she found she had no stamina for the actual writing; she was seventy-eight at that point and preferred company to computer screens. She also hated the genre itself, finding it—at least in her parents' examples—unrelievedly self-serving. And there was something else, too, that would become apparent later.

At the time, though, she asked if I was interested in writing it with her. Or even without her. Or if I thought she should return the advance and forget about it. "If it's not fun, why do it?" she said. "But wouldn't it be fun if we did it together?"

I read the pages she'd written thus far, mostly about her childhood.

The stories were good, but they all seemed to flatline, as if she'd grown tired of telling them partway through. Something was wrong with the voice, too; it sounded a little like Mary, but stiff and muffled. In actual conversation, her every sentence was filled with juice; the punch lines let the juice squirt out. Every part of the utterance was energized. But her draft read like a memoir written by a hostage still locked in the bunker.

I suggested we throw those pages away and start over together—not writing but talking. For as long as it took to cover her entire life in conversation, we'd meet and gab while I typed and prodded. Eventually, when we had enough, we'd use the typescript as raw material.

Mary agreed, but we hit that other snag before we even got started. For another three years, she vacillated about moving forward, nearly canceling the contract several times. Her fundamental fear, as I finally understood it, was the same one that had rendered her first attempts remote. The fear was hypocrisy. If her brand was frankness, how could she withhold anything? And yet there were things—not many—even she did not wish to say.

This made her probably the first would-be memoirist in history to get stuck on that particular qualm; autobiography is the art of obfuscation. I wasn't willing to force her hand, but I saw the solution as simple: Be transparent about keeping things in the dark. To offer 100 percent honesty about 95 percent of her life, while keeping the remaining 5 percent to herself, was, in a story like hers, a damn good bargain.

By the time she turned eighty, in 2011, she was ready to make that deal with herself. After the publisher and agents were satisfied, we began meeting twice a week for three or four hours, usually starting at nine in the morning and spilling over into lunch. When she arrived at her appointed spot on the couch—which she repeatedly instructed me was properly called a sofa—she was sometimes joyful, sometimes pissed off, sometimes stuck until I found a provocation that unstuck her. She liked being provoked. I told her she habitually confused jealousy and envy, both as words and as concepts. She told me I mispronounced "lingerie"—"as well you might." When I accused her of internalized sexism (for having avoided working with other women for so long) or of the casual racism typical of her era, she'd get excited. "Let's keep that!" she'd exclaim, though I didn't in every case.

What excited her was the drama of the interchange. "Wouldn't it be more fun as a dialogue?" she would ask. Certainly, we were having a ball; without the pressure of turning stories directly into copy, and without the eternal ear of a tape recorder eavesdropping, she was utterly uncensored, only on three or four occasions saying "not for publication" or "don't include that unless she's dead"—that last about Alice Hammerstein, whom she mostly liked. When I got her to cackle or to stick out her bottom lip by sometimes taking her parents' side, she would invariably ask how we could get that kind of back-and-forth into print. And though I was sure that the best version of a book about Mary Rodgers would be one that sounded as if she were talking to a friend without interruption, I began to see her point.

In any case, there was another problem with the full-on, unfiltered Mary approach. Talking to a friend, she would never have said, "My father, Richard Rodgers, the theater composer" or even "my father"; in conversation she almost invariably called him Daddy, and her mother, Mummy. (Her draft defaulted to RR and DR, as if she were writing a psychiatric case study.) Nor in conversation did she have to stop to explain who someone like Temple Texas was, let alone Phyllis Newman. Yet many readers would not recognize such names. When it occurred to me that we could solve that problem and also create at least a little back-and-forth tension by annotating her voice with exegesis in mine, she of course knew where I'd gotten the idea. It was the trick she and her mother had used, for a different purpose, in *A Word to the Wives*.

But time was running out by then. We'd been talking for more than two years, and Mary was beginning to decline. If I didn't realize how precipitously, it was partly because she didn't like to show it and partly because I didn't want to see. Even so, I was shaken by the difference in her condition between the Juilliard gala that honored her on April 30, 2012, and the gala performance of *Once Upon a Mattress* by the Transport Group on June 17, 2013. She was a glowy dinner hostess under the Damrosch Park tent after the Juilliard event—and, the next day, a vivid critic of it, for (among other things) omitting her first three children from the filmed tribute. But a year later, the process of getting to the stage for the conversation that followed the performance of *Mattress* almost undid her. From my seat I recognized the panicky look hovering beneath her big frozen smile: She could not catch her breath. Only after an excruciating couple of minutes did she finally find enough wind to speak, at which point she immediately proceeded to charm the audience with her dirty grandma routine. "George Abbott agreed to take on the show," she said, "and I didn't even have to sleep with him."

The final year of our work together was intermittent and occasionally grim. Her recollection and insight were as sharp as ever, but she got tired—"fuzzy," she called it—after an hour instead of three. Often, she canceled. When we did meet, she expressed impatience to move from the talking phase to the writing phase, while at the same time acknowledging that we had not yet covered all of her life. Nor was I very far along in investigating her stories, though the few I had checked by then checked out. Even though they were meant to be taken as anecdotes, not history, they usually proved to be both.

I say that with some surprise; when I started working with Mary, I assumed that the stories she was sharing existed on a different axis of facticity than objective truth. I asked myself whether I would need to pull those axes into some sort of alignment, as one would in a biography, or whether, as in a memoir, which is to say a reconstructed book of inherently unstable memory, they could simply be left askew. These considerations proved to be moot. Research bore out pretty much everything she told me, no matter how outré, or perhaps even more so the more outré it was. What research did not bear out I corrected. As for those few things that were not even checkable—matters of opinion, trivia buried too deeply in the pre-Internet past, tales existing in competing versions in the many books written by and about her circle—my aim has been to say: This is how Mary saw it. Or, really, with one more wrinkle: This is how I saw her see it.

In any case, when I at last started writing, our plan was that I would draft pages and she would mark them up. Because Mary was eager to avoid the cardboard mouthfeel of her parents' books, she wanted us to open with something zingy and gossipy and nonchronological. I immediately thought of beginning with games, which we'd discussed many times and in many variations: those she played with her parents, those she played with her friends, those she played with her children. I pulled the threads together from my hundreds of pages of single-spaced notes and rewove them to introduce this character called Mary. Then I emailed the result to her.

When we next met in the yellow room, she was unwell and unhappy. She hated the oxygen that she needed in order to breathe comfortably, even just sitting on the sofa; the cannulas reminded her of her mother. But she was also, clearly, unhappy with the pages, which she kept picking up and putting down; I could see the pencil marks she'd made on them but not what they said. Was she troubled by my use of "Mummy" and "Daddy"? Did she find the games angle too obtuse? Had I taken too many liberties with her phrasing?

None of those. "Make it funnier," she said. "Make it meaner."

I was taken aback; it was already plenty of both for a first bite; the section was even called "Hostilities." But as I heard her out, it became clear that if she was going to talk about herself for a few hundred pages, she wanted two things to happen: She wanted readers to have a good time, even when learning about the times she did not, and, on the assumption that those readers were no saints, she wanted them to know that she wasn't, either. You could have a good life without being dull and without being perfect or great, she said, if you jumped in and kept your eyes open. Niceness was not, on its own, a virtue: It needed to be expressed in action.

That turned out to be our last working session.

The stories "Mary" tells in this book are the stories she told me. They are often in her exact words, albeit cherry-picked from multiple conversations separated by months. When the words are not hers, they are, at her suggestion, my best ventriloquizing of them; she encouraged me to think of "Mary" as a fictional character of my own devising, but one who happened to have lived within a true, if unusual, story.

That wasn't difficult. After the hours I'd spent listening to her, her verbal rhythms and characteristic constructions were second nature to me—or maybe first nature. I'd been playing her music since childhood, after all. You couldn't sing the octave leap to get to the word *shy* in *Once Upon a Mattress* without re-creating in yourself, if just for that moment, the personality of the woman who wrote it: eager, bighearted, bigmouthed.

"Shy," sung by Carol Burnett on a kinescope of *The Garry Moore Show*, opened Mary's Town Hall memorial on Monday, November 3, 2014. A choral performance of "Something Known," from *The Member of the Wedding*, ended it. In between, friends related their best Maryisms; Alec showed the Cool Whip commercial; Julie Andrews introduced herself as Burnett, and vice versa, saying it must be freaky Monday; and everyone talked about the dirty-martini cackle.

The emotional highlight came when Sondheim took the stage. At the piano, he played a "song without words" based on the first bar of "Fair Lady," a number he and Mary had written for *The Lady, or the Tiger?* more than sixty years earlier. No one could have missed how apt a portrait of Mary it made, with its restless melody, tangled figures, harmonic conflict, and inevitable last-minute return to the tonic.

But where would Mary herself return? The disposal of bodies had never been a priority in the family; the whereabouts of Dick and Dorothy remain undetermined. And now Mary's children had not just her ashes but also Hank's to deal with. Friends suggesting a back-to-nature theme like the beach at Quogue were barking up the wrong tree, and there was no right tree. "The whole ocean-mountain-forest thing just wasn't them," Alec explained. "They were city people"—and, more specifically, that subgenre of city people known as theatricals.

So, having transferred Mary's cremains, or as much of them as would fit, into an empty vodka bottle, and Hank's into a bottle of Scotch, they headed after the memorial to West Forty-sixth Street, where without undue ceremony, and before they could be caught, they poured their parents into the weather-beaten wooden planters in front of Joe Allen, within laughing distance of the wall of flops and just a few feet from the bar.

ACKNOWLEDGMENTS

The richest and most accurate source of information about the life of Mary Rodgers Guettel proved to be Mary herself. But missing details and backup were generously provided by many of her collaborators, friends, and acquaintances from the theater, including Susan Birkenhead, André Bishop, Ken Bloom, Patrick Brady, Michael Feinstein, Steve Hamilton, Emma Walton Hamilton, John Kander, Charles Kopelman, Ann Morrison, Marsha Norman, Bill Rudman, Richard Sabellico, Scott Schwartz, Stephen Sondheim, and Mark Waldrop.

Mary often worked with and complained to Ted Chapin, who, until he retired in 2021, was president of what is now called Rodgers & Hammerstein. Perhaps in tribute to Mary's own style, he has been remarkably frank and generous with tales and information. What's more, he showed me the actual Johnny Mop.

I consulted several libraries, research centers, and archives, including the Billy Rose Theatre Division at the New York Public Library; the Tamiment collection at New York University's Bobst Library; and the Paley Center for Media, where Barry Monush and Rebecca Paller helped me track Mary's work for television. At my behest, Bianca Rhea spent hours at the main branch of the New York Public Library, often paging through old phone books on microfilm. Malcolm Thaler, M.D., advised me on the many medical matters that were part of the life and everyday conversation of a woman who read *The Merck Manual* for pleasure. The theater critic and historian Steven Suskin swept up my stray Rialto facts; any that remain unswept are my fault, not his.

Suskin is the author of two classic works of theater history I also consulted: *Second Act Trouble: Behind the Scenes at Broadway's Big Musical Bombs* and *The Sound of Broadway Music: A Book of Orchestrators and Orchestrations*. Another in the same category is Ken Mandelbaum's *Not Since Carrie: Forty Years of Broadway Musical Flops*. Highly informative as well were Gary Marmorstein's *A Ship Without a Sail: The Life of Lorenz Hart*; Andrew B. Harris's *The Performing Set: The Broadway Designs of William and Jean Eckart*; and *Dear Genius: The Letters of Ursula Nordstrom*, collected and edited by Leonard S. Marcus. Less informational, but a bigger hoot, was Paul Rosner's roman à clef *The Princess and the Goblin*, which, though mostly based on the supposed lesbian relationship between Mary Martin and Jean Arthur, features the insulting caricature of Mary Rodgers that Mary thought was so funny when I read it to her.

Stories about Mary's circle have wormed their way into too many books to mention, but among the ones I found most useful, whether for corroboration or contradiction, are two memoirs by Arthur Laurents (*Original Story By* and *The Rest of the Story: A Life Completed*) and two biographies by Meryle Secrest (*Sondheim: A Life* and *Somewhere for Me: A Biography of Richard Rodgers*). Sondheim's own "Hat Box" set—*Finishing the Hat: Collected Lyrics (1954–1981) with Attendant Comments, Principles, Heresies, Grudges, Whines and Anecdotes* and *Look, I Made a Hat: Collected Lyrics (1981–2011) with Attendant Comments, Amplifications, Dogmas, Harangues, Digressions, Anecdotes and Miscellany*—was, and will always be, invaluable. And though memoirs bordering on fantasias by Mary's parents had to be taken with a cut-crystal shakerful of salt, the three by Dorothy (*My Favorite Things: A Personal Guide to Decorating and Entertaining*, *The House in My Mind*, and *A Personal Book*) and the one by Dick (*Musical Stages: An Autobiography*) provided a helpful framework. The Dorothy-Mary collaboration *A Word to the Wives* provided something even better: the idea for the format of this book.

Finally, of course, there are Mary's own works for young people: *The Rotten Book*, *Freaky Friday*, *A Billion for Boris*, and *Summer Switch*, all of which reward adult rereading—and the ghostwritten *Freaky Monday*, which doesn't.

I spent hundreds of hours in the Guettels' Central Park West apartment, where the household staff, including Aicha Chafi, Leila Valera, and Nafe Badrudeen, made me feel as welcome (and as well-fed) as family. The office staff, which during my time there included Hilary Leichter and Ruchika Tomar, both now successful novelists—that's the kind of joint Mary ran—did everything possible to keep Mary, and thus the book, teed up. William Baldwin Young, Mary's longtime secretary, who could have written these tales in his sleep, was the key that unlocked thousands of memories, manuscripts, insights, file drawers, and ephemera.

It was probably asking too much of her surviving children—Tod Beaty, Nina Beaty, Kim Beaty, Adam Guettel, and Alec Guettel—to be resources in the writing of this book without giving them any say over it, but that's what Mary did. Surprisingly, yet also unsurprisingly, they were quick to answer, in unsentimental detail, anything I asked them and left me alone otherwise. Also carrying on the family tradition of "knee-jerk transparency" was Hank's grandson, Tom Carr. Guettel family friends including Susannah Clark (a daughter of Judy Abbott) and Adam Brien (the son of Nancy Ryan) were able to confirm some of the unlikeliest of Mary's many unlikely assertions. I was especially lucky to have Mary's cousin Sarah Crichton, now the editor in chief at Henry Holt and Co., read *Shy* in its earliest phases and again in its latest. She knows Mary's exact voice by heart.

That Jonathan Galassi, the president of Farrar, Straus and Giroux, edited the book in its entirety is really only a fraction of the story of his efforts on its behalf. It was he who persuaded Mary to work on her memoirs in the first place, and then repeatedly re-persuaded her to do so as her doubts mounted and her energy flagged. In agreeing to Mary's suggestion that I write it with her, he indirectly provided me with some of the best, most hilarious days of my life.

The other best days of my life were and are filled with my husband, Andrew Mirer, and my children, Erez Mirer and Lucas Mirer, all of whom loved Mary and Hank as quickly and fully as I did. My friends Sara Sklaroff and John Cantrell read and advised me on portions of the manuscript, just as they had for my previous one. My agent, Cynthia Cannell, and my editors at *The New York Times*—and before that at *New York* magazine— were all more flexible and accommodating than I had any right to hope in allowing me to disappoint everyone a little by splitting my time among everyone a lot.

It was while profiling Adam Guettel for the *Times Magazine* in 2003 that I met Mary and Hank, and it was while (some would say) deboning Arthur Laurents for *New York* in 2009 that I got to spend time with them again. Both articles were assigned by Adam Moss; Megan Liberman edited the earlier one ("A Complicated Gift") and Jared Hohlt, the later. (Jared gave the Laurents profile its dead-on title: "When You're a Shark, You're a Shark All the Way.") To them and all patient editors everywhere, a writer's complicated, sharklike gratitude.

If Mary and I had gotten around to writing a dedication before she died, I wonder if hers would have been to Hank. And yet she'd already honored him that way, in *Summer Switch*. There was only one family member she never thanked in the front of her books, the one she felt had earned it most and needed it least: her father. By a similar logic, I would have dedicated this to my mother.

ILLUSTRATION CREDITS